Fantasy Football Guidebook
Your Comprehensive Guide to Playing Fantasy Football

By

Sam Hendricks

"Fantasy Football Guidebook," by Sam Hendricks. ISBN Softcover 978-1-60264-020-7. Hardcover: 978-1-60264-022-1.

Library of Congress Control Number: 2007929163.

Manufactured in the United States of America.

Preface

This book is not about selling you anything. You are not asked to subscribe to a premium website service. No newsletters will be pushed. You have to go it alone, without any special one-time offer or discounted drafting service. I simply wrote a book to share all (or most) of my fantasy football knowledge. My goal is to help everyone improve his or her game of fantasy football. I hope that the competition gets better and brings more enjoyment for all.

This Fantasy Football Guidebook (FFGB) is a labor of love. It is the result of playing this wonderful game for more than 17 years. Along the way, I wondered about the history behind such a fun game. I remember my first draft, and the nerves and disappointment that were inevitable as a result of the outcome that first year. I swore to better myself. I am competitive at everything: from Dominoes to Scrabble to first car in the driveway. Therefore, I studied, researched, and learned the game of fantasy football. I think you can learn a lot from your mistakes. And mistakes I made. However, you can also learn from good owners, and I did that too.

I first started looking at the available literature on fantasy football four years ago. There was nothing on the topic. I made inquiries at all the bookstores and asked them to do online searches for "fantasy football," but few books turned up. Some were only self-promotions for the authors or advertisements for their "premium" services. The few books that were actually honest examinations of fantasy football had very basic information, and did not even cover auctions, keeper leagues, or IDPs to my satisfaction. It is my hope that this book will give you, the reader, more information on these and other areas, and allows you to learn and grow with this wonderful hobby.

Fantasy Football Guidebook (FFGB) is about mastering the game of fantasy football. Use this book as a reference. Read it and pass it on, or put it on the shelf by your computer so that it is a handy reference guide, within arm's reach in a moment's notice. Future editions will come out to update the strategies and expand on other critical areas.

This book is for beginners and experienced fantasy football players alike. The beginner will find an explanation of all of the major aspects of fantasy football. Experienced players will find draft tips, explanations of draft strategies, and a list of rule variations, as well as help in understanding what is successful and what is not. This book started out as a clinical approach to fantasy football. Somewhere along the line, I decided to sprinkle in some humor and sarcasm too, just to keep you honest. I hope you enjoy the almost 400 pages of fantasy football wisdom and guidance.

Dedication

I dedicate this book to my late father, Sam, who worked so hard for his family. He is missed everyday. I also dedicate it to Cynthia, my mother, otherwise known as "Fannie," because she is always there with a smile. Also to my sister Trish, who is the most caring individual I know. And, most importantly, to my loving wife Birgitte, who loves me enough to let me watch all that football. I love her dearly.

Acknowledgements

A special thanks to my sister, Trish Hendricks, who served as my first copy editor to "make sure the manuscript looked good enough to edit." I think this is like cleaning up before the cleaners arrive to clean your house, but it worked. I would be remiss if I did not express my sincere thanks to Alice Faintich for her invaluable insight into the editing world. It is with great thanks that I acknowledge my peer reviewers Bobby Floyd, Ned "Neckless" Rudd, and Mike "Smy" Smyth. Their tireless efforts to review this book are greatly appreciated. And thanks to Rob Zarzycki for taking the time from his busy schedule to review and comment on my book.

A big thanks to Kimberly Hancock for the tremendous editing job she did and to Bobby Bernshausen, also at Virtualbookworm.com Publishing, for his help pushing me along the publishing process.

In addition, Jorgen Magard, my father-in-law, deserves praise for his good advice on all things book-related.

Contents

About the Author

Sam Hendricks was born and raised in Lynchburg, Virginia and graduated from the University of Virginia in 1986. He joined the USAF and flew RF4C fighter jets in Germany during the Cold War. He transitioned into the F15E Strike Eagle and earned three aerial achievement medals during combat missions in Operation Desert Storm.

He left the Air Force in 1993 to work for McDonnell Douglas as an F15E instructor, a job he has performed for over thirteen years. Sam spent the last ten years in the Middle East and Europe. He and his Danish wife, Birgitte, recently moved to Virginia and now live in the foothills of the Blue Ridge Mountains.

Sam enjoys golf, chess, poker, writing, and, of course, fantasy football.

He participates in the World Championship of Fantasy Football (WCOFF) and has won numerous league championships during his seventeen-year fantasy football career. He has been the commissioner in leagues on three continents and continues to perform those duties to this day. He also is an Outstanding American Award winner.

Abbreviations

3RR	3rd Round Reversal	KO	Kickoff
ADP	Average Draft Position	KR	Kickoff Return
AAP	Average Auction Position	LCG	League Championship Game
AAV	Average Auction Value	LB	Linebacker
CB	Cornerback	LT	Long-Term
DBC	Defense by Committee	LTFA	Long-Term Free Agent
DEF	Defense	MLB	Middle Linebacker
DH	Doubleheader	MB	Message Board
DL	Defensive Lineman	MNF	Monday Night Football
DE	Defensive End	NFL	National Football League
DSD	Double Serpentine Draft	OL	Offensive Line
DT	Defensive Tackle	OLB	Outside Linebacker
EDP	Estimated Draft Position	OT	Offensive Tackle or Overtime
FA	Free Agent, Free Agency	P	Punter
FAAB	Free Agent Acquisition Budget	PPR	Points per Reception
FCFS	First Come, First Served	PR	Punt Return
FF	Forced Fumble	PT	Playing Time
FG	Field Goal	QB	Quarterback
FS	Free Safety	QBBC	QB by Committee
FMV	Fair Market Value	RB	Running Back
FP	Fantasy Point	RBBC	Running Back by Committee
FPPG	Fantasy Points per Game	RD	Round
FR	Fumble Recovery	R/FA	Rookie/Free Agent
GL	Goal Line	ROT	Rule of Thumb
GM	General Manager	SB	Super Bowl
HC	Handcuff	SLB	Strong Side Linebacker
HO	Holdout	SOS	Strength of Schedule
HSL	High Stakes League	SRB	Stud RB Theory
IDP	Individual Defensive Player	SS	Strong Safety
ILB	Inside Linebacker	ST	Special Team or Short-Term
INT	Interception	STFA	Short-Term Free Agent
IR	Injured Reserve	TD	Touchdown
K	Kicker	TE	Tight End

TFP	Total Fantasy Points
TMTS	Too Many Teams Syndrome
TO	Turnover
TP	Total Points
VBD	Value-Based Drafting
WLB	Weak Side Linebacker
WR	Wide Receiver
XP	Extra Point

Chapter 1 Introduction

What is fantasy football? Only the greatest way to enjoy NFL football games ever invented. Watching NFL football on TV is like connecting to the Internet with a dial-up modem, whereas playing fantasy football is like using high-speed broadband/DSL.

Imagine watching Detroit versus Arizona on Sunday afternoon. ZZZZZZZZZZzzzzzzzzzzzzzzz.

Now imagine that you have a reason to root for Kevin Jones (Detroit RB) because if he scores a TD you get points; or for every 50 yards rushing you get points; or if Arizona's defense can stop Kevin Jones and Detroit from scoring, you get points. Now that "laugher" of a game is not so boring. I actually have seen grown men cry when a last second score in a lopsided 34-0 game meant giving up some bonus points by their defense. Okay, maybe no actual tears, but you get the idea.

Do you think you could be a better coach than Bill Parcells? Maybe that is a bad example, since Bill has recently given up the game, but you get the idea. If you think you can handle T.O. on your team, then draft him. If you think you can do better than Marty Schottenheimer; try fantasy football. Try to take a team through the season and into the playoffs. There is a great sense of pride in putting together your "hand-picked" NFL team and coaching them to a championship; especially when it means beating your friends and neighbors. In fantasy football, you are the owner, GM and coach of a team of NFL players. Complete with all the decisions that go with it, but without the millions of dollars it would cost.

Here's how it works. You name your team and then in a draft (preferably live), just like in the NFL, you get to pick players to fill your roster. You will be drafting with 7-13 other "owners," so the draft is usually the most fun of all as you wheel and deal and try to outfox the others to get the best team. From this roster of individual players who are unique to your team (i.e. no one else can "own" your players at the same time) you will decide whom to start each week and whom to bench. As the GM, you can make trades with other teams (if they agree) or drop players who are not performing and pick up others from a free agent pool (players not drafted in the live draft or dropped by another owner). Your objective is to have the best regular season record, advance to the fantasy football playoffs and eventually win the Super Bowl. Throughout it all, the experience is a major ego trip since you drafted them, you own them and you started them.

How much time will it take? Fantasy football is a pursuit that takes as little or as much time as you want to give it. I have friends whom I have introduced to the game who become very engaged (read obsessed) and devote many hours trying to get an edge. I have others who spend an hour or so on Saturdays before the games and use that time to set a lineup. The most fun comes in the bragging rights of knowing you met your opponent in a head-to-head matchup and came out with a victory. Remember, the winner of the fantasy football Super Bowl will have a years worth of bragging rights.

What is the draft like? Just imagine Christmas and double the pleasure; that is draft day. How does the draft work? Lets say my team, Slam's Slammers, has the first pick and I select Peyton Manning. He is no longer available for the other teams to pick. This draft goes on for a certain number of rounds in which each team will draft, on average, 2

QBs, 3 RBs, 3WRs, 2TEs, 2 Ks, and 2 Defenses/Special teams, in any order they wish. A typical draft may have your team with the following roster:

QB 1   P Manning (IND)

QB 2   T Brady (NE)

RB 1   S Jackson (STL)

RB 2   R Brown (MIA)

RB 3   Reggie Bush (NO)

WR 1   R Moss (NE)

WR 2   C Johnson (DET)

WR 3   K Johnson (CAR)

TE 1   T Gonzalez (KC)

TE 2   H Miller (PIT)

K 1   N Rackers (AZ)

K 2   J Feely (NYG)

D 1   CHICAGO

D2   WASHINGTON

Extra 1 N Burleson (SEA)

Extra 2 N Davenport (PIT)

Each week you, as the owner, must decide which of your players start and which sit on the bench. You must start 1 QB, 2 RBs, 2 WRs, 1 TE, 1 K and 1 DEF/ST each week. Therefore, you have to ask yourself many questions and make many decisions, such as; will Randy Moss score more points or should he be benched in favor of Keyshawn Johnson this week? Each fantasy team will play another fantasy team in the league in a head-to-head matchup. Whichever team scores the most points will get the win. The fantasy football season occurs during the first thirteen NFL games (all teams will play each other once) and then the league will have their playoffs during weeks 14 and 15 and their Super Bowl in week 16.

How do you score points? Basically, I have tried to keep it simple enough to where you can do some of the math just by watching the games or the two-minute ticker at the bottom of the screen. Every time your players rush or catch a TD it is worth 6 points. If they throw a TD it is worth 4 points. Every 50 yards rushing or receiving is worth 1 point. Every 100 yards passing is also worth 1 point. For example, if P Manning throws 3 TDs in a game and passes for 240 yards, and I started him, my team, Slam's Slammers, would get 12+2= 14 points. However, if my opponent (Birgitte's Mad Danes) started B Favre and he had 4 TDs and 399 yards passing, she would get 4 x4 +3= 19 points. At the end of each week, the TFPs (total fantasy points) for all starters are compared and the winner of the head-to-head match is given a victory. At the end of the season, half of the teams advance to the fantasy football playoffs.

This is a very basic, yet fun, version of a fantasy football league. It is by no means the only version of fantasy football. That is what makes this game/hobby so much fun. There is no right or wrong way to play it. There are no golden rules nor ancient royal society that decides what is official and what is not. You make the rules, you live by the rules, and you win or lose by the rules of the league(s) you choose to play in.

What is the attraction of fantasy football? I am asked this all the time!

Top 10 Reasons to play Fantasy Football

1) You want to affect the outcome of a football game in a way you never could before.

2) Competition with other football fans. Players enjoy the opportunity to match their skills against coworkers, friends, and family members. One survey reports that 3 out of 4 fantasy sports participants play with others they know personally. Most men are competitive and this allows us to compete without getting off the couch.

3) You love to watch football and your home team is driving you crazy.

4) The social aspect of belonging to a group; not to mention social networking or sharing a hobby with your children or spouse.

5) Fantasy football gives you one more reason to cry, laugh, yell, scream, rant or jump for joy while watching NFL football. It is like gambling but without the guilt.

6) Fantasy football makes for better NFL fans. We are more educated about the nuances. We know the players more intimately. We care about the rules and the changes each year brings. We are more attuned to the NFL.

7) Fantasy football helps you appreciate all the talent in the NFL, not just that on your favorite team.

8) Sometimes you watch a game to see how one or more of your players will do. Other times it is to see how your opponent's player does. Still, other times it is to see how a player on your watch list is doing.

9) It prevents you from having to cut the grass on Sundays or watch NASCAR with your extended family.

10) You want to win, have fun and have something to brag about around the water cooler at work. It is the adrenaline rush of winning.

The main purpose of participating in fantasy football is to have fun. It is sort of like a neighborhood poker game, only on Sunday afternoons.

Why are fantasy footballers so committed to the game? The reason fantasy football is the most popular fantasy sport is because it is played once a week and every game counts. In fantasy baseball, hockey or basketball, you can have over 100 games, so you have a situation where the games don't have that much meaning. In fantasy football, it is all about Sunday games or Monday night. It is instant gratification that lets you enjoy it for a few hours.

Another reason might be that the games restore a feeling of ownership that slipped away from many fans with the advent of free agency. I am a big Minnesota Vikings fan, but I do not have the same connection to them as I used to. Now players come and go from the "Vikes" roster every season. You need a scorecard just to keep up with who is new through the draft, through a trade, through a free agency pick up, and who is off the team due to suspension (no boat jokes) or other reasons. Players used to stay on a team for years. Now it seems as if they are there two years at the most. Now I put more of my emotions into my fantasy teams. Why? Because I control who makes the team and who starts. Fans who are not located near a major football team can become more active in the NFL by playing fantasy football and turning that devotion, which would have gone to a local market team, toward their own fantasy franchise.

Some people say that fantasy football fans are not loyal to their professional favorite teams. Hogwash. I love my Vikings; I just don't trust them. To win, that is. I do not have every single hat, shirt, tie, sweatshirt/pant, shorts, jacket, pajama or boxers from the Minnesota Vikings. Nor have I ever. I love the Vikings but I am not "crazy in love" with them. I am a fan of the game of football. I love to spend Sunday afternoons yelling at the coaches and players of the NFL, cursing my own stupidity or basking in my own stupendous glory and bemoaning the fate of my Vikings. Up until sixteen years ago (1991), I wallowed in self-pity as my Vikings self-destructed every season. Then a friend introduced me to fantasy football. Now not only can I cry over the collapse of Minnesota, I can also get enjoyment as my own fantasy teams pull out "come-from-behind victories" or crush rival teams.

What are the arguments against Fantasy Football?

1) Fantasy Football is for nerds. Ouch! That hurts. With over 10 million people playing fantasy football, that is a lot of nerds out there. Lots of non-nerdy people must be playing for the NFL, Fox, ESPN and CBS to all jump on the fantasy bandwagon. Okay, maybe that's because they smell money.

2) Fantasy Football is gambling. Oh my! If a hobby that asks for an entry fee (to pay for the costs of running the thing) and gives a few baubles (bucks) back (and maybe a trophy) to the winner is gambling, then so is golf, bowling, bridge, and so on. Gambling should be where everyone has an equal chance of winning. Fantasy football is not a place where everyone has an equal chance of winning. Just ask Big City (the code name for an owner in my local league). He has won the Super Bowl three out of eight years. Or ask another owner who has yet to make the Super Bowl or even the playoff semifinals in those same eight years. You win by preparation, some luck, skillful drafting and season transactions. Gamblers play against the house. Fantasy football players play against their friends.

3) It takes up too much time. Actually, it will only take as much time as you want to put into it. If the family wants to go to Wally World on Sunday, take them. Just make sure you tape the games so you can watch them when you get home. And don't leave the house until your lineup is set.

What is fantasy?

Fantasy is the creative imagination; an imagined event that fulfills a wish or psychological need. First, let me explain that fantasy football does not involve people who pretend to be real NFL players. This is not a fantasy role-playing game where you will be taking on the persona of Brett Favre while slaying trolls or dragons. Although if it were, Brett would definitely get points for endurance and speed; but I digress… It is not about lonely, anti-social men who never marry and think that Britney Spears will someday show up on their doorstep and ask for help with her computer. Stop these stereotypes now!

Why is fantasy football called fantasy football? That name does kind of creep some people out. I start to think of fantasy and my wife hits me over the head because I get that faraway look on my face and she knows I am in the Bahamas with Courtney Cox during her early "Friends" years. I remember early in my fantasy career (football that is) typing "fantasy football" into a search engine but forgetting to put quotation marks around it (thus inviting any hits on either fantasy or football to be displayed). Wow; porn on a new level. A recent Google search of the words "fantasy football" produced nearly 3 million results. Now that I think about it, Fantasy Island did a lot to hurt the sport. Why not call it "Armchair Coach" or "Tuesday Morning Football" or "You Make the Call" or "Madden something-or-other?"

I have experimented the past two years and have found an interesting phenomenon. Every time I am around four people, I ask if any play fantasy football or know someone who does. The majority of the time, someone in that foursome says yes! Usually it is someone else they know who plays. I think this hobby is bigger than we all think. Try it yourself.

Now it is time to wow you with statistics. Depending on which article you read or which survey you use, (the Fantasy Sports Trade Association (FSTA) is quoted the most,) the average fantasy football fan is a male in his upper-thirties with a bachelor's degree, working a white-collar job earning somewhere around $75,000 a year. Are you the average fantasy football fan? To be more precise, the average fantasy football player is an educated professional living in the suburban US. The average age is 36 (although this may have gone up to 38 by now; the surveys were a few years ago). Also, 92% are male and 77% are married (again this may have taken a hit too since the survey was a few years ago). What is the ratio of fantasy footballers who are getting married to ones getting divorced? I would say fantasy football might have pushed a few marriages over the edge, so this percentage may be lower by now. About 86 percent own their own homes, 71 percent have a bachelor's degree and 92 percent attended college. Additionally, 59 percent make over $50,000 annually.

There are approximately 15 million fantasy sports players, of which 65% play fantasy football. That means that close to 10 million people, give or take two or three, are playing fantasy football each year; and the numbers are growing at 7-10% per year. Of those 10 million, approximately 1 million are women. Okay single guys, chalk up another reason to play. To meet females. Actually about 97% percent of those buying fantasy sports content (signing up for website membership or purchasing magazines) are men. However, that masks the higher number of spouses who play jointly with their husband on teams. Women could be anywhere from 10-20% of the fantasy football population.

This leads to the classic story: Girl marries boy. Boy watches a lot of football. Girl hates football. Girl must choose whether to hate boy and football or learn to love football and boy. Girl takes up fantasy football. Girl wins league. Boy and girl live happily ever after.

I am going to use the pronoun "he" throughout this book. Why you ask? It is easy and I am lazy. I realize that there are large numbers of women who play fantasy football. There are women who play quite well. I am not attempting to make light of that fact, just pointing out my laziness. Please, ladies, do not take offense or throw burning aromatherapy candles through my living room window.

There are 10 million fantasy football players. Denmark had a little over 5 million people in the entire country according to a census in 1999. You may wonder why I am using that little-known Scandinavian country in my comparisons or why I am picking on Denmark. I am merely using it to help my Danish wife (and father–in-law) understand how big fantasy football really has become. My aim is to decrease those shrugs of "I hope he knows what he is doing!" It never hurts to prop oneself up in front of the in-laws.

However, these "he must be crazy" looks are not just coming from my relatives. While I was writing this book, when people asked what I was doing, I would say writing a book. They would brighten and enthusiastically ask me what type. When I said fantasy football, their cheery demeanor would change. They would get this worried look on their face as if to say… "Sam sure has gone around the bend quickly. But he seems so normal on the golf course."

Here are some actual questions from people I have met at parties and social gatherings:

"So, do you really own those players?" (Hello…..who's in fantasyland now?)

"Do you have to add up all the scores yourself? How do you get all the stats? From the box scores? (No, we use this little thing Al Gore invented called the Internet.)

"So, do you act out the different positions and wear different jerseys? (It depends on if there are any women in our league… No we don't act out their positions.)

Most fantasy footballers are educated, moderately wealthy, middle-aged family men who play to have fun and beat the pants off their co-workers. They play fantasy football to escape and return to those glory days without dumping the older wife for a newer model or blowing the family's retirement fund on a new red Corvette. You are my target audience.

Author's note: Some articles state that 20 million people played fantasy football in 2006. I think that is either the total number of all fantasy sports players or the total number of participants in fantasy football leagues. (Most players are in more than one league.) Is it possible that there are only 14 players and they play in 1.5 million leagues? Think about it.

Other surveys have come up with the following results regarding the fantasy player:

1) Game attendance by fantasy sports enthusiasts is very high in comparison to the general fan. Only 9% of general football fans attended a game whereas 47% of fantasy players attended a game.

2) Most players spend three hours per week managing their team(s).

3) Here is a shocker: 55% of fantasy sports players reportedly watch more sports television since they started playing fantasy sports. Duh. I would hope so…

But what has fantasy football done for the economy? Fantasy sports have a $1 billion to $2 billion annual economic impact within the fantasy industry and a $3 billion to $4 billion annual impact across the sports industry as a whole. The average fantasy sports enthusiasts have played for nine years and play in six contests or leagues in a year. The average annual cost to these individuals is $500, in terms of entry fees, magazines, online content, Alka-seltzer, Tums, etc.

So I ask again, what is fantasy football? It is a way to enjoy the game of football on a higher level. It is a method of competing while watching the sport you love. It is also a hugely popular social event. Anyone who has ever attended a draft knows the camaraderie and excitement of this one day of the year. It will be something to look forward to year after year. It is Christmas in August. It is about using your brain to best your friends in a challenging yet non-threatening way. It is about getting together, laughing at other's picks, sharing outrage as your pick is snatched from you and looking forward to the upcoming season with optimism. It is the ultimate extension of the football season. It gives you a reason to watch the NFL draft and the first half of any preseason games you can. It rationalizes your desire to park your butt on the couch in the living room for ten hours on a Sunday and intake ample amounts of popcorn, pizza and beer. (Did I say that out loud?)

Whether you are a newbie who wants to learn what everyone (and I mean everyone) is talking about, a casual player who wants to know more about the game, or a serious fantasy football competitor who wants to learn some more tips, this book is for you. In the chapters that follow, I will show you the history of fantasy football and what makes up the very basics. I will also show you the different types of leagues, of which there are many. I have included a decision tree to help make that decision a little easier and to concentrate on what is best for you. Next we examine the scoring systems: if you like TDs, then perhaps a TD-only league is for you. If you like big plays then perhaps a distance scoring system is best for you. If you like to see a little of both, then a combination league might be more your style. Do you want to draft with slots and picks like the NFL or would you rather be in an auction where every owner has a chance to bid on every player with you? Options, options, options, there are so many. I will get you through it. But how do you know who to draft or bid on? Ranking players will outline how to come up with your cheat sheets and how to use them wisely. Draft day strategy examines popular theories in use today and offers many tips on what to do and what not to do on draft day. If you think you would like to draft with an auction format, be sure to read chapters 11 and 12 for the draft tips and strategies unique to that format. Regardless of whether you are in a serpentine draft or an auction draft, chapters 13-15 will fill you in on all you need to know to improve your team after the initial draft. From start/bench decisions to adding players through free agency and the all-important trade, these chapters will help prepare you for those midseason tweaks. Later, once you have digested the bulk of the book, come back and use it as a reference guide, especially the rule variations and commissioner information chapters. If you are in this game for the long haul then you will want to check out the keeper leagues.

Anyone will be able to find exceptions to this book and pick things apart with "my league does this" and "my league does that." Just remember: The answer to many questions is "it depends." It almost always depends on your scoring system or rules, or both. Sometimes it will depend on your willingness to take risk.

And no matter why you start (whether it be a local work league or a way to stay in touch with old friends or reconnect with a child), once you start, I guarantee you will be hooked. Don't say I didn't warn you!

Chapter 2 The Basics

What is fantasy football? It is a game played in the minds of NFL fans where they become the owner, GM and coach of their own NFL team, which is made up of players they pick. Their teams then compete with other such teams (owned in many cases by their friends or other fantasy football fans) using a scoring system similar to the NFL rules, but with a few modifications.

Simply put, it is 8-16 football fans who each think they know more than their friends and is willing to put their reputation on the line to prove it. Each "owner" gets to pick his players during the draft. By the way, "The DRAFT" is the most important, and some say the best, day of the fantasy football season. I, for one, agree. During the draft, owners take turns picking the players who will form their team. Generally, you (as the owner) will pick starters and extra players from each position in your lineup. Once the draft is over, it is up to the "coach" (you again) to set his lineup by picking which of his players to start and which to leave on the bench. Those players that he starts will accumulate points based on their performance that week.

The draft order is usually assigned by drawing numbers from a hat. Many Internet leagues have a random generator assign the draft order to teams arbitrarily. The draft is then carried out in a serpentine method. This means the order of the draft is reversed every round. So if you are in a 10-team league and have the tenth (last) pick in the first round, you would get the first pick in the second round (and every other even-numbered round). This makes the draft infinitely fairer, although there have been recent grumbles about the fairness of the system and several new variations have sprung up. (See Chapter 19 – Commissioner Information.)

Once a player has been selected and drafted by a team he is no longer eligible to be drafted by any of the other teams. For example, once Peyton Manning goes, no one else can have him on their team. The number of rounds your draft has will depend on the number of starters and bench players you are allowed, but for fairness, an even number of rounds is necessary. There should be a time limit designated for how long you can take to make your draft selections.

For live drafts, I highly recommend that a draft board be purchased by the league (www.draftkit.com is my favorite). These boards come with different color stickers for different player's positions and have individual player's names on them. For example, one of the yellow (QB) stickers will say P Manning; one will also say E Manning. If everyone cannot attend the draft in person, there are many ways to conduct the draft live over the Internet.

Positions

Most leagues have the following positions: QB, RB, WR, TE, K and DEF/ST. Some leagues have other variations, which will be discussed in chapter 4. Your weekly lineup will be a set number of players from each position.

Scoring

Scoring can come in many forms, which will be elaborated in chapter 5. Basic scoring uses the NFL scoring method, with one small exception. Six points are awarded to any player who rushes or receives a TD; players passing for a TD are awarded three or four points. Any FG is worth three points. PAT's are awarded one point and two-point conversions are worth two points to anyone who actively participated (i.e. if the RB rushes for two points, he gets two points; if QB throws a two-point conversion to the WR, they both get two points). DEF/STs get six points for any TDs they score; either by a turnover returned for a TD or a P/K returned for a TD. Safeties give a defense two points also. Keep in mind the exception mentioned earlier; QBs pass for many more TDs than RBs and WRs, therefore many leagues only give QBs four points (sometimes only three) for passing TDs and some leagues limit passing for a two-point conversion to only one point for the QB.

Basic scoring is great for the beginner in that you can watch the games and keep track of your score and your opponents' scores with just a piece of paper and a pencil, since the scoring is so similar to that of the NFL. The networks help this process with their fantasy stat trackers and "game break" updates. However, the more experienced you become at fantasy football, the more you will want to tweak the scoring system for your league, for more enjoyment.

Each week your team will play another team. You each will set your lineup of starters (typically 1 QB, 2 RBs, 2 WRs , 1 TE, 1 K and 1 DEF/ST). Then as each player performs in his game for that week, you will get points based on the league's scoring system. After the Monday night game, all results will be final and whichever team has the highest fantasy points total will get the win for that week; the other team gets the loss. The season is played out like this every week of the fantasy football regular season (usually the first 13-14 games of the NFL season). Then the "Fantasy Football" Playoffs are held to determine who the champion is. The champ is the winner of the league's Super Bowl usually held in week 16 or 17.

How to form a league of your own.

1) First, you need to gather some like-minded individuals to be team owners in the league. Anywhere from 8 to 16 owners will work. For a thirteen-game regular season, having 14 owners would be ideal. An even amount of owners is always preferred so that you do not have any bye weeks in your league. If you have an odd number, my suggestion is that you have the team who does not have an opponent in any given week play against the average of all the other teams. That way every team has the same amount of win-losses and no team has more byes than any other team.

The other owners should be football diehards just like you. Do not drag in friends just to get more teams involved (although they will likely become addicted to fantasy football and become diehard fans). Some of these dragged-in friends will not want to put any effort into fantasy football and thus become deadweight teams or "dependable doormats"– teams that always lose because no effort is put forth to make them competitive. They will start bye week players because they won't look at the website for a week. They will drop their #1 draft picks because they get off to a slow start for the first few weeks. They will forget to start superstars who were on a bye week the previous week. They will not pick up prime waiver wire players and let other better teams get them. These actions will cause discord among the real fantasy enthusiasts and hard feelings when another team does not get the "gift" of a win from these loveable losers. Instead, only select owners who are knowledgeable about football and will put in at least a minimum amount of effort to insure a competitive team.

2) Decide on the type of league you want. (See Chapter 4 – Types of Leagues.) Then decide on the rules the league will use. This is very important: Make sure the rules are written down somewhere and are distributed to every owner. There is nothing worse than being in week 8 and some owner doing something he thinks is legal, but isn't, and then having to argue about whether it is a rule or not. Agree on the rules before the season starts and then write them down. The rules must be official BEFORE the draft is held because the rules and scoring system will influence the ranking of the players.

3) Pick a commissioner. If possible, the commissioner should be a neutral party, so not an owner in the league. Of course, this is rarely the case as it is hard to find someone who wants to take on this responsibility but who has no stake in the league. He/She should be trustworthy and someone who puts the league first, before his own team interests. All owners should approve him. Finally, some incentive should be provided to them for doing this thankless job. A free entry fee is usually just enough to show how much the league appreciates his hard work.

4) Determine the schedule (if in a head-to-head league). Many online services do this for free after the draft order and draft information is entered. No schedule is needed for a rotisserie league or TFPs league.

5) Conduct a draft. This can either be a traditional serpentine draft or an auction draft. The best time to hold the draft is when everyone can attend; the closer to the start of the NFL season the better. Late August or early September is generally best and Saturday or Sunday is perhaps the easiest time to get everyone together at once. The closer the draft date is to the start of the season, the better informed all owners can be about starting players on the NFL teams and injuries, etc.

6) The commissioner enters the draft information into the Internet website or computer program and then begins the fantasy football season. He should post the starting lineups prior to kickoff. Any messages from the commissioner can come through e-mail, phone or the message board at your league website.

7) Owners should set their lineups each week. If you do not set it, it will automatically be the same lineup as the week before.

8) Compile scores based on your league rules and scoring system. This is usually done with the help of an Internet site.

9) Execute transactions. From the beginning of the season until some point before the playoffs (around week 10), teams can drop players from their rosters and add other players who are available. Teams can also trade with one another.

10) Postseason. Some teams will make the playoffs and advance to the Super Bowl. Others may go to a "Toilet Bowl" to determine the worst team in the league.

Don't forget to have fun!!!

If you do not want to form your own league or cannot find enough players then join an Internet league. If you have some friends who want to play against you, then have them join your Internet league too. That way you all can have fun without the required number of players. One perk to this is that someone else will be the commissioner and undertake those responsibilities. There are typically three types of Internet league: free leagues, small stakes leagues and high stakes leagues.

Even if you do not have a computer to play in an Internet league, you can always go to a public library or Internet café. The public library usually offers free use of a computer. A simple stop at the library on Sunday morning or Saturday afternoon will allow you to do the minimum required to participate. If you feel that computer access will be a problem, consider a magazine contest. Many magazines offer salary cap contests (for small stakes) that require either Internet or phone use.

The following are some of the different leagues and their approximate prices. If you are just starting out, try a free league at Yahoo, ESPN or CBSsportsline. If you want to try something else, look into the intermediate leagues. If you want to be the best in the world, try the WCOFF, NFFC or AFFL games.

Beginner	Yahoo, ESPN or CBSsportsline.
Intermediate	Sporting News games ($25 leagues)
Advanced	WCOFF or NFFC satellite ($200 leagues)
Expert	WCOFF, NFFC, AFFL ($1000+ leagues)

Who can you expect to play against?

Types of Players

1) Fair-weather friends or "boneheads" – Just playing because they were dragged in by the commish or some of the other owners, or a co-worker who wants to be in on the fun but does not know anything about fantasy football. He follows his favorite team but does not know much about the other 31 teams. He does know who Peyton Manning is and knows he has a brother but is not sure if his brother plays. He will forget the bye weeks, start injured players and draft players just released or injured for the season. He should be considered a part-timer, since he shows up with no prep work done. These are the teams you should always win against.

2) Experienced and competent but not an expert – He enjoys watching NFL football and loves to play fantasy football. He has not one, but two, fantasy football magazines he uses to reference for draft day. He has ESPN, Yahoo and CBSsportsline stored as his favorite websites and uses them to get "the scoop" but does not spend hours combing the Internet looking for that gold mine of secret information. He does not do his own rankings but instead modifies his one favorite magazine cheat sheet. He plays for the bragging rights but does not let it get obsessive and ruin his family life either. He is a good guy but will never quit his day job to play the WCOFF. He is like most fantasy football fans. He wants to win but does not care if he loses a few games.

3) Experts – Play fantasy football religiously. Have all the magazines and books. Subscribe to at least one service with customized cheat sheets, news, etc. Wants to win badly and will spend some time to get the win. He wants to win every game.

4) Homers – They show up wearing their Eagles jerseys and hats and you know right away who they will be drafting in the first 3 rounds. Homers are inexperienced players who draft based on their favorite NFL teams or divisions, or players that have played on their fantasy teams before or, heaven forbid, for his old college. Who only drafts former University of Miami players, etc.?

5) Cool Hand Luke's – The player you should try to be. They do not let emotions get in the way of their judgments. They do their homework. They are gamers. They create their own cheat sheets from scratch. They know every starting offensive skill player on every team. They are a wealth of knowledge and skill. They make the playoffs every year and win the championships more often than not. Confidence is their middle name.

Now that you know the basics of fantasy football, you have no reason not to try it.

Chapter 3 History of Fantasy Football

Contrary to popular belief, Fantasy Football did not arise from the Rotisserie Baseball craze that started in1979 with Dan Okrent meeting friends at La Rotisserie Francaise (hence the name). According to NFL.com, Fantasy Football got its start much earlier, on a rainy October night in 1962, when Wilfred "Bill" Winkenbach, Scotty Sterling and Bill Tunnell became the founding fathers of Fantasy Football. Bill Winkenbach was a limited partner of the Oakland Raiders; Sterling was an Oakland Tribune sports writer and Bill Tunnell was the Oakland Raiders PR manager. They were relaxing and having some cocktails in a Manhattan Hotel, (now the Milford Plaza), as the eventual 1-13 Oakland Raiders finished up a three-game, 16-day East Coast road trip (Boston, Buffalo and finally New York). This is where the rules began. They created a set of rules in which individuals could draft skill players from professional teams and play weekly games against their friends. Fantasy Football was born. In fact, Bill Winkenbach may be the father of Fantasy Baseball and Golf as well, since he based fantasy football on some other fantasy sports games that he had been playing since the 1950's, but that is for another book.

Of course, no great event is completed in a single session and the three men got together with George Ross, an Oakland Tribune sports editor, once they returned to Oakland and fine-tuned the draft rules.

GOPPPL

Their league was called the GOPPPL, The Greater Oakland Professional Pigskin Prognosticators League. Try saying that three times fast! There were four others who would play the next year (1963), to bring the total to eight team owners. Many of the owners took on partners or coaches. For instance, George Glace grabbed 24-year-old Ron Wolfe (former Green Bay GM) as his co-owner.

The "Club Owners" of GOPPPL:

- Raider owner Bill Winkenbach (and first commissioner)

- George Ross, Oakland Tribune Sports Editor

- Scotty Sterling, Oakland Tribune Sports Writer

- George Glace, Oakland Raider Ticket Manager

- Bob Blum, Oakland Raider play-by-play announcer

- Bill Tunnell, Oakland Raiders Public Relations Manager

- Phil Carmona, Raider Season Ticket Seller

- Ralph Casebolt, Raider Season Ticket Seller

The first draft was held in Winkenbach's basement, known as Winkenbach's Rumpus room. Other drafts and playoff dinners (at the end of the season to award prizes) were held at local restaurants. The only requirement to join was a journalistic or administrative capacity with professional football, or you had to have purchased or sold ten or more season tickets for the Raiders (four of the original owners fell into this category).

Bill Winkenbach served as the first commissioner of Fantasy Football (remember this for Bar Trivia later), and as such he prepared weekly reports that were delivered to each GOPPPL owner on Tuesday morning of game week. He also was the first to deal with the same kind of squabbles that plague many leagues to this day. He collected money, got starting lineups and prevented owners from colluding, long before many of us were born.

The GOPPPL had many of the trappings of today's leagues.

– The first draft was eight teams, 20 players with a serpentine format.

– The order was determined by a deck of cards.

– Of the 20 players chosen, teams had to draft the same amount from the positions listed and start the same amounts, so there was no stockpiling at RB.

– They had a loser's trophy that the ultimate loser had to display on his mantel for an entire year.

– They had IR rules.

– The following year's draft order was based on previous year performance.

Andy Mousalimas partnered with Scotty Sterling and later opened up the Kings X Sports bar in 1968. The first Kings X draft was held in 1969. There was only one division then, but it soon grew to five divisions by 1972. No women were allowed to play, but in 1974 Al Santini suggested an all-women's division and the Queens division began. This marks one of the first written documentations of women and Fantasy Football. By 1974 the game had over 200 participants.

Previously published histories of FF note that it spread from the Kings X in Oakland to San Francisco, and then the entire Bay Area. Then in waves (like ripples on a pond), people would talk about FF at the Kings X and then take it to their hometowns. These players, in this, the first Fantasy Football league, then became disciples and spread the word along the West Coast. Individuals would call and request the rules. However, many groups faltered because of the cumbersome and time-consuming act of scoring. Remember, there were no Yahoo leagues to provide instant totals or stat trackers back then.

The media was not much help either in finding the young stars or sleepers. Those owners with more experienced "coaches" usually found themselves at the top of the leaderboards. Back then, Street and Smith was the bible for research, just as it is now.

The rosters had to be submitted in person on Friday by midnight (except for Thanksgiving, when the deadline was Wednesday at midnight). No changes could be made before kickoff or after Saturday's injury report. Many of the owners came to watch the Sunday games at the Kings X bar and cheered their own fantasy players, not NFL teams, causing some confusion. Sunday scores were posted Monday at lunchtime and Monday Night Football packed in the crowds. Tuesday lunch became standings day. The scoring was done manually, of course, with one person scouring the sports page with paper and pencil. Let me reiterate: there was no Internet, no sports talk radio and no fantasy football magazines or books. This probably explains why the sport did not catch on. Many were intimidated or simply turned off by the amount of number crunching that was involved in transforming the box scores on Monday's sports section into league scores and standings.

There also was a rules committee, consisting of a committee czar and appointees from each division, and they met twice a year to hear grievances and organize for the upcoming year. Originally a RB, Rec or QB received the same points regardless of TD length. In 1970, however, points were increased based on the length of the TD (modern-day distance-scoring rules).

In 1971 the league moved from a TD-only league to a performance league based on yardage scoring as well. That year also saw "defensive and return players" changed to "defensive and return teams;" DEF/ST was born. Interestingly, no trades between teams were allowed for fear of collusion (although some owners wanted trades). In 1979 the league added a midseason draft because teams were not allowed to add players until their position was depleted by IR.

The Kings X owner, Andy Mousalimas, asked the media types involved to keep it low-key, fearing for gambling rules that might be used against the bar. Of course, the media was not as receptive then as they are today. Many times you would not know who scored in other games until reading it in the Monday paper.

Fantasy Football spread slowly due to the problems with scoring, although it was easier than fantasy baseball to score. The computer made calculations easier. As software became available, interest increased. The Internet (thank you, Al Gore) proved to be the big catalyst that propelled FF into fame. The Internet took FF from sports bars and office lounges into individual homes and turned the hobby into a money-making enterprise. Today, fantasy football is big business.

Now commissioners could easily download a stat file with all of the previous week's statistics. Then the software would generate the scoring reports, league standings and other pertinent information, savings hours of work. Next came high-speed Internet, live scoring and real time stats, so that an owner could see how his team was doing against his opponent instantly. Fantasy Football has progressed from small local leagues which used paper, pencil and the Monday box scores to automated websites that give you live scoring.

Information resources have changed too. The transfer of information has gone from snail mail newsletters to websites with injury annotations and projected customized lineup suggestions.

The NFL did not embrace fantasy football as soon as it could have. Instead, it kept its distance because it feared the gambling label that some use with Fantasy Football. Now, in the 21st century, the NFL has opened its arms to the hobby. One does not have to look much further than NFL.com or the commercials with NFL players (Reggie Bush is in one) about fantasy football. My all-time favorite is the T.J. "Hoos-your-mamma" commercial from 2006. I also like the "Kickers go fast; take them early and often " commercial, that the NFL network runs.

Timeline for Fantasy Football History

1954 – Football's popularity soared when TV became popular because scheduling games on Sunday afternoons meant more men could watch from the comfort of their couch on Sundays while at home.

1962 – Fantasy Football rules born in NYC Hotel Room.

1963 – First league formed, the GOPPPL.

1965 – Fantasy Football spread to San Francisco.

1966 – NFL and AFL merge; color TV becomes popular.

Jan 15,1967 – the first Super Bowl was played (although it would not be called a Super Bowl until the 5th Championship game was played).

1969 – First Kings X Fantasy Football leagues formed.

1970 – Conferences used AFC and NFC. GOPPPL starts distance scoring

1971 – GOPPPL turns to performance scoring and to DEF/ST versus defensive players.

1972 – Kings X Leagues now fill five divisions.

1974 – First known Ladies Division (QUEENS) at Kings X Bar

1979 – GOPPPL adds midseason draft; one of the longest actively running leagues "Wagon Wheel Fantasy Football League" based in Spokane, Washington begins.

1987 – "Fantasy Index" Magazine was first published.

1989 – There are 1 million fantasy sports players in the US.

1990 – "Fantasy Pro Forecast" Magazine was first published.

In the 80s and 90s, pioneers in fantasy football provided the innovative products that spawned the growth of the sport and led to the present Internet-based explosion of fantasy football.

1990 – The World Wide Web debuts as a new interface for the Internet.

1997 – FSTA (Fantasy Sports Trade Association) formed and is the oldest and most prestigious non-profit fantasy sports trade association.

The 90s showed explosive growth in the number of fantasy football participants, due to computers, to between 7 and 8 million players.

The twenty-first century saw fantasy football become more mainstream.

2002 – The World Championship of Fantasy Football (WCOFF) begins.

2003 – There are approximately 10 million FF players.

2004 - NFFC and AFFL begin

2005 – Yahoo stays free.

2006 – There are approximately 12 million FF players.

2006 – CDM Fantasy Sports wins battle with MLBAM over rights of player's statistics. On Aug 8, 2006, Judge Mary Ann L. Medler gave a strong opinion, siding with CDM on every point. That's baseball, you say. It has the potential to affect fantasy football too. Twenty years ago, commissioners sorted through the Monday and Tuesday sports sections of their local newspapers in an effort to decipher the publicly available stats to run their leagues. Now those stats are processed much more efficiently, thanks to technology. But that same information should, in my humble opinion, continue to be publicly available.

2006 – The Anti-gambling bill has fantasy sports carve out language. It says that fantasy games are exempt from the gambling law (they were targeting offshore betting sites; think poker and gambling) as long as they meet two requirements:

1) Awards and prizes must be stated prior to the game starting and not be determined by the number of participants or total entry fee revenue and
2) Winning outcomes are determined by skill for contests that use results from multiple real life games.

In essence, it solidifies the fact that fantasy sports are games of skill, not luck.

Chapter 4 Types of Leagues

Outside of the scoring system you choose, the type of league is the most characteristic feature that identifies your league; but the choices are difficult.

If you are a beginner, your best bet is to go with the simplest of leagues to learn the ropes. This will most likely be a free fantasy football league on Yahoo, ESPN or CBSsportsline. I suggest you choose a public league with the lowest number of teams and the basic scoring method. Try to minimize the number of teams so that the talent pool of NFL players is large. That way you can jump into FF and still be familiar with some of the players at the end of the draft (versus picking out names from a magazine list).

Unfortunately, the simpler the league, the more luck plays a persuasive role. Generally, the more complex (within reason) the more skill is needed to win. Below you will find a decision tree. It will help you wade through as many variables as possible to make different decisions in starting or finding a league.

Whether you are looking for a fun league (co-workers, neighbors or bar buddies and no big money) or a high stakes league (experienced players, serious money), this information should help you find the right league.

A detailed explanation of each step follows the decision tree.

League Decision Tree

1) Free or pay? (If pay, is it a one-time entry fee or will transactions/errors cost?)

2) Will league need a stat management service? (If free and using Yahoo or ESPN or CBSsportsline, then no stat service is needed; if yes, who to use?)

3) League type: Head-to-Head, Rotisserie, Points, Survivor

4) Draft type: Traditional or auction and how will it be conducted (live, online or e-mail?)

5) Number of teams (between 8 and 16, preferably an even number)

6) Scoring System (Basic, Performance, Bonus, Distance, Combination)

7) Scoring Rules (PPR, negative values, decimals)

8) Starting Roster (Flex vs. No Flex, IDP vs. DEF/ST, TE vs. No TE required)

9) Total Roster Size (8-25). Prefer an even number if having a serpentine draft so that it will be fair to all teams.

10) Transactions and Free Agent (FA)/Trades: (No trades vs. trades allowed, Limit on number of transactions, FA bid vs. waiver wire, first come, first served (FCFS) vs. waiver wire, waiver priority basis, time limits on add/drops/trades.)

11) Super Bowl in week 16 or 17 (this will affect the playoffs).

12) Number of Playoff Teams: Usually 50% of league teams or less. Does #1 seed get a bye? Do all teams start over in playoffs or do some points carry over from regular season? Is there a consolation bracket?

13) Ownership: Keeper League vs. Non-Keeper League (also called re-draft leagues). If keeper league, will it be dynasty, minimal keeper or somewhere in between; will contracts be used to keep?

14) Prizes: If prizes are offered, will it be all or nothing or spread the wealth?

1) Fee or no fee; if there is a fee will there be prizes?

A free league can be fun and you are playing for bragging rights anyway, right? But the idea of having a trophy appeals to some, so how do you pay for the trophy? Perhaps have the last place team buy the first place team his trophy every year to keep it free to all. Ultimately, it may be better to "put your money where your mouth is" and play for a nominal amount of prize money. Usually the fee involved, if there is one, will be to cover the costs of running the league. These costs occur when opting to go for specific league management software instead of the free sites available. A draft board will cost $20-$30, unless you decide to make your own. Once the upkeep costs are covered, prize money and trophies can be added in if desired. What is too expensive? What is the cutoff between high stakes and low stakes? Most would say a $100 entry fee is expensive but okay. Most draw the line at $200. The high stakes leagues, (WCOFF, NFFC and AFFL), all charge over $1,000 to enter. If there is a fee, you need to find out if it will be a one-time entry fee or if other things will cost too. Some leagues charge a small fee for transactions such as adding another player from the free agent list or executing a trade. Other leagues make the last place team throw a Super Bowl party or bring the beer for next years draft. Any such requirements should be mentioned up-front and put in writing.

2) Stat management service or not?

The answer to this question will determine what other options below you can use. If you elect to use a stat service, your league will have to have an entry fee to cover the costs. Normally they will run from $50-$150, with discounts for early signups. Generally, you get what you pay for with these sites. I have had great luck with http://www.myfantasyleague.com. Add in a draft board and you have in excess of $100, but when split between ten or more owners, this is small change. In Yahoo it is free but the live stats service is $10 extra per owner or $120 per league. Most owners elect to pay this on their own, so have a vote. Many owners will be willing to pay $10 extra for a stat service that provides live scoring and all the options that you can think of below. So if you can find a stat service that provides live stats and great management, grab it. What do you want in a stat service? Live scoring, flexible scoring options and rules set up, dependable service and a reasonable price. That's all you need from a stat service. Remember, oftentimes you get what you pay for.

3) Head-to-Head, Rotisserie or Fantasy Points?

The first decision is whether to have a head-to-head (H2H), rotisserie or fantasy points league. All leagues have their advantages and disadvantages. H2H is perhaps the most common type of league since it incorporates more of the NFL style of competition.

Purists to fantasy football will say that only in a Rotisserie league will the real fantasy football expert be crowned a champion year in and year out. Fantasy points leagues are a lot like Rotisserie leagues but use total fantasy points.

H2H

In a H2H league every team plays another team each week based on the schedule. The TFPs from your starters are compared with the TFPs of your opponent's starters, and the higher scoring team gets a win. If both score the same amount of fantasy points, then either a tie is awarded to both teams or a tiebreaker system is used to determine a winner and a loser. The scheduler should make every attempt to have every team play every other team in the league at least once. A 16-team league with a 14-game regular season will not allow this. Subtract 1 from the total number of teams in the league and that is the length of the regular season required so that each team plays all of the other teams once. Therefore, 14-team leagues usually go with a 13-game regular season and 12-team leagues like WCOFF go with an 11-game regular season. If you have more regular season games than the above formula (total number of teams minus 1), then you end up with some teams playing each other twice. That can be unfair, but then again it happens in the NFL, so tough! Some leagues have divisions; some have just one big division. If your schedule allows teams to play each other more than once in a season, then divisions are recommended so that those who play each other more than once will be in the same division. Thus, those who play each other more often will end up competing directly for playoff spots. In 10-team leagues, two divisions of 5 teams each (North and South or East and West, etc.) work best with a 13-game regular season so that each team is played once and every team within the division is played twice. In 12-team leagues, three divisions of 4 teams each will work (North, Central, South or East, Central, West, etc.), with an 11-game regular season so that everyone plays once. Another option is a 14-game season so that everyone plays once and you play the other three teams in your division twice. Head-to-head leagues offer just that, real NFL-like matches, where two teams meet in competition with no one else affecting the outcome except those two team's players.

Advantages: NFL-type schedule, rivalries, more trash talking, individual wagers on individual outcomes.

Disadvantages: Possibility for teams to score more points over the season but not make playoffs (this is called the boom-bust phenomenon); luck plays a larger part possibly; may leave out week 17 due to players not playing.

Rotisserie League

In a rotisserie league, all teams turn in a lineup each week just like H2H leagues. That is where the similarities end. When the games for a particular week are over, all the scored stats are added up. A rotisserie league involves all teams ranked in differing categories. The categories can be anything but are usually the same scoring criteria as seen in the next chapter, "Scoring Systems." As an example, a league may have the following seven categories: rushing TDs, passing TDs, receiving TDs, rushing yards, passing yards, receiving yards and total kicker points. If you wanted to have ten categories, you could add in QB interceptions (the lower the number of interceptions, the higher your rankings and points awarded) and tackles and sacks for individual defensive players (IDPs). Teams get points for each category ranking (for example, in a 10-team league, first place in a category gets 10 points, last place in the category gets 1 point). If there were seven categories and 10 points for the first place winner in each category, then the most points a team could have would be 70. In a 14-team league with seven categories, 98 would be the most points possible (7 x 14 points for first place = 98).

At the end of the season, (usually the end of the NFL regular season), all of the teams are ranked based on each category. The payouts (if any) usually go to the top three or four teams, depending on how many played. Usually the payouts work out as 60% for first place, 30% for second place and 10% for third place, or something similar. Many times the entry fee is the third place prize and first place takes 50% or more of the prize money.

There is no H2H schedule and no playoffs in a rotisserie league. Each owner plays until the end of the NFL regular season (week 17). At the end of the season, points are totaled based on category rankings and the winner is the team with the most points. One advantage to this format is that all 17 weeks can be utilized. Another advantage is that no H2H schedule is needed so bye weeks are not a problem like with odd teams in a H2H league. Another advantage is that no "easy schedule" or "hard schedule" excuses can be used. This involves teams that are better than their records indicate because they played other teams that they should have beaten but played them when they had their "best week of the year." The opposite is true when lesser teams have better records because they got lucky and played better teams when those teams had bad weeks (due to injuries or bye problems). These excuses cannot be used in a rotisserie league because there is no schedule. There are no playoffs in which it is single elimination. There is no scoring system used so no need to decide how many points to award passing TDs, etc.

In rotisserie, points are awarded for the ranking within the category and the rankings are simply based on the amount of that category's statistics accumulated. For example, the end of the season may find Slam's Slammers the #1 team in Passing TDs, with 49 (think P. Manning in 2004), and Thumpers, the #2 team, may have 41. The Slammers would get 14 points in a 14-team league, while Thumpers would get 13 points even though the Slammers are 8 TDs ahead of them. Rotisserie leagues really do present the best team with the trophy at the end of the year. If you use "yards per carry, catch or pass" as a category, you may want to put a minimum number of throws, catches or rushes. Otherwise, an owner could get a RB who has only carried twice, but for long runs, and thus his YPC will be inflated and at the top of the category. Tiebreakers may be important here too, so have a system in place (such as the team with the most total TDs, etc). Rotisserie leagues require balance to win. If you lead a rotisserie category by too much (for example Passing TDs) and you are in first place with a 24 TD lead, then you have also probably sacrificed in another category. Rotisserie is the least popular method, probably because it is so "baseballesque."

Advantages: No H2H schedule (thus great for odd number of teams); all weeks used; no single elimination playoff format; less luck/more skill; no scoring system needed.

Disadvantages: No playoff or Super Bowl excitement; harder to find owners to play this format; once you fall too far behind it's easy to lose interest; no spoiler magic; boring.

Points League

In a points league you set your starting rosters each week and accumulate fantasy points. The team with the highest total fantasy points at the end of the season is the League Champion. It differs from a rotisserie in that you do not have categories and rankings but instead use the scoring system in the rules. Using the above Passing TD example, Slam's Slammers would receive 196 points (49 TDs x 4 points = 196) and Thumpers would received 164 (41 x 4 points = 164). So, in this format, the Slammers would be rewarded for having a player who was head and shoulders above the rest that year. This format does not require as much balance as the Rotisserie leagues. This type of league is also losing popularity by the year. However, many leagues have gone to a H2H league format while including the high-points teams in the playoff spots. For example, the Top 3 H2H teams make the playoffs and then the team with the highest TFP is allowed in as the fourth playoff team.

Advantages: No H2H Schedule; all weeks used; no single elimination playoff format.

Disadvantages: No rivalries; no playoff excitement; harder to find owners to play this format; once you fall too far behind it's easy to lose interest; no spoiler magic.

Other variations of leagues:

Draftsmasters – this involves drafting more players at the draft and then never having a FA system. Who you draft is who you have for the entire season. In addition, some leagues will not require a lineup but instead will use whichever players score the most for the starting positions on your team. For example, you have T. Brady and P. Manning. Whichever player scores the most points in any given week will be considered your starter QB for that week.

Survivor Leagues – In these leagues, the team that scores the fewest points in any given week is eliminated from the competition, so it behooves you to draft a well-balanced team. Survivor leagues are less common in fantasy football and more prevalent in football picks. If you get knocked out early, you have nothing to look forward to.

4) Traditional or Auction Draft or Contest

A traditional draft occurs when owners pick players in order, one at a time, to fill all of their roster spots. Usually it is a serpentine draft, which means the draft order reverses itself at the end of every round, like a snake. In this format, with 14 teams, whichever team had the fourteenth pick in round 1 would also have the first pick in round 2 (order reversed at end of each round). The owner who was lucky enough to get the first pick in round 1 would not pick again until the fourteenth pick in round 2 (the 28th pick) but would then have the first pick again in round 3, (hence back-to-back picks in rounds 2 and 3). Auctions use a bidding system in which owners bid play money from their salary cap (usually $100 or $200) for each player and the owner with the highest bid wins that player. As an example, in one WCOFF 2006 Auction League draft, Larry Johnson went for $76 out of a $200 budget.

Whether you choose to have a traditional draft or an auction, you still must decide whether you will have it live, online, via e-mail or staggered. A live draft involves all owners being present at the draft or available by phone, as the case may be. An online draft will involve all owners logging into the draft website or allowing their computer to auto draft, as discussed in chapter 8. An e-mail or staggered draft can take weeks and involves players making their picks with a time limit of 24-48 hours. Of course, not every owner takes the full 48 hours with every pick, but some owners can be away from their computer for long periods and thus delay the draft significantly.

A contest is where you are given a list of names and you pick the players you want based on a salary cap or one from each category, etc. Normally a contest is a "pay for a chance to win" contest. Contests usually allow multiple teams to have the same player, as long as the team remains under the salary cap. For example, P. Manning is worth $5 million. Any team can have him as long as they remain under the salary cap of $100 million with him on their team.

Many contests have roster limits. In this instance, you can only have a certain number at each position. This may be a minimum, a maximum or a required amount. If the limit was a minimum of one TE then you would be required to always have at least one TE on your roster at all times, but you could carry more. If the limit was a maximum of six RBs, then you could never have more than six on your roster. If the rules required a certain amount then you would have to have that amount at all times. A common roster requirement is 2 QB, 3 RB, 3 WR, 2 TE, 2 K and 2 DEF, at all times.

5) Number of Teams

An even number of teams is desirable if in a H2H league. If you have an odd number then one team will be without an opponent every week in a H2H League. An odd number of teams can be fixed by using a rotisserie format, by playing each team every week, or by averaging the scores for all teams and having the bye week team play against that average.

Leagues can have any number of teams from 6 to 24, although 24-team leagues are really smaller leagues disguised as divisions, in which they have their own draft. Most leagues consist of 8-14 teams. Some do have 16 but this is stretching it, for various reasons discussed below. If you have a rotisserie or points league, some of the arguments below will not apply since you will not have playoffs. However, when you begin to consider 16 or more teams, take into consideration the amount of players drafted and the limited supply of certain positions (QB, K, DEF) with only 32 NFL teams (see Table 9.3). If your league will have 16 teams and require each team to own two QBs, kickers and defenses, then there will be none available to pick up in free agency. On the opposite side of the spectrum, you can do a league with only six teams but it really is too small to have much good competition. In 6-team leagues, everyone has great QBs and RBs, so it is less about skill in drafting and more in luck of who gets hurt or escapes injuries. Eight teams is realistically the minimum number of teams.

With a 16-team league, you would need to play a 15-game regular season for each team to play every other team once. If you do not play a 15-game season, then inevitably some owners will complain that others had an unfair advantage because they did not have to play the tough team in the league or, vice versa, they got to play the easy team in the league. Better to avoid these types of situations if possible. To avoid this, in a 16-team league you would have to have a 15-game regular season and then a one-week Super Bowl (week 16) or a one week playoff (week 16) and the dreaded week 17 Super Bowl. Even then, the playoffs would be limited to four teams in order to get two for the Super Bowl. Only 4 of 16 making the playoffs may be a bit too harsh.

For all of the above reasons, 12 or 14 team leagues are the best fit. With 14-team leagues, you would have 13-game regular seasons with six or seven teams making the playoffs (one or two teams get byes), and the playoffs last through week 16's Super Bowl. Additionally, 12-team leagues are perfect for 14-game regular seasons, with each team playing its division opponents twice each. The playoffs occur in week 15, with four teams (3 Division Winners and a wild card team). The Super Bowl occurs in week 16. An 8-team league means there are too many good players on each team (with large rosters) or on the FA list. The more teams you let play, the more emphasis on combining WR/TE into one position. Some have suggested that with the recent 6-team bye weeks (started in 2006), a 14-team league is no longer tenable since some owners will not have a serviceable QB, TE, K or defense. Having 32 teams with a kicker, 6 teams on bye week, leaves 26 kickers available for 14 teams, but if any team has more than two someone could be left out.

More teams means less players available in free agency, which means a harder league. More teams also mean more money for the prize, but more competition. An odd number of teams can cause problems as well. If you have an odd number of teams then one team each week will be left out and not have an opponent in a H2H league. This is easily fixable in leagues where you can customize the stats. Have the team who is the "odd man out" submit a starting lineup as if he is really playing someone, because he will play the average of all the other teams. If his score is higher than the average of the other teams that week he gets a win, if not then a loss or a tie. The only disadvantage is that the owner has no one to trash talk with on this week. Beware if your league uses a free web/stat service such as Yahoo, ESPN etc; these leagues may have limited stat editing and may not handle an odd team. Yahoo will allow between 4 and 20 teams but I have yet to play in a league with an odd number there.

6) Scoring Systems (Basic, Performance, Bonus, Distance, Combination)

Refer to Chapter 5 – Scoring Systems, for a discussion on these types of systems.

7) Scoring Rules

PPR – One variation that has gained popularity is the points per reception rule. In this case, a player who catches a pass is awarded one point. A WR who has an 8-catch day would score eight points on his catches alone. This rule tends to help even out the playing field between RBs and WRs. It also helps the lowly TE, since in many cases he does most of the dirty work over the middle, catching numerous passes but for short yardage and infrequent TDs. Think twice about using the PPR rule in basic leagues as this may give too much power to pass-catchers.

Negative Values – Another decision will need to be made about whether or not to allow negative values, as in if a player throws four interceptions and no TDs. The result would be negative four points. Some leagues do not penalize a player or allow him to have negative points since you cannot score negative points in the NFL. Other leagues allow individual players to have negative points and take the chance that a team will one day perform so poorly as to have a negative score.

Decimal values – You should decide in advance if you want to have scores in decimals or whole numbers. Decimals can get messy and distract from the purity of the game since the NFL cannot have a decimal for a score. Many leagues elect to round down if decimals are awarded. The best way to avoid this is to have your scoring rules set up so that only whole numbers are awarded. However, if you award points for yardage (one point for every 10 yards), then you must decide if you want decimals or not as many stat sites will simply divide the yardage by 10, as in the above example, and 73 yards would result in 7.3 points. The advantage to using decimals is that it cuts down considerably on the number of ties in a league, virtually eliminating ties in some cases.

8) Starting roster requirements

Most leagues require as a minimum one QB, one RB, two WRs, a kicker and a defense. This is the very basic starting roster. At some point, 92% of all leagues had a QB, RB, WR, TE, K and DEF/ST. The other 7% had replaced the DEF/ST with IDP. The remaining 1% had many different variations. The rationale here is that this is what every NFL team has as its starting lineup of scoring positions. Many leagues add another RB. Some will add a third WR as well.

TE or No TE? – Notice there is no TE in the lineup above. There is a great debate about whether to include the TE in the starting roster. Those *for* TEs insist he is a basic ingredient in the scoring positions. They also point out that the TE position has become more valuable in recent years, with valid arguments for a strong group of at least 15 TEs these days. Those *against* TEs say that it is an insignificant position. The pro-TE camp counters with examples of Tony Gonzalez and Antonio Gates. Many leagues have concluded that the TE is valuable but should not be mandatory, so they have included a flex position that can be either WR or TE. This has helped sway some of the pro-TE camp to eliminate it as a permanent member of the starting roster. Therefore you must decide whether TE is a required position on the starting roster.

Flex Position – Do you want to have a position called Flex, where a RB, a WR or a TE can be started? Some flex positions are limited to WR or TE only.

IDP or DEF/ST – In this case IDP stands for individual defensive player. (See Chapter 21 – IDP and Defenses.)

Most common starting rosters: 1 QB, 2 RB, 3 WR, 1 TE, 1 K, 1 DEF (THE MOST COMMON)

1QB, 2 RB, 2 WR, 1 TE, 1 K, 1 DEF

1 QB, 2 RB, 3 WR/TE, 1 K, 1 DEF

1 QB, 2 RB, 2 WR, 1 TE, 1 K, 1 DEF, 1 Flex
(RB/WR/TE)

1 QB, 1 RB, 1 WR, 1 TE, 1 K, 1 DEF/ST, 2 Flex
(RB/WR/TE)

Some leagues allow different formations each week; others force you to pick a formation and stick with it for the entire year. The following formations are typical:

Traditional (pro set)   1 QB, 2 RB, 2 WR, 1 TE

West Coast   1 QB, 1 RB, 3 WR, 1 TE

Run and shoot   1 QB, 1 RB, 4 WR (no TE started)

Formations allow for different draft strategies and weekly lineup strategy.

Some suggest that the flex position favors the "stacked" teams the most and thus only helps those with great RBs or less injuries.

Flex Players:

(W/T) Means a player can be either a WR or a TE.

(W/R) Means a player can be either a WR or RB.

(W/T/R) Means a player can be either a WR, TE or RB.

Some leagues have head coaches as a roster spot. Some have IDPs, (replacing DEF/ST) which will be addressed further in chapter 21.

Simpler lineups are better for beginners whereas complex lineups (flex, formations, etc.) are better for more advanced players.

9) Total roster size

A ROT for total roster size is twice the number of players starting (can be as high as up to three times starters – a big roster). So, if 8 players start then 16 will be the roster size. This allows you to have extra players for bye weeks and injuries. The larger the number the longer the draft will take. The larger this number the harder it will be to find replacements. The larger this number the more skilled an owner needs to be in drafting since more players will be selected and less will be available for free agency. Most leagues allow anywhere from 14-20 players on a roster with 16 being the average. If you start 8 (QB, two RB, two WR, TE, K, DEF), then you would want to allow 14 as a minimum so that owners can have a backup at each position. Whether they choose to do so is another topic discussed later in the book. Even this gets problematic with injuries and bye weeks. Once teams have more than 20 players to draft, it can be a little monotonous at the end as everyone is scraping the barrel for players. Some believe this is where the draft is truly won or lost. Smaller rosters usually force more transactions due to injuries, suspensions, benching, etc. Large rosters mean fewer transactions are needed because you can keep a player on the roster and wait it out. As an example, imagine the difference between a 24-man roster and a 14-man roster in leagues that only start eight players. In the 24 man-roster, I have 16 players as backups. I can have two players at each starting position (so I start two RBs and have four as backup). Now in the 14-man roster I only have six total backups. I am limited to, at best, one backup per position. IR rules are more for smaller rosters to help with injuries. Smaller rosters are generally designed to prevent hoarding of players. For example, a 24-man roster in a 16-team league that starts eight players could see some teams with three kickers or QBs, thus squeezing out some teams and forcing them to carry only one QB or K and be screwed on bye weeks. 20 players on a roster with 12 teams or more make the FA listings pretty poor. Half the fun is picking up someone off the FA list that performs for you that week. Teams with two of everything and three QBs, and five or six RBs and WRs do not leave much to pick from. You would like to have an even amount of players on your roster so that the draft will be an even number of rounds.

Small rosters = large FA lists = better for beginners.

Large rosters = smaller FA lists = better for advanced players (less luck, more skill).

10) Free agency (FA)/Trades

Let's first define Free Agency, waiver wire and trades. Free agency is any player that is not on a roster. That player is available for any team to pick up. Players on the waiver wire have been released by their previous owners (placed on waivers). Normally, players who are dropped go on waivers for two to three days and then become free agents, if no team makes a waiver claim for them. Trades are exchanges of players, draft picks or, in some instances, salary cap money between teams. Usually all players dropped from a team will go to the waiver wire for a certain amount of time. This can be anywhere from a few days to the entire week. This allows all owners the opportunity to see who has been dropped and is now available. Otherwise, if they went straight to the FA market, then another owner, who just happened to be online and see the player get dropped, could add him without other owners having any chance to get him. This would hurt owners who were not online 24/7. All players remaining after the draft will either go to free agency or go to the waiver wire for the set length of time and then become free agents. Many articles and references will use the terms free agent and waiver wire interchangeably. In some leagues, the waiver wire is where a player goes for a certain period of time after release from a team. In other leagues, the wavier wire is a system for determining which players can be added each week. In some cases, see the bidding system below, there is no dedicated waiver wire since all players are bid upon to secure their addition. In these cases, the rules often refer simply to the FA system (which is both players not on a team and those just waived from a team).

Some leagues do not allow you to add players throughout the season. Fantasy Auctioneer has a Beat-the-Expert league where you draft your team but cannot add, drop or trade players. Some leagues allow unlimited free agency and some put a limit on adds and drops. A limit can be in the number of transactions per week or per season. Limits per week can hurt a team that is faced with catastrophic injuries or demotions. Limits only make sense if you are running the league by phone and doing all the work by hand. In that case, a limit of three moves per week seems reasonable to prevent the commissioner from going crazy; otherwise, why handcuff an owner's strategies. Some leagues will place a deadline on trades and other transactions. Many leagues do not allow trades after week 11 (week 12 in a 14-game regular season). Once the trading deadline passes, no more trades can occur. Usually the trading deadline comes before the playoffs and then other transactions (if they are going to be stopped) will be prohibited during the playoffs. Some leagues stop transaction after the last bye week. There is nothing worse than watching your team lose to another owner who raided the FA market and got lucky with a sleeper the day of your playoffs.

Free agency comes in many forms:

First come, first served is a simple way to conduct free agency. In this system, if a player is available then the first team to select him gets him. This system benefits the fantasy football geek who has no life and spends his entire time ear to the ground listening for snippets of news. He will be the first to know that Shaun Alexander slipped in his kitchen on his pet wiener dog and may be out for this week (remember this ESPN commercial?) and thus he gets Maurice Morris (Shaun's backup) before anyone else even hears about it a day later.

Waiver Wire – this sets up a priority for awarding players at the end of a certain deadline. For example, at the end of the week, a day before the first game of the week, the waiver wire is conducted and awards players requested (free agents and those waived from other teams) based on your overall ranking. If both Team A and Team B want Morris on Saturday, the team with the worst overall ranking is awarded him. It can also be set up so a team with the least points scored will win him. Or, my least favorite, to the team with the lowest points scored that week. This seems unfair, as the best team in the league (8-2) may have a bad week and then gets the #1 waiver wire priority.

Free agent bidding – This is usually a blind bid process where owners have a set amount of imaginary money for bidding on FA. Blind bidding starts everyone out with a budget for FA, often referred to as the Free Agent Acquisition Budget (FAAB). Owners submit bids before the agreed upon deadline (usually Friday nights up until Thanksgiving for players each week). No other owner knows whom you bid on or how much you bid. There is a minimum bid (usually $1) but no maximum, except for the entire FA budget amount. Whoever bids the most gets the player and has that amount subtracted from his FAAB. You can only bid as much FAAB money as you have left; once that money is used, you cannot get anymore free agents. This is the most democratic and economic methods of FA. It is much more equitable than "whoever is on 24/7 gets the player," or "fastest mouse wins."

Trades

Most high stakes leagues do not allow trades in order to prevent collusion. Collusion occurs when two or more teams attempt to help one team get an unfair advantage over the other teams in the league. The easiest way to do this would be for Team A to trade all of their best players to Team B, thus giving Team B a great chance of winning the league. In sixteen years of playing fantasy football, I have never seen this occur. I hope I never do. Having said that, when the money is higher than $100, I do not want to play in a league where trading between teams is allowed because it would be too tempting to unscrupulous owners.

Decide when transactions can occur and when the deadline is for them, if there is one.

Roster Deadline – Roster deadlines occur when a league chooses to close the FA/Waiver wire system down for the rest of the season and playoffs. This deadline is usually two weeks before the playoffs start. It prevents teams out of contention from "dumping" good players onto the market for other teams to pick up. It also prevents owners with legitimate needs from picking up players. I suggest leaving the waiver wire open but restricting it to only players not on a roster after a certain date. Having cut players go onto the waiver wire for a set time period (2-3 days or a week) also prevents this from happening (unless the team that wants them is highest on the waiver priority list).

Supplemental Drafts – Some leagues do not allow FA transactions at all, but instead have a supplemental draft at some point from the middle to the end of the regular season. Many times you can drop a certain number of players and then replace them (and add a few more) with the supplemental draft.

Allowing trades increases owner interaction.

The more restrictive the transactions are, the more important the draft becomes.

The less restrictive the transactions are, the more that skills in management of a team become important.

11) Super Bowl in week 16 or 17?

This is another age-old FF question. Do you use all of the NFL regular season (play the Super Bowl in week 17) or do you only use the first 16 weeks (play the Super Bowl in week 16)? More leagues avoid week 17 than play in it. The problem with having the Super Bowl in week 17 is that many times NFL teams who have clinched their playoff spot and have nothing to gain in week 17 will sit their stars on the bench or play them sparingly. This drives fantasy football fans nuts if they have a Super Bowl in week 17 and their starting QB P. Manning is not playing or only plays the first quarter in order to avoid injury. Better to avoid week 17 for your Super Bowl because there are almost always some players who do not play that week for this reason. Yes, the same things can happen in week 16, but they are far less likely to occur that soon and most coaches do not want their team to get too lackadaisical about their game performance. Of course, 2006 proved to be so competitive in the NFL that week 17 saw very few players resting on the bench. Just because it did not happen one year does not mean it will not happen the next year. Of course, your choice of when to play your Super Bowl will also affect your playoffs and potentially how many regular season games you play.

12) Number of playoff teams/format

Your choice for determining the league champion is either no playoffs, multi-week playoff or single championship game. If no playoffs are desired, then at the end of the regular season the team with the best winning percentage wins the league championship. One advantage to having no playoffs is that the regular season can be played through week 17. Another advantage of the no playoff system is that all of the teams in the league get to compete for the entire season. If you want just one championship game, do you want to use week 16 or 17? I suggest week 16 for the reasons mentioned before. The two teams with the best record or the one with the best record and the highest scoring team could meet. If you do want some type of elimination playoffs, how many teams do you want in the postseason tournament? Playoffs can start as early as week 12 or as late as week 16. The advantage of a playoff format is the excitement and intensity of single elimination. The downside is that owners who do not make the playoffs have little to play for (having a bonus for high points each week helps create motivation for such teams).

How many playoff teams? The regular season should mean something. Once you allow more than 50% of the teams into the playoffs (hmmm… NBA), you start to make the regular season worthless. If more than 50% go, then teams with losing records make it and that distracts from the league and lessens the importance of those all-too-few regular season games. Not to mention this is the NFL, not the NBA, where every team with a pulse makes it to the postseason. Therefore the number of teams allowed in the playoffs should be 50% or less. You should always strive to have at least a 4-team playoff, so somewhere between 4 and 8 (if there are 16 teams and 50% are allowed, then 8 would be the max). Most leagues require three weeks for the playoffs, including the Super Bowl.

Do all teams start over in playoffs or do some of their points carry over from the regular season? Do the top seeds get any bonus points? Is there a consolation bracket?

Does the #1 seed get a bye?

Do you want to have five teams in the playoffs? If so, allow the top three teams to get a bye and have one wildcard game in round 1 to determine who joins the other three teams in round 2 of the playoffs.

Having six teams in the playoffs usually means that two teams will get a bye in the first round of the playoffs and then will meet the two winners from round 1.

Having seven teams in the playoffs usually means that one team will get a bye in the first round of the playoffs and then meet up with the three winners from round 1.

Having eight teams in the playoffs usually means that no teams get a bye, as the winners from the four games in round 1 will advance to play in round 2, and those two winners will meet in the Super Bowl.

NOTE: Having 16 teams with a 15-game regular season results in a two-week playoff format (week 17 Super Bowl) and only four teams in the playoffs. Most 14-team leagues use six teams making the playoffs in week 14 (#1 and #2 seeds get a bye) and the playoffs continue in week 15 with the Super Bowl in week 16. Usually 12-team leagues go with four playoff teams and have playoffs in weeks 15 and 16 (if week 17 is used for Super Bowl, then six can make playoffs and #1 and #2 seeds get byes in week 15). Most 10-team leagues use two divisions of five teams and a 14-game regular season with four teams making the playoffs.

13) Ownership: keeper vs. redraft

Redraft is the easiest way to go about starting a new season. Every year you start with nothing. It is a complete do-over. Keeper involves more skill. Redrafters say that keeper leagues benefit the owners who have more time to find the sleepers and who get lucky enough to draft the stud players. Eventually, keeper leagues will have those on the bottom who resent those at the top, which is why they advocate doing the draft all over every year to give everyone an equal chance. Plus, the draft is the best part of FF. If a keeper league is the format, will it be a minimal keeper, a Dynasty league or somewhere in between? (See Chapter 22 for additional keeper information.)

14) Prizes

You also have to make many decisions regarding the awarding of prizes. How much of the entry fee will be distributed? How much of the entry fee remains after administration costs such as league management service, draft board and trophies? A good ROT is first place gets 50%, second place gets 20% and third place gets their entry fee back. You do not want to award prizes to too many places. The object is to win! Remember to have some prize money for weekly high scorers, a week 17 mini-tourney, an NFL Playoff tourney and to award regular season high points team and playoff winners. Some leagues are free. You just play for bragging rights. However, these leagues tend also to be the ones where apathy sets in and they become less fun as some teams do not participate. Prizes are best when everyone has a chance to win something, even if not in a playoff hunt. A weekly prize for the highest scoring team works great for weeks 1-15. (Week 16 is the Super Bowl and thus the highest scoring team that week is going to win the big prize.) Some argue that prizes should be all or nothing. In this case, the champion would get all the prize money. Again, these leagues breed apathy when an owner is out of contention. I think the best format is to award prizes each week so that everyone has a chance at those and stays competitive, and then award bigger prizes for the top three finishers only.

15) Tiebreakers

Are tiebreakers based on win/loss record or total points? If a weekly game ends in a tie, is the tie broken? If so, how? Some leagues go down the list of starters and whoever has the starter with the most points, starting with QB and working down, wins. Some leagues start with DEF and work up; some use bench points, still others do not break ties. For further information on tiebreakers, see Chapter 18 – Rules Variations.

Chapter 5 Scoring Systems

Often what sets a league apart from another league is the scoring system it implements. For some leagues this has been a lifelong pursuit, with growing pains and yearly tweaking to get it exactly right for the owners. Other leagues picked a system early on and have never changed it. Therefore you may want to establish in the rules if your scoring system (or rules themselves for that matter) can be changed, and if so how?

The scoring system should be the same from year to year if possible. Do not make changes lightly. This makes comparisons easy and league records consistent. However, you can and may want to tweak your scoring system to either add some excitement to a league that is getting boring or address some area that has a deficiency. The bottom line is that you want the league to be fun and if it is not fun because of the scoring system, you need to fix it. The NFL tracks and makes available to the public endless categories of statistics from each week's games. This opens up limitless possibilities for scoring rules. No rule is wrong, some are just better than others for certain leagues.

Fantasy Scoring History

The early scoring systems tried to quantify a player's performance in relation to how his team performed. In the NFL a team succeeds by scoring TDs and TDs are scored by gaining yardage. Thus players were rewarded for scoring TDs initially and eventually for gaining yards. The early scoring systems also believed that a rusher rushed; passer passed and receivers... well, received. This meant that only QBs got passing yards and passing TDs, only RBs got rushing yardage and rushing TDs, and only WRs got receiving yardage and receiving TDs. Eventually these systems evolved so that any skill player could score points via a pass, rush or reception. But fantasy football fans began to realize that QBs scored more TDs and threw for more yards than RBs and WRs. To even it up, QB points for TDs were reduced to 4 and their yardage was increased in relation to rushing and receiving yards. All of this was in an attempt to make the position's relative value equal. Now that QB scoring was reined in, leagues faced the dilemma that RBs score more than WRs. Thus the next wave of scoring, which introduced PPR, points per reception. PPR awards points to a player based on the number of catches he makes (usually 1 point per reception). Realize that changing the number of starters can also affect the relative value of that position. Some leagues require that only one RB start, which decreases demand and thus increases supply. Still other leagues combine the WR and TE positions, thus reducing the need for all but the best TEs. Some leagues require that three WRs start, thus increasing demand for that position and increasing the relative value of a WR.

Scoring systems have become more of a scoring philosophy. There are three main camps when it comes to scoring philosophies: the purists, the realists (performers), and the stat geeks.

1) The Purists – The purists believe that to truly make FF more than just fantasy you have to make it as close to the NFL as possible. Therefore rules and points mirror those of the NFL. You receive 6 points for TDs for RBs or WRs. You receive 3 points for FGs and 1 point for XPs. The biggest difference is that some leagues will adjust QB passing TDs to

either 3 or 4 points. Then again the purest of the purists (try saying that three times fast), will keep it at 6 points or even give 3 points to the QB and 3 points to the WR. This obviously makes RBs more dominant. Scores typically are in the 30-40 range but can be in the lower teens or even single digits. This means the scores are just like the NFL too. The bottom line is that these leagues want to be like the NFL and they are. As with anything, there are problems as well.

Purists (disciples of the basic scoring system) want the scoring system to be directly related to NFL scoring. Therefore, TDs, FGs, XPs and two-point conversions are **ALL** that are scored. No yardage or catches are accounted for. This leads to many leagues decided by luck. The luck factor is just too great when only TDs are used to score points. In 2003, Tiki Barber rushed for two TDs on 1,216 yards and caught 69 passes for 461 yards and one TD. He was the NYG workhorse that season but did not have many TDs. And what about the RB who rushes all day long and every time he gets the team to the goal line the "Bus" (or some other goal line vulture) comes in and scores the TD? Does J. Bettis' three rushes for 3 yards and three TDs really deserve to be rewarded more than W. Parker's 200 yards rushing and no TDs for that game? Purists say that TE should be a mandatory position. Why? 1) Because every team has a TE and uses it to varying degrees. It is part of the sport. 2) It makes the draft more diverse with more players. 3) It is one more skill position to exploit by better owners.

2) The realists say that performance scoring means less luck and more skill when it comes to drafting and winning a championship. The games are more exciting. And the more variables added, they argue, the more advantage a skilled owner has. Performance scoring assigns points for yardage. It does veer a bit from the realistic, yet it is directly related to how a player performs and makes other positions more equivalent in terms of draft day. Yes, W. Parker did contribute to that Bettis TD by rushing for 95 of the 96 yards on that drive. Performance leagues are the most common format for high stakes leagues and several studies have shown that they are less luck-based than basic scoring or distance scoring leagues.

3) The stat geeks use anything and everything. Their weekly scores are 1,184.45 to 1,173.16. It can be a combination of attempts, number of incomplete passes, yardage per play, first downs made, YAC, etc. Most would argue that too much of a good thing is bad.

Before I get into the nuisances of scoring systems, I want to start with one basic difference between leagues. In most instances, rushing and receiving TDs are worth 6 points. Passing TDs however, are usually only awarded 3 or 4 points, since there are generally many more TD passes than TD runs or catches. If the QB was awarded 6 points for every TD pass thrown then that position would become much more valuable than the other positions. Another argument against awarding 6 points for passing TDs is that it takes away the advantage of a rushing QB. If you awarded all TDs 6 points, then the rushing QBs Dante Culpepper and Mike Vick would be undervalued when compared to the Drew Brees and Peyton Mannings of the world.

Note: Some leagues do award 6 points for all TDs, so beware!

So, the first scoring difference between leagues is how many points they assign to a passing TD. This will have a huge impact on your draft order (QBs will be worth more and thus drafted earlier, as well as LaDainian Tomlinson (LT) who throws a few TDs each year on the option.)

There is no set scoring method that must be used in fantasy football. In fact, that is part of the beauty of it; there are so many variations on how to score points in different leagues. This is unlike the scoring practices of fantasy baseball, where there are less variations. Each year the number of different scoring systems in use by fantasy football leagues increases. Most will fall into the following broad categories: Basic, Performance, Bonus, Distance or Combination.

Basic Scoring

In basic leagues (also sometimes called TD-only leagues), the scoring is an attempt to mirror the NFL as closely as possible. In most instances, rushing and receiving TDs are worth 6 points. Passing TDs, however, are usually only awarded 3 or 4 points. Two-point conversions can either be worth 2 points for each individual involved in carrying out a successful two-point conversion pass (i.e P. Manning gets 2 points, as does Reggie Wayne) or, as some leagues believe, because only 2 points were scored only 2 should be awarded. In this scenario, Peyton and Reggie would each receive 1 point. Rushing two-point conversions are awarded the full 2 points.

Kickers get 3 points for every FG they kick and 1 point for every successful extra point. In keeping with the basic principle of being "just like the NFL," defenses are awarded 2 points for safeties and 6 points for any TD scored by the defense or the special teams unit (i.e. a kickoff or punt returned for a TD). One example of a basic scoring system is:

Rush TD = 6   Receiving TD = 6   Pass TD = 4

Two-point conversion rush = 2

Two-point conversion pass = 1 for passer, 1 for receiver

FG = 3

XP = 1

Safety = 2

DEF TD = 6

KO/PR TD = 6

Leagues that use the basic method of scoring tend to have scores that are closer in amount and numbers to the NFL. The basic scoring method is the easiest method to use. It also results in the lowest scores of any of the other methods, simply because basic scoring is used as the base for all other scoring systems, which then award points for more events. The basic system is easier to keep track of by individual owners on a Sunday afternoon because it only involves scoring TDs by their players. So 6+6+FG and 2 extra points equal 17 total points. Your final scores end up being 24-20 or 17-15. The owners can keep track of every team's scoring with just a pencil and a piece of paper. The downside to this is that they tend to be a little hit-or-miss. Your RB can rush for 200 yards but be taken out for some rest and the fullback (or third down back) comes in and scores 3 TDs. You end up with zero points while the "TD" back (think Brandon Jacobs) scores all the points. It is very frustrating to see your starting RB bust one loose and run 85 yards only to be tackled at the 2 yard line and then come out for some much needed oxygen, as someone else gets the TD rush. For these reasons, some feel that basic scoring, while having its advantages, is a bit unfair. Some even say it is boring. This is precisely why the yardage scoring rules came about.

NOTE: Of course there is no right or wrong way of scoring. Some of the examples given can be modified as your league desires. Use what you want and disregard the rest. The bottom line is that when a particular way is not preferred, the reason for that decision will be explained here.

In the examples shown in this chapter, all individuals can score points for the actions. The player does not have to be a QB to get points for throwing a TD pass or have to be a WR/TE to get points for catching a TD pass. LaDainian Tomlinson (LT) has caught, thrown and rushed for a TD in a single game. He would get 6 points for the TD catch, 4 for the TD pass and 6 for the TD rush, for a total of 16 points in the basic format above. If he kicked the extra points for all three TDs, that would be 3 more points, bringing the total to 19.

Performance Scoring (Sometimes called yardage scoring)

Performance scoring involves the basic format but adds points for yardage. The most common method is to award 1 point for every 10 rushing/receiving yards. The passers also get 1 point for every 20 yards passed (sometimes this is per 25 yards, if 20 yards is too much of an advantage). So if your RB runs for 200 yards but no TDs in a game; he still ends up with 20 points (200/10 = 20). Some leagues use decimals (i.e. points less than 1) and some only use whole numbers in their calculations. I find that using whole numbers makes it more like the NFL and less like a math contest. The advantage of yardage scoring is that it makes the games more fun to watch because now every play means something for your players. In the basic league, if you are watching your RB and he is backed up in his own red zone, each rush is not significant unless he breaks one for a TD or they drive down to the opponent's red zone. But in yardage leagues, now every rush from scrimmage can offer the possibility of points. Three 4-yard rushes now give you 1 or 1.2 points, depending on the format for that league. Purists will say that it is not fair to award someone points for just rushing up and down the field. That does not win games in the real NFL and it should not win games in fantasy football either. In the NFL you have to get the pigskin in the end zone and it does not matter if you rush for 300 yards; if you don't score you probably will not win. Ah the debate continues. On the other hand, I hate to see my players have a good day (95 yards rushing against a tough defense) and get nothing for it. The other disadvantage to this scoring system is that the scores can be quite large and thus hard to keep track of at home without a computer to give you live stats. It is not quite as fun when you are asked what the final score for the week was and you say, "I won 154 to 147." Kickers get involved too because in many leagues yardage scoring for kickers means getting points for how long a FG was. Any FG inside 30 yards is 3 points; any outside 30 is worth the distance divided by 10. So a 48-yard FG is worth 4.8 points, or 4 points if dropping decimals. The defense had to have their yardage compensation so they are awarded points for how many points they give up (or, less often, how many offensive yards they give up in a game). In many formats a shutout equals 10 points and holding your opponent to under 7 is worth 5 points and under 14 is worth 3 points.

The most common performance scoring method is:

1 point per 10 yards rushing/receiving

1 point per 25 yards passing

6 points per rushing/receiving TD

3 or 4 points per passing TD

-1 point for interceptions

FG = yardage/10 (with a minimum of 3 points)

1 point for extra points

Defense/ST

1 point for sacks and turnovers

2 points for Safeties

6 points for TD

DEF = 10 points for allowing no points to opponents; 5 points if score is 6 or less; 3 points under 14

Note: The points a defense gives up should only be based on what the DEF/ST gives up and not what the offense gives up. For example, if the final score is 10 for your defense's opponent but 6 points came when the QB threw an INT that was run back for a TD, that score does not count since your defense was not on the field to give it up. They did give up the XP since they could have blocked it.

Bonus Scoring (also known as milestone scoring)

Bonus scoring developed for those who liked the idea of spicing up the basic format but were afraid of getting too complicated and taking the game out of the hands of the owners and putting it on a computer with advanced mathematics to tally the score. The result was bonus scoring or milestone scoring. In this format, players are awarded bonus points for exceeding a set amount of yardage in rushing, receiving and passing. The most common bonus points are for 100 yards rushing or receiving and 300 yards passing. You will notice that many of the halftime, pre- and post-game shows focus on these achievements in their announcing. These achievements are easy to track during Sunday's games. CBS has a great ticker at the bottom of the screen to show game scores and individual stats for QB/RB/WR/K/DEF. It was initiated for the fantasy football fan. Fox, unfortunately, does not give as much information but both provide details at halftime, and during and after the games.

Passing 300 or more yards = 3 bonus points (1 point for every 50 yards after 300)

Rushing 100 yards or more = 3 bonus points (2 points for very 50 yards after 100)

Receiving 100 yards or more = 3 bonus points (2 points for very 50 yards after 100)

Kicking a FG of 50 or more yards = 2 bonus points (on top of the 3 awarded for every FG)

Defenses would get a bonus for shutouts = 10 points

Note: Bonus scoring can be just as frustrating as TD-only scoring. For example, if Steven Jackson rushes for 102 yards and then loses 3 yards on the last play of the game to finish with 99. Or if you see your WR hovering at 98 yards but then cannot get another catch to go over 100. These emotions are just as heart-breaking as watching your RB dragged down on the 1-yard line after a 35-yard rush only to be replaced by that "goal line vulture" or QB who gets the TD plunge.

Distance Scoring

Distance scoring takes the basics of performance scoring and adds points for the distance of the TD play. This "bonus" only applies to plays that score TDs. Generally, any TD play of more than 40 yards will get a bonus of 2 points. In distance scoring, if Larry Johnson rushes twice in a game for two TDs; one of 65 yards and the other 34 yards, then he would get 6 points for each TD rush and 2 points for the distance TD over 40 yards. He would also get 9.9 points for his total rushing yards of 99. This would mean a FP total of 6+6+2+9.9 = 23.9. Some leagues award more points the longer the TD play. For example, a TD rush that is over 80 yards may be worth 6 additional points! This is also sometimes called the "big play league" since TDs are worth more the longer they are. It does not reward the "plodding warhorse," but instead the "speedy stallion."

NOTE: The same example would warrant only 12 points in both the basic and bonus leagues since he did not gain 100 yards.

In this format, FGs are also rewarded based on longer distances. FGs inside 39 yards are worth 3 points; over 40 yards are the distance divided by 10. A 45-yard FG would be worth 4.5 points. A field goal from anywhere between 40-49 yards is worth 4 points in leagues without decimals and 50 or greater yard FGs are valued at 5 points.

Combination Scoring

This is the most common format and, as the name implies, it takes factors of the other methods and comes up with a unique system of scoring.

Common Combination Scoring System:

4 points for passing TD

6 points for rushing/receiving TD

1 point for every 10 yards rushing/receiving (20 passing yards)

1 point for every reception (PPR)

Minus 1 point for interceptions and fumbles lost, missed XP

2 points for two-point conversions (2 each for passer and receiver)

1 point for every XP

1 point for every 10 yards of successful FG (3 point minimum)

1 point for turnovers, blocked kicks and sacks

2 points for safety

6 points for every DEF TD and KO/PR TD

10 points for shutout, 5 points for allowing 10 or less points, 3 points for allowing 13 or less points

Fans of combination scoring will point out that even in low scoring NFL games you can still find something to root about with a combination scoring system. (For example, yardage.)

Miscellaneous Scoring Rules

Points per Reception (PPR): This method typically awards 1 point for any reception made by an individual player. This is called the great equalizer. In many leagues the RB is more powerful because he scores more TDs than the WRs and TEs. So to give the WR and TE more value and a better chance to score fantasy points, 1 point is awarded for every reception. This is especially helpful in leagues that require a TE on the starting roster. TEs will rarely score and do not usually rack up huge yardage or distance numbers but they will make many catches and this equalizes that position among QBs and RBs. Don't count all the RBs out of this category. Many RBs also catch the ball out of the backfield, like Steven Jackson and LT. Now the question becomes is it too much of an advantage? Tony Gonzalez catches eight balls for 79 yards and thus gets 8 points for the receptions and 7.9 points for the yardage, 15.9 points total. Is that truly equal to 159 yards rushing or a TD and 99 yards rushing?

What happens if you give 1 point per reception? The WR and TE will get the biggest boost, then the RB. The QB will get no boost and thus drop further down the food chain (drafting order). What you will find is that QBs, RBs and WRs will all be much closer in the number of points scored. In one league where I looked at both no-PPR and PPR (1 point), the no-PPR league had two WRs in the top 25 players, in terms of scoring. The PPR league had thirteen WRs in the top 25. The effect is not as dramatic as you might think. We are boosting all WRs and TEs, so that does not really make any of them more valuable in terms of drafting. The top WRs will score more but so will the last starting WRs (WR36 in a 12-team, start three WRs league). QBs are the ones who get dumped on here and end up losing about one round of draft value. If Brady was going in round 2 in a non-PPR league, he would go in round 3 in a PPR league. PPR definitely helps the top 10 TEs. The ones who catch more than 40 passes a year are more valuable than before. The decline in the position is still pronounced, thus making it a priority to grab an early TE.

The purists hate PPR. How do the realists justify it? The realists will argue that it is much harder to catch a ball (especially coming across the middle and having a MLB about to take your noggin off), than it is to take a handoff in the backfield. Not to mention most of the RB passes are dump offs coming out of the backfield. Sorry S. Jackson and Reggie Bush; so rewarding a catch is only right, due to the degree of difficulty. Catching a moving object while running down a field and avoiding other players is quite a miracle when you think about it. If anything, the realists will sometimes admit that 1 point to a RB is too much and thus only PPR for WRs and TEs has become more prevalent in some leagues.

If you want to devalue the RB position, consider only starting one RB per team. That will take the emphasis off of them somewhat, since now there will be less demand and thus more of a supply of them. Of course, if you only start one RB you can't have a flex position that involves a RB or you will face the same problem. In leagues that start two RBs and a flex with the possibility of a RB, you will find RBs have even more emphasis. RBs tend to have more consistency. That is why RBs taken in the second half of the draft are more "handcuffs" (HC's) or sleepers than anything else. Is PPR the new standard? Some studies have reported that over half of all leagues use some form of PPR format. PPR helps to even out the receivers, but what can we do to help the defense/ST?

Defensive points for turnovers: This is very common in many leagues. Usually 1 point is awarded for every forced turnover recovered by the defense. Some leagues even dare to give 2 points for them.

Defensive points for sacks: Award 1 point for every sack by the defense. The problem here is that a good defense can now outscore your individual players because of this equalization. For example, a 4-sack game with three turnovers and holding the opponents to 10 points would be 4+3+3 = 10 points. Is that worth a 100-yard rushing day? Probably, but some will think this favors the defense too much.

Sacks, however, are a poor measure of a good defense. When I say this, I mean that teams with lots of sacks do not necessarily provide good defensive coverage. A sack on third down is great and forces the other team to kick the ball. A sack on first or second down, while demoralizing, is not a show-stopper like a turnover or third down sack. Perhaps a better measure would be stops or goal line stands.

What makes a defense great? Is it giving up fewer points or yardage? I would argue that giving up the fewest points is more important than yards, since a team can stop the rush and be winning by two TDs late in the fourth quarter and go into a prevent defense, thus giving up a lot of easy passing yards (underneath routes but nothing deep; "garbage yards"). Some have suggested that a way to give defenses more relative value would be to take away sacks and incorporate fourth down stops and punts. Fourth down stops would be just as valuable as a TO and thus valued at 2 points. A punt would only be worth 1 point. This would increase team defensive average scores to around 10 points per game, on par with the average starting WR.

Does ST (K/P returned for TD) count against DEF? (See Chapter 18 –Rule Variations.)

Other Individual Scoring Items

Negative points for interceptions and fumbles lost by players

Negative points for allowing over 35 points by a defense

Negative points for missing an extra point

Kicker penalties	Minus 3 points for a missed 30 yard or less FG
	Minus 2 points for a missed 30-39 yard FG
	Minus 1 point for a missed FG over 40 yards

Some ask why you would penalize for FGs over 40 yards, since those are not automatic, and say that you should not penalize a kicker trying a 50+ yarder.

I like it because it holds kickers accountable, but not for missed FGs over 40 yards. What about the weather? It will force a few misses due to wind or rain, right? Weather can have an effect on a FG. And INTs too, and fumbles too. Yadda yadda yadda…

Purists will point out that you cannot score negative points and thus you should not be able to score negative points in FF. Subtracting one point for INT, fumbles, missed XPs and FGs are taboo to them.

Some scoff at penalties for miscues because blocked kicks, tipped passes or QB-RB exchanges are to blame and that often gets put on the wrong person.

Of course, each new item complicates the ability to keep score at home on your sofa without being tied to a computer.

See Chapter 21 – IDP, for rules about individual defensive players and their scoring rules.

How do you determine which scoring system to use?

The aim may be to put things on an equal footing. If 100 yards rushing is the same as scoring a TD then it should be worth the same fantasy points. If 100 yards = 6 points then 15 yards = 1 point. Instead many leagues use 10 yards = 1 point and thus a 100 yard game is worth more than 1.5 TDs. Additionally, if 250 yards passing should be worth a TD (250/6), then every 40 yards passing should be worth a point. Note: We round to make the numbers easier to remember and calculate while watching TV.

What is the objective of your scoring system? Do you want to equalize the big three skill positions (QB, RB and WR), or do you want to be exactly like the NFL? Before deciding on a scoring system, consider that the average NFL team passes for slightly over 200 yards and rushes for 120 yards, per game.

More Radical Scoring Rules

Completions 1 point (So an INT would be a net of 0 points, +1 for completion -1 for INT)

Incompletion -1 point (My QB loses points every time T.O. drops one that hits him in the chest.)

Passing or rushing or receiving for first down   1 point (no objection)

Big plays (over 10 yards)   1 point (no objection)

For Punters:

Touchback -1 point

Inside the 20 = 1point

PR yards 10 yards = 1 point

KR yards 25 yards = 1 point

KO touchback = 1 point

Decimal Scoring

 Decimal scoring awards .1 points for every 1 yard, versus 1 point for every 10 yards. If LT rushes for 11 yards (a poor day indeed) then with decimal scoring he would be awarded 1.1 points. With the other system he gets just 1 point. Decimal systems will almost always eliminate the possibility of a tie in head-to-head games. Of course, decimal scoring is less realistic but rewards the player for his effort. With this type of scoring, 19 yards is worth 1.9 points instead of only 1.

Misc

Some leagues will use a PPR to elevate the WR and TE. Others give TEs 2 points per catch versus 1 point for WRs, to help the TE. Still others give higher points per yard to TEs. Finally, some leagues just do away with the TE position completely. Opponents of these systems will say that they devalue the QB position. If you give more to one position to bring it up, then you lower another position and the QB position will be the one with no love. Some use this as their entry into the starting two QB mentality.

Reasons for Starting two QBs:

1) Helps emphasize the most important position in football – the signal caller.

2) We start two RBs and there are only 32 starting RBs, so why not start two QBs?

3) Adds emphasis to QB for trades because it takes them off the FA list. (Many leagues will have six or more QBs available as free agents at any one time; not so when you start two. They will be non-existent on the FA list and thus more valuable in trades.)

4) Improves QB value and thus makes the draft more fun when two QBs are needed. (i.e. owners cannot just wait until everyone else has their QB1 and then pick up theirs.)

Those against starting two QBs will point to the fact that in a 12-team or greater league there will not be enough QBs to go around. Having 14 teams needing two starters each equals 28 QBs, and on those bye weeks when six teams stay idle, 32-6 = 26; oops! Also, the purists will bring up the fact that each NFL team only fields one starting QB at a time.

Chapter 6 Types of Drafts

The draft is like Christmas day. You have your eyes on something special and you hope you get it. On draft day you are like a kid wondering what you are going to get; losing sleep the night before and the anticipation of the event building up in the weeks before it. Sound familiar?

Draft Date

The ideal time to hold the draft is after the last game of the third week of preseason. You should have some idea of the starters on each team and all of the starters are probably going to be benched for the last game anyway. The later it is (closer to the NFL season kickoff), the more information the owners will have to make informed choices. Remember to pick a date that everyone can make. Usually this will mean a Saturday afternoon. Of course now that the NFL has a kickoff game on Thursday, that has taken one key Saturday away from draft availability. I find it hard to believe that some leagues are holding a draft in May (right after the NFL draft) or June. You really are in the dark on so many things, but the rational goes that the better owners (read well-informed) will have an advantage because they will know more than the average owner who is still waiting for his outdated magazine to arrive. I still prefer a date closer to September than July.

Draft Location

Try to conduct a live draft instead of an online draft. Live drafts are the most fun. The point is to get away from the wife and kids and have some cold ones with your buds. The ultimate is to have the draft on a trip away from home for the weekend. Have everyone meet on Labor Day weekend in Vegas or some other suitable destination (golf can be included too). If this event is held in Las Vegas or another place away from home, then consider hiring some "outside talent" (nudge, nudge, wink, wink, say no more) to help with the presentation.

Any location that is quiet, large enough and easy to get to, will work. Back yards and garages work well because they can be hosed down easily. In many cases the draft will be at the home of the commissioner or some owner who volunteers his abode. No matter where it is held, make sure there are enough comfortable seats and room for everyone attending. This will include co-managers and any spectators. Are you going to allow visitors to the draft? If so, make sure they know to be quiet and not disturb the actual draft process or assist the other owners in any way.

The owner of the draft house has some advantages and some disadvantages. The main advantage is the familiarity factor. He knows his house and will be comfortable in the surroundings. He will not have to drive to the draft so he can partake in some frosty beverages if he chooses. He can use the extra time saved (what would have been travel time to the draft) to prepare for the draft. And, perhaps most important, he can have the latest information from his computer right up until the other owners arrive.

The problems with being the host are the distractions that can occur if coordinating the party (food, beverages, etc.). On the day of the draft, some time will need to be spent arranging furniture and cleaning up before the guests arrive. Once the draft starts, as the host, it may be easy to get distracted by helping the guests with food, bathrooms, beverages, etc.

On draft day, there are some key ingredients to a successful event. Have food but do not let people eat until after the draft. Order pizzas or grill later, but no eating the main food until after the draft. One reason is that it will distract from the "pageantry" of the draft. Another is that the grill master or pizza organizer will be stressed out over the details during the draft. It is best to conduct the draft first, and then when all is said and done, fire up the grill for those burgers and dogs; try to avoid nuts and dips, as the messes they make are not worth the effort. Popcorn and pizza are great and can be delivered or prepared easily. And what draft would be complete without some buffalo hot wings? I have found that it is best to cook out before or after the draft, just not during it.

Of course, you will need lots of beverages to wash all the good food down. Make sure there are enough beverages for everyone (including sodas and water). DO NOT DRINK AND DRAFT YOURSELF THOUGH!

Many leagues have moved the draft (and thus the stress) out of private homes and into public places such as a bar, restaurant or conference room. If you do conduct your draft at a public place, make sure you have some privacy and are not near the band, jukebox or TV. In 2006, Buffalo Wild Wings (BWW) Grill and Bar offered their restaurants as draft locations, along with offering free wings. I cannot think of a better place. Okay, maybe Hooters, but that is the best place. BWW and CBSSPORTSLINE also teamed up to offer fantasy football leagues, and the last time I sat at the bar I noticed a game machine (usually the ones that have poker or trivia on them) with fantasy football on it. Do we live in a great country or what?

Draft Rules

All of the draft rules below should be covered in the league constitution. Make sure that all draft rules are in writing and that all owners have a copy well before draft day. Then on draft day go over all the rules again so that everyone is clear on them. If an owner does not show up for the draft, call him and try to establish if he is just late or cannot make it. After a reasonable time period (say 30 minutes), if he still cannot be reached, start without him and have another owner draft for him if possible.

Any player not in college and eligible for the NFL can be drafted. This prevents college players from being taken before they become eligible for the NFL but does not prevent you from drafting NFL Europe, CFL, unemployed or retired players who may make a comeback. For example, Ricky Williams was a keeper on a team in 2004 while he was retired; he then played in 2005 for that owner.

What about time limits to make picks? Anywhere from 1-2 minutes is normal, with 90 seconds as the most common. The use of a clock is recommended and I suggest you give a 30-second and 10-second warning before time is up. Some leagues allow less time for the first half of the draft (as an example, one minute since it is easier to make picks) and more time for the second half of the draft (possibly two minutes).

Keep in mind that the longer the time limit the longer it will take to finish the draft. For example, a 14-team league with 18 rounds would equal 252 picks. If two minutes were allowed per pick, theoretically you could be drafting for 504 minutes or over 8 hours. Most players do not take the full time, but some do and all can if they want. A 14-team, experienced league with 20 rounds, utilizing the one and two minute time limit in the example above, can finish their draft in approximately four hours.

If an owner does not make a pick in the time allotted, he forfeits his pick and the next owner goes on the clock. You must stick by the limits. Do not let someone who is ill-prepared or who cannot make a decision ruin everyone else's fun. There will be frustrated owners, who had their picks stolen from under their noses a round earlier, ready to go for blood if you bend the rules here. After that owner picks, return to the indecisive owner, only allowing him five seconds (depending on your rules) to make his pick (but only after the owner originally after him has picked). Each subsequent time he misses the deadline he will move back a slot and get five seconds to pick. Once time expires, even if that owner blurts out a name, he has forfeited his pick until the next owner makes his pick, then the passed-over owner gets another five seconds to make his previous pick. You might initiate a policy where passed picks are made up at the end of the draft (essentially penalizing them to a FA pick). This is a pretty hard-core penalty and not even the NFL does that. Isn't that right Minnesota? Note: Some leagues allow ten seconds to make a missed pick instead of the five mentioned earlier.

What if an owner selects a player already drafted or violates the roster limits with his pick (such as: maximum of three RBs and he drafts a fourth)? The penalty can be monetary or libationary, whichever you prefer. Another common penalty is postponement of their draft pick until later. The most common penalty is that they lose one slot for buffoonery or owe everyone a drink after the draft.

Some other considerations for the draft: Think about banning computers. Is it really fair to those without laptops that some owners can use them during the draft? Also, be sure to tell all the owners what colors the stickers are for each position on the draft board in advance of the draft. Some programs for ranking players allow you to customize the colors used for positions, thus giving a jump ahead of the competition since the cheat sheet matches the colors on the draft board.

Traditional Draft Format

There are three possible formats for the draft order. They are the serpentine method, the standard method and the random pick method. The serpentine method is the most common. The standard method is used in R/FA drafts in keeper/dynasty leagues.

Most drafts will use a serpentine method. In this format, the draft order "snakes" back and reverses on every round. The first round would be picks 1-12, in that order. The second round would go in reverse order. Team 12 would get the first pick in round two and Team 1 (who picked first in round one) would get the last pick. Team 1 gets back-to-back picks for every pick except the first and last rounds. Team 12 (or the last team in the draft) always has back-to-back picks. Odd rounds comply with the original draft order (1-12) and even rounds are the reverse (12-1). So the first four rounds would look like this: 1-12; 12-1; 1-12; 12-1.

If you have an odd number of rounds then with the serpentine draft some owners will have an advantage because they will have higher draft picks in the last round of the draft. For example, if you have a 17-round draft, in the 17th round the draft will go from Team 1 through Team 12 but Team 12 will not get the first pick in the next even round to balance things out. It is always best to have an even number of draft rounds and thus an even number of roster positions (14, 16, 18 or 20 work well). If you do have an odd number of rounds in the draft, perhaps you should repick the draft order for the last round so that it is another chance for the teams that got the last pick in the main draft to get a better position in the last round. Plus it creates more "pageantry" of picking a draft spot.

The other draft format is the standard draft order, which is what the NFL uses. In this case, the same draft order repeats every round. For example, the first three rounds would be 1-12, 1-12 and 1-12. R/FA drafts in holdover leagues use this format the most.

Another draft order format, although rarely used, is the random pick method. In each round owners are randomly given their draft spots. So you may have the fifth pick in the 10th round and the third pick in the 8th round, etc. It is a logistical nightmare and prevents any coherent "box out" strategy from occurring.

Draft order can either be known well in advance or decided right before drafting on draft day. If they are to be known in advance, they can either be ordained by the rules (reverse order of finish) or drawn at random. Leagues that use the reverse order of finish for a draft order will have the order known at the end of the season. These teams will have over six months to mull over their draft spot and the strategies that go with it. It also allows more time to think about trading draft picks. Picking spots at the actual draft eliminates these advantages. But if you wait until draft day, when everyone is present (by drawing numbers or cards out of a hat), it is hard to be challenged as to the fairness of who got what pick. It also prevents the owner who gets the last draft pick from deciding to quit. Once the owners are at the draft munching on a hot dog, it is hard to abandon the league. However, it takes away some of the strategy from owners and also distracts from some of the water cooler banter leading up the draft. Another problem with determining the draft order in advance is the difficulty in getting all 12 or 14 owners together. It is hard enough just getting everyone to the draft, imagine trying to get them all together just to decide the draft order. If done in advance, a system such as reverse order of finish or allowing the league software to randomly assign picking order a few weeks before draft day may be the best solution. You could also do it when all owners are at a league end of season party (Super Bowl).

How do you determine the draft order using a random method? One way is to use a deck of cards. Take out the same number of cards of one suit that you have of teams. For example, in a 12-team league take out the top 12 hearts, ace through queen. Place these twelve cards on the table face down and mix them up. Announce that the best picks go to lowest cards, so ace is low (first pick of draft) and queen is high (twelfth pick of draft). I have seen numerous owners select the queen or king and be overjoyed because it is a high card in poker terms. Allow owners to pick cards one at a time. Any new teams to the league should pick their draft card first. Have the commissioner get whichever card is left over. If you have more teams (say 14) then use the king of hearts as the 13th pick and then add a joker (or any other card) as the 14th pick. For 16 teams use the ace and deuce of spades, with ace of spades being 15th pick and deuce of spades being the 16th pick. Some leagues use ping-pong balls that have numbers painted or written on them. This is even better than cards because it seems more like a lottery plus you know what pick you have instantly (versus "I got a jack. What is that worth again?"). If you choose to use the ping-pong ball or a similar method, be sure to underline the six or nine in some way to indicate which is which.

If possible, have someone else place the labels on the board or write the player's name. Two extra helpers are best; one to watch the clock and one to place the labels. The individual placing the labels should have some idea of football players, teams and positions. Make sure owners know to clearly announce the full name of the player selected (there are several Clarks, Smiths, etc.), the team he plays for, and most importantly, the position he plays. If using a draft board (highly recommended) then the positions will be color-coded on the player's names sheets, making it much easier to narrow down the search for a player's label. Offer the helpers free food and drinks for assisting in the draft. Who knows, maybe they will want to become owners next year!

Some owners do not want to take a break because it gives their opponents time to recover and catch up with the draft if they were behind. Teams can use breaks to their advantage by updating their drafts, mapping out strategies or discussing trading draft picks. Unfortunately, a draft can take four or more hours and thus at least one break is recommended. A ten-minute break in the middle to let everyone go to the bathroom seems fair. Be sure to take the break at the end of an even round, that way the next owner is Team 1 and he just had a pick so there is no real pressure on him with breaking before his next pick. This way no teams have any unfair advantage with a long break before their picks. At the end of the even rounds, the draft snakes back on itself again. If you have a really long draft (over 20 rounds), consider a ten-minute break every 10 rounds.

Auction Drafts

Recent studies show that 95 percent of fantasy owners who have tried both the serpentine and the auction draft methods prefer the auction method! That is a significant percentage. In my experience, I have not seen 95 percent of fantasy owners agree on anything. In fact, if someone were handing out free money at the post office; only 80 percent would agree it was a good idea to go to the post office. In fact, I have never heard of a league switching to auction format, not liking it and switching back to a traditional draft.

As a fantasy owner in a traditional draft, you cannot select NFL players that were drafted prior to your turn. Therefore, unless you are lucky enough to have the first pick of the draft, your favorite player may not be available to you when it is your turn to select. If you have the 10th pick in a 12-team league, you know you will have every NFL player to choose from except nine (the nine taken with the first round picks in front of you) and then with your second round pick you will have a choice of every NFL player minus 14 players. If you know your draft pick in advance you can know who will not be available in most cases. In an auction draft, however, ALL players in the NFL are available to you. Your only limitation in an auction draft is the amount you are willing to "spend" on a particular player. If you bid the most of your salary cap "money" on a player then he goes to your team. After each draft selection, your "salary cap" is reduced by the amount of "money" you "spent" on the player just drafted. This continues until all rosters are filled on each team. This way, each team has an equal chance of drafting an NFL player. It is the highest bidder who ultimately gets him.

There are so many auction advantages; the biggest of which is the fact that draft position no longer matters. You will never miss out on a chance at a player unless you "cap out" by spending all of your cap money. Auctions are more fun because every few minutes a different player is up for auction and everyone needs to have a vested interest in what happens, versus waiting 30 minutes before the next pick comes back to you in snake draft. Auctions have more strategies too; if you want to spend most of your money (70%) on two or three 1st round picks from a traditional draft, you can. Or, if you do not want to risk big money on a bust, you can get more 2nd-4th round players from a traditional draft at less of a price. Or if you love the Minnesota Vikings (who doesn't), you can try to get ALL Vikes on your team. It is much easier in an auction than a traditional draft. If you want an all-star WRs team, you can have that. Any player you want is yours, as long as you can afford him.

There are many auction misperceptions. These will be hauled out occasionally by entrenched owners who have never tried an auction. "Auctions are time-consuming;" not anymore than a traditional draft, if you stick to time limits. Auctions will go faster in the later rounds as owners run out of cash and cannot afford to bid. "Auctions are complicated;" only if you cannot add or subtract. Or, the most famous refrain of all, "But we have always drafted traditionally." I reply with "A traditional draft compensates those who have not done their homework." Why play in a league that rewards laziness? Instead, try a league that has as its mantra: "Any player you want, just not every player you want!"

Auctions allow every owner a chance to get his favorite players. No owner is ever excluded from the option of getting his favorite player. If he wants Larry Johnson (LJ) and is willing to pay any price for him, he can probably have him in an auction. The price is sometimes too painful for him to compete, if he gets in a bidding war with another owner who also desperately wants LJ.

Auctions add a salary cap and bidding process to the snake draft we are all familiar with. These two things turn the slow snail-paced snake draft into a strategy and guts game (much like poker). Auctions reward smart thinking and planning. Knowing who is overvalued and undervalued goes a long way toward winning in an auction league. Also, auctions are more fair because your draft position just does not matter anymore.

Auctions are all about how you manage your salary cap money. Do you spend on the "studs," do you wait on "bargains" or do you mix and match for the perfect team? How much you spend, when you spend it and on whom are the keys to an auction draft. In a serpentine draft the keys are what draft spot you have and who the other owners take.

Running an Auction Draft

The location for an auction does not have to be any different than the location of a serpentine draft. As long as there are enough chairs, tables (for cheat sheets, beers, laptops, etc.) and lighting for everyone, and bathrooms. Auctions do not require a draft board, but one is recommended. Breaks at the halfway point and ¾ point are recommended so that remaining salaries can be calculated.

Just like a traditional draft, before the auction you need to know how many teams are in the auction, roster sizes, starter requirements and scoring rules. However, the one unique thing is the salary cap, the actual amount that can be spent on players.

A good ROT for the salary cap is $10 multiplied by the number of players on the roster. If 20 players on on each roster then $200 makes a good salary cap. The cap can always be rounded up but I would not round down because this $10 ROT is on the low side. For a first time auction league, perhaps use $15 per player. This allows you to have enough money to have bidding wars but prevents the auction from dragging on for hours, because owners have so much cash. If there are 14 on the team and you are using $15 per player then $200 will work (14 x 15 = 210). If you have an 18-man roster, then $240 may be a better salary cap. Most leagues use $100, $200 or $240. The minimum bid will be determined by the cap. For $200 and $240 caps, a minimum bid of $1 works well. A minimum bid of 50 cents may be better for $100 caps but the hassles of 50 cent bids make me lean toward $200 caps and $1 minimum bids.

Owners acquire players by being the highest bidder. Once they are the highest bidder and that player is "sold" to them, the player is then added to the team roster and the team's salary cap decreases by the amount of the winning bid. How does the nominating proceed? Normally it will proceed around the table in a set order or it may be up to the winning owner to suggest a player for auction.

There are two types of auctions: open and blind auctions. An open auction is what you are probably already familiar with; an auctioneer says, "Going once, going twice, sold to Slam's Slammers for $45." Blind bidding auctions are a version in which the owners do not know how much the others are bidding for players. The object is to acquire players for the least amount of money but still bid enough to get who you want. Most leagues of this sort will have a minimum bid amount and a cap. It is much easier to do this type of auction online. Many leagues also require that the amount bid stays with that player regardless of his status. Therefore, if he is traded, dropped or placed on IR, his salary stays with him and the team that drafted him.

You will need an auctioneer. If you cannot get someone to volunteer to be an auctioneer and sit for five hours in front of the drunken slobs that make up your league then use the poker-style auction. In a poker-style auction, the bidding goes around the table clockwise from the individual who nominated the player. If an owner does not raise the bid then he is out of the bidding. It continues around the table until no one else bids and the last bidder wins that player. The nominating process must also go clockwise around the table, since there is some advantage to where you are in the bidding order in this format with lower priced players.

The commissioner must keep track of everyone's cap dollars and move the nomination process along. He does not have to keep the draft board updated, as each owner should move to the board and place the player he selected on it. This is another reason why I do not like the "winning owner nominates next" rule.

An easy way to keep track of the amount of money an owner has left is to use monopoly money, poker chips or real money and have the owners pay for their players as they go. If real money is used then the amount of the entry fee is your cap. This way an owner cannot overpay for a player with funds he does not have. Another advantage is that the entry fee has to be paid before the auction because that money is used for the auction (for example, if you use $100 as the salary cap and $100 is the entry fee).

Auction Rules

The honor of bidding first can either be determined at random (highest card drawn from a deck of cards) or be last year's winner or loser. There is no advantage to bidding first. That is what makes auctions so great; the luck of the draft pick is removed.

The owner who is on the clock to nominate a player should only have 60 seconds. The time limit for auctioning a player should also be 60 seconds from when a bid hits the auctioneer until he says, "Sold." "Going once" at 40 seconds, "going twice" at 50 seconds, and then 10 seconds later "Sold." That way the 60 seconds to nominate combined with the 60 seconds to auction a player off will give you a two-minute window per player, just like the traditional drafts.

Another decision you have to make is whether the salary cap money will only be used for the auction or if any leftover money will go to an FAAB. If just starting to use an auction format, then keep it simple. Just have the salary cap money be for the auction. So it is "use it or lose it." Money left over after the auction is lost. Next year the salary cap assigned can be used for the draft and FAAB. This involves more skill in budgeting for both the draft and FA. You force the owner to manage his money throughout the season. Some leagues use an FAAB for the season (say $100) and a draft cap (say $200). What remains after the draft can be used for the FA blind bidding process.

Chapter 7 Ranking Players

"The more you average the picks, the more average your results will be."

Let's start with the cold dark truth about your rankings. They are not going to be great. In fact, they will be horribly flawed to some degree. Injuries, blown opportunities and breakout players will all skew your rankings in a way that will make you pull out all the hair in your head. The good news is that every owner in your league will also have a flawed ranking sheet. The key is to have the least flawed sheet at the end of the season. In other words, your rankings do not have to be perfect, just better than all of the other owner's at the draft.

1) About 50% of the top 12 players at each position make it back each year. Some positions have more consistency than others (kickers and defenses have no consistency; RBs and QBs have more). Why will the other half not repeat? Injuries, holdouts, retirements, supporting cast changes (this includes player and coaches). Your job is to predict who will not make it back and who will make it in from below.
2) The "experts" are not going to go out on a limb and try to predict the rankings other than last year's stats becoming this year's stats, with a few modifications.

Why do the experts have this group think? Why will no one go out on a limb?
1) Too much work to actually think for themselves.

2) No one wants to look dumb. If you take some chances you will be wrong sometimes, and that will make you look dumb. Others will criticize you for going out on a limb and this may lead to being "outside" the experts circle.

3) Money is the biggest reason. No one wants to lose customers by not having the consensus or not being close to it. If so, then you look out of touch. You cannot afford to lose customers by taking chances.

So look for experts who differ from the crowd. Look at their lists and see if they take some chances. If they do, you will have found a valuable source to use in compiling your rankings.

Remember: ***"Dare to be noticed, dare to be different."***

There are three ways to do your rankings:

1) Let someone else do it for you. Remember the problems we mentioned above. If you let someone else do it for you, then you will use a pre-printed cheat sheet out of a magazine or a customized cheat sheet from a website. This is the lazy way.

2). Do it yourself. This will involve some spreadsheet work and projecting the players. Creating your own customized cheat sheets is half the fun. Watching others draft from the outdated magazine cheat sheets is like shooting fish in a barrel. Creating your own personal cheat sheets is your first huge advantage over the other owners who use outdated magazine copies. You need to rank every player that will be drafted on the categories of stats that your league uses. I can hear the whine now, "But it's too haaaaaaaaaaaaard." Would you like some cheese with that whine?" You are already doing some of the work

---

now. Do you rank the players at each position based on who you think will be better? Do you make a list of QBs and think to yourself, "P. Manning is best, then comes C. Palmer and I think McNabb will rebound?" If so, you are halfway home. The problem is comparing your #3 QB to your #1 TE. That's why you need to know what their individual stat projections are; so you can determine how many fantasy points you can expect them to post. See projections.

3) Let someone else do it for you but then you tweak the data.

Magazine Cheat Sheets

Cheat sheets that are created by someone else in the printed media (magazine, newspaper, etc.) are not based on your league's scoring system. The cheat sheets should say somewhere on them what scoring system they are based on. They are great for the beginner FF player. It gives him (or her) a ranking of players based on their positions. These are a great way to start a draft if you know little about what is going on. In fact, in my league in the UK there have been times when one or more of the owners cannot make it to the draft due to certain situations. Thus, we will assign an owner to draft for him and give him a generic cheat sheet so that he can be an honest broker in the draft process. It does not guarantee a win for this absent owner, only that he will get a competitive team with which to begin the season. What he does with it after that, through trades, adds and drops, is his business. On more than one occasion, within 24 hours that absent owner has dropped the majority of his late round picks and added his own sleepers. Such is life, as we all do not agree on who will break out and who will fall on their face.

There are many reasons why you should not use a magazine cheat sheet. First, it is outdated. The minute they print that thing it is old news. Someone has been hurt since it was printed, someone else has retired, and still another has been suspended. All of these events will affect that outdated cheat sheet. The second reason not to use it is that it is probably not based on your league's scoring system. I wish I had a dollar for every draft I have participated in where an owner drafted P. Manning in the first round, not knowing that passing TDs in the league were only worth 4 points, not the 6 points stated in his magazine. Know your scoring rules. The cheat sheet is probably not set up exactly like your scoring rules. Many owners are in multiple leagues and they will either use the same cheat sheet (from an outdated magazine, no less) for all the leagues or customize a cheat sheet for their thinking (sleepers/busts/etc.) but not customize it for the scoring system used for the league. If you do not believe that player rankings will be different in different scoring systems, please let me know because my league can always find room for you. Your league's own uniqueness may be another reason. If you are a keeper league, who will be kept this year? If you have some "Homers," how do you factor in their obvious drafting schemes? Owner tendencies are a factor. Finally, some of them are just "politically correct" popularity contests. Yes, believe it or not, some magazines simply make the lists based on who everyone else thinks will be there and this just perpetuates the popular players over and over again. How will you know you have real thinkers versus "lemmings"? Look at the lists; scan them for oddities like a player much higher or lower than everyone else. If you find any of these, the list is probably by someone who truly does not care what others will say and is basing their predictions solely on what they think will happen. As an example, take C. Palmer after injuries in 2005; 2006 cheat sheets had him primarily at 6th or worse. But Yahoo, fantasyguys.com and fantasyinsights.com listed him as #2 behind P. Manning. They were ranking them like they saw it, believing that he would recover from injury faster than the naysayers predicted.

Customized Cheat Sheets

Customized cheat sheets are only as good as the people doing them. Ask yourself these questions:

1) How often are updates?

2) Can you customize them exactly for your leagues rules?

One league I am in awards 3 bonus points for rushing over 100 yards. The custom cheat sheet gave 1 point per amount of yards. But 1 point per 33.3 yards is not the same as 3 points per 100. If a RB rushes for less than 100 yards he gets nothing in our league, but the cheat sheet expects to give him 2 points for 67-99 yards.

Ranking the players yourself

For those who want to create their own rankings, there are many different theories on how best to do it. Some involve making rankings first and then determining their projections. Others have you create the projections first and then the rankings will come from the projections.

Ranking Theories

Rank first, then project

1) Old fashioned gut check – Take all of the QBs that will be drafted and rank them in the order you think they will finish in terms of fantasy points. Now divide the list into three groups: the top 33%, middle 33% and bottom 33%. Rank them again within each group: the top half and the bottom half within each 33% grouping. See if there are any changes you want to make. Now is the time to move from group to group if you thought a player was misplaced. You should end up with six groups of players and every player within each subgroup should be of the same value. Repeat with all the positions to be drafted.

2) ADP Set – With this method you take a consensus of player rankings (from experts, etc.) or use the ADP. This will represent how others think the players should be ranked. It is kind of like having your opponent's thoughts on paper. You then adjust the rankings based on your own theories. You may downgrade players based on injuries in preseason, poor OL or injuries there, RBBC situations or suspensions. Other players may be moved up due to opportunities or improved supporting players. Players who you think are prime targets for a breakout year should be moved up as well.

3) Fantasy Points scored method –

A) Come up with the 32 starters at each position this year by using depth charts and local media.

B) Take the starters from last year, of the 32, and rank them based on how they did according to your league's scoring.

C) Move the remaining players based on what their previous year looked like. (i.e. look at what NYJ RB#1 did last year and use that for this year's replacement). You now have more information than many cheat sheets. The cheat sheets do almost the same thing, only in April, when starters are much less defined.

D) Look at weekly points based on your scoring system. Throw out the top two weeks (lucky freaks of nature) and the last week, when many are resting for playoffs. This leaves 13 weeks of data. Finally, give more weight to weeks 11-16 since this will be a good predictor of next season Look at how many times the player went over a certain threshold and how consistent he was. Take half the FPs to break any ties that may exist between players. Now move these players up in the rankings due to their consistency.

E) Avoid new teams (players who move to new teams, who have new head coaches or new schemes.)

F) Look at SOS and adjust accordingly. RBs go down if faced with tough defenses. QBs and WRs generally get a boost in rankings if playing tough defenses.

G) Look at early season matchups and your FF playoff matchups. Move players up based on a favorable early schedule or FF playoffs.

H) Avoid players who turn over the ball. There is nothing a coach hates worse than a fumble or interception. That is the fastest way to be benched in the NFL (ask Drew Bledsoe). Move these players down your list.

Projections first, then ranking –

1) Three year average- Take a player's statistics from the past three years, add them all together and divide by 3 to determine the average. This method gives equal weight to all years and thus undervalues younger players and overvalues older players, therefore a three-year weighted average is better. It also devalues rookies with no history.
2) Three year weighted average – (Year x is the most recent.)

.50 x (Year X) + .35 x (Year X-1) + .15 x (Year X-2) = Projection

3) Trend analysis – Simply increase or decrease last year's stats based on trends from the previous year. If a player increased his stats by 10% from the previous year to this year, then assume he will do the same and bump up his last year's statistics by 10%.
4) Team projections – With this method you determine stats for the entire team then allocate those yards, catches, rushes and TDs to players on the team based on their percentages from last year. For example, if P. Manning is projected to throw 33 TDs then M. Harrison will get 13, R Wayne 11, D Clark 6 and three individual TDs to three other players. The player stats must add up to the total team stats. These are very tedious and complicated calculations.

Checklist for Rankings

1) How have they performed in the past? Past performance is no indication of future performance but it should be a consideration. Consistency is the key.

2) Was there a trend in the second half of the season? Positive trends may mean breakouts next year, especially for younger players; negative trends can be indications of a breakdown for older players.

3) Have they been promoted/demoted (WR2 to WR1, rookie to different position than in college)?

4) Will they also get touches as a kick or punt returner?

5) Age factor – Most RBs and WRs peak at 27. QBs need time to mature (2-3 years holding the clipboard) so there is no set age for them. Is he one of the exceptions to the "rule"?

6) Has the player changed teams? Is it to a better, same or worse team? Will he be under pressure to perform? (WR2 to WR1)

7) Offensive Line – No changes are good for building chemistry at this position. A weak OL leads to more sacks and rushed throws and less of a running game because if the passing game does not hold up then the defenses just stack the middle with 7- and 8-man fronts. Injuries, holdouts, retirements and inexperience can all lead to a weak offensive line.

8) Has the passing or running game changed due to the addition or subtraction of personnel? The success of one often helps the other one improve.

9) Has the defense changed dramatically? If not, expect the same as last year. A good defense might allow the offense to run more. A bad defense might force the offense into a passing shoot-out, or set them up to get some garbage time points.

10) Is a player being pushed by the backup? Players play better when pushed by competition, but if they lose the battle… beware!

11) Is there an early 1st round draft choice that's going to see the field at some point?

12) Has the coaching changed? New head coach or offensive coordinator? Has a player's positional coach (often a mentor role) been added, deleted or changed?

13) Will there be a new offensive system to learn? Has the player worked in a similar system before? Is the player suited to the system? How complex is the new system and how much learning curve might be expected? RBs learn systems quicker than QBs or WRs.

14) Is there an indication that the team wants to focus more on running or passing this year? Judgment call: is it legitimate or just hype?

15) Is there an indication that the team wants to shift focus in the red zone? Judgment call: is it legitimate or just hype? Will TEs be more involved or another goal line RB?

16) Will a RB become more (or less) involved in the passing game?

17) Is a player being taught or forced to change his style or tendencies? (Such as a scrambling QB being pressed to stay in the pocket or a RB carrying the ball another way to avoid fumbles?)

18) Are they coming off an injury from late last year or the off-season? Is it one of those that take two years to truly recover from, as in an ACL injury? Have they recently picked up one of those nagging minor injuries? Do they have any key teammates with injury concerns?

19) Are they in much better (or worse) shape than last year?

20) Are they in a contract year and thinking about money? Did they just sign a big contract? Are they holding out during camp/preseason? Are they dealing with personal or legal issues?

21) Do they have a renewed focus? Do they have something to prove this year? Have they been putting in overtime studying the playbook and game films?

22) Team morale – What's the focus level of their surrounding teammates? How does the head coach affect team attitude? It can be infectious, whether good or bad. What city is the team in? Have they accomplished any goals recently?

23) Does the schedule this year look significantly easier or harder than last year's?

24) Is there potential carryover from the end of last year? Did they end last year on a hot streak and, if so, was that just luck or had they finally gotten it together? Did they end last year in a slump (and was that just luck or had the opponents finally figured them out)?

25) Are they in the coach's doghouse for some reason? Is the coach forceful enough to do something about it? Is the player talented enough that the coach probably has to play them regardless? (The T. Owens rule.) Has the player done something to gain (or lose) the respect of his teammates?

26) Who signed what free agents. How will they impact the team? If it is a big offensive improvement (say a great RB improvement or QB) then perhaps the defense will get a boost as well, since they will not have to be on the field as long every game.

Creating your own projections:

1) AVT Method (See Chapter 10 – Advanced Draft Strategies)

2) Take last year's stats for all players who played every game and return to the same team as much as possible. If a player was out for two games or more prorate his stats for a full season; if out for eight or more games, look at the prior season; for rookies, use last year's starter's stats if he starts or backup stats if he is the backup.

3) Determine what the team is going to do then divide them up between the QBs, RBs, WRs and TEs.

If a player has an injury coming into the season, you need to factor that into projections. Once you have the season projections, divide by 16 and subtract that amount for every game the player is expected to miss. (Factor in half of another game to be conservative.)

Player Rankings

QB Rankings

1) Are they the starter? Do not take chances with backups until the late round and even then only as a sleeper, not as your backup, unless you have a very reliable QB1, as in P. Manning.

2) How consistent are they at TD passes?

3) Don't forget rushing TDs.

4) Do they have quality WRs? Look at Tom Brady in 2006 after he lost D. Branch and D. Givens.

5) OL concerns

6) Offensive scheme/Head Coach

Tip: Put QBs who are competing for the job on the same line. Separate them with a slash, with the first name being the one you think will win the position battle (for example, Garcia/Simms). They should be pretty far down in your rankings based on the unknown of who will start; definitely no higher than the required number of QBs in the league. For example, if you must have two QBs and are in a 10-team league, then QBs 1-20 will be drafted; therefore place them 21st or worse, because you do not want to draft a QB that may not be starting. Caveat: if in this situation you have a QB who would be a good QB2, if not in an unknown situation, then you may take a chance on him. Do so if your QB1 was solid and had a late bye week, that way you could find another QB2 before the bye week if needed.

Why would you ever value a QB high overall? If your league requires that two QBs start or if the scoring rules give you 6 or more points for a Passing TD (the same as for a rushing or receiving TD), then QBs should be ranked higher overall.

RB Rankings

1) Are they the starter or are they RBBC?

2) Average TDs over the last couple of years?

3) Does he stay in for GL carries?

4) OL concerns

5) Offensive scheme/Head Coach

6) Are they healthy coming out of preseason?

7) Do they play on well-balanced offenses (teams with QBs expected to pass for 3200+ yards, 20+ TDs, have a 60% or greater completion rate)? These are teams that can throw the ball well and prevent the eight-men-in-a-box defenses that shut down the run game.

WR Rankings

1) Are they starting? Are they #1, #2 or #3 WR on their team? WR#3 rarely produce enough to be worth drafting unless they come from a passing offense like Indianapolis or Cincinnati.

2) Past production?

3) Who is their QB?

4) Possession WR or deep threat? Possession WRs catch more balls (great in PPR leagues). Deep threats score more TDs and get more long-yardage TD passes.

5) Offensive scheme/Head Coach

6) Are they an end zone option? Look for tall WRs. Size matters and so does speed. Diminutive speedsters such as S. Smith, and S. Moss are becoming more of a trend as WRs adapt.

7) Is he the QBs favorite target?

TE Rankings

1) Do the rules require you to draft one? If not, skip the position unless a top 5 TE is available.
2) If you do have to draft a TE, can you get away with only drafting one until his bye week? Some leagues have a minimum number of players at each position. If you have to draft two then rank 2 times the number of teams in the league. If there is no minimum, I suggest drafting one TE and then using the other roster spot on a sleeper RB or WR.
3) Do they use the TE position a lot?
4) Is he a pass-catching TE or a blocking TE?
5) Look for second and third year TEs: tall with great leaping ability (former basketball player in college)?

Kicker Rankings

1) What is his FG percentage inside 40 yards? If he missed more than two FGs inside the 40 last year then he may be on a short leash this year. Avoid, if possible, since drafting a kicker who will be fired is no advantage in most leagues.
2) What is his FG percentage over 40 yards? This may be worth more points in some leagues so know your rules. Make sure he only has a few misses or no less than 70%. Has he tried any 50+ yarders? Has he made any? This may indicate whether the team will let him try some again this year.
3) Offensive scheme/Head Coach
4) Defense – A good defense can give the offense the ball inside the opponent's territory and even if the offense cannot move the ball, it will give your kicker FG attempts.

-The difference between the top kicker and the medium kicker is only a few points per game.

-A Top 5 kicker from last year could end up just about anywhere in the final rankings the next year. Many of the Top 5 kickers come from the Top 15 kickers the year before. 2006 Top 5 predicted kickers (actual finish): Rackers (8), Vinateri (11), Graham (9), Feely (19) and Vanderjagt (released).

-Denver Broncos kicker Jason Elam is one of the most reliable FP scorers.

-Even good kickers have a few bad weeks because their offense does not put them in position to score.

-If you are penalized for missed FGs, look into kicker's averages.

-The more FG attempts, the more FPs a kicker will score. Duh!

-Most of the Top 10 kickers of the past have had at least an 80% FG kicking accuracy.

-Studies have shown that 75% of the Top 5 kickers came from the Top 10 scoring offenses. Over 50% of the Top 5 kickers came from the Top 10 yardage offenses. So scoring, even TDs, does not hurt a kicker FP-wise.

Qualities to look for in a kicker (Top 5 to be)

1) Ranked between 6th -15th last year
2) Successful FG rate of 85% or greater (ignore FG attempts over 50 yards)
3) Team has same kicker, QB, Head Coach, holder and long snapper from last year
4) Top 10 Scoring Offense or Defense
5) Home is a Dome. (This is not a disqualifier if all of the qualities above are met; more of a tiebreaker.)

Defense/ST rankings

1) Safeties, turnovers, and DEF TDs are hard to predict and tend to be based on whom the defense plays and what kind of QB they face. Sacks and points/yardage allowed tend to be the most consistent statistics among defenses based on the talent on the field. Look for 40 or more sacks as a good indicator. Pittsburgh, Denver, Miami, Dallas, Jacksonville and Baltimore are all good bets for a good defense. These teams have consistently played good defense year in and year out as reflected in sacks, points/yards allowed.

2) DC/HC
3) Is offense high scoring?
4) Look at whom they have gained and lost due to FA, retirement, trades etc.
5) Look at injuries to key players last year and anyone hurt or out this year.

In general, last year's top defenses probably will not slip too much and last year's terrible defenses probably will not improve drastically. Defenses will usually move one way or the other, but in small increments. About 80% of the Top 5 defenses stay in the Top 15 the following year.

How many players from each position should expect to be drafted?

If your league has fixed roster requirements (i.e each team must have two QBs, three RBs etc.), then simply multiply these numbers by the number of teams and "voila," you have your draftable players. If, like most leagues, you have a starter requirement and a max roster size but that is it, then you must estimate the number of players drafted at each position. For example, in a 14-team league that requires one QB, two RBs, two WRs, one

TE, one K and one DEF/ST, a good place to begin is a starter and backup for each position. So in a 14-team league, 28 QBs, 42 RBs, 42 WRs, 28 TEs, 28 Ks and 28 DEF/STs should be ranked. Some teams (including yourself) may skimp on an extra TE, K or DEF and go with an extra RB or two and a WR. In this case, bump up the RBs and WRs to 50, just in case. Add 2 to QB for Mom and the kids and we have our draftable numbers. 30-50-50-28-28-28.

**Once you have players ranked, adjust their positions based on injuries, suspensions and position battles during preseason. When a player becomes injured, he needs to be downgraded. How long will he be out? Add an extra game to the prognosis and move him down based on the percentage of the season he will miss. Upgrade his backup for the same amount. Look at how his absence affects the other skill players on his team. (QB is out, WR is down too; unless they are familiar with QB from practice squad. RBBC, injuries, suspensions, players entering the coach's doghouse – like Mike Shanahan for fumbling all affect the situation)

I suggest you use an ADP set and adjust it up until draft day, then use AVT for statistical projections based on rankings.

ADP

ADP is the average draft position of a player based on numerous mock drafts. The ADP will vary depending on the scoring system, starting lineup and number of owners. ADP is useless if applied to leagues that have scoring or starter rules that encourage teams to stock up on WRs or QBs first or even to stockpile RBs. To be beneficial, it needs to be modified to fit your league's rules. The best way to do this is to adjust it based on league tendencies. Tendencies can be determined by league drafts from the most recent years.

EDP is the estimated draft position of a player. This is based on scoring system, starting lineup, number of owners and owner tendencies, if known.

What does ADP data look like? In many cases it will provide an ADP, the highest pick a player has been drafted and the lowest pick a player has been drafted, along with the number of drafts used to calculate the data. If the ADP data includes high pick and low pick, you can use it as a window of opportunity for when you may be able to draft that player.

Sample ADP for Chad Johnson:

Player	Pos	Team	ADP	High	Low	# Drafts
Chad Johnson	WR	CINN	2.6	1.10	3.06	53

Chad is expected to go somewhere between the tenth pick in the 1st round and the sixth pick in the 3rd round. The ADP is sixth pick in the 2nd round. Notice that the high and low need to be based on a certain number of teams in the league. A player's overall ranking will depend on how many teams in the league format the ADP used. In a 10-team league, his ADP overall is 16th. In a 16-team league it would be 22nd. You need to know what it is based on. Sometimes ADP data will be in the form of an overall draft ranking such as 35th pick or 41st pick.

What good is ADP? You can use it to determine which player is undervalued (ADP is lower than you expected). You can use it to find those players who are overvalued (going earlier than you think). You can use it to find players that you are not aware of, but who have a following. Ultimately, it answers the question: when will players be drafted in my league? However, be careful. ADP can get old very fast; for instance if C. Portis gets hurt and is out for six weeks. Watch how quickly he drops on the ADP. On the other hand, if you do not get and use the latest ADP, you will not have the current trend.

How good is ADP? The best ADP would be what you have after your own draft, or with the help of a time machine. The next best would be if you got all your owners together and mock drafted a few times. That would give you a good idea when players will be drafted. The next best data would be from many leagues exactly like yours. These are all unlikely. The best data that is realistically available will most likely be from leagues with the same number of teams as yours and rules that are similar. This ADP data is the most accurate for your league. The worst thing you can do is blindly follow ADP that is from all different kinds of leagues and scoring systems. It is not worth the paper it is written on.

Using ADP to predict your draft –

1) Look for trends in your opponents draft picks over the years. (For example, if he always takes a RB or never takes a Bears player.)

2) The top 10 or 15 overall are usually the same players in slightly different order. After that is where the real differences appear.

3) The first five rounds of your local draft can be scripted based on tendencies (WR-WR), player profiles (Homers), and the cheat sheet they use.

4) You can bet that the player from the "Homer's" team or the player always on "Owner B's" team will be drafted by them a round earlier than what the cheat sheets say.

AVT

There are two methods for calculating AVT.

1) Average of FPs for past three years (some use five years but I think the data and trends are outdated). Range of FPs by position, which allows you to adjust player performances based on their own strengths and weaknesses.
2) Weighted average of FPs over the last three years. Not much difference from average for three years, so not used as often.

(Refer to Chapter 10 – Advanced Draft Theories, for more information on AVT.)

Tiering

What is a tier system? Sometimes called "drop-offs," "bucketing," "maximizing value" or "categorizing." A tier is a group of players with similar expected performance for the season (fantasy points). It is good to get any of the players in that tier because they are all of equal value. Players not in that tier (or level) would represent a significant drop off in fantasy points.

How do you tier players? When you start, you will have players ranked from one through the number of players at each position you expect to draft, plus a few extras.

1) Determine what the tier drop off number will be (usually 10-20 points). This number will depend on what you use for projections. Is it fantasy points? If your league is a basic scoring league (average of 5 points per player per game) then perhaps 5 points will work. If it is a high scoring league (12 points per player per game) then 15 or 20 is probably more appropriate. Is it X values, as discussed in chapter 9? In this case, the tier drop off number will be less, so 5 or 10 points may work. Every league will not be able to use the same generic 5, 10, 16 (one point per game) or 20 points.

2) Subtract that number from the fantasy points (FPs) of your #1 player in that position and then draw a line below the last player to have that many points or more. For example, LT is the #1 RB with 340 FP projected. Using 20 points as my tier level, 340-20=320, so all players with 320 or more FPs are in the top tier in this league. Repeat with the top player in the next tier and subtract the same amount from his FPs to determine who is in the next tier. Repeat until all players at the position are tiered.

3) Look at the tiers. Do they make sense? Players tiered together should offer the same risk/reward.

Make sure the tiers are not too big. If 23 of your 50 RBs are in one tier, something is wrong. By the same token, 28 tiers for 50 RBs means your tiers are too small. You should feel completely comfortable drafting anyone within the tier and also feel that someone in the upper tier is better than someone in the lower tier. If a player is in the lower tier but should be one tier higher, just move your line. This is the "art" of tiering. You can adjust as you see fit.

4) Repeat for all other positions.

5) Repeat with the overall list.

Note: I highly recommend using the X values found by using a value-based drafting system like those discussed in chapter 9.

Some individuals start tiering at the last player in a position and work their way up. Just realize that this method will mean not subtracting the tier number from Step 1, but instead using it to group players with FPs within that number starting from the bottom.

Some experts suggest a simpler method: Tier based on Top 3, then 4-11 then 12-19, 20+. The rationale is that normally there are three players in the top tier at each position. There are between six and eight players in the next tier (depends on position, but second tier WRs are getting larger every year) and after that around eight at each of the other levels. This is the easiest and quickest method but it does not capture the essence of tiering, which is trying to group players of similar expected performance on the same level. A player ranked 19th may be so similar to the 20th ranked player that they both should be in the same group.

How does tiering help?

Tiering prevents you from becoming so focused on taking a certain position with each round of the draft, for example: RB-RB-WR-TE. It helps you find value and avoid drafting lower players in positions at the expense of much better players at other positions. Tiering will show the drop offs in productivity at each position and how many quality players are available at each level (tier). It also allows you to determine value in the draft by getting talented players from different positions before all the talent at that level is gone. Once a group, or tier, is depleted and the next tier is available and has many players available then there is no need to immediately draft from the new tier (reaching too high) since it has more of a supply. Instead, you can target another tier in another position that is on the verge of being depleted. As an example, tiering can help you determine whether you need to grab a RB because there will not be any second tier RBs left when you pick or if you can wait and grab a first tier WR before he is gone. Tiering allows you to get the most value from the draft choices available. It also helps avert the "big freeze." This occurs when the player you want is grabbed by an owner who picks before you do. Now you are on the clock and look like a deer caught in the headlights. The clock is ticking. What is your pick, sir? Now any player in that same positional tier will do. Remember a tier contains a group of players that you would be just as happy to draft versus another. You can then pick the player in that tier that you feel best about (based on SOS, bye week, previous injuries, other players on your team, etc.). The point is that every player in that tier is equal and getting one of them is better than settling for a player in a lower tier.

Miscellaneous tiering issues

1) Tiers do not have to have the same number of players

2) Tiering is less important in the late rounds since you will be drafting sleepers and backups based on bye weeks and possible matchups. Not to mention, the values of the lower ranked players all start to merge and the tiers become larger.

3) Tiering helps in auctions too. Why overbid for one player when there are several others in his tier still available?

4) Some recommend that you target players with favorable FF playoff matchups. You would place an asterisk by their name, or a plus or minus sign, depending on their FF playoffs matchups. These symbols would be used as discriminators between players in similar tiers or to move them up or down a tier. *Authors Note: I disagree. If they are on the same tier that should mean that all those players are expected to put up about the same FPs. If you select players from the tier that should do better in the playoffs, then they should do worse during the regular season because at the end of the season their FPs should be the same. Example: Two 160-point RBs (expected to average 10 points per game); one is expected to do better in weeks 14-16. Lets say instead of his average 30 points (10 per game), he will score 45 during that 3-game stretch. That means that he has to score less in the first 13 games or a lot less in his last game of the season. 160-45=115 averaged over 13 games = less than his 10 points per game average. You could almost go the opposite way and pick players in the same tier who are not going to do well in the playoffs. That would mean they do well in the regular season. So should you pick players based on predicted playoff performance? No. Make acquisitions and trades midyear based on expected fantasy playoff performance. Do not draft based on fantasy playoff performance. Things change. RBs get hurt and teams improve or go down the drain by week 14.*

5) Rule of Thumb – When drafting, always remember to draft from the higher tiers first, draft from the shallower tiers when the high tiers are exhausted, and wait to draft from deep, lower tiers until absolutely necessary.

6) I suggest putting red lines on the draft cheat sheet to draw your attention to where the tiers are.

Tiering – {example of tiering using 20-point tiers)

RB

Player	Team	Bye	FP
L Tomlinson	SD	3	340
L Johnson	KC	3	335
S Alexander	SEA	5	322
S Jackson	STL	7	273
B Westbrook	PHIL	9	269
R Johnson	CINN	5	265
C Williams	TB	4	211
C Portis	WASH	8	208
E James	AZ	9	199
L Jordan	OAK	3	179
R Brown	MIA	8	175
R Bush	NOR	7	169
W McGahee	BALT	8	169

WR

Player	Team	Bye	FP
S Smith	CAR	9	223
T Owens	DAL	3	222
L Fitz	AZ	9	215
T Holt	STL	7	203
C Johnson	CINN	5	199
M Harrison	IND	6	192
A Boldin	AZ	9	182
R Moss	NE	3	177
S Moss	WASH	8	177

Question: You have the 10th pick in a 12-team league. In the first round, your cheat sheet looks like this (tiers are indicated by horizontal lines). Who would you draft?

RB

Player	Team	Bye	FP

C Williams	TB	4	211
L Jordan	OAK	3	179
R Brown	MIA	8	175
R Bush	NOR	7	169
W McGahee	BALT	8	169

WR

Player	Team	Bye	FP
S Smith	CAR	9	223
T Owens	DAL	3	222
L Fitz	AZ	9	215
T Holt	STL	7	203
C Johnson	CINN	5	199
M Harrison	IND	6	192
A Boldin	AZ	9	182
R Moss	NE	3	177
S Moss	WASH	8	177

The choice here would be C Williams because he is the only RB left from the third tier. If you were thinking of taking the top WR as your first pick since the top RBs have been depleted, a quick scan of the WR tiers shows that there are four in the top tier. Knowing that two owners will be drafting twice before your next pick, the odds are in your favor that one of the four WRs will be available for you in round 2. The only way for none of the four to be available would be if both Owner 11 and Owner 12 took WRs back-to-back as their picks in rounds 1 and 2 (Picks 11, 12, 13 and 14). If Owner 11 takes a RB and a WR and Owner 12 takes two WRs, you have this left for your second round pick (pick 15):

RB

Player	Team	Bye	FP
R Brown	MIA	8	175
R Bush	NOR	7	169
W McGahee	BALT	8	169

WR

Player	Team	Bye	FP
T Holt	STL	7	203
C Johnson	CINN	5	199
M Harrison	IND	6	192

A Boldin	AZ	9	182
R Moss	NE	3	177
S Moss	WASH	8	177

If you wanted a top WR, now will be your last chance to get him since there will be 18 other picks before your pick in round 3. Therefore T Holt is, in this case, the pick for a top WR.

Rookies

A rookie being taken in the Top 5 of the NFL draft is an indication of an elite player and one that will play soon. In the case of a RB, he will contribute from the beginning. (RBs have an easier transition to the field than any of the other offensive players besides kickers.) Expect the RBs drafted in the Top 5 in the NFL draft to be used heavily. You don't pick a guy that high (pay him that much money) to let him ride the pine at RB. QB and RB are a little different in the systems they have to learn. Rookie QBs – They usually hold the clipboard and thus do not start in the first year. Yes these teams probably have weak offensive lines (that's why they are drafting in the top 5), but the RB can make the lines look better and that makes the team look better as a whole.

Rookie RBs – A 1st or 2nd round rookie RB usually ends up as a low RB2 at best. They tend to disappoint as far as value for their ADP is concerned. So whatever the ADP says they should go as is usually pretty close or they disappoint. Rarely does the market underestimate a rookie RB. To get the most value from a drafted rookie RB, stay with them all year, because they are more likely to perform better in the second half of the season. (This is in part because they may not start week 1 but will eventually get their chance.) This is another reason that their value, as expressed by ADP, is usually not as good; because they do not start all 16 games from the get-go. Rookie RBs who are backing up an elite RB (top 10 RB) will have much less chance of success. If the rookie is behind a RB that is outside the top 25 RBs then he has the best chance of success. Duh! A rookie RB may get a quicker chance if he is on a losing team or a team that is out of playoff contention by week 12 or 13 (going into your fantasy playoffs).

Rookie WRs – Approximately 1 in 6 rookie WRs drafted in the NFL's first three rounds becomes a fantasy starter that year. Statistically only about 5% will make the Top 25 WR list. Therefore you have a 1 in 20 chance of any rookie WR picked making the Top 25. Most are undervalued because many owners base rankings on last years stats (thus no stats for a rookie) and many owners have a "don't draft a rookie WR" mentality. Many rookies will be hyped by the media; your problem is finding the 1 in 6 (or the 1 in 20 that breaks the Top 25) that are really going to have a fantasy impact. Opportunity and situation will dictate who plays and excels. Will they be replacing the retiring veteran or working their way into a WR heavy corps? The situation is the offensive style, head coach, QB, etc. First rookie drafted is not an automatic, though it should give him some playing time. With your last pick, instead of grabbing a benchwarmer, take a gamble; a 1 in 6 gamble on a rookie WR drafted in the first three NFL rounds, who has opportunity and situation playing to his advantage. Of course, a rookie WR in a keeper league is worth more than in a redraft league. (See Chapter 22 – Keeper Leagues.)

Rookie kickers may take some time adjusting to the balls, coming straight from college. Do not expect as good a performance from a rookie kicker as they did in college.

Character Issues

Another critical discriminator in ranking players is the character issue. Just as the NFL commissioner, Roger Goodell, has made player character a major emphasis point in his early policy decisions, so should you. Add the possibility of off-the-field issues, which can hurt an individual player's career and your season, to the list of things to evaluate (such as a players work ethic, game tape study, and body conditioning) for your rankings. The risk is much higher now for "bad boy" players who have had previous problems or who may have future incidents. The message sent by the commissioner (with recent offseason suspensions) is anything that reflects poorly on the NFL will be punished and result in missed game time. Keep this in mind when comparing talent. There even may be a premium on "good guys" in fantasy drafts.

Mock Drafts

Aren't mock drafts a waste of time and energy? And besides, I am not going to use my real picks and strategies and give that away to others, am I? So the mock is just a bunch of fanatics who are kidding each other about who they will pick. NOT TRUE! First of all, you do not have to mock with owners from your own league. In fact, it is probably better to mock with other owners from different leagues who use your same scoring and roster rules. The scoring rules should be the same so that the values of players are based on the same system. It is silly to mock where the players get a point per reception (PPR) if your league does not use that rule, since WRs will be more valuable. Another important thing to note is the roster rules. Some leagues will require a minimum number at each position; still others will have different starting players. It makes no sense to mock in a draft where three WRs start when your league only starts two or in a mock where TEs are required to start and you must have two on your roster, and in your league they are optional. Apples to apples.

Mocks are important for several reasons. 1) they let you practice making time-critical decisions, 2) they let you practice recognizing trends, 3) they show you selection trends (i.e. where there is depth and where there are shortages), 4) you can make sure your rankings are not too far off. Check to see where players are drafted in the mock. If they go much higher than you expected, reevaluate them; maybe there is something you missed. What about players you have never heard of? Again investigate; maybe there is something you don't know. What if some players slip further down the draft? Maybe these can be your sleepers.

Other advantages of mock drafts:

1) Helps to rank players

2) Good practice for draft strategy

3) Allows you to predict when the runs will occur

4) Helps determine when your sleepers will be drafted

5) Allows you to determine if a draft day trade of picks is worth it

When you do a mock draft:

1) Make sure everyone shows. One owner on computer-pick or auto-pick can ruin the entire draft.

2) If you really want to know where a player will fall, do not draft him yourself and see where he is drafted.

3) Use the mocks to determine average draft position and rankings if you need a starting point. The good news is that if the number of teams and rules are the same it should be a good proxy for how your league's draft will go. The bad news is that situations change from when you mock to when you actually draft and owner tendencies in your league will affect the outcome.

4) Ignore the mock if there is an owner who is obviously just picking to ruin it for others. This fouls up the results. For example, if someone picks all kickers, takes all Cowboys, or three TEs with their first picks.

Cheat Sheets

Cheat sheets are like getting your opponent's game plan in advance. Armed with that knowledge you should be able to plan a strategy to get your top guys before the other owners. Cheat sheets are usually based on last year's performance or past performance. (And like a mutual fund statement – past performance is no indication of future returns.) But that is the building block for our rankings. The freshest thing in our mind is last season, when that player flopped or excelled. If you do the rankings in June, that is only four months removed from some of his performance, if in the playoffs. Cheat sheets at a minimum should have player's name, rank by position and overall, bye week, ADP, and a place for notes (injuries, team issues, suspensions, SOS, etc.). Rob Zarzycki in *Drafting to Win* goes further "I also like to list teams, bye weeks, sleeper potential (denoted by asterisks)".

Rankings are used to create your cheat sheets. I use a cheat sheet or two for various tools. One is to get a consensus on the experts, another is to use when drafting for absent owners should I be asked, and yet another, I know several of my opponents use them so I keep that as information on their plans. Always have an overall sheet of first 100 picks. It helps prevent excessive page turning (going from player ranking to player ranking) in the first rounds to get you to break time. Have your player rankings on three pages at most. Have RB and WR on the first page, QB and TE on the second page and K and DEF on the third page. This gives you five pieces of paper to carry to the draft (overall list, QB/TE list, RB/WR list, K/DEF list and a draft-tracking sheet). Do not throw away your cheat sheets after the draft. Use them for evaluating trades, add and drops, and creating a watch list. Then you can use it next year to evaluate how your projections were.

Auction Cheat Sheets

The number one thing about auction cheat sheets is that they have to add up. A good auction cheat sheet allocates the right amount of dollars to the right amount of players. You want the total value of all players sold at the auction to add up to the total money spent. As an example, say you have a 12-team league with 20 roster spots to draft with $200 in salary cap money. At the end of the auction $2400 (12 x $200) will have been spent on 240 players (12 x 20). The total value of the top 240 players overall on your cheat sheet should equal $2400 and then all other players should be worth $0. If your league starts three WRs and the cheat sheets only start two, then WRs are more valuable in your league. If PPR are used in your league but not on the cheat sheet then WRs, TEs and pass catching RBs (L. Jordan, S. Jackson, R. Brown, B. Westbrook) are undervalued on the cheat sheet from what they are worth in your league.

Cheat sheet values vary by roster size, number of teams in the league, scoring rules, keeper or not and waiver wire rule. What if you have a cheat sheet you trust but it is for a different amount of teams? Simply apply a conversion factor. Calculate how much money will be spent in the draft for your league (# teams x salary cap). Divide that by the cheat sheet's current value, which is the total value of all players sold overall (# teams x # roster spots). So, if I want a 12-team league with a $200 salary cap and I have a cheat sheet that has $2800 for the first 240 players (12 x 20 roster spots), then I need to multiply all the values by 2400/2800=.857. Because the cheat sheet was built for 14 teams and is thus overvalued, you would multiply all the values by .857 to decrease them.

What if I play in a keeper league?

How do I adjust the cheat sheet for those keepers? You would not keep the keepers unless they were a bargain, right? Who would keep J. Lewis for $20 from last year if they could get him for $15 this year? Add up the prices for all the keepers and subtract that from the salary cap of the league; then subtract the number of keepers from the total number who will be drafted. In my 12-team, 20 roster, $200 cap league, we have 20 keepers at a value of $500, so 2400-500=$1900. When you subtract 20 keepers, that leaves 220 roster spots to fill, paying $1900. Add up the top 220 and they should be going for much less than $1900. In my example they go for $1600. Multiply each player value by 1900/1600=1.1875 to get the true value after keepers.

The goal of an auction cheat sheet should be that you would not care who you got off the cheat sheet as long as you spent your $200 and had the correct roster size. In other words, make sure it has the values you think are correct. If you do not want T. Owens, mark his value down or eliminate him if you could never find it in your heart to root for him. I do not think it is a good idea to eliminate based on feelings. Your emotions should play very little part in fantasy football. Another way to look at your cheat sheets is that if the computer randomly drafted all the teams you would not care which team you received because they all were of equal value based on the values you give. Indifference is the key word regarding your cheat sheet.

Does the average of all cheat sheets work?

Does pooling or averaging cheat sheets work? In this scenario you take the cheat sheets from several reputable sources and combine them or average them to come up with the cheat sheet of justice. Is this really worth anything? The answer is … it depends. The short answer is yes; it will work if you are a newbie or have not had time to do any research. That document will guide you and probably do better than two-thirds of the individual experts. It will be a very big picture of the available talent. It may help you realize a trade has happened that you did not know about. For example, if a player is ranked much higher or much lower than you thought, that is a clue that you do not know something and need to research it more. The long answer is that it will not help you if you are a serious FF owner. **The more you average the picks the more average your results will be.** If you want to win you need to pick the diamonds in the rough, not the next guy in everyone else's list. If you pick strictly using this expert consensus then you will have middle-of-the-pack results. To get the edge you need to put your own analysis in there. Evaluating the players is what differentiates the middle-of-the-road owners from champions.

Research

1) Watch college games late in the season and make notes on the big names who are seniors or juniors who may turn pro. Watch a few key players each game like you are a scout. Compare your observations with what the pundits say. Trust your gut.
2) Stay informed of off-season developments.
3) Watch at least the first two rounds of the NFL draft.!!! Watch even more if in an IDP, dynasty or deep roster league.

Determining League Draft Tendencies

Unless league rules change drastically, drafting tendencies will probably not change much from year to year. You can use a weighted average (better, but more complicated) or just last year's data to determine: a) How many players from each position are taken in each round? and b) How many players from each position are drafted in total after each round? Information from question "a" can be used to generate an answer to question "b" and all of this can be retraced from last year's draft data.

In Table 7.1 below, I have taken the two-year-average for a local league, Lakenheath Fantasy Football League (LFFL). It is a 14-team, keeper-2 performance league. The two keepers can only come from players drafted after the 8th round and to keep them you pay a stiff four round penalty. I did not use 2004 data because we were a 12-team league then and are now a 14-team league. This league is somewhat unique in that all 14 teams must have the same number of players at each position after the main draft. Each team must have 2 QBs, 3 RBs, 3 WRs, 2 TEs, 2 Ks and 2 DEFs at the end of the main draft. The total number at each position is already predetermined in this league, unlike most leagues where any number of RBs or WRs, etc. can be drafted. A supplemental draft is then held to draft four more players from any position.

Table 7.1 – Two-Year-Average for LFFL

Round	QB	RB	WR	TE	K	DEF
1	1	12	1	0	0	0
2	0	9	5	0	0	0
3	5	4	4	1	0	0
4	5	3	5	1	0	0

5	3	3	6	2	0	0
6	1	2	6	4	0	1
7	2	2	3	2	2	3
8	2	2	4	2	3	1
9	2	2	2	1	5	2
10	3	0	3	3	1	4
11	2	1	2	3	3	3
12	0	0	1	5	4	4
13	1	1	0	3	6	3
14	1	1	0	1	4	7
Total	28	42	42	28	28	28

Observations:

Early Rounds, 1-5: Round 1 is a RB run; Round 2 is 65% RB and 35% WR; Round 3- QB; Round 4- QB and WR; Round 5- WR

Middle Rounds, 6-10: Round 6- WR and 30% TE; Round 7- Every position including K and DEF; Round 8- WR; Round 9- K; Round 10- DEF

Late Rounds, 11-14: Rounds 11-14- Backup TEs, Ks and DEFs

Notice that 21 RBs were taken in the first two rounds. Stud RB theory anyone?

In rounds 2-6, of the 70 possible picks, 26 of them (37%) were WRs. All the starting QBs were taken by the end of round 5. The top defenses (top 4) were taken before a kicker but then by round 8 the kickers had caught up.

In rounds 11-14, on average a total of 11 TEs, Ks and DEFs are taken per round. Can you say backups?

The 2005 breakdown is almost exactly the same. The only significant difference was in the 7th round when 6 defenses and 3 kickers were drafted.

Next, we have a four round supplemental draft where owners can take any positions. See Table 7.2 – Two-Year-Average for LFFL Supplemental Draft.

Table 7.2 – Two-Year-Average for LFFL Supplemental Draft

Round	QB	RB	WR	TE	K	DEF
15	3	10	0	1	0	0
16	1	9	4	0	0	0
17	0	8	5	1	0	0
18	3	7	4	0	0	0
Totals	7	34	13	2	0	0

Table 7.3 – Two-Year-Average for LFFL Entire Draft

Round	QB	RB	WR	TE	K	DEF
1	1	12	1	0	0	0
2	1	21	6	0	0	0
3	6	25	10	1	0	0
4	11	28	15	2	0	0
5	14	31	21	4	0	0
6	15	33	27	8	0	1
7	17	35	30	10	2	4
8	19	37	34	12	5	5
9	21	39	36	13	10	7
10	24	39	39	16	11	11
11	26	40	41	19	14	14
12	26	40	42	24	18	18
13	27	41	42	27	24	21
14	28	42	42	28	28	28
15	31	52	42	29	28	28
16	32	61	46	29	28	28
17	32	69	51	30	28	28
18	35	76	55	30	28	28
Total	35	76	55	30	28	28

Table 7.3, Two-Year-Average for LFFL Entire Draft, shows the entire draft in all its glory. Great but what can I tell from this information? Starting RBs are taken by round 4. Everyone has a starting QB by round 5. Starting WRs are gone by round 7. The last of the starting TEs go in round 10. The first kicker or defense goes in round 6 or 7. No one gets more than 2 kickers or defenses and rarely take more than 2 TEs. The average team consists of 2.5 QBs, 5.4 RBs, 4 WRs (3.93 rounded up), 2 TEs, 2 Ks and 2 DEF/STs, or 2-3 QBs, 5-6 RBs, 4 WRs, 2 TEs, 2 Ks and 2 DEFs. The supplemental draft sees a run on RBs every round so get them early.

RBs are drafted in rounds 1-8; after that only 5 can be taken. If in the 7th round I see that only 5-6 more RBs are needed by other teams and I like all remaining RBs equally, then I can wait and draft my last RB (RB3) with my last pick in the main draft (14th). This gives me a potential RB keeper who, if he pans out, I can keep for a 10th round pick next year.

The same applies to WRs. If I need my WR3 and it is the 9th or 10th round I need to see how many have been drafted (lets say 39) and compare that to how many have to be drafted (42) to determine how many more WRs will go in the main draft. In this case my

WR3 and two others will go in the next 4-5 rounds. Again, if I like who is left, why not wait to draft him in the 13th round and get a potential WR keeper for a cheap price (9th round pick next year)? So, RB-WR-RB-TE-WR-QB-QB-DEF-K-TE-K-DEF-WR-RB appears to be a good initial strategy for this type of league.

Now use ADP data (preferably based on league size and scoring system) and apply that to your draft to mock out who goes where. For example, in round 1 I know that usually 1 QB, 12 RBs and 1 WR are drafted. If the ADP says the top QB drafted is P. Manning, the top WR is S. Smith and the top 12 RBs are… then I can predict the first round of my draft:

Round 1	P. Manning	QB
	S. Smith	WR
	L. Tomlinson	RB
	L. Johnson	RB
	S. Alexander	RB
	T. Barber	RB (based on 2006, before his 2007 retirement)
	S. Jackson	RB
	C. Portis	RB
	R. Johnson	RB
	L. Jordan	RB
	B. Westbrook	RB
	C. Williams	RB
	R. Brown	RB
	W. McGahee	RB

Now you can get a great idea of who will go in what round of your draft. It will eliminate some of the panic of not knowing who goes where. Do the same for every round of your draft. Add keepers in the rounds they will go in; also add in tendencies of the other owners. If an owner always takes Broncos players for his team, throw that in the mock. Try to calculate when the skill players for Denver will go in a regular draft then have him draft them a round earlier to beat everyone to the punch. Then take that position out of the equation if you think he will go WR in round 4. In the example above, if you think he will take J. Walker (Den WR), then put Walker as going in round 4. Now find out the other 5 QBs, 3 RBs and 4 WRs (plus a TE) who will also be drafted in round 4. Factor in tendencies with the modified ADP data and you have your draft prediction.

If you do your own projections

1) Look at your projections from last year. Is there a position that you are weak at projecting? Do you always miss on QBs or WRs? If so, do some more study in those areas next year. Create realistic projections. Don't have P. Manning throwing for 4000 yards but his WRs, TE and RB only receiving 3000 yards. Compare your rankings with others for a sanity check.

Eliminate (do not erase, just mark so that you do not draft) players whom you do not want to risk drafting this year; players whom you think are way overvalued or who are too risky (C. Portis in 2006).

2) Preseason – Ignore it. WRs who know they are guaranteed a starting position will not go the extra mile for a catch down the middle of the field during preseason. Watch how many RBs will take the easy road and step out of bounds in preseason versus turning their body up field and trying to ram through a LB. They know it does not count and so should you. However, injuries do count; watch out for a QB with throwing arm or hand injuries or a RB with leg or foot injuries.

3) Statistically speaking:

a) Studies show that if a QB was in the top 12 the previous season, then he has a 50% chance of making the Top 12 the following season. Approximately 66% of the top 6 QBs would stay in the top 12 the following year. Most likely, two of the six would again place in the top 6 and two more in positions 7-12. What does this mean to you? There is not a lot of difference between the 7th and 12th QB, so wait on picking them. P. Manning is the stud at this position, and is the only one likely to repeat in the Top 6 year in and year out.

b) A RB in the Top 12 last year has a 50% chance of returning. More of the top 6 RBs do well, though if he is in the 7-12th position he has a better chance of staying or slipping out (freak season).

c) With the exception of the four stud WRs (Steve Smith, Chad Johnson, Torry Holt, Marvin Harrison), a WR has little chance of returning to the Top 12. The top 4 are the top 4 for a reason. The other 8 in the top 12 are fluky. The top 4-6 are the ones to grab; after that, the chance of the WR repeating a great performance from year to year diminishes.

d) The TE position is the most reliable for repeating past performance. What this means is that the Top 6 TEs usually finish in the top 12 the following year. Because there are so few good TEs they tend to dominate year in and year out.

e) Kickers are the most unpredictable. If a kicker made the top 5 the previous year, that is usually the kiss of death and he probably will not return the following year. If you pick the #1 kicker, odds are that he will not finish in the top 15 next year. If anything, the #5-10 kickers have a better chance of staying there or moving up. Likewise, the really bad kickers (20th or worse) tend to stay bad.

4) Don't ignore coaching changes. More so at head coach and to a lesser degree at OC and QB coach. The new coach's style and personality will influence how a player performs.

5) What percentage of yards go to whom?

There are four main passing systems with regards to WRs:

1) Typical system with a good WR1, WR2 and WR3
2) "Go-to Guy" system where the WR1 gets more passes (A. Johnson in Hou)
3) "WR Duo" system where there is little degradation from WR1 to WR2 skills. (M Harrison and R Wayne in Ind)
4) Committee System where no WR is really much better than the others. (Jacksonville with Matt Jones, E. Wilford and Reggie Williams)

The typical system has passing yards distributed about 30/20/10. WR1 gets 30%; WR2 gets 20% and WR3 gets 10%. TE1 sees 15% and TE2 only 4%. RB1 has 10% and RB2 has 5%. That leaves 6% to others. In a "Go-to Guy" system, WR1 gets 5% more (now at 35%) and they usually come from WR2's numbers (now at 15%). If both WRs are good (WR Duo) then both get about 25%. In all these cases WR3 sees his 10% untouched. A committee system has all three WRs getting 20%, with WR2 and WR3 possibly getting a little less and WR1 a little more.

Teams with a Top 5 TE will see up to 30% of the passing yards go to that TE1. Likewise, teams that do not have a good pass catching RB in the backfield may see WRs with as much as 45% of the passing yards. If the offensive focus is on the pass (56% or more of plays are passes) then all the WRs will rank higher than if the offense employed a more balanced (50-55% of plays are passes) approach. A primary run scheme (49% or less are pass plays) will yield the lowest rankings for all WRs.

Summary:

The following steps will guide you in the ranking process. Steps one and two may be reversed depending on which method you use to develop your projections. In any case, you will want to tier the positions and overall ranking of players. Next, find ADP data that pertains to your league size and rules. Finally, incorporate all of these elements into your own customized cheat sheets that break down each position and the top 100-120 players overall.

1) Create your rankings

2) Project your statistics for the next season (projections)

3) Tier your players

4) Determine ADP using ADP data or mocks

5) Create customized cheat sheets

Chapter 8 Draft Day Tips

Draft day is the most important day of the FF season. If you are brand new to it (a draft virgin), then what is the objective on draft day? I cannot say this enough: **Your main objective at your first draft should be to not look stupid**. You know nothing about what you have gotten yourself into. You probably have been railroaded by a buddy who needs a designated driver to come to this fantasy football draft and fill in for an owner who recently had his kitchen pass revoked for playing too much twister with the babysitter. Now you are thrust into this madness. Remember, objective #1 is to not look stupid, so read on and minimize the WAGs (Wild Ass Guesses) until another year.

Some "experts" say that "Fantasy football championships are lost in the early rounds of the draft." I disagree. It is hard to make a real mistake in the early rounds (picks 1-5) unless you are asleep. Still other experts say, "Fantasy football championships are won in the middle rounds of the draft." Others say, "Fantasy football championships cannot be won in the draft, but they can be lost in the draft." I say you can neither win nor lose it on draft day, but it will be a lot harder to win it after a poor draft. It is much easier to win after a strong draft and then adjust your team with season adds, drops and trades to strengthen your team even more. Ultimately winning takes good start calls, waiver wire skill and some luck (with injuries especially). Some experts say that "Who you start and sit and pick up on waivers has more affect on the championship than who you draft." Think again. Most of the players you are basing the start/bench decisions on come from... you guessed it, THE DRAFT. So if you drafted poorly you will be stuck with poor choices for starting/benching. I love the analogy to rearranging deck chairs on the Titanic. While the rare championship occurs with a great team and no moves, consistent success comes by having a good draft plan and staying up-to-date on the available players.

Drafting is a combination of art and science. Of gut emotion and numbers. Each draft takes on a personality of its own. You need to have information and a "feel" for the game. Some say it is more science because of the increasing use of statistics and drafting applications. I still see it as an art. It is something that requires observation, analysis and lots of practice. You become part-scientist and part-showman. Never forget that chance favors the prepared mind.

Let's face it, drafting these days is easy. There are a bazillion websites to help you customize your cheat sheets. Even my grandmother knows that the three main tips these days are RB early, kickers late and wait on QBs. Knowing this and not being comatose, why do owners still come out of the draft shaking their heads and wondering how Slammers made it look so easy? You can make the draft and managing your team very easy. Staying one step ahead of everyone else in the draft is the best feeling in the world and the easiest way to achieve drafting success. For the veteran, it is always a good idea to review the basics of good draft preparation. The novice will find many useful tips below.

General Tips

1) Arrive early to get comfortable and get a good seat. Look for a seat near the bathroom but not in it, and comfortable but not too much so. You need lots of room for your stuff. Try not to be near the buffet table but close enough to grab a bite.

2) Ignore the preseason. Many starters will have less impressive stats and their backups will have huge numbers. That RB who scored two TDs and 114 yards was running against the 3rd string unit for Houston. He will not be starting so forget about him, unless as a HC or sleeper. Do not be swept up in the preseason emotion of player performance. Coaches are trying to see which players can make it in game conditions. For this reason they will start lots of 3rd and 4th string players in order to find their #2 backup. Not the backup but the #2 backup. Similarly, who cares what S. Jackson does in the preseason? It does not count for anything; no contract bonuses, fantasy football points or NFL wins will come from a preseason game. The real professionals are just trying not to get hurt and the coaches play them at a minimum to make sure that it doesn't happen. No injuries equals a good preseason. How many times has the 4-0 preseason team won the conference championship? Point proven.

3) The draft becomes much more important in a transaction-limited league. If you are in a league where you draft a huge roster but can make no transactions and a league with a smaller roster but unlimited transactions, the draft is more important in the larger, non-transacting league because those players cannot be changed. Leagues that restrict acquiring other players to replace your injured, suspended, retired or just lousy players place more emphasis on a good draft, because there is no way to fix a bad draft.

4) Draft the best player, from the highest tier within a position with the smallest amount of players in that tier first. Example: it's your pick and you cannot decide between RB or WR. The RB tier has two players and the WR tier has three players. You should pick a RB because that is the tier with the least amount of players and is more likely to be depleted faster. Of course, if you see that the four picks after yours (and before your next pick) are sure to be mostly WRs, you might pick a WR to grab him before the other two owners draft twice in front of you. However, if they go RB-WR, then you have lost your chance at the RB from the tier but you will get to draft the WR from the tier.

5) A player's value is not in his fantasy football numbers, but rather in what pick he was drafted. Most of us know who the top 10 RBs are going to be but if you get a top 10 RB that no one expects and draft him later in the draft; that is true VALUE!

6) Rookie Information – Most QBs need time to learn systems and the defensive schemes they will be shown. Avoid rookie QBs as they will most likely hold the clipboards. RBs adjust much easier but coaches worry about their ability to block pass defenders and pick up the blitz to protect their QB. For every rookie RB star (Edgerin James) there are three busts. WRs can be productive but most take 2-3 years to learn systems, adjust to their QB and learn blocking assignments. Only 1 out of 6 WRs will succeed in their first year.

7) Take only educated, rational risks in the draft and then only in the second half of the draft. With information, analysis and trends you can predict more (hunches) than you think. Follow through on those hunches because you will never know how right or wrong you are until you do. If every year your hunches stink, then consider making less of them or getting more advice.

8) Holdouts do not practice with the team and will require some time to get it together with their teammates after they return. Rookie holdouts are the worst. They will be set back a lot. Veterans can practice on their own and recover quicker than a rookie. Do you draft the holdout and hope he comes to his senses or do you pass on him and risk missing his production if he returns? Holdouts are worse than injuries because you never know

when a holdout will return, if at all. With an injury, you can get an estimate and then add a game to be conservative. Holdouts (HOs) are unknowns. I stay away from them. Let someone else take the chance on them with an early pick. Gambling is better for the later rounds.

9) There will always be some discriminator between players after the 1st round. Use these to your advantage to get value.

10) Have a plan. Even if it is RB-RB-WR-RB-WR-TE/WR-QB, at least it is a plan. This type of plan is often called the "draft by numbers" plan. It may not be the best plan in the world, but at least it is a plan and it works fine; however you should not limit yourself to drafting a given position within a certain round. Another variation of this is to draft all your starters first, in a certain order, such as RB-RB-QB-WR-WR-TE-K-DEF.

11) Avoid players on a new team (new system, new head coach or moved to a new team). They will be overvalued on draft day. They will take half the season to adjust and will thus underperform for the first half.

12) Highlight players you want in one color; highlight players you want to avoid in another color. This helps you get to know your draft board.

* One bad pick can snowball into a terrible draft, especially if you let it get to you. On the other hand, making a good pick that you have confidence in can go a long way to building a positive attitude toward your entire draft. If you get thrown out of whack easily by the unknown, the best way to stay on firm ground is to be prepared. The more homework you do, the less likely you are to be caught off guard when someone says, "I will take S. McNair in the fifth."

Do Not Draft a QB/WR Combo

If there are three WRs to choose from, all in the same tier, I would not draft one from same team as your QB1. I also would not get one with the same bye week as RB1or RB2. All of this is because I want consistent points. The points lost are negated somewhat by the backup. Say I lose 15 points and my backup is good for 10 points. In effect I see a decrease of 5 points at that slot when my WR is on his bye. If I combine that loss with another letdown at QB (because both have the same bye week) then my loss may be another 3 points. Now I am down 8 points because of the combination. If I combine that 8-point loss with RB1 or RB2 on the same bye week, that is about a 15-20 point reduction. Losing 20 points is a guaranteed loss that cannot be made up. If I spread those point reductions over six games (QB1, RB1, RB2, WR1, WR2, W3) then my team is only losing a few points every week and I have a better chance of overcoming each reduction. Another reason for avoiding the combo is if the QB gets hurt then the WR will probably lose some productivity. Think back to what happened to S. Smith when J. Delhomme went down with an injury for a few weeks in 2006. Don't use any combos and do not get starters on the same bye week. It also goes without saying that you should not draft more than two players from the same team (not counting kickers). This can mean that if the QB or RB is hurt, the others may suffer too.

Perhaps having three or more players on the same bye week is better. You are stronger in more games and weak in only one game. Kind of like a Homer with all his Denver players. I need to analyze it in more detail . It is either better to have them all on the same bye week or none on the same bye week.

DRAFT PREP

Know every player who will be taken in the entire draft. If you hear a name that you do not recognize it better be someone who was cut last week and thus you flushed them from your memory. Participate in some mock drafts. It will loosen up your drafting nerves, practice makes perfect, and you can get a feel for where players are going (why waste a 6th round pick on someone who others will not take until the 8th round) and who the sleepers are according to others.

Next try to conduct a mock draft in your league based on your league's tendencies (look at the past year's results; are RBs all in round 1; do WRs mainly go in rounds 4 and 5; etc.) and owner tendencies. This lets you see who may be available to you and gives you a "craniums up" on the hard decisions you may face, such as, S. Jackson or R. Johnson with pick 1.06? Be flexible. The draft will not go as planned but if you have your act together you can roll with the punches and not fall apart when the dynamics of the draft change.

Best Drafting Tips (Strategies to employ on draft day regardless of your "Big Picture Strategy")

1) Have a plan. Use a theory or system; it does not matter which theory you use, just have something to go with. The plan may fall apart by round 4, so be flexible. You wanted to go RB-RB-WR-WR in the first four rounds. After getting two great RBs and a good WR you now have your fourth round pick and find another good RB still available. You expected him to go in the early part of round 3, but a sudden run on TEs has dropped him into your lap. What do you do? Your plan will be dramatically altered if you go for RB3 here, but can you pass on the value he offers? No, draft him and change the plan. Adapt and change, but if you have no plan to start with it is hard to change your strategy to adapt.

2) Know the rules (drafting method, scoring, and starter positions/roster limits). Do you have a flex position? If so, will more RBs be picked in the early rounds than normal? Many owners will draft according to starter positions. They will pick their starting QB, two starting RBs, two starting WRs and starting TE in the first six rounds. In other words, by getting a QB and TE earlier than you they leave lots of good RBs and WRs for you to draft as flex players/backups/bye week replacements/trade bait. Then you can grab a serviceable QB and TE in rounds 7 and 8. *Note: Many owners like the QB position although it isn't the most important in most leagues. Therefore, inexperienced owners will draft a QB early (rounds 2-4) and may get a QB2 in round 7, so watch for a run or depletion on QBs in these leagues.*

Why do I need to know my scoring system? Whether QBs are awarded 3 or 6 points per passing TD, will determine how valuable P. Manning is. He threw for 31 TDs in 2006. B. Favre threw for 18 TDs. If your league awards points for yardage then Chad Johnson in 2006 would have been more valuable than in a TD-only league. "Ocho Stinko" only had seven TDs but 1369 yards (his second best year).

3) Don't get caught up in runs. Every draft will have a run on positions. Typically it is some TEs in the 4th, QBs in the 5th, 7th and 8th and WRs in the 3rd and 4th; kickers and

defenses will have their run in the later rounds. What is a run? When in any given round or succession of picks a certain position is picked predominantly. For example, if in the 5th round you have the last pick (14th) and 6 of the last 9 picks have been QBs, then that would qualify as a QB run. It will naturally make you want to grab a good QB before they are all gone. Runs are powerful psychological forces. You say to yourself, "Everyone else is getting a QB, I do not want to miss out. They must know what they are doing." AVOID THIS MENTALITY! You have a plan. You know when to draft a QB or whatever position is running. Suggest or start a run by saying out loud "Hmmm… looks like a lot of QBs are being picked," or the less obvious, "Here comes the TE run." Let the lemmings of the group chase after these runs and be reactive. You are going to be proactive and get value with every pick. Runs occur when owners begin to pick the same position with pick after pick after pick. This develops into a herd mentality. I have to get my TE before everyone else gets their TE. Do not fall into this trap. It will make you abandon your strategy and lose value in the draft. If you know what position and players you are going to target in round 6 (WR3) it should not matter that four TEs in a row have been drafted ahead of you. It only helps you now, in that a better WR may be around.

4) Don't get stuck in the past. Some owners love veterans even to the point of drafting them when they are past their prime. You need to evaluate all of the talent: old and new. Don't get stuck and find yourself saying "Well Bubba Franks is always good for a few TDs." Know before you draft if they are worth it. Do not rely on name and past performance only.

5) Avoid the rookies or do not draft them too high. "Big City" always reminds me of the draft where he took E. James as a rookie with his second pick. Occasionally rookies will pay off big, but my question back to him is "Was he worth a second round pick?" The answer is no. If he had gotten him in the fourth round that year then he would have been a steal, but traditionally rookies do not produce big. Rather they are over hyped and drafted too high. Avoid rookies and the mess (underperforming against high expectations) they bring to a fantasy team. Some "experts" say that you should never draft a rookie as high as 25th overall, while others recommend no higher than 35th. I disagree with both. Draft a rookie where his rankings project him, just realize that, at best, he will perform at that level, but not any higher.

6) Look for the breakout players (2nd-4th years) who have either learned the system, came on strong in the second half of last year, acclimated to a new team or grasped the system or QB. These players will give you that little bit extra to make the playoffs and win the Super Bowl.

7) Ignore the preseason stats but watch the injuries, suspensions, demotions, etc. Many owners do not follow the ins and outs of the preseason position battles. This is where, in the late rounds, you can get tremendous value simply by knowing who is hurt and who is not.

8) Work in tiers. On your worksheet, have tiers of the same quality players at each position. For example, after P. Manning, the next 7 or 8 QBs may all be the same. Have them as second tier QBs. Draw a line under the last QB of roughly the same quality. When it is your turn to draft and you need a QB, you do not have to draft the #4 QB on your list. You can either: a) draft the #4 QB because you want him, b) draft another QB in the same tier (remember they are all of the same quality) because he has a better schedule or a different bye week than your stud RB, or c) pass on a QB this round because you know

you have four more in this tier and the odds of them being picked before your next pick are slim. Therefore, you will get one of the QBs in this tier the next round and can choose another position with this pick. Tiers are the key to maximizing your draft.

Top 15 Drafting Mistakes

1) Not having a plan or rankings, or sticking with the plan no matter what. Showing up to the draft with nothing, not even a magazine cheat sheet is the worst thing you can do. Preferably, you have developed your own customized rankings. *Note: This is a necessity if you are in an online league since computer problems, power outages or unseen emergencies can prevent you from being on the website to draft live.* Usually the owner with no plan ends up drafting his starters first, then backups. In the meantime he loses value because he is grabbing his kicker and defense while everyone else is getting good RB and WR backups. What about the owners who come to the draft with a plan (WR-RB-RB-WR-QB) and stick to it regardless? This is the guy drafting at the end (pick 11 of 12), who is given a gift when three other owners grab a stud WR in the first round and another takes Peyton at QB, leaving him with a chance at the #7 RB with the 11th pick, but he instead sticks to his plan and drafts the #4 WR. The 12th owner nearly jumps out of his seat when he sees he can grab the #7 RB (last in his tier) with pick 1.12 and get the #5 WR (one of 3 left in that tier) with his next pick, 2.1. Our owner, with the next pick 2.2, scratches his head and wonders why he never gets that lucky since he now has to dip into the next tier of RBs. Roll with the flow and change on the fly. Flexibility is the key to FF dominance.

2) Fails to work in tiers. They just move right down the cheat sheets, not realizing where the drop offs are and that A. Brooks is way less valuable than T. Green, even though Brooks comes just one player ranking less than Green in the QB section.

3) Getting caught in runs on positions. Panicking in the middle to late rounds when names you have never heard of are called for TE and kickers and then jumping in with both feet to get a player at those positions that you know. Rookies tend to follow these runs for several reasons. First, they think the other owners know exactly what they are doing so if they are drafting QBs in round 5 then so should they. Also, they are afraid that all the good players at that position will be taken. If you are at the tail end of a run you are more likely to get a poor player at that position. Better to buck the trend and get value somewhere else.

4) Picking the "hyped" players. If T.O. has been in the news, he will get high priority. Did Oakland go 4-0 in preseason and look good? Expect the rookies to grab Oakland players. Do not draft a player just because he is on your favorite NFL team or just because he is dating Carrie Underwood or Jessica Simpson. You draft the best players available, not the most popular. It is not a popularity contest; it is fantasy football, where you try to score the most fantasy points you can, week in and week out.

5) Picking veterans because of their name or association with favorite teams, not based on what they are projected to do the coming year. Don't live in the past. B. Favre is not the great QB he once was. Too many owners will draft a player based on seeing or hearing his name and remembering how great he did last season or during his career. Past performance is no guarantee of future performance. Another big mistake is drafting players from your favorite team. Yes, this may bring added fun on Sundays as you watch not only your favorite team do well but your fantasy team as well, but realistically most teams only have

a few key players and to draft many of them you will have to reach too early in order to get them. This also leads to having too many eggs in one basket, and too much risk of one injury affecting the entire fantasy team catastrophically. The flip side to this is avoiding players on teams you hate (Dallas players anyone?). Try to avoid this too, as you should be interested in anyone who can get you to the championship.

6) Picking rookies because they are new. He is someone you have heard about on numerous occasions. The name gets ingrained in your brain, so he must be good.

7) Cannot predict the hidden sleepers. If the magazine they buy or ESPN does not predict it then they will not know it.

8) Being unaware of late preseason changes. Whether it be injuries or position battles, don't expect many of the fantasy football rookies to know it (or some veterans either). You need to know who is injured and who was traded, who has a new coach and who has a new contract. All of these things influence the chances of a player returning to form or performing better/worse than last year

9) Draft to fill out their lineup first. You can expect them to get 1 QB, 2 RB and 2 WR in their first five picks. Then they will draft another WR, if starting three WRs. Next will be a TE, K and or defense. You do not have to have a complete starting roster until the end of the draft!

10) Draft QBs sooner and more likely to have three. They drool over the numbers QBs put up. They score the most points and thus must be the most valuable right? Inexperienced owners will draft Manning in round 1, and if not then whoever is left at QB in round 2 or 3. Drafting a QB in the first round is crazy, unless it is Peyton and you are in a league that rewards the QB position a lot, such as 6 points for every TD pass and 1 point per 20 yards passing. If it is a standard 3 or 4 points per TD pass, skip the QBs until at least round 5, and even later is better.

11) Taking kickers and defenses early and often, and their backups as well. That means a few less on the waiver wire than if in an experienced league.

12) Drafting too many players in one position with the same bye weeks; if you draft 2 QBs and both have the same bye week, you are screwed. Either you do not have a starter on their bye week or you trade/drop one and pick up another with a different bye week. You could also drop another player and use that spot to pick up QB3 with another bye week. Any way you look at it, that was a mistake in the draft. When you drafted your QB2, I am sure there were several to choose from, and of those, some had different bye weeks than your first QB. The same goes for any positions that you only start one of and have two (TE, K, DEF) on the same bye week. If you have 6 RBs on your roster and start 2 and a flex player, and three of those RBs have the same bye week, then you better hope that the three not on that bye week are all healthy.

13) Drafting injury-prone players. One of the keys to a good draft is who you do not draft. Injury-prone players can sink a team faster then you can say "Houzmanzadee." Taking a gamble on one is okay, but having too many or too high a gamble (high draft pick) on an injury-prone player can put you from first to worst very quickly.

14) Drinking and drafting. The casinos in Las Vegas give out free booze for a reason. It impairs your ability to think straight. Thus, you should give out booze freely on draft day. Bring a case of beer for the others but don't drink any yourself until after the draft.

Distract the other owners by showing some porn on the TV or having a baseball game on (muted of course). Anything to distract the other owners will work. Use distractions to your advantage and do not get distracted by others.

15) Ignoring the middle and late rounds. Normally once the excitement of your first few picks has passed and you have your first break out of the way, many owners will let their guard down. They will not pay as close attention to the draft as before (maybe have a beer or two) and they will take a lazy attitude into the later rounds. Maybe they will stop keeping track of picks or grab a player from the same position on the same bye week. They don't finish strong. Remember that every draft pick counts. The fifth RB you get in round 12 is just an injury away from starting for your RB3 during his bye week. Also, the ultimate sleeper is usually found in those late rounds and he will be more special the later you grab him and have more value as well.

Most Common Draft Day Tips (truth or myth)

1. Don't draft a kicker until the last round. (Good advice unless you need two kickers to start, in which case… you get the point.)

2. Load up on RBs. Get 3 RBs with first six picks. (Good advice in general if you start 2 or more RBs.)

3. Take 2 RBs with first three picks. (Good advice unless playing in a 3 WR or PPR league, then go with a WR or two in first three picks, or 2 RBs and 2 WRs with first four picks.)

4. Take a QB in later rounds. Skip the QBs in round 3 or 4. (Good advice unless in a 6 points for passing TD league.)

5. Don't fall for the runs. TEs, Ks and DEFs usually all start to be drafted together. Don't follow the crowd. (Best advice!)

6. Do I take the #10 RB or #3 WR? Always go with the higher-ranking player. (Terrible advice. You should use VBD and your teams' need. If you already have 2 RBs and your league only starts 1 RB (no flex), then #3 WR is the best choice; if you already went WR with your first round pick then #10 RB with pick 2 may be the right choice.)

7. Think outside the box. Draft P. Manning with pick 4 after LT, LJ and Shaun Alexander (SA) are picked. (Hmmm… as with most advice, know your scoring rules. If yours is a 6 points for passing TD league then maybe it would be good. If in a standard 3 or 4 points per pass league, I would not pass up on the #4 RB for the #1 QB. The advantage is that Peyton has never missed a game so you are guaranteeing yourself an injury-free first round pick. But then again, the Colts may have wrapped up the playoffs by week 11 and he may sit the last few weeks.)

8. Using the most common performance scoring method, RBs are the most important followed by the top 5 or 6 QBs and then the top 3 WRs; so WRs can wait until the middle rounds. Wait on TEs, kickers and defenses until the last rounds of the draft, with the exception of the top 3 TEs. The top defense, if reasonably assured of staying intact, can also be drafted a little before the last rounds. (Sounds very

good, but remember it depends on if PPR or not. TEs get more value in PPR, especially the Top 10.)

Worst Draft Advice

1) Draft your QBs real life backup as your QB2. That way you will always have a QB who is playing. What about the bye week? What if the backup is not nearly as good as other viable QBs available? This also eliminates any chance of QB2 being good enough to trade.

2) Never think you can get away with only one QB. What if I am in a 10-team league? At the most there will be 19 QBs taken, one of which will be mine. Why should I draft a QB #2 when I have 13 others on the free agency list just waiting? No, use the pick to get a sleeper RB or WR and grab a QB#2 when you need him (hopefully in a late bye week scenario).

3) Play it safe. Go with the aging veteran?

4) Pick six sleeper picks? What about storing up strong backups for RB or WR? Handcuffs? But not sleepers here.

5) Get a top kicker in round 7 or 8. Top kicker in round 8? That is too much of a reach for a kicker who may or may not be a Top 5 contender at the end of the season.

6) QB-WR hook up is best. Not! See QB-WR Combo, earlier in this chapter.

7) Always HC RBs. Always? What if backup is no good? Do you HC RB3?

8) Draft five RBs if rules allow. (What if 8 starters and 12-player rosters (leaving four on the bench)? This means that three of the four on the bench are going to be RBs. Only one WR on bench and start two?

9) It's okay to take a QB in first round. (Scoring rules? With first draft pick?)

10) By round 4 have QB, 2 WRs and RB? This is a recipe for disaster.

How to use your Draft Board (Cheat Sheets)

1) Look at intangibles. If you have three equal players, compare their age, injury history, team expectations, attitude, SOS, consistency, bye weeks, etc.

2) Draft for upside (especially later in the draft); young gun or aging vet? Go with young gun.

3) Know the player's ADP. Are you getting him later? It is a steal.

4) Track overall draft (who has what spots filled, not individual players unless co-manager). The real pros hate the big draft boards because it gives everyone the same advantage they had when tracking the draft on their own.

5) Think backups, yours and your opponents. If you can trade within the league, then grabbing your opponents RB1 HC can pay off handsomely.

Keys to a Good Draft?

1) Get a good night's rest. Have a good meal, a relaxing evening and do not stay up too late.

2) Show up prepared. Bring the following:

a) Money for entry fee. There is nothing worse than showing up without the money to pay your entry fee. It is embarrassing and shows a lack of interest in the league right off the bat. Some leagues will not allow you to draft without first paying your entrance fee. (And for good reason; what if you have a terrible draft and then decide to not play, forever cursing you in fantasy football leagues around the world?)

b) Cheat Sheet (perhaps the most important tool). Make certain that it is customized for your league rules and your strategy. These documents should each be position-ranked accordingly and have an overall top 100 ranking. (See Chapter 7– Ranking Players.)

c) Several pencils, pens and highlighters; use one color for your picks – I like yellow for picks and blue for sleepers already marked.

d) Old magazine to loan to the newbie who shows up without a cheat sheet or to use for the friend who cannot make the draft and asks you to draft for him. (You really do not want to use your customized, experienced cheat sheet for him, do you?) It also gives you something hard to write on.

e) Clipboard so that you have something hard to write on when there is no table to draft from or when the newbie borrows your old magazine.

f) Draft tracker (see appendix). Sheet to track what positions (and money if in auction draft) have been chosen by other owners.

g) A plan; some strategy that can be executed or ignored, but at least you have a plan.

h) A folder to hide your stuff from prying eyes.

NOTE 1: Do not bring anything else to the draft. Too much stuff overloads the system and prevents clear thinking.

NOTE 2: Do not use the old magazine you brought or be tempted to bring a magazine to use or other devices such as a computer. Remember the KISS principle. Keep It Simple Stupid.

3) Show up to the draft. Do not let your friend, the commissioner or a computer draft for you. Sure, all of those options are better than not being in a league at all but lets face it, is your friend really going to have your best interests at heart? I have drafted for others before and can say I try hard… but not 110%. If I am drafting for a friend and myself at the same time, which team will get my full attention and which team will get some attention? Case in point, I have #2 pick in 14-team league and friend has #12 pick. This is convenient because each of our picks is spread out. If my pick was #8 and his was #6, I know that some of his 90 seconds would be used for my teams next pick and I sure would not grab for him the player that I was hoping would fall to me in two more picks. I would pick him a good choice but one that is not on my list of three possible choices. That way I get who I want. The lesson to be learned here is that being present at the draft is your best

option. Letting a computer automatically draft for you may be better than having a friend draft because at least with a computer you can set up your cheat sheets in advance and let the computer use them. (How does it know whom to draft? See Online Drafts below.) On the other hand, that is a double-edged sword because that cheat sheet needs to be current right before the draft, (updated for injuries, demotions, etc.) so an old cheat sheet for a computer is just as bad as none for a friend. If you are not going to make the live draft, ask a friend who is not an owner to go and draft for you and give them precise instructions if they are not a fantasy football fan like you.

4) A few hours before the draft check on the latest injuries and news reports. Stay up on injuries, suspensions, demotions, etc. and update your cheat sheets accordingly.

5) Have a bye week list handy (or have them listed on your cheat sheets beside the players names) so you can see which teams are out when. Highlight the teams in each bye week that have favorable matchups, especially for QBs. *Strategy tip – Choose the backup QB, K and DEF for their matchups when your #1 players are on a bye week. That way you maximize the return from the backups, unless you were lucky enough to draft backups almost as good as your starters.*

6) Don't drink and draft. It might be fun to have a few beers with the boys, but this often leads to poor decision-making. Case in point, Slam has two Strongbow Ciders... only year not to make it to the playoffs. "Big City" has some Strongbow Cider and with #2 pick overall went with P. Manning (After his 49 TD season) instead of LT. (He still made the playoffs and won the SB, so maybe that is not a good example.)

QB Tips

1) QBs rarely if ever follow a record-breaking season with a similar or better season.

2) Don't rush to get a QB and don't wait to get your second, especially if you waited to draft QB#1. QB#2 may prove to be better than QB#1 and every bit of improvement helps. What I am saying here is that by selecting two middle of the road QBs you improve your chances of getting one that will shine. If you draft one middle of the road and one dreg of the league, your chance of having one be a big help to your team has been halved. QBs are prone to injury too. Drafting a good backup may be better than a good QB#1. Look for offensive scoring machines (Denver, St. Louis, Kansas City) versus good defensive teams that have poor offenses (Tampa Bay, Baltimore, Cleveland). Remember that the number one requirement for your backup is that he is the clear starter in the NFL. No need to pick up a rookie who is holding the clipboard or a QB who is #2 on the depth chart. That will not help you when it is time to call him from your bench.

3) QBs go in rounds 1-4, but fantasy owners rarely pick two QBs before 6th round.

4) The QB pool is deep and will have lots of value later (you only start 1 QB versus 2 RBs).

5) Some studies have shown that QBs are at their best between the ages of 28-29. I think they perform well regardless of age.

6) Another reason to wait on QBs: Look at 2006 when there was such turnover at the QB position due to injuries (Hasselbeck, Delhomme, Brooks, Culpepper) and benchings (Warner, Bledsoe, Collins, Culpepper).

RB Tips

1) 75% of the first two rounds will be RBs. Bet on it!

2) Draft RBs early and often.

3) Draft a rookie RB as your RB3 if you can get him for value.

4) Avoid RBBC situations. Save yourself the headaches and the work of scouring your resources for the definitive word on game day of who will be the primary back.

5) There may be three RBs in first 4 rounds but rarely four RBs in first 4 rounds.

6) If a RB makes it to the free agent list they usually get gobbled up quickly. Lowest supply and the highest demand (most leagues start two RBs and some allow a third at flex). With only 32 NFL teams and some of those doing the RBBC shuffle you can see why everyone is screaming supply and demand with regard to RBs. You need a RB who will get lots of touches (20 or more is the magic number). Catches out of the backfield are just as good as a touch (especially in PPR leagues).

7) Avoid older players (RBs over 30, same applies to IDPs) the older they get the more likely they are to lose a step, have an injury or retire. Some studies have shown that RBs tend to peak between ages 23-25, from 26-28 they have slight declines, after age 28 the declines are more pronounced and after 30... well...

8) Seek RBs that are healthy throughout preseason and that play on good balanced offenses (to avoid 8-men-in-the-box scenarios)

9) Watch the RBs with over 370 touches from last year (add ½ rushing touch for every pass reception). They tend to break down more often the next season and or get less carries than the previous year. Don't say I didn't warn you. LT had 348 rushes and 56 catches in the regular season. In the short postseason he had 23 rushes and 2 catches. That is almost 400 touches for the entire season. LJ is another one to watch.

10) In regards to your #3 RB (your backup), a good offense is a strong defense. By that I mean your backup RB should be a starter who can replace your #1 or #2 RB on bye weeks (that would be 2 of the 13 or 14 games during regular season where you will benefit) or be the flex player more weeks than not. Of course, having a starting RB#3 will mean drafting him in round 3 or 4 in most leagues. So, RB-RB-WR-RB may have to be your strategy, but look at the alternatives. If there are only 32 starters and you are in a 10-team league, he should be available in round 4 as other teams take a WR, QB or TE in round 3 or 4. If you are in a 14-team league then you may have to reach for RB#3 in round 3. If you are in a 16-team league then just be happy to have two starting RBs. But what if you cannot get a starter as your #3 RB? What is your next plan? Look for the good backups who play behind an "injury-prone" RB. Also, look for backups who play for teams with good offenses, good OLs and a good defense. This will mean that if your backup starts in the NFL then he has a good chance to excel. Finally, look at the goal line vultures. They are not consistent but may be better than a backup who might not see the field all year.

WR Tips

1) Some studies have shown that WRs tend to peak around age 26-27, then decline gradually after that.

2) Back up WRs. Their stats are affected by their skills, the QB throwing to them, the OL giving the QB protection and the RB who can keep the opposing defense honest. Look for WRs who have all of these things in their favor. If you are in a performance scoring league, go with possession receivers as backups first, since they will be consistent in yardage. Look at the #2 WR on passing teams (St. Louis , Cincinnati, Indianapolis), often the second and sometimes third best WR on a passing team is better than the #1 WR on a run-oriented team (Baltimore, San Diego). Finally, look to pick up a sleeper or two. The sleepers are more likely to come from the 2nd-4th year players. Second year players are being used more now than ever. (The NFL's "Win Now" attitude means less development time and more show time for the younger players). Third and fourth year players are in the prime zone for a breakout year, so a possession receiver on a passing team who is in his 2nd-4th year has sleeper written all over him.

TE Tips

1) Some studies have shown that TEs tend to peak at 25, then decline after that. Tell that to Tony G.

2) There is no reason to reach for backup TEs. The drop off from the top 5 to top 15 is huge. You either get one of the big names or not. There is no reason to go fishing for a TE#2 until the late rounds. I mean last five, especially if you have to get a couple of kickers and defenses. Look for the same attributes as a backup WR. Make sure he is a pass-catching TE and not a primarily blocking TE, and look for a 2-4th year player who may break out.

K TIPS

Ask yourself these questions: How many teams are in the league? How many players per roster? Is there a minimum or maximum number of kickers required? How many kickers start? Can a kicker be picked up on the waiver wire? Do you have to draft a kicker?

Seven Strategies for When to Draft a Kicker:

1) Draft them soon. Get one of the Top 3 kickers (10th-12th round) before the run on kickers kicks off (excuse the pun). If you get your top choices, just hope they pan out because you paid a high price for them. The best reason not to draft a kicker early is that if he gets off to a slow start you feel obligated to stick with him, rather than cutting him and going with a better option from FA. (See Chapter 20 – Psychology of Fantasy Football.) If you are not heavily invested in your kicker (high draft pick), then you are more likely to look at improving that position.

2) Draft them later. Wait until a few kickers are drafted then jump in at round 13 or 14. You get the top 6-10 ranked kicker and do not pay as much.

3) Draft two with good matchups that complement each other. Use SOS and kicker lineup strategy to select a kicker with the best chance to score the most points each week, also known as kicker by committee (KBC) method. For example, if a warm weather kicker is playing outside in cold weather in a northern stadium in December then have your other kicker in a dome that week. Pick the kicker with the best matchup.

4) Pick them last. Only draft one kicker, late in the draft, who has the latest bye week among those ranked highest so that you can wait longer to get a bye week replacement, thus giving your sleeper picks (one of whom replaced K2) more time to either blossom or bust. You also will have more time to find a kicker who is doing well and still on the FA list. This strategy will depend on your answers to some of the questions above. If your league starts two kickers and you wait until the last two rounds, you may not get two in a 14-team league. Know how many can be expected to go on draft day. If 6-8 will remain on the FA list then, by all means, wait to draft one.

5) Don't draft them at all. Wait and pick one up on the waiver wire right before game time, that way you can watch some of your sleepers in their positional battles. This is for leagues that allow it and that draft early.

6) Draft a kicker from the same team as QB1. The theory goes that even if the QB does not score TDs at least the kicker gets FGs.

7) Draft a kicker with strong SOS in your playoff weeks. This strategy is better for adds or trades in midseason than to start the season. If he is going to do well in weeks 13-16, chances are his performance during weeks 1-12 will be less than average.

Option 1 is based on the top kickers usually providing a point or two more than the rest of the kickers per game. A problem arises in finding the Top 3 kickers every year. Some say look to the highest scoring NFL teams and you will have yourself a high scoring kicker. There are two problems with this. First, it is hard to predict the top scoring team. Second, they do not always guarantee the highest scoring kicker. In fact, if you could magically know the top 5 scoring teams it would not always give you a Top 5 kicker. Generally, though the percentages are with you, the more a team scores the more his kicker should score. Another fact is that the worse a team scores the worse a kicker scores. There is more to this than the Top scorer correlation. If you want to avoid a terrible kicker, avoid the bottom five or six scoring teams. Their kickers are terrible. Summary: The top kickers do not always come from the top scoring teams, but if you pick kickers from the top 5 scoring teams you should have a top 10 kicker or so. The difficulty in doing this makes Options 2 and 3 more promising. Whatever you do, do not draft a kicker from a team that you think will be in the bottom five in scoring. That is a recipe for disaster.

Reasons why you should grab a kicker with the next to last or last draft pick

1) A kicker's performance is too hard to predict. You cannot even rely on them getting on the field on their own. They need others to put them in a position to take the field, unlike QBs, RBs and WRs, who will at least take the field on several possessions during a game and get a chance. Can the offense stall enough times to get the kicker lots of FG attempts? How is the kicker's defense? Will the team be behind in the second half and by so much that they do not go for FGs but instead go for TDs? Last year's #1 kicker has little chance of making the Top 5 again, so why bother drafting them any higher than with the last pick?

2) The difference between the #1 and #12 kicker is very small. Last year, in many leagues, the difference between the #5 and the #17 kicker was 10 points. That is less than 1 point per game. Granted, the top three kickers did slightly better but they are too hard to predict.

3) Kickers on the waiver wire can be just as good. Many times a kicker that starts off good in the first few weeks will continue to do so.

4) The kicker and defense are the easiest positions to get thrown into a trade to give it some extra value. So chances are, if you trade you can get a better kicker or defense sometime in the season. Plus, who is the first to be dropped when a waiver wire/FA becomes available? You got it; K2 or DEF2.

Look for the following in a kicker:

1) Kicker's performance tends to follow their team's performance. High scoring teams = High scoring kickers.

2) FG attempts last year and where they were from. Many from inside the 29 are botched red zone forays and any improvement in the offense (even just a year older and wiser) may result in more TD celebrations and XPs for that kicker but a reduction in FGs and thus FPs. Look also at kicks from 40+ yards. Those may turn into more chip shots (inside 39 yards) the following year.

3) For kickers in domes, the weather will at least be favorable. Studies show that FG percentage and points per game are higher in domes than outdoor stadiums. These numbers apply to visitors playing in domes too. Therefore, kickers in a division with lots of opponents in domes are a good choice.

4) Kickers with good defenses since they keep teams in the game till the end and give your kicker more opportunities to score.

5) Kickers with a strong leg, especially if your league rewards for distance on FGs. (Like Elam kicking at Mile High, the thinner air doesn't hurt either.)

6) Performance Method – Draft a kicker who has the same coaches and players and has done well in past. This is the simplest approach.

7) Draft the SB winning kicker. If they have the same head coach and QB and a Top 10 offense, they have a 5 in 8 chance of going back into the Top 5 the following year.

8) Extra Point Method – A team with a high amount of TDs last year, with the same QB returning, usually scores more FGs the next year. Regression to the mean?

9) Backup kickers – Last pick of the draft, since your #1 kicker was the next to last pick of the draft. Someone will draft last year's #1 kicker. Let them and you wait for your sleeper in the last rounds. It's better to draft just one if allowed and play waiver wire.

Kicker Thoughts

1) Some owners try to draft from a high-powered offense, but if they score more TDs all you will get is XPs.

2) Some look for great defenses with struggling offenses. The theory is that the defense will give the offense the ball in opponent territory and then the offense will stall and kick FGs.

3) Some look at the schedule to see when and where they play. Favor domes and warm weather locations and schedules (divisions with domes –NFC South) with these.

4) Some look at Denver for its favorable altitude if distance is rewarded.

5) Some just take the best kicker left with the last draft pick and do not waste too many brain bites on it.

7 Strategies for When to Draft a Defense

1) Draft them soon – Get a defense in the 8th or 9th round. Again you get your top choices, just hope they pan out because you paid a high price for them.

2) Draft them later – Wait until a few defenses are drafted then jump in at round 11-14. You get the top 6-10 ranked defense and do not pay as much.

3) Defense by Committee (DBC). Draft two with good matchups that complement each other. Use SOS and defense lineup strategy to select the defense with the best chance to score the most points each week.

4) Pick them last – Get one defense with next to last pick.

5) Don't draft them at all- Wait and pick one up on waiver wire right before game time, that way you can watch some of your sleepers in their positional battles. This works well in leagues that allow it and that draft early.

6) Draft a defense with a strong SOS in your playoff weeks. This strategy is better for adds or trades at midseason or later IMO.

7) Another technique is to wait and draft a defense after the first two have been picked. This may start a run on defenses (always good after you have picked yours) and that is the perk to using this strategy. A backup defense should be one of the last picks.

Defense Tips

1) Watch out for SB champs. They usually have a crosshair on their back and everyone prepares well for them. Not to mention the defensive players get to go to more dinners and eat way too many meals and end up weighing more than their lean and trim SB weights. SB win equals decline in defense the following year. Injuries and losses to FA can also hurt a defense and make it lose some performance year to year.

Know your scoring rules. Some award points for TO only, others for yardage allowed or points allowed. Remember ST points from KO and punt returns. Teams are lucky to have even one kickoff or punt returned for a TD. Look for that special play maker who can make a difference (Dante Hall– STL, Devin Hester– Chi). Kansas City, before they traded Hall to STL and Chicago average more than one TD, giving them a big advantage at Team DEF/ST, that some owners overlook.

2) Team defenses are usually taken in the latter part of the draft, especially if scoring is based on unpredictable TDs and turnovers, but if your league uses yardage and/or points allowed for team defenses, then this may move their draft spot up some. Most team defenses will score between 2-4 TDs on defense. In fact, many times a fumble occurs on a sack and many fumbles returned for TDs come from sacks, so you can see that the more times an opposing offense is throwing the more likely good things will occur for your defense. So look for defenses that have offenses that score often. Good defenses are often a product of a great offense and a favorable schedule. But know your scoring rules. If your

league gives negative points for yardage or points allowed then this type of defense may not be good, since they will be giving up plenty of yards in their prevent defense and may even allow some garbage points at the end of the game. If your league only penalizes defenses that allow 35 or more points, then you are safe with this type of defense.

3) Backup defenses - don't. If you can get by with just one defense, do it. If not, try to get a backup with favorable matchups when your main DEF is on a bye. Most defensive points come from plays that are pass oriented. Points come from sacks, interceptions, safeties and TDs from INT returns, all of which happen when the offense attempts to pass. Other points such as fumbles for TDs are less rare.

Backups

When do you draft backups? The most important thing to remember is do not draft all of your starters first. There is no reason to draft your starting kicker or defense before your RB backup or even WR or QB backups. How early to get backups will depend on the scoring rules, the size of your league and roster limits. If you play in a 10-team league and all teams are limited to 3 RBs then there will be only 30 drafted and two starters left over for free agency. This "lessened" demand may allow you to draft other starters earlier. On the other extreme, a 16-team league with no roster limits, starting two RBs and a flex, will see 32 RBs chosen just as starters and probably another 8-10 as main flex players, so in this case 42 RBs (10 of which are not starters) could be drafted in the first four rounds easily. Assuming your league uses a pretty standard scoring system, then RB will be the first backup to be chosen (a good ROT, if all else fails, is to get your backups in the order you drafted your starters). If you drafted RB-RB-WR-QB-WR then do the same with your backups, going on the premise that they were important enough to warrant that order. Supply and demand will dictate RBs since they are chosen first and go rapidly in rounds 1-3, diminishing their availability. Your WR backups will be critical too. The WR position has fewer injuries but also has more sleepers who break into the Top 10 and more busts. A good number of WRs is a must.

Once again, the value of each position (does it score the most points and have the biggest drop off in points from tier to tier?) and the depth of that position will influence backup selection. But you will already have figured value and depth out in determining your initial draft strategy. To do this look at last year's statistics (and optimally the last three years) with regard to your scoring rules. In other words, see who the top starters were at each position and how many points they scored. Now graph this to see the differences. What position scores the most points? Which position has a flat line when graphed, showing little drop off in productivity? Does one line drop sharply? There is your tier cutoff. Does one line cross another? The intersection is where the higher line has replaced the lower line (player position) in terms of value. Use MS Excel spreadsheets and then select the graph function to illustrate these points.

Draft your backups as if they are a completely different team. Do not draft them based on bye weeks alone. Some owners just zero in on who will be the best player to have on their RBs bye weeks. Is drafting a backup based on how well he should do in one week a successful way of drafting the best player available? No. Don't draft a backup who is on one of your bye weeks unless he happens to be a steal and the last remaining player from that positional tier. In that case, grab him. The chances that your RBs will both be healthy are not as good as you think. Often the backups will have to be started more games than you would like. By the same token, when deciding on which backup to pick from a tier, look at their bye weeks. If you have three RBs in the same tier to choose from, then use bye weeks as a discriminator to weed out one or two. You have two starting RBs (RB #1 and RB#2), use their bye weeks to eliminate some of the choices. If one of the other three RBs has a bye week the same as your starters then cross him off the list since he will not be able to fill in when the main RB is on a bye, since he will be on a bye too. So now you are down to two backup RBs to choose from and you have 65 seconds left on the clock. Look at who they play on the two bye weeks. Go with the backup who you think will have the better matchups on the two bye weeks you will have to start him.

Know your Opponents

Look at what other owners do every year. Does one always draft RB-RB? It is my experience that most owners do not have any preplanned pick scheme in mind at every draft. It will depend on your draft position and the depth at positions and who is drafted before you. Drafting is DYNAMIC. If you have no historical data for the league but you want to know how many of each position will probably go in each round, use ADP to calculate it. Just use the ADP list as if it were your draft. Note that the ADP data needs to be consistent with your league size and rules. Some owners will fill out their starting roster and then move onto backups; note if specific owners do this and plan for it.

Look around the room on draft day and look at what materials your fellow owners are using. Specifically look at the magazines they use. Are many owners using the same magazine? Do they use the cheat sheets inside religiously? Advantage to you. How many have their own cheat sheets (either handwritten or typed but not PRE-PRINTED)? The same can be said about online drafts. In these instances, the league's pre-draft rankings are provided. How many owners just follow this blindly? Use that to your advantage. If you watch the owners and note which ones are just using the website cheat sheet (just like using a magazine, since it was not updated recently), you can take advantage of them. Say you want a WR with your third draft pick (3.10) and then another RB with your fourth pick (4.3). There are three players in the same tier at each position. There will be four players chosen by two different owners after you pick your WR. If they are both just following the pre- draft rankings list you can see who they will pick. If all three RBs are on the list next, but only one of the WRs is scheduled in the next 5 picks on the pre-rankings, then you should draft your RB in round 3 and then grab your WR in round 4 after the other owners draft their RBs according to the rankings. Another advantage occurs when the owner is absent and lets the computer pick for his team. Often this will be annotated with a symbol by the owner's name after the first few rounds. Remember two things about this; first, they should be fairly predictable (using rankings and whatever positions they assign to the rounds). and second, they are NOT going to use much time off the clock so be ready to draft immediately if you have a few auto drafting teams in front of your team.

Know the other owners. Most leagues (except a dynasty) will only have 4-5 serious owners. These are the guys who will likely be thinking like you and are more than likely to steal a player before you get him. Watch where they are in the draft; note their positions relative to you. Hopefully they are all lined up at the other end of the draft so you can take advantage of the weak members of the herd down at your end.

Online Drafts

If drafting online, make sure the computer is in a comfortable room with no noise (close door to family, turn off other computer applications, etc.) and have a few beverages and snacks to keep you company. Have a table or tray stand to put your draft materials on. Reboot your computer approximately 15 minutes before the draft to make sure all is well. Schedule your draft for a time that suits you. Many online drafts will allow you to pick a league based on several variables, one of which is the date and time of the draft. Most online drafts will give you 90 seconds to make a pick. I suggest you use the draft board's draft queue (pre-selection block) to list players you want to target with your next pick. Then you can see them disappear if drafted by others in front of you. When it is your time to pick, you can go with the highest player left that you targeted. Another advantage is that if your PC hiccups or the connection dies, you will at least have a player you want in the queue who will then be drafted automatically by the website when your time elapses (due to your computer problem). Then you just need to get the problem fixed as soon as possible to log back into the draft.

How does an Auto Draft Picker Work?

First, get used to the idea of an emotionless draft. There will be very little trash talking. Somehow, typing "Hey Mike, your team always sucks like a vacuum cleaner," does not have the same effect.

There are two types of auto drafts:

1) Single List Drafts –This is the most common auto draft type. You compile a master list of all the players you want to draft in the order you want to draft them.

2) Multi-List Drafts – You compile separate ranked lists for each position. You also provide a list of what position to draft in each round. This is more like what you would do if you were not going to make your live draft and trusted a friend to draft for you.

Multi-lists are better if you know what draft spot you have beforehand. If you are 12th of 12 then you can set some strategy for what picks to go with in each round. As an example, with the 12th pick you may want to go with WR-WR to start out as you may get WR1 and WR2 since most other owners are going RB. Then you can target RBs in rounds 3 and 4, and maybe even 5. The problem with a multi-list is that you cannot do any exceptions. In the example of you giving lists to your friend to use, you may tell him draft WR-WR with 1.12 and 2.01 unless there are two RBs in your top 10 still available, in which case get them. You cannot do that with a multi-list but you can do it with a single list because they will still be the Top Players in your overall list. The advantage of a multi-list is that you will draft exactly the right amount of players at each position that you want. If you only want one K and DEF then pencil them in on the rounds you want and that's all you will get. In a single list you may get more than one K or DEF.

Logic used by most auto drafts

1) All teams will draft starting lineups before backups. So if your 12-team league starts 8 (1 QB, 2 RB, 2 WR, 1 TE, 1 K , 1 DEF, 8 bench) then after round 8 the following will be drafted:

12 QBs, 24 RBs, 24 WRs, 12 TEs, 12 Ks, 12 DEF/STs

What does this mean to you? Plan accordingly. You will have a QB in your top 12, two RBs in your top 24, two WRs in your top 24, a TE in your top 12, a K and a DEF/St in your top 12.

2) The computers will fill a roster first so do not worry about three kickers right off the bat, but do not rank them too high either.

3) The computer will prevent stockpiling by giving each team a predetermined bench, so you may get one bench player at each position plus an extra at a skill position.

Tips

1) Do not use the site's pre-ranked list. It will have last year's studs but no changes for injuries, suspensions, retirements, etc. It will also be what other lazy owners use. Use it to your advantage when planning strategy, but always take the time to develop your own rankings.

2) Use VBD to make your list of top 75 players. The first five players are critical and you want the best players available.

3) Rank each position based on its value. Look at your VBD cheat sheets based on the league's scoring rules. What position is at the top (probably RB)? Which position has many players of the same value (QB, TE)? Deep positions should be ranked lower on your list. The more valuable, scarcer positions should be at the top of the list. Most leagues will be valued as follows: RB-WR-QB-TE-K-DEF. Once you know what positions are most important, fill in those positions with starters plus two bench players for every team. So in our 12-team league that starts two and has a bench of two, which would be four per team, I would list 48 RBs first. Remember, once the computer gets your two starters it will fill in other spots. But you want RB to be the first bench player it selects too. After those 48 RBs put in the 48 WRs then the 24 QBs. Next you would put in the 24 TEs, 24 Ks and finally the 24 DEFs. You are forcing the computer to draft smarter for you.

4) After the draft, hit the waiver wire/FA listings as soon as possible to take advantage of any value that remains after the draft. Look at your strengths and weaknesses. Do you want or need more RBs or WRs? Are there any bye week problems (notorious from auto drafts)? Can you drop an extra TE, K or defense now and get extra skill players? If your family shares the PC, print out your roster now so you do not have to keep looking it up.

5) Get your HCs now if they are still available.

6) Look at your opponent's rosters right after the draft and suggest trades to fix their bye weeks or get them HCs while helping your team.

Instructions if someone else is drafting for you

Precise instructions would involve a top 100 overall list to use for the first several picks (with some caveats like "don't draft three QBs in first 6 picks," etc.), a cheat sheet with players ranked based on positions and a flow chart or rule list. The flow or rule list can have rules to follow like "Do not draft a QB until the 7th round or later," "if I have the first pick draft Larry Johnson" or "Get two RBs in the first 3 rounds." A flow chart would list which players to draft in which rounds. Someone who always likes to draft Denver Broncos might create a flow chart that looks like this:

Rd 1 (Best RB Available)

Rd 2 Travis Henry

Rd 3 J Walker

Rd 4 J Cutler

Rd 5 Another RB

Rd 6 Denver Defense

Note: if any of the above players go in early rounds adjust this flow chart accordingly.

He ends up having all Denver players and their defense and his fantasy team is a reflection of how the Denver Broncos are doing. Denver's bye week will be a terrible time for him. He is the ultimate "Homer".

Ways to Manipulate the Draft

1) Trading for draft position. Are there three clear-cut studs and you want one of them? Or is there a lot of doubt about abilities and you do not want the top picks and will trade them away? What about the middle picks? Will the talent at RB run out before the second round gets back to you unless you trade down for a lower first round pick, but better second round pick? Do you need the last first round pick to get the value at RB and WR that you need? Plan for it and if possible trade to get into the position you need and want.

2) If faced with a decision between two or more equally qualified players, look at who you can hurt the most. If the next owner is a Philly fan and your decisions are B. Westbrook or L. Jordan, grab Westbrook to torment the owner after you. If you hear muttered curses soon after announcing your pick then you have succeeded. A trade may be in the works.

3) Chart what positions (not names, as they are too hard to keep up with) the other owners are taking. This will allow you to manipulate the draft board. (See Appendix B: Draft Tracker)

4) Some teams will take two RBs and a QB before their second WR, if in a start 2 WR league. Watch for this and use it to your advantage.

5) Start a position run. Grabbing a top player from a position first is a great way to stay ahead of the crowd. Just don't do it too early; know when to start a run and when to walk away from one. If you can start a position run then you get a high-ranked player at that position and the other owners waste picks taking other players at that position who are less

valuable than your player. Try to time a TE run or a backup QB run. A starting QB run is best avoided due to the depth at that position early in the draft (4th or 5th rounds).

6) Plan ahead. Know who you want before it is your turn. Target 3-4 possible players and then allow the draft to eliminate them as you get closer to your turn. Rank them in your mind and look at what upcoming owners may need Then when it is your turn, announce your decision decisively and quickly. This puts more pressure on every other owner because now they cannot use your precious draft time to make up their minds. The owner behind you will hate you for forcing him into the hot seat so soon, so often.

7) Play your hunches and go with your gut in the second half of the draft. If you think someone is going to break out, grab him in the draft. You may have to get him a round or so before someone else will get him (use ADP), but as long as you do not reach too early then you can celebrate your great ability to pick talent. And if he flops; oh well, you took a chance and he was a late round pick anyway.

8) Be flexible, but if your plan is broken or if value falls in your lap, you need to alter the plan. You may have planned on RB-RB-WR-RB with your first four picks at the 9th spot. However, with your 3rd round pick (3.9), if you see that the three owners after you in the wrap-around all have WRs, you may want to rethink the WR at 3.9 and go with the third RB that is still in the 2nd tier left on the board. At most, probably only one or two more WRs will go with the next six picks by the three owners. So your WR may still be on the board at 4.4. Rather than being inflexible and going WR and then having to grab a lesser value RB at 4.4, try to manipulate the draft.

9) Blocking is drafting the next best player at a position your opponent needs. Usually occurs at the 3 or 4 position or 9 or 10 position in 12-team serpentine drafts. If you have the 2nd, 3rd or 4th pick or the 9th, 10th or 11th pick, you can look at opponents needs/trends and get more value for your picks by choosing players they need, before they do. This takes advantage of the "wrap-around" by "boxing them out."

10) If all of the other teams have their starting QB by round 6, why would you need to pick your starting QB in round 7 or 8? Most teams will be filling in starting rosters.

Who do you pick and when?

My friends (and I do have some) ask me if there is any player that I would not draft? I always say no. I will draft anyone depending on how far they have dropped. I would even take a player I hate, if he drops far enough, with my last pick. So no, there is no one who I rule out on draft day, just some I like more than others and my cheat sheets reflect this.

Early Rounds

In the early rounds of the draft work off your overall list. Use it to figure out the first few rounds and anticipate who will be available. I do not include K or DEF in my overall top 100 list. I never draft them until late rounds. I avoid the top QBs too, regardless of where they are on the overall list. If I can get Peyton in round 4 I will take him, but someone always grabs him in round 1 or 2 at the latest. After round 4, team needs become more important than getting the best overall player. Too much of a good thing can be bad for you. Four RBs with the first 4 picks when you can only start two may not be the best idea. Early round busts kill teams. Be conservative in the early rounds as you build up a core team.

Middle Rounds

Use your position cheat sheet for the middle rounds. The middle rounds are the time to "turn on the magic," when you can get great value. The other owners are off the playbook because the top 50 players are gone, their cheat sheets are calling for a kicker and they are fighting back the urge to blindly follow ("I'll take Neil Rackers"). This is where you make your money. If only about half of the top 12 in most positions return, then where are the other 50% coming from? You guessed it, the middle rounds. Consider the following points for those middle draft picks:

1) Better to go with a 2nd-4th year player than an aging veteran if both have same projections. Think upside potential and opportunity in the middle rounds.

2) Go with players on way up versus on way down.

3) Grab the sleeper before your opponent. If you really want him, grab him a round earlier so that you do have him and you can let everyone know how smart you were next year.

4) Grab a QB2 that starts rather than the hopeful superstar. You get more points from a starter than you do from someone holding a clipboard.

5) Avoid players on new teams; favor players on teams who lost the vet they backed up.

6) Target RB1 backup (Handcuff) if ADP dictates.

Late Rounds

Late rounds are for K, DEF, low-end TE, sleepers and rookies. Keepers too, if in that type of league. In the late rounds, do not pass up a Top 10 player at any position except K or defense, and then if Top 5 grab him for a sleeper pick. There are no gifts in FF. You need to concentrate hard on the middle and last rounds of the draft too, because when the injury bug comes, nothing will save you except a solid core of backups. Sleepers, rookies and breakout players are for the second half of the draft.

How to succeed in the draft

1) Spend more of your time looking at the middle to lower ranked players than the top players (the top 10 at RB or WR, top 5 at QB or TE) at each position. Say what? You heard me right. Spend some time on the top players at each position but spend more time looking at the others who will be drafted in the middle to late rounds. This is what separates the men from the boys, the newbies from the experts, the winners from the losers. Anyone can draft a top 10 RB or WR. Heck, most of your customized draft boards or cheat sheets are going to be pretty much the same. Of those 10 RBs you have, the other 11 owners probably have 90% of them in their top 10, just ranked a little (very little) differently. So are you really going to get a steal in the first four rounds? No. Can you

mess up? Sure, but only by drafting a stud who just got hurt. But you can get some great value in the middle rounds by digging deep into that player grouping.

2) WR is the most unpredictable when you talk about the middle rounds. Target a few in the middle rounds hoping for success. Look for QB changes, head coach changes, OC changes, SOS. Gain or lose a star RB or WR? Does he have a preseason leg injury (especially hamstrings and groins, both take a long time to really recover and can be nagging all year)? Did he do well in the second half of the season? (Confidence is a great thing!) Is he in his 3rd or 4th year (the more experienced the better)?

3) Don't get too carried away with HCs. Handcuffing is insurance, usually on your stud RBs. Look at RB durability before wasting a pick on his HC. Is it LT who has rarely missed a game? Pass on the HC and use that pick for a sleeper. Many head coaches don't use their depth charts. Minnesota's Chester Taylor goes down in week 13 of 2006. Instead of Mewelde Moore or Ciatrick Fasion he starts Artose Pinner? What? Who saw that? That lying son of a gun. A. Green goes down. V. Morency or N. Herron? You make the call. Think about HC if backup is a strong back on his own (J. Norwood, M. Barber) who may see GL carries or be traded to another team to start.
So HC top RBs only if injury-prone or if HC is a strong back himself (maybe traded in the season). Actually in the LT example above, M. Turner is such a good back on his own that he is worth a HC for LT, because he gets some points just as the backup.

4) Look at a TE in round 5 or 6 if he is a consistent TE; better to have a TE who can give you points each week than a reach for a WR. TEs are getting more passes because safeties are too small to cover them and LBs are too slow. More teams are involving the TE in offenses more effectively.

5) DON'T grab a K or DEF until later. If you are in a 12-team league, at most there will be 24 Ks and 24 DEFs drafted. That means 8 of each are left over in the FA pool. So between your two kickers and the other eight FA you have ten kickers to choose from every week to find a good matchup. The same applies to defenses and if you only draft one of each then you still have ten to choose from each week, your one and the nine in FA.

6) Avoid injured players. By this I mean the stud who is out until week 6 and can be had in the middle rounds. Avoid the temptation to get him for a steal. There are three main reasons for this. First, he will take up a roster spot for six weeks that could have been used to find a sleeper or to pick up bye week substitutes, thus your injured wreck is just dead weight on your team. Next, most injuries take longer than the experts predict to fully recover from, so he will likely be out at least a week longer than expected and may not be fully recovered even then. Last, he is more likely to reinjure or aggravate that injury.

7) Avoid "group think." If all the experts are saying "WR A" will have a great year then his value will go up, he will rise up the draft boards and ADP will rise. If you don't think he will do as well as others say, then he will be overvalued for you, but that might make his teammates undervalued and thus a steal for you in the middle rounds. Then "WR B" becomes very valuable as a round 8 pick. Sell high and buy low. The best time to buy is when everyone else is selling a player because someone else is being bought. The best time to sell is when everyone else is buying the hype of a player.

8) Take a few calculated risks. Don't go for all sleepers but if the opportunity presents itself you can go off the cheat sheets and grab a sleeper or two in the middle rounds. If they hit, you are on your way to the championship.

ADP Data

1) Use ADP to prevent any gross reaches for a player. For example, taking them more than a round before they should have gone according to ADP is a reach.

2) Use ADP to draft value within tiers. If you have three WRs to choose from, take the one with the best ADP. That way the other two may be around for your next pick. Other owners think the WR you picked was the better WR, based on ADP.

3) Watch the high pick and low pick differential with ADP. If a player has wide H/L pick differential, it means you cannot necessarily wait until the ADP for a player. On the other hand, if a player has an ADP of 7.01, a high pick of 6.7 and a low pick of 7.6, then you can be fairly certain he should go in the 6th or 7th round. A player with a 7.01 ADP, a high pick of 4.4 and a low pick of 10.01 has a varying degree of interest.

4) Look for players with upward moving ADPs.

5) Use mock drafts, ADP, Homer allegiances and FF owner's tendencies to predict where players will go in your draft. Use this knowledge to get who you want, when you want them.

Prepare a "Perfect Team List." This is a list of whom you want on your team realistically. If you could have a great draft, this is whom you reasonably could expect; not LT, LJ and SA all on the same team. We all have had this dream but let's face it, not very realistic, is it? No. I mean, if you have the 7th pick, go figure out who will be available for the first several rounds. Fill in your starters using ADP. Figure out when your sleepers can be snatched. Plan for a perfect draft, and ask yourself: Would I be happy with this team? Too many times you come out of the draft and say "I hate my team," and it is because you followed some cheat sheet or used some VBD application and lost sight of the big picture. You waited too long to grab all your favorite sleepers and you watched as they were stolen one-by-one right out from under you and you were left with an old injury-prone vet that you hate. Do not do it! Plan now. Think about drafting a sleeper a little earlier (a round or two) if it looks like someone else has the same ideas as you. He is not a sleeper if you don't have him.

Do a worst-case scenario and a best-case scenario. In the worst-case scenario, it would appear that all the other owners know all your secrets, sleepers and tricks. They will be one step ahead of you. In the best-case scenario, everything will fall your way. Obviously, on draft day something in between is more likely to occur but this way you know what the range of possibilities are. Don't do the entire draft if your rosters are bigger than 16. The later rounds are not as important, especially if everyone just grabs Ks and DEFs in the last three rounds anyway.

Know the ADP so that you can know when players will be picked in your draft. Use this to know when you need to strike to get the players you want. There is nothing better than hearing those three beautiful words, "I wanted him," from a fellow owner who is getting hot under the collar. Use your knowledge of the other owners and ADP to estimate how the first eight rounds will go. After that, those positional needs, handcuffs and sleepers will determine who goes where. Also consider recent news with regards to ADP right before the draft. If a player has just been named a starter yesterday and the draft is today, expect his ADP to be moving toward the high pick.

Deciding between Two Players of Equal Value (Discriminators)

1) Always anticipate what players will be around when you make your next pick so you will have the luxury in advance of making those decisions.

2) Avoid players with bye weeks on the big bye weeks (2006 had weeks 6 and 7 with six teams on a bye each week, in 2007 it will be weeks 6 and 8). There are so many more teams (6) in those bye weeks than the other weeks (4). If you can avoid having any of your stars (QB1, RB1, RB2, WR1, WR2) on those big bye weeks, you are that much better than a team with two of their stars on one of those bye weeks. Avoid players with bye weeks the same as your starters.

3) If deciding between two players, take the player on the more explosive offense.

4) Avoid players on a new team (new system, new head coach or moved to a new team). They will be overvalued on draft day. They will take half the season to adjust and will thus underperform the first half of the season.

5) Avoid more than two players on the same team.

6) Avoid QB-WR combos.

7) Avoid injury-prone players.

8) Look for players with favorable playoff schedules.

Draft Tracking

By tracking what others have done, you can better predict what they will do. If only one other team needs their first QB along with you and you have three left in the tier, then you can skip a QB this round and maybe next and focus on other position needs and still get a QB from the tier in a later round (but before the other teams start to get their second QB). Know what you need and target a few players from each position (tiering helps in this too) for your next pick and see who comes available. Look into the future and try to predict what the other teams will do with their next pick.

Some owners do not even bother to track draft choices from other teams. Still other owners have a roster sheet for each team and record the actual player's name at each position for each team when drafted. This is fine if you have an assistant co-manager helping but it is too time-consuming and wastes valuable time that can be spent elsewhere. So throw away those antiquated team rosters and go to the draft with a simple draft tracker (See Appendix B Draft Tracker). It is only important to know WHICH positions are drafted, not WHO is drafted. Sure, when the players name is called out you should scratch it off your overall player list and cheat sheet list under his position, but who cares who owns M.Vick. If you have a co-manager he can use it to track who might need a HC and estimate a player who may not be taken due to bye week conflicts, but this is too much for a single owner to analyze in the heat of the draft. It is far better for you to track which positions have been drafted by which owners.

It makes your draft much easier if you only track the positions drafted. You can see who needs what positions, how many TEs have gone and when backups are coming into play. In addition, you will have less stress because you will not be writing down every friggin' players name in those little boxes under each team in your draft matrix. Some basic examples just ask you to write a big Q, R, W, T, K or D based on the positions drafted in the traditional matrix of teams at the top and rounds down the side. An even simpler way is to create a draft tracker with teams and squares to fill as positions are drafted. For example, if your draft is for 16 players and your rules state each team must draft 2 QBs, 4 RBs, 4 WRs, 2 TEs, 2 Ks and 2 DEF/ST, then you can create a draft tracker with each team and enough squares under each position that is required. Then, as the draft progresses, simply put an X in the box under the team and the position taken. You can instantly see who has taken QBs and who has not. You can see who needs a TE and who does not.

The only thing you cannot see is "runs" in positions and maybe that is a good thing. If tracking all the owners is too much, try tracking just the two owners ahead or behind (depends on which way the draft is going (odd numbered round versus even numbered round). It is easier and will still give you some insight into what you may be able to let slip to the next round. I also recommend adding the bye week number to the X in the draft tracker as occasionally it will provide a clue as to which player an owner should not take (the player with the same bye week as his stud at that position). Use your cheat sheets with tiers, ADP, your team's needs and other team's needs that will draft before your next pick to determine the optimal draft pick for that round. (See Tables 8.6, 8.8 and 8.10 for examples of a draft trackers use)

Past Draft Results

1) Look at the last three year's drafts and calculate (average) how many players from each position are drafted.

2) Determine how many players (on average) from each position are drafted per round. This helps with projections. (How deep will the free agent pool be at position X, Y or Z?)

*If you have no historical data for the league (ask the commissioner, they usually have it) but you want to know how many of each position will probably go in each round, use ADP to calculate it. Just use the ADP list as if it were your draft.

** I like to use a three-year weighted average for most calculations. I use a 50% weighting for the last year of record, 35% for the next to last year and 15% for the third year (earliest). If only two years of data exist (like below) then I use a 60/40 weight.

Let's look at leagues where any number of players from a position can be drafted. First let's look at WCOFF, where 12 teams are in each league and they start 3 WRs and have a flex (R/W/T) player. See Table 8.1 below.

Table 8.1 – Average of several random WCOFF Leagues for 2006

Pos/Rd	1	2	3	4	5	6	7	8	9	10	11	12	13	14	15	16	17	18	19	20	Total
QB	0	1	0	0	3	2	2	2	4	1	0	1	4	2	0	1	2	0	2	1	28
RB	11	5	4	5	4	5	3	2	2	7	4	2	3	5	3	4	4	3	1	1	78
WR	1	6	7	7	3	5	3	6	5	2	6	3	2	3	5	5	2	5	0	2	78
TE	0	0	1	0	2	0	4	2	1	1	2	2	1	2	1	1	0	0	0	0	20

K	0	0	0	0	0	0	0	0	0	0	0	0	2	0	2	1	2	2	4	5	18
DEF	0	0	0	0	0	0	0	0	0	1	0	4	0	0	1	0	2	2	5	3	18

What does this analysis reveal? QB runs in rounds 5 and 9. RB runs in rounds 1, 5, 6 and 10. WR runs in rounds 2-4, 6, 8, 9 and 11. TE run in round 7. No kicker run. (Indication of an experienced league). Defense run in round 12.

You can also expect about 80 RBs and WRs to be drafted and approximately 30 QBs. There will still be plenty of TEs, Ks and DEFs left on the free agent list since only a little over half of the starters are drafted at these positions. A realistic overall 100 list should last until the 8th round and include 10 QBs, 40 RBs, 40 WRs, 10 TEs and no Ks or DEFs, because that is how the draft should fall out.

Most of these analyses are only good in the first half of a draft. After that, owners are OBE (overcome by events) drafting HCs, considering bye weeks, shortages, their own strategies and boxing other owners out.

Now lets examine some averages from 10-team Sporting News leagues (with 4 points passing TDs; 6 for others and 10 yards=1 point rushing/receiving; 25 pass yards =1 point. See Table 8.2 below.

Table 8.2 – Average of several 10-team Sporting News leagues

P/rd	1	2	3	4	5	6	7	8	9	10	11	12	13	14	15	16	Total
QB	0	1	1	2	2	2	1	2	0	3	2	0	4	1	0	1	22
RB	10	6	2	3	4	1	2	4	4	1	5	1	1	0	2	2	48
WR	0	3	7	3	2	5	4	1	5	4	1	3	4	5	2	1	50
TE	0	0	0	2	2	1	2	2	0	1	0	2	0	1	2	0	15
K	0	0	0	0	0	0	0	1	0	1	0	2	1	1	1	4	11
Def	0	0	0	0	0	1	1	0	1	0	2	2	0	2	3	2	14

Not only does this analysis tell you where the runs will be but also how many players from each position you can expect to be drafted and thus, the depth needed. In this league 3 WRs are started from your 16-player roster. Thus more WRs than RBs are started on a weekly basis. RBs have their usual run in rounds 1 and 2, but also a mini-run in rounds 8, 9 and 11. QBs do not have a run (maybe a backup run in round 13) but expect one or two to go every round. WRs have their run in round 3 and again in rounds 6 and 9. So every three rounds in the first part of the draft lots of WRs are taken. This is a very experienced league in that kickers and defenses are not drafted in runs and go at the end of the draft.

* Remember that if you are in a keeper league the results will be skewed, because keeping players will change the dynamics of who you need to draft, and if you pay a penalty to keep them that will also throw off this analysis.

After the Draft

1) Save rankings for later. Use them to evaluate trades and determine how good your cheat sheets were.

2) Check that you have the same players you drafted on the draft board.

3) Examine your team for strengths, weaknesses, bye week problems, trade bait. (see example below)

4) Check the waiver wire to see if any players are available that are better than who you drafted. Now is the time to correct any mistakes you may have made.

5) Check injury and starter status for your players.

6) Set your first week's lineup just in case something happens and you cannot set it later. You can always update it and refine it later.

7) Study your opponents for weaknesses (trade exploitation). Does Team C have both his QBs on the same bye week? (Suggest a trade to help him out while upgrading your QB position.)

Examine your Drafted Team

Look at your roster for strengths and weaknesses. (See Table 8.3)

1) Look for bye week conflicts. Are any players from the same position on the same bye weeks? As an example, two kickers on your team both having a bye in week four is bad. How many starters are on the same bye week? If QB1, RB1, WR1 and TE1 are all on the same bye week, that is not necessarily a good thing. Not a deal-buster but something to watch out for.

2) What is starter strength? Do you have great RBs or WRs or a great QB?

3) Where is your starter weakness?

4) What is your best backup strength? Do you have an exceptional RB or two good WRs?

5) What are your backups lacking?

6) Which players are possible trade bait?

Table 8.3 – Sample draft result from 2006

Pick	Overall	Pos	Player	Team	Comments
1.6	6	RB	R Johnson	CINN	Only stud left
2.5	15	RB	WMcgahee	BUFF	Had potential
3.6	26	WR	T Owens	DALL	TD's baby
4.5	35	RB	C Taylor	MIN	Great value at 35th

5.6	46	TE	T Heap	BALT	Value
6.5	55	WR	D Driver	GB	Steal
7.6	66	QB	M Bulger	STL	Steal
8.5	75	RB	J Addai	IND	RB4
9.6	86	RB	T Bell	DEN	RBBC but sleeper
10.5	95	WR	L Coles	NYJ	Steal
11.6	106	RB	M Barber	DAL	Gifts from heaven
12.5	115	WR	M Clayton	TB	Bust
13.6	126	QB	A Brooks	OAK	Bust
14.5	135	WR	E Wilford	JAX	Good early, Bust
15.6	146	DEF	Miami	MIA	Great late
16.5	155	K	M Stover	BALT	Excellent

Here is my roster in this 10-team league that starts 1 QB, 2 RB, 3 WR, 1 TE, 1 K and 1 DEF/ST.

Table 8.4 – Roster from Sample Draft 2006

Position	Player	Team	Bye	
QB	Bulger	STL	7	
QB	Brooks	OAK	3	
RB	R Johnson	CINN	5	
RB	W McGahee	BUF	8	
RB	C Taylor	MIN	6	
RB	J Addai	IND	6	
RB	T Bell	DEN	4	
RB	M Barber	DAL	3	
WR	T Owens	DAL	3	
WR	D Driver	GB	6	
WR	L Coles	NYJ	9	
WR	M Clayton	TB	4	

WR	E Wilford	JAX	6	
TE	T Heap	BALT	7	
K	M Stover	BALT	7	
DEF	Miami	MIA	8	

Draft Analysis

1) Bye week problems. None except week 7, when my only TE and K will be on a bye week and I will need to pick up two replacements. The good news is that it is late into the season (week 7) and I will have some idea of who has panned out by the time I need to drop players to add a K and TE in the same week. M. Clayton and E. Wilford (my sleeper WRs) both proved to be busts by then and I dropped them to make room for a TE2 and K2 going into the second half of the season.

2) What is starter strength? Three strong RBs and three strong WRs but no backups.

3) Where is your starter weakness? QB is solid. TE may be a problem if Heap gets hurt. What are the odds of that? Miami defense may not be as strong as past years with new QB.

4) What is your best backup strength? RB. I have several who are getting touches and chances in Bell, Addai and Barber.

5) Where are your backups lacking? WR, TE, K and DEF. I have sacrificed the WR position to get quality RBs.

6) Possible trade bait? RB 4-6.

Sample Draft

Let's look at a sample draft. Through pick 3.09 it went as follows:

Table 8.5 – Sample draft through pick 3.09

Rd/Team	1	2	3	4	5	6	7	8	9	10	11	12
1	R	R	R	R	R	R	R	R	R	W	R	W
2	W	R	W	W	W	R	R	W	R	Q	W	W
3	R	W	R	R	T	R	W	R				
4												

Our draft tracker looks like this:

Table 8.6 – Draft Tracker through pick 3.09

Pos/Team	1	2	3	4	5	6	7	8	9	10	11	12
QB1										X3		

QB2												
RB1	X6	X6	X7	X3	X5	X4	X4	X7	X8		X5	
RB2	X5	X8	X5	X9		X4	X6	X9	X7			
RB3						X6						
RB4												
RB4												
RB5												
RB6												
WR1	X7	X9	X8	X6	X5		X5	X4		X6	X4	X7
WR2												X6
WR3												
WR4												
WR5												
WR6												
TE1					X6							
TE2												
K1												
K2												
DEF1												
DEF2												

What can we tell so far? Have any mistakes been made? What do you think?

1) The first nine picks were RB. Pretty standard and hard to make a big blunder with your first pick since there are no bye weeks to worry about, etc. Teams 10 and 12 did not like the RBs left at the end of the round and decided to shake things up a bit by going WR. Who knows, maybe Team 10 convinced Team 12 to go WR with his pick.

2) Round 2 saw Team 12 employ the WR-WR strategy. Both WRs are on different bye weeks so that is good. Team 10 may have made a blunder by grabbing P. Manning (QB) in round 2. It is not necessarily a mistake to grab Peyton in the 2nd round; if anyone is worth it, he is, depending on the scoring system. But Team 10 has decided to go WR-QB. He is dangerously short on RBs and now must wait 18 picks before he drafts again. He has forced his hand now and must go RB-RB with

picks in the 3rd and 4th rounds. His opponents around him (Teams 9, 11 and 12) should note this and use it to their advantage. Teams 5 and 6 have drafted their two stud players on the same bye week. Team 6 especially has both of their RBs on the same bye week, a big mistake.

3) The third round went pretty predictable with teams getting their RB2 or first WR if they already had 2 RBs. Team 5 reached for A. Gates (TE) with his third and Team 6 realized that both their RBs were on a bye in week 4 and corrected it by drafting a RB instead of the more valuable WR.

Now it is Team 9's pick. He is debating between a RB or a WR. By looking at the draft tracker, he sees that 11 WRs have gone and notes that he has 2 WRs left in Tier 2. 20 RBs have been drafted and he has 2 left in Tier 4. He also notes that Teams 10 and 12 will have to draft a RB, maybe two, since they have none. The smart pick here is to go with a RB before Teams 10, 11 and 12 grab the next 5. Chances are very good that both Team 10 and 12 will go RB-RB. Team 11 will probably go RB-WR. That means that one of the two 2nd Tier WRs will be left for pick 4.04. TEAM 9 SHOULD DRAFT A RB WITH PICK 3.09.

The draft continues to pick 5.09

Table 8.7 –Sample draft through pick 5.09

Rd/Team	1	2	3	4	5	6	7	8	9	10	11	12
1	R	R	R	R	R	R	R	R	R	W	R	W
2	W	R	W	W	W	R	R	W	R	Q	W	W
3	R	W	R	R	T	R	W	R	R	R	R	R
4	Q	W	T	W	R	W	W	W	W	R	W	R
5	W	R	W	Q	W	W	T	T				

Table 8.8 – Draft tracker through pick 5.09

Pos/Team	1	2	3	4	5	6	7	8	9	10	11	12
QB1	X6			X5						X3		
QB2												
RB1	X6	X6	X7	X3	X5	X4	X4	X7	X8	X6	X5	X8
RB2	X5	X8	X5	X9	X7	X4	X6	X9	X7	X5	X7	X3
RB3		X5				X6			X5			
RB4												
RB4												
RB5												

	1	2	3	4	5	6	7	8	9	10	11	12
RB6												
WR1	X7	X9	X8	X6	X5	X3	X5	X4	X6	X6	X4	X7
WR2	X8	X4	X5	X3	X7	X5	X8	X9			X6	X6
WR3												
WR4												
WR5												
WR6												
TE1			X7		X6		X4	X9				
TE2												
K1												
K2												
DEF1												
DEF2												

What happened from 3.09 to 5.09?

1) As expected, Teams 10 and 12 took two RBs in rounds 3 and 4. There was a WR run in round 4.
2) In round five, team 6 with pick 5.06 has a choice between two WRs, one with bye week 3 and the other bye week 5. They correctly took the player with bye week 5.

Team 9 now faces a choice between a QB or a WR. Team 10 already has his QB but teams 11 and 12 do not and both get two picks after team 9's 5th rounder. A quick look at the tracker shows that three QBs have gone and he has three more at his 2nd tier. Even if teams 11 and 12 go with a QB, there will still be one left for team 9. Team 9 takes a WR who is not on bye week 6.

The draft continues to pick 6.11.

Table 8.9 – Sample draft through pick 6.11

Rd/Team	1	2	3	4	5	6	7	8	9	10	11	12
1	R	R	R	R	R	R	R	R	R	W	R	W
2	W	R	W	W	W	R	R	W	R	Q	W	W
3	R	W	R	R	T	R	W	R	R	R	R	R
4	Q	W	T	W	R	W	W	W	W	R	W	R

5	W	R	W	Q	W	W	T	T	W	W	Q	R
6			R	T	Q	Q	R	Q	Q	T	R	T

Table 8.10 Draft tracker through pick 6.11

	1	2	3	4	5	6	7	8	9	10	11	12
QB1	X6			X5	X8	X7		X4	X3	X3	X4	
QB2												
RB1	X6	X6	X7	X3	X5	X4	X4	X7	X8	X6	X5	X8
RB2	X5	X8	X5	X9	X7	X4	X6	X9	X7	X5	X7	X3
RB3		X5	X6			X6	X5		X5		X6	X4
RB4												
RB4												
RB5												
RB6												
WR1	X7	X9	X8	X6	X5	X3	X5	X4	X6	X6	X4	X7
WR2	X8	X4	X5	X3	X7	X5	X8	X9	X7	X8	X6	X6
WR3												
WR4												
WR5												
WR6												
TE1			X7	X5	X6		X4	X9		X8		X4
TE2												
K1												
K2												
DEF1												
DEF2												

Team 9 took a QB (he had two in his tier to choose from) in round 6.

It is now team 2's pick with 6.11. He has either a QB or WR on his cheat sheets. Who should he pick? The WR of course. Team 1 already has his QB. There is no logical reason for team 1 to reach for his QB2 anytime soon. So team 2 can wait until at least pick 7.02 to even consider a QB. Once he looks at his positional cheat sheets he sees that he has four QBs in tier 3. A quick scan of the board reveals that only three other teams need a QB. Team 2 can probably wait until round 9 to pick a QB (pass on QB in round 7 then if the other three teams grab a QB in rounds 7 and 8, team 2 can pass again in round 8, hoping that team 1 does not get his QB2 with his two picks). So team 2 should target a WR. Who should he pick from his three choices, assuming all have equal projections?

WR(a) bye week 9, great matchup in week 4

WR(b) bye week 7, great matchup in week 9

WR(c) bye week 5, great matchup in week 3

WR(a) should be eliminated because he is on the same bye week as WR1 already drafted. WR(b) has a different bye week than WR 1 and 2 and has a favorable matchup when WR1 is out with a bye. WR(c) has a different bye week but has a favorable matchup when WR 1 and 2 will be starting so it will not help.

WR(b) is the one to draft. And what about pick 7.02? Since seven (eight if team 1 grabs one) TEs are gone, wait on them too, as many good ones are gone. Instead use pick 7.02 on a RB and then another WR at 8.11 followed by your QB at 9.02.

With pick 6.12, team 1 has two QBs on his overall list, well ahead of his remaining RBs or WRs. Should he draft a QB because VBD indicates it is the best move? NO! VBD does not account for positions you have already drafted. C. Palmer in the 4th round is a great QB, you do not need another good QB at the expense of a backup RB or WR. Picks 6.12 and 7.01 should be a RB and WR and not a QB. He can consider a TE but for the same reasons team 2 should wait on them; so should team 1. Too many good TEs are gone.

Analysis after six rounds

Table 8.11 –Analysis of Sample draft after round 6

Rd/Team	1	2	3	4	5	6	7	8	9	10	11	12
1	R	R	R	R	R	R	R	R	R	W	R	W
2	W	R	W	W	W	R	R	W	R	Q	W	W
3	R	W	R	R	T	R	W	R	R	R	R	R
4	Q	W	T	W	R	W	W	W	W	R	W	R
5	W	R	W	Q	W	W	T	T	W	W	Q	R
6	R	W	R	T	Q	Q	R	Q	Q	T	R	T
	1	2	3	4	5	6	7	8	9	10	11	12
QB1	X6			X5	X8	X7		X4	X3	X3	X4	
QB2												
RB1	X6	X6	X7	X3	X5	X4	X4	X7	X8	X6	X5	X8
RB2	X5	X8	X5	X9	X7	X4	X6	X9	X7	X5	X7	X3
RB3	X7	X5	X6			X6	X5		X5		X6	X4
RB4												
RB4												
RB5												
RB6												
WR1	X7	X9	X8	X6	X5	X3	X5	X4	X6	X6	X4	X7
WR2	X8	X4	X5	X3	X7	X5	X8	X9	X7	X8	X6	X6
WR3		X6										
WR4												
WR5												
WR6												
TE1			X7	X5	X6		X4	X9		X8		X4
TE2												
K1												
K2												
DEF1												

DEF2												

Team 5 is going to have some trouble with both studs at RB and WR on a bye in week 5 and again in week 7 when his RB2 and WR2 are both on a bye. He can fix this by trading.

Team 6 is really in for it when both his RBs are on bye in week 4. He can fix this with a trade as well.

Team 10 has both his RB1 and WR1 on byes in week 6.

Otherwise, teams have used the short side very well.

To try to forecast the long side of the draft (the longer picks before you go again), I suggest you use previous drafts or ADP specifically adapted for your draft spot.

If you are in the 8th spot and the long side has 14 picks from your even rounds until your odd round pick, then use probabilities for how many players will be predicted based on previous drafts.

In the above draft example, you saw how the draft tracker helps draft decisions. Use VBD then forecast who might be left over the next time you draft; it may be because of depth at that tier or no/low chances of them being drafted by others.

If you still have a decision, then:

1) Between two players go with one without bye week of other starters at that position (example: RB1 has bye week 4 and you are contemplating two RBs, one with bye week 5 and one with bye week 4, draft the one without bye week 4, because that corresponds with the bye week of RB1.)
2) Draft player who does not have bye week of any of top 4 draft picks.
3) Draft player who is on least number of other starter's teams. Example: if you have two players both on the same bye week as two Top 4 picks, draft the player who is not on the same team as the others. If RB1 and WR2 are both from Indianapolis with bye week 5; RB2 has bye week 4 and is from Tennessee, WR1 has bye week 5 and is from Baltimore and you have the choice between a player from Baltimore or Indianapolis – Go with Baltimore to avoid having too many players from one team.

Conclusion

In conclusion, some say "the more you know, the better the draft," but I would disagree with this to some point. Yes, you need to know the rules, and your league inside and out and be aware of the preseason injuries, etc., but too much knowledge (that KC gives up 3.2 yards per rush on grass at night) is confusing. The key is to know what is good information and what is deception. Garbage in, garbage out, as they say. You need to know what you need to know. This chapter outlines tips for drafting. The next chapter explores strategies for drafting.

Chapter 9 Draft Theories/Strategies

Your plan going into the draft should not be to have a position dedicated to certain rounds (i.e. I will draft a WR in round 2 and a TE in round 4). Having a general RB-RB strategy for the first two rounds is probably okay but going into the draft with a hard and fast plan (RB-WR-RB-QB-WR-TE for the first six rounds in that order) is too rigid. The draft will take on a different twist as soon as the first few picks are made. Your #2 pick is more important than your #1 pick. The #1 pick is a given for most owners. Which RB do I pick? And the choice comes down to who is left and what pick you have. The #2 pick is where you start to decide which direction the team is going. It will influence your 3rd and 4th picks, etc. For example, if you take another RB with pick #2, now #3 has to be WR or possibly TE; if you went WR with #2 now pick #3 has more options.

Whatever strategy you use will be based on scoring rules, roster spots, league type (keeper, etc.), draft rules (maximum number at that position, etc.), tendencies of opponents, position drafting from, and your flexibility (things will change and opportunities will occur). Tailor your strategy to your personality: conservative, middle-of-the-road, or aggressive. They all will depend on how much risk will be involved.

RISK

At every draft, you, as the owner, are doing a risk versus reward analysis. There are the studs who put up big numbers and who rarely have problems (injuries, suspensions, issues with coaches/teammates). Those players are easy; grab them early and often. Then there are the players who will not get enough playing time to score any real points anyway so they are never drafted. Scratch them off the cheat sheet. And then there are the tough choices. Basically, you have the steady eddies who consistently put up average numbers without fail but who do not produce big games, and the talented players who are hot and cold or have problems that hinder their ability to produce like the studs. *Note: Issues with coaches/teammates did not used to be a problem but has become an increasing nuisance lately.*

How much risk should you be willing to take?

This will depend on your league. Is it a playoff league or a non-playoff league? In a playoff league, typically you have to finish in the top 50% or better to advance to the playoffs. Once in the playoffs, it is basically a single elimination tournament to see who the champion will be. In effect you have two seasons, the regular season where you need to finish in the top half or so and then a postseason where it is one and done. In a non-playoff league, typically the team with the most points or best record wins the league at the end of the regular season (which is all 17 games). In which league should you take more risk? Owners in the non-playoff league would be best served by taking on more risk.

Why? In a playoff league (lets say there are 14 teams and 6 make the playoffs) all you need to do is finish in the top 6 and then you will have a 1 in 6 chance of winning the championship. In a non-playoff league you have to finish first, which in a 14-team league would be 1 in 14. It is smarter to take on less risk in the league where luck (playoffs and single elimination) is more of a factor. It is better to take on more risk in the league where luck is less of a factor. If you take on more risk in the playoff league, the reward is either finishing at the very top, if successful, or not making the playoffs if unsuccessful. In the first case, you really have not gained that much for your risk of missing the playoffs. You get no tangible benefit from finishing 1st or 6th. On the other hand, if you take on less risk and (big assumption for sure) only make the playoffs in the 5th or 6th place, then you have traded points for consistency and a playoff spot. Of course, this assumes that points from the regular season are not carried over into the playoffs and that byes are not given to teams finishing first in the regular season. Both of these variations can eliminate some of the luck of single elimination playoffs and would lessen the need to go more conservative in the draft.

In general, the larger the bench the more risk is rewarded. The smaller the bench spots the less risk is rewarded. Consider two leagues: my first commissioner job was in a league that started with 14 players on the roster. We started a total of 8: QB, 2 RBs, 2 WRs, TE, K and DEF, and had a bench of 6 players (14-8 starters=6). Then a few years later we added four more spots for a total draft of 18 rounds (10 bench spots). In the first league (6 player bench) I have an extra roster spot for each position if I choose to do it that way, so an extra QB, RB, WR, TE, K and DEF. This way, on bye weeks or if someone is hurt, I can plug in my backup and get some points. In this league conservatism is rewarded over risk. My backup QB should be a steady eddy-kind of player who will score consistently when he steps in on the bye week or due to injury. If he is a high risk/high reward type of player, I may not get any points (or heaven forbid negative points) when I need him. Because I do not have as many choices, I need to draft conservatively, so I do not hurt my team on those bye/injury weeks. Now look at the league a few years later. Same starters required, but now I have four more roster spots. Assuming I draft a backup for each position, I can now use those four extra spots to take some chances on high risk/high reward players. If they pan out or have a great matchup, I can start them; if not I have a steady eddy to go in too. The more bench roster spots, the more risk you can take.

How you run your bench will also dictate how much risk you can handle. In the previous example, if I planned to use a rotation for DEF or K, I could take on more risk. If I drafted a DEF with a late bye week (say week 9), or planned to do a DEF by committee approach, where I simply added the best available defense in FA each week, then I would not need to use a bench spot for another defense. This "extra spot" could be used to take a chance on a sleeper RB or WR. I could take on more risk with the style or strategy of how I ran my bench. This is why so many teams that score more points than others end up with worse records; it is not about scoring the most points in the regular season (or maybe it is if that is written into the rules), it is about advancing to the playoffs based on winning the most games. You can outscore your opponents by 100 points over the season, but if you have a losing record, you will not make the playoffs. Which would you rather do: score 50 points every week or 80 points one week and 20 points the next for the rest of the season? The steady eddy (50 points) will have a chance of finishing above .500 whereas the high point/low point scorer will probably finish right at .500, because he will win all the high scoring games and lose all the low scoring games because they are so divergent. Who will make the playoffs? You need to know how many points it takes to win games and make the playoffs, then draft for that consistency. Who would be better in a league where the highest TFPs team was the champion? The team that has a shot at scoring more than the average, of course! A conservative strategy in a TFPs league just means mediocrity. The high/low team will have a chance of winning the title if he can get some sleepers to come through. Owners need to realize what league they are playing in and draft accordingly.

So where do I take risks? If I am in a playoff league with no carryovers, points or byes, and have a small bench and no room to play bench strategies (rotating TE/K/DEF not an option due to mandatory minimum position numbers; aka must have two defenses on roster at all times), then I draft conservatively and take the chance that I can add/drop/trade or pick starters better than the other owners. If I am in a TFPs-only league with 10 bench spots, I will take on much more risk knowing that I have to go for broke to win the championship and I have lots of room to take chances on sleepers.

So there are leagues where risk pays off and leagues where consistency pays off. Who do I draft and where, in each type of scenario? In leagues where I am risk averse (consistency is the key), I will draft only those players who have no outstanding issues. By this I mean no players who are injury-prone, have a history of suspensions or management problems, etc. If T.O. has a contract beef, scratch his name from your draft board. Pass on him; let him be someone else's nightmare. Clinton Portis out for game 1 and future games unknown – another player I don't have to worry about drafting. P. Manning and B. Favre, both having starting game streaks – sign them up. Eddie Kennison still on the board in round 6, I will take him – all he does is deliver constant production. W. Parker versus B. Westbrook? One a workhorse, the other some injury issues; I'll take Fast Willy, thank you.

If I am in a league that rewards the risk taker, T.O. looks much better now. Who knows, maybe even Mike Vick makes my roster this year, because eventually he has to break out right? Even if I do draft a bust or two or three, it is okay because I drafted six RBs and six WRs and I only need three of each to do well during the season, so my few busts will be jettisoned by late season and a few more potentials will be added.

Now that you are aware of risk/reward strategies, lets see what some of the drafting strategies are.

Draft Theories

There are many draft strategies out there. Ask a diehard fan what his strategy is and he will either say he cannot tell you (because it gives away too much info) or he will go into an hour-long diatribe on the intricacies of his preferred strategy. There is no "perfect strategy" that will always win you the championship. Do not believe the hype in the books and magazines that sell you their winning, time-proven strategy. If it worked so well, then they would be at WCOFF or NFFC every year taking home the trophy and prize money. If there was a single fantasy football theory that always worked, then fantasy football would be a boring game. Fortunately, there are quite a few common theories and we will explore most, if not all, of the most common ones. Just for kicks, we might even delve into some of the uncommon ones.

First a little history lesson on the progression of draft strategies; the first theory must have been the superstar theory. If you look back at the first draft in 1963 G. Blanda was the first pick and thus the superstar theory was born. Here was a true superstar who could play multiple positions. The Stud RB theory may well be the first theory widely used and talked about once fantasy football became more well-known. Some give it credit for starting in the 1990s, but I think it was used before then, just not published. Next came the Stud WR theory, which has gained even more momentum recently now that the illegal contact rule for WRs is enforced more. The 21st century brought us the Stud TE theory when Tony Gonzalez started to shine. Let's look at the early theories and work our way up to the more current ones.

Superstar Theory

This is the foundation upon which most of the other theories rest. It is to always go with the superstar in the first round. Don't go out on a limb, don't draft the guy who is hurt but has lots of potential. Play it safe in the first round and get a reliable, consistent, proven money player. Your championship cannot be won at the draft, but it can be lost at the draft. If you grab a rookie who is going to be the hottest thing, but he does not start, your season is toast if you wasted a #1 pick on him. If you draft that injured player who should be in the top 12 if healthy and he does not return to form, you have lost the championship before you even get started. If you draft a great player who is holding out on signing and he does not play for the first six weeks, you can kiss the league trophy goodbye. The point here is that you can lose the season in the first round of the draft by going out on that limb. Don't do it! Wait for the other owner to do it and fall on his face. You go for your sleepers and chance-takers later when you can take a chance and not risk the whole season. It happens every year; a player (sometimes a rookie, sometimes a player who goes to another team/system, or returns from an injury) who is the surprise pick of the first round of the draft. Don't be the owner who does this. The risk versus reward is too great.

Stud RB Theory (SRB)

This may be the most common draft strategy. RBs win championships so get as many of the good ones as you can. This theory goes that RBs score more of the points (again league scoring rule-dependent, but most leagues have RBs as the most important scorers other than a few QBs or WRs) so you need to have all of your starter RBs early and even a bye week or injury backup ASAP. Grab a RB in the first two rounds, a third very soon thereafter and a fourth pretty quickly too. If you do this, the theory goes, you will get consistent, high scores from your RBs. The corollary to this theory is that you will also decrease the number of RBs available to your opponents thus decreasing their productivity at this most valuable position. RBs are also less deep than WRs or QBs (see Table 9.3 – Supply and Demand, later in this chapter); at the RB position there are the top 3, 5 and 10 and then you usually have another tier of 10 or so and then the rest of the starters are questionable at best. Once we get out of the top 20 or so the pickings get slim. At the WR or QB position the quality drops too, it just does not drop off so dramatically. Another factor is the "expert" issue. If you examine many of the expert cheat sheets the RBs tend to be very similar (i.e. little disagreement; L Johnson is either #1, #2 or #3, but not #7). The opposite is true with the WR positions according to the experts. So where are you more likely to pick up a valuable pick that is still on the draft board? WR! Here you might find your top 25 pick after 40 or more WRs have gone. Why? Because some other cheat sheet did not rank him as high or slightly lower on another and the other owner did not draft him because of his bye week. Thus you have your #25 WR fall in your lap after 40 other WRs are drafted. This rarely, if ever, happens to a RB. They are ranked very close and get gobbled up and hoarded on draft day.

When we say you need two or more RBs early in the draft, we are talking about franchise RBs, a top 15 and a top 25 RB if possible in the first two rounds. Herein lies the disadvantage of this strategy. Many times once the top 10 backs are gone, the run on RBs will continue. It is at this point where teams are sacrificing great players at other positions simply to "get a RB." When, in fact, that RB they reach for in round 2 or 3 is not the best player on the draft board available. So while this is good advice, if it is taken to extremes (three RBs in first 3 rounds when only two start and no flex), then your team will be weak at other positions. Much more so than the owner who took a RB in rounds 1 and 2, but then went to a WR in round 3 or got his second RB in round 3. Don't get me wrong, RBs are the most important position of most drafts and they get hurt the most. The real question here comes down to: do you draft for depth (assuming an injury will occur or you can trade them later) or do you go with the best player at any position after round 1? Of the 32 starting RBs in the NFL, by the end of round 1 (in a 12-team league) 1/3 can easily be gone. By the end of round 2 well over half of the starting RBs could be drafted and lets face facts; the remaining RBs are going to be in an RBBC, coming off injury or have some other question marks in all likelihood. I have even been in some leagues where 20 of the first 24 picks are RBs. The only other positions picked were P. Manning and the top 3 WRs. So grab those RBs early but do not take this theory too literally and get them all early and leave the rest of your team hanging. The problem with this theory is that if you do get 3 RBs with your first four picks then your WR situation is going to look pretty thin.

Generally, the more teams in your league and the more RBs that need to start, the more valuable the theory. There are about 20 or so teams that have one dedicated RB, the rest will have RBBC or platoons of more than one RB or a GL back, too. So if there are only 20 sure thing RBs, your league starts two RBs and there are 12 teams in the league, then some owners are going to be left out. The more teams, the more reason to stick to two RBs with the first two picks.

Other reasons for choosing the Stud RB Theory:

1) RBs are the most reliable position as far as consistency. Unlike QB, WR and TE, RBs in the top 25 tend to perform in the top 25, barring injuries or suspensions, more so than the other positions.

2) RBs are given a longer time to pass or fail, unlike QBs who are blamed for poor passing pretty soon after things go to pieces.

Stud RB theory is also a self-fulfilling prophesy. By this, I mean the more owners who practice it, the more it looks like it has to be done. Suppose every owner intentionally did not draft a RB in rounds 1 and 2 (except for you), then the theory would fall apart. Those who did draft a RB in rounds 1 and 2, mainly you, would see that the other owners took all the great QBs, WRs and TEs. Now in round 3 they (the non-SRB majority) have lots of RBs to pick from and you, the only stud RB guy, have no QBs, WRs or TEs to get and another RB will not do you any good. So in a 12-team league after 24 picks, your two RBs would be off the board and 5 QBs, 4 TEs and 13 WRs. Who is in the best position in this draft?

STUD QB THEORY (SQB)

In this scenario you take a stud QB with your first pick of the draft. The only time this theory may apply is if you have a league in which the rules favor QBs or if you start two QBs, thus making them more valuable since there may not be much left at the QB#2 spot. There are usually a few stud QBs that stand out, and if grabbed early, they can give you a significant advantage at that position. But be careful after the first few stud QBs, then their tiers tend to be deep and one QB in that tier has just as much chance of outscoring the others as any other in that tier. In other words, if you do not get a stud, then you can afford to wait on your QB, even in this QB-friendly scoring system, because no one can predict which of the next 10 or so QBs will do the best, as opposed to RBs where predictions can be better at who should perform to higher levels. Be wary of fantasy football books that give cookie-cutter advice and statistics. Some examples are "In 2004, QBs dominated fantasy football leagues" or "In 2000, seven of the top 10 fantasy scorers were QBs." Remember not every league is the same. They have different numbers of teams, scoring rules, starting roster requirements, trade/waiver rules and different roster numbers. So how can anyone make a claim like "C. Palmer dominated fantasy football leagues in 2005"? He scored lots of touchdowns, I will grant you, and was probably the best QB in the NFL. But did he really do that much better than P. Manning? Would Shaun Alexander have been a better pick in the first round? It all depends. Some will laugh at the Stud QB theory but one benefit is what I like to call the "Stress-Free Starter" benefit. No matter what, you know P. Manning is starting for you at QB because he is the best. That is an easy lineup decision every week. It also means you can wait on QB2 until much later, giving you an advantage. The QB by committee (QBBC) approach will always point out that they can draft two QBs later and play the matchups. But do you think you can really play every matchup correctly?

QB by Committee (QBBC) Theory

The theory is that QBs are not that much different when it comes to stats and the differences occur when they play tough defenses. In other words, most are the same; they just play tougher defenses on certain weeks. P Manning is the one exception to the rule. Of the top 8 QBs in 2005, six threw for either 23 or 24 TDs, four of the top 7 threw for 23 or 24 in 2006. So rather than waste a high draft pick (3rd or 4th round) on a QB, go with a committee approach where you get two middle-type QBs in the 7th, 8th or 9th round and use them when the matchup is favorable for one or the other (in fact, draft two that have complementary schedules). This allows you to grab a RB or WR earlier than normal and helps spread the QB risk out in case of injury (if you draft P. Manning with a 2nd round pick and he gets hurt, you are screwed). QBBC theory says that you can create the best production at QB by swapping QBs based on matchups. Rather than draft a top 5 QB with a high draft pick, go with two middle of the road QBs that have favorable matchups on differing weeks. Or, grab three weak QBs late, in the hope that one of them will do well and make the Top 10. DO NOT grab a QB until the 6th round or later, preferably round 7, and then QB#2 in round 9 or so. If so, you can get two RBs, two WRs, a stud TE and backup RB before QB #1. You are looking for QBs with upside potential and a favorable schedule for passing. During the season, use the QB with the best matchup (playing worst pass defense) or the one who is far above in performance (may be hot). This strategy may also employ three QBs; if so, I recommend getting a sleeper QB in late rounds. The disadvantage is that it is hard work figuring out who to start when both are similar. Be careful in a start two QB league because it may be harder to get two QBs with complementary schedules due to higher demand.

QB delay strategy

Drafting a premier signal-caller in the early rounds may provide you with a championship team, but another theory suggests that waiting to draft your QB can pay off handsomely as well. It is known as the QB delay strategy since you delay drafting a QB until basically everyone else has their QB. The theory goes that if you do draft a QB early, you are sacrificing a quality player at another critical position (RB, WR or even a stud TE). By waiting to draft a QB in the 6th or later round, you effectively guarantee that you draft two or more good RBs and 2 good WRs These extra quality players will more than make up for the drop in the QB position.

The difference between the #5 QB and the #11 QB is 1 point per game, on average, or 16 points per season in a standard performance league. Why jump on the #4 or #5 QB in the third round when you can draft your third RB or second WR (after a stud WR earlier)? If you are going to get the stud WR without sacrificing the all-too-important RB position, then you will have to give up ground on the QB and that position can afford it. If you do draft two middle-of-the-road QBs and they do not turn out to be good, you always have those two and a minimum of four more in free agency to shuffle in and out to play the matchups. But do not wait too long, watch what the other owners are doing. Always get a QB before the last owner gets his, avoid being the last owner to get a starting QB because it might be too late. Some of the other owners are going to get panicky and will grab their second QB (that's right, the backup) in the later middle rounds (about 7 or 8) and you do not want to be forced into picking your QB#1 while others are drafting their QB#2 as there may not be much left to pick from. Better to wait and take your QB#1 right after the third from last owner gets his QB or sometime after the 5th round. The theory goes so far as to suggest that you draft two QBs in rounds 6-8. This gives you two QBs who can be rotated based on matchups if needed. Target QBs who scramble and get rushing TDs and those who play for pass-oriented teams. How does this differ from the QBBC strategy? In the QBBC, you pick two or three QBs based on their schedule. With the delay QB strategy, you simply pick QBs later but with no complementary schedule plan. Any two QBs will do.

What if QBs are awarded 6 points for TD passes? Does this mean they will need to be drafted earlier? If the logic of "wait because they are all similar" works with 4 points, why not 6? It does not work; more points mean the top QBs are worth more. P. Manning and C. Palmer. Draft them sooner.

STUD TE Theory (STE)

If your league forces you to start a TE then get the best TE you can because that is one position where you can outscore opponents week after week. This used to be called the "Tony Gonzalez theory." From 1999-2003 Tony Gonzales ruled the TE position and was the #1 TE every year. A. Gates took over that role in 2004 and now we have several (usually four or five) TEs that can be said to dominate their league. What makes this theory so good is that the TE position usually does not produce many points. Therefore, to have a TE that scores eight or more TDs is a huge advantage to your team. The conventional wisdom is to try to get a stud TE pretty early, usually in the 4th or 5th round (A. Gates in the 2nd or 3rd), but if you don't, then forget about them because separating the #6 TE from the #14 TE is very difficult. However, with the emphasis on the 5-yard chuck rule, more TEs are becoming bigger parts of their offenses. The Heath Millers and the

Vernon Davis' are changing the field these days. But also remember that if your league does not require you to start a TE every week nor has a flex player which can be a WR or TE, then the stud TEs are not as important than if every team has to start a TE week in and week out. Also remember that if the league has PPR rules then TEs become more valuable depending on their offensive scheme.

Stud WR Theory (SWR)

This came about based on seeing everyone drafting RBs and the occasional stud QB. If everyone is depleting those resources then that must leave another high scoring position open to some value picks. This may work best in PPR leagues. So if all the RBs are grabbed, the top WRs will be on the board and you can get them before anyone else does. This also helps because generally there are the first tier WRs (M. Harrison, T. Holt, T. Owens, etc.) and the second tier WRs (C. Johnon, R. Williams, D. Driver), and then from 10 through 35 it is a crap shoot. This theory is usually only employed by owners who have the late pick in the first round. By this time the really solid RBs (and maybe a QB or two) are gone. Thus when faced with getting a solid but less than stud RB or getting a stud WR (see Superstar theory), these owners grab a WR. So by getting the proven performers early you secure the best WR production and you start your own run on WRs, which leads to the next theory.

WR-WR Theory

This is an extension of the WR theory. Basically, if it is smart to get a WR in the first round, maybe it is just as smart to get one in the second round too. The only owners who will employ this are the ones drafting late in round 1. If you are in a 14-team league and have the 13th or 14th pick, the RBs are out of stud tier 1 and stud tier 2 by the time the draft gets to you. With the 13th pick (or 14th and then 15th pick) you can grab a WR, then know that after only two more picks you get another pick in the second round. Both picks can be stud WRs who will produce big time and now you have started that run on WRs (probably not until the third round, but who knows). You no longer have to worry about WRs and can focus on RBs in rounds 3-5 when the others are scooping up the #20 WR. Another advantage is that you just threw off everyone's draft board. No one expected you to go WR-WR, especially if you do it with a 9th or 10th overall pick. Wow, the other owners are calling the insane asylum for you by now.

The disadvantage is that your RBs will be thin. You will have to take some chances as you are looking at the #20-25 RB with your third pick (35th overall). The other disadvantage (and this is really why I don't like it) is that you are counting on two people staying healthy, not one (as opposed to the Stud RB theory). What I mean by this is that you need both your WR and the QB throwing to him to stay healthy in most cases. Imagine what would happen to M. Harrison or C. Johnson's numbers if P. Manning or C. Palmer missed a significant part of the season. Do you really want Jim Sorgi or Anthony Wright throwing to those guys? Not having Carson Palmer at QB, in the words of Chad Johnson, is "like Star Trek with no Captain Kirk." Keep in mind that those two positions get injured less than the RB position. Another problem is the predictability it brings. You almost have to go RB-RB with the next two picks.

In many cases, this theory is used in the 2nd and 3rd rounds by teams with the top picks in round 1. Let's say you picked S. Alexander with pick 1.1 and now at 2.14 and with 3.1 (back-to-back) you take R. Moss and Chris Chambers, who are available. You have your stud RB and then you forgo a quality #2 RB to secure two top WRs. Not a bad strategy. Another scenario that may make this more viable is if your league has a PPR format. In this scenario WRs are worth more than pure TD-only leagues or performance leagues. The biggest disadvantage is the flexibility it removes. If you go WR-WR, then you can no longer get the best available player in rounds 3-5, as you are forced to get a RB in each of those rounds.

Defense by Committee (DBC)

Rather than reach for a defense with your 8th or 9th pick, try a rotating defense approach. With this strategy you draft two average defenses (higher ADPs than the Top 5 defenses) that by virtue of their schedule will play several bad offenses on differing weeks. Then you start the defense that plays the worst offense in the hope for higher fantasy points. So you play the matchups with your defense. What do you look for? Defenses ranked outside of the top 15, that way you can wait to pick them later than most everyone else can. By using the rotating defense, you hope to approximate a Top 10 defense. Look for defenses with compatible, easy schedules (weak offenses).You do not want to have both your defenses face the easy teams on the same week. Look for defenses on winning teams. Teams that win games usually lead in those games and force the other team to pass and take chances. And finally, defenses that have a chance to improve from last years numbers (their ADP is based more on last year than on anything else).

Stud Team theory

Draft the QB, RB, K and even a WR or two from one of the top offenses in the league. The advantage is that when you score big, you score really big. Every Manning to Harrison TD gets you 11 points (4 for pass, 6 for receiving TD and 1 for XP). Two of those and a rushing TD give you almost 30 points, not counting yardage. However, there are too many eggs in one basket with this theory. An injury to one (QB or RB injury or even an OL injury) could ruin the entire team as the QB, RB, WRs and kicker suffer (simply because the replacement tackle cannot protect the QBs blind side). The bye week is almost an automatic loss when you have so many of your starters out. The backups will score some points but not as many as your starters. For this same reason, I suggest not having more than two starters on the same team or bye week. Why? You want consistent points. If all six starters are out in the same week, you can expect a reduction in FF points of perhaps 50%. If I spread those point reductions over six games (QB1, RB1, RB2, WR1, WR2, K) then my team is only losing a few points every week, (3 points one week, 5 points the next week, etc.). You have a better chance of overcoming each reduction this way.

The Anti –Draft Theory

With this theory, you buck all conventional wisdom and go for studs in other categories. A typical draft and your draft may look like Table 9.1.

Table 9.1 Anti-Draft Theory

Round	Normal Draft	Pos you draft

1	RB	WR
2	RB	WR
3	WR	QB/TE
4	WR	RB
5	QB	RB
6	RB	RB
7	WR	RB
8	Best available	Best available

You get stud WRs and a stud QB/TE and hope that two of your four RBs turn into something. Help yourself out by going with both RBs in an RBBC so that you can at least get some RB help. Look for the GL (Goal Line) vultures here too.

QB-WR Combo Theory:

In this theory, you get the QB and his #1 WR. When they connect for a passing TD you get 10 points (4 for pass and 6 for receiving TD) plus yardage. A two or three TD day for Manning to Harrison can be huge for you. However, there is a huge disadvantage with this theory. One injury now affects two of your players. If J. Delhomme is hurt and out that will also affect Steve Smith and vice versa. Just look at 2006 and Steve Smith, when Jake Delhomme was out.

Another problem occurs when they are on their bye week; you will have two starters out and the loss in productivity (your bench players will not be as good) is tough to overcome. Better to have only one starter out per week as this loss is much easier to win with.

OTHER DRAFT STRATEGIES

1) Handcuffing (HC)

Handcuffing is when you draft or trade for the backup. Thus, the term handcuff, because you are handcuffing yourself to that player and his backup (usually done for one or both starting RBs and sometimes your QB1). Why? Because if the primary player becomes injured their production is not replaceable otherwise. But if you have the player who will replace them, then you get those FPs replaced and prevent another owner from getting them. Think of it as insurance in case your top draft pick is out for some reason. The HC must be the assured backup and should be a good player if he does step on the field or else it does no good to waste a roster spot on him. Usually teams employing this strategy will handcuff (HC) their RB1 and think about handcuffing RB2 if they have a deep enough roster. When considering a HC, think about the potential for injury from your starter and also the potential of the backup if he plays. HC's for P. Manning or B. Favre are worthless since these tough guys never get hurt (jinx for 2007). The same goes for LT, but M. Turner is an excellent backup and in some cases scores junk points on his own just "spelling" LT on a series or two. He is worth a HC. One caveat, at the first hint of an injury to a starter that is not handcuffed, you need to get his backup. You want to be proactive not reactive. His HC is probably available in free agency, if you act early enough. Another HC advantage can occur if that backup is traded by his NFL team.

Handcuffing a QB can be dangerous because you are forced to get another QB for bye weeks (thus have three QBs on roster). This insurance is too expensive unless it is for a backup QB who may be a sleeper. (See Chapter 23 – How to Find a Sleeper.) Matt Leinart or Vince Young in 2006 would have been handcuffs who became starters. What are the disadvantages of a HC strategy? The backup is taking up dead weight on your bench (a sleeper could be there instead). If you HC, you lose a chance at taking another player who, if left out, could help your opponent.

2) Draft for easy early strength of schedule

Some argue that you should draft solely based on the first half of the regular season. So, draft based on what the players will do in weeks 1-6 or 7. Why? After the midpoint of the season, you are going to be affected by injuries, player situations, etc. You are more likely to be aggressively managing your team. The first few weeks are letting the studs start and seeing how the NFL starts to shape up. No way will you bench your #1 and #2 RBs or WRs for your sleepers until the sleepers prove they can perform. So the draft is really based on how well you can do for the first half of the season. Then (and perhaps a little earlier) you will start to massage your team to maximize matchups, bye weeks and injuries, etc. If you can start fast (4-2 or 5-2) you will be a lot closer to the playoffs than if you start slow (2-4, 3-4), so why not draft for a fast start and worry about the second half of the season when it gets here. By then things may be OBE (overcome by events). At worst you can trade the players who have performed well at a high price and trade for players who should perform better in the second half (based on SOS). Sell high, buy low. Trades are better evaluated after some games anyway, so why not draft for the first half and trade/add/drop for the second half. Also, look for teams who will start slow but have an easy schedule in the second half of the season. These will be the players that you want for the stretch. It is also easier to play the playoff matches in the second half of the season because teams have shown their true colors, so look at trades that will get you valuable players during that period too. It is much easier to evaluate the playoff matchups your players (or potential players) will face after eight games have been played than in August before the season starts. If targeting two players at RB who have favorable remaining schedules (after week 7), weigh your playoff weeks a little heavier. If he faces a weak run defense in weeks 15 and 16 but the other faces weak run defenses in weeks 11 and 12 then give the nod to the player who will do better in your playoffs.

3) Draft for playoff stretch

In this case, you draft players who will give you the best matchups in your playoffs. If you make the playoffs this theory should give you a better chance of winning the championship. Notice the big "if." Matchups that looked good in August have a way of changing from good to bad by December. You could find yourself with bad matchups or players from August who are not even starting anymore.

4) Avoid West Coast Teams

This strategy attempts to minimize any uncertainty about players before game time. It is best if your league has a "roster lockdown" rule, in which all roster decisions must be in before the start of the first game on Sunday. West coast teams tend to play in the late games (4 p.m. EST.) when they play at home. Teams that play in the late games will not have player's status available by the time your roster is required. Any player listed as a game time decision will still be hours away from a decision. Thus if you can avoid the west coast teams you have a better chance of avoiding situations where you must make start decisions without team information. (See Chapter 19 – Commissioner Information, for more detail.)

5) Stockpile Theory

He who has the most wins. In this theory, you attempt to monopolize a position. If you have all of the good TEs, then other owners will not have them. They are forced to trade with you to get them. The problem with this theory is you cannot stockpile all of the RBs, so having many of them to the detriment of other positions is foolhardy. Better to stockpile RBs and WRs to increase your chance of hitting a "breakout" player, not to "corner the market."

Overall Strategies for the Playoffs

1) Try to target players who will do well in the playoffs and hope that you make the playoffs; then you should do well.
2) Target players who should do well in the first half of the fantasy football season (this gets you a good record and assures playoffs) then trade or add/drop bench depth to get studs who will come through in playoff weeks.
3) Draft a team that is best available with emphasis on players that will perform well in the playoffs.
4) Draft the best players available and hope that you make the playoffs and do well.

Draft Strategies based on Draft Rounds

Most drafts are analyzed as having two or three parts. I like to take it in three equal chunks (the early rounds, the middle rounds and the late rounds). (See Table 9.2 Draft Strategy 20-Round League). If your draft is shorter or longer than 20 rounds you will need to adjust accordingly, but most drafts will be 16-20 rounds unless you are in a dynasty or IDP heavy league.

Early Rounds (1-7)

Rounds 1-3: These rounds should be scripted. You should know pretty well which three players you will have after these rounds. If you know your draft position and the ADP and the other owners' tendencies, then you should have a very good idea who will fall to you in these early rounds. Two RBs in the first three rounds is almost a given depending on the league scoring/starter rules.

Round 1: RB unless you have a later draft pick and want to grab a stud WR. You should know who you want. Do not sweat your first round pick. It will probably not break you one way or the other unless you take a risk. Don't take a risk! Focus on having a good overall draft. Concentrate on picks 2-XX.

Round 2: Most likely RB, especially if you can start more than two RBs (i.e. through a flex option); if you can get a top WR and there are still RBs in your tier available next time, then go with a top WR (i.e late 2nd round pick). RB or WR, whichever you did not take with first pick, is a great generic strategy.

Round 3: Depends on whom you took with picks 1 and 2. Do not be locked into a certain position. Go with whom you need and who is the best value.

Rounds 4-7: Focus on what others have done and need. If everyone has a QB by now, you can afford to wait on your QB so look to a top TE or whoever is the best value on the board. Stock up on RB and WR talent. Start a run on a position before anyone else does (as long as it is not a K or DEF).

Round 7: If you only have two RBs and two WRs by now (i.e. took a QB and TE too), get a third RB and WR soon.

Overall: Two WRs in first 6 rounds. Do not get too many WRs since they have so much depth, unless you are in a start three WR and flex league, in which case three WRs in the first 6 rounds is a must. Three RBs and three WRs by round 6 is a good generic strategy. Historically there are 1-2 elite QBs and TEs but grabbing one before round 3 is probably a reach. The higher draft pick you use on any QB1 or TE1, the less value you get from the player. In other words, if you use a high draft pick on them they had better produce as expected, and if they do not produce, you will be hurt.

Middle Rounds (8-14)

Go for QB in round 7 or 8 and QB2 soon thereafter. This will start a run on QB2s and can buy you some time. Draft for depth at RB and WR. Look for a starting TE if you do not have one by now. Avoid K and DEF (there will be runs on them in later rounds 10+). Get a HC for RB1 if not already taken.

Rounds 8-10: Add depth or finish out lineups? Best available players? Look for breakout candidates.

Rounds 11-13: Handcuffs, catch-up with RB or WR (by now should have 2 QBs, 4-6 RBs, 4-6 WRs, 1 TE)

Round 14: Think about K or DEF if top one on board with late bye week.

Late Rounds (15-end)

Take K1 and DEF1 with the last picks of the draft or a round earlier. Notice only 1 K and DEF, not two if allowed. Get your TE2 in a bye week different from TE1, K1 and DEF1 if you are not getting a K2 or DEF2. Look for sleepers and HCs if needed. The number of sleepers increases if you decide to forgo TE2, K2 or DEF2. Not drafting one or more of these will give you more room to grab another sleeper pick. Again, sleepers should be RB or WR.

Rounds 15-17: HC, bye week fill-ins, players with potential (sleepers).

Rounds 18-19: K or DEF if not already taken or K2 and DEF2 if required by rules.

So your final rosters will either be 2-3 QBs, 5-7 RBs, 5-7 WRs, 2 TEs, 2 Ks, 2 DEFs or 2 QBs, 6-8 RBs, 6-8 WRs, 1 TE, 1 K, 1 DEF or somewhere in between. Personally, I think fewer TEs, Ks and DEFs and thus more RBs and WRs gives you the better team.

Table 9.2 – Draft Strategy 20-Round League

Rd	Position	Comments
1	RB1	This could change if late round draft pick
2	RB/WR	Opposite 1st pick; gives more options
3	RB	
4	WR or TE1	WR unless Top 3 TE
5	RB/WR	Top 50-60 player you want to target
6	RB/WR	Depends on team need
7	RB/WR	Depends on team need
8	QB1	What have other owners done at QB?
9	TE1 if needed	
10	QB2	
11	RB1 HC or WR	Use ADP to decide if round 11 or 13
12	Best available	
13	RB1 HC or WR	If HC taken in round 11, then go WR
14	TE2	
15	Sleeper#1	
16	Defense1	
17	Kicker1	
18	K or DEF ?	
19	Sleeper #2	
20	K or DEF ?	

1) Pick three players that you want to target for the year. One should be a Top 15 player, the other a Top 40 player and the third a Top 50-60 player based on ADP. Pencil them in on rounds 1, 3 and 5.

2) Next, find the HC to your expected RB1 and find his ADP. Can he reasonably be expected to be around in round 13? If yes, pencil him in there, if not pencil him in round 11 or one round earlier than his ADP/EDP.

Drafting by Numbers (Or first three picks by player position)

1) RB-RB-RB: Classic Stud RB theory taken to extreme. You better have some good QB and WR options later. This can also hurt other teams that waited to take RB2, as there may not be much left for them. Better used in flex leagues.

2) RB-RB-WR: One of the most common strategies. You get two good RBs and then a shot at a good WR. Probably the safest generic advice if you do not know anything about the league.

3) RB-WR-RB: Hopefully RB2 is good enough to warrant the WR at pick 2. WR1 is a strong addition to the team and RB2 can be too, depending on which spot you have. This may be weaker than RB-RB-WR, unless you start three WRs or are in a PPR league.

4) RB-WR-WR: Great start at WR and probably are far above the rest, but still need a RB2 and pickings will be slim at pick 4. This forces your hand a bit too, with a RB in rounds 4 and 5 likely. Best if you have a late round pick so that pick 4 comes quickly.

5) WR-RB-RB: Best if you draft late. RB1 will be solid but RB2 may need to have lots of upside potential.

6) WR-WR-RB: Must be the last pick of the draft and can get two RBs back-to-back with picks 3 and 4. Even then, the supply of RBs at picks 36 and 37 can be frightful. High risk/high reward.

7) WR-RB-WR: PPR league?

8) WR-WR-WR: Come on, really?

Be disciplined, be honest, have a set of rules and follow them no matter what and control your emotions, yet be flexible and go with what the draft sends you as far as steals. That is how you do well.

Strategies based on Pick Position

Draft strategy per round based on 12-team league, redraft, starting 1 QB, 2 RBs, 2 WRs, 1 TE, 1 K, 1 DEF/ST

Draft Spot #1 –

A great spot to be drafting from, but actually I prefer #2. So this is not, without a doubt, the best spot to draft from, unlike some "expert" testimony to the contrary. Of course, 2007 and LT makes #1 desirable. You get to pick whomever you want from the top of your draft cheat sheet as long as he is a RB! Not only that, but you will get three of the top 25 players and five of the top 50 players on your sheet. You can plan a great strategy by simply knowing these few things. One major disadvantage is that you will not be able to box out any opponents and you cannot plan for other opponents' picks too much, since you will always draft two picks back-to-back and then have to wait as 22 more picks are made. One alternate strategy is to get another RB with pick 2 and then target the best WR or TE with pick 3. Since you have the best RB from pick 1, you have a lot of flexibility with the next two picks. However, one should be a RB so that you have two starting RBs before pick 4 comes around (48th pick of the draft), since waiting on RB2 will be costly. Of course, if all the other owners have targeted RBs exclusively you may find that the pickings are so thin that two outstanding (top tier) WRs give you more FP potential. If so, definitely target two RBs with picks 4 and 5. The downside to this draft pick is that you could find yourself a victim of a positional run. If you wait too late to get your QB1 for example, and then with the next 22 picks the other owners target their QB1 and a few QB2, then by the time your pick comes around there may not be any serviceable QBs left. You can get caught holding the bag at a position or two.

Typical Flow: RB-WR-RB/WR/TE-WR-RB-WR/TE-QB (note the order for picks 2-3, 4-5, 6-7 etc. do not matter since you draft back-to-back)

Advantages

1) 1st pick so best RB in round 1

2) three of top 25 Players; five of top 50 players

3) Possibility of trading down to gain better picks, especially if two or three stud RBs all ranked same.

Disadvantages

1) Cannot employ box out strategy

2) Could be caught in positional runs

Draft spot #2 –

Also a good spot and perhaps even better than #1 because you can box out and play owner #1's picks. You have the second best RB (many times it may be your first pick anyway). You get two of the top 23 players, three of the top 26 players and five of the top 50 players. With your second pick, try to evaluate what owner #1 will do. What has he done in the past? Is he a Stud RB theory guy? Will he go WR-RB, RB-RB or WR-WR? How you estimate his direction with his next two picks will determine what you need.

Advantage

1) Can use box out strategy

Draft spot #3 –

Now you start to lose some choice in the top RBs. Still a good spot, but may be the leftover stud RB or may get lucky and be left with who you would have drafted anyhow. Remember, there are four picks between your 2nd and 3rd picks. Analyze what the owners in front of you will do. Most likely you will see them go WR-RB. So plan on two RBs and two WRs off your list. If you go with two non-RBs with picks 2 and 3, then RB needs to be one of next two (4th or 5th) picks or both.

Advantages

1) Can play the box out even more

2) Can get better feel for bottom half of draft and play both sides

Draft spot #4 –

Probably going to be RB with first pick and you just have to decide which is best leftover after picks 1-3. You get to draft before those owners in round 2, so you can start to build some advantages based on who went earlier in 2nd round and then who went in 3rd and 4th rounds. Your 4th round pick is where you start to make some money as you can determine what owners 1, 2 and 3 will likely do with their next two picks and use that to get the best value with your picks in the 4th and 5th rounds.

Draft Spot #5 –

At 5th it is still too early to get sidetracked from RB 2nd tier with first pick. However, if no RB or one of the top tier WRs are still on board for your 2nd pick, you could take a chance here.

Advantages

1) Get 2nd tier RB

2) May be a chance at top tier WR

Draft Spots #6-9 –

These spots are very similar in that you will scramble for a third tier RB with your first pick and then hope for one of the same with pick #2. RB-RB is what most owners will go with here, to get two serviceable RBs and a good start. If you do not like the RB choices left over in round 2, then a top tier WR may be a better move. If so, then you must target two RBs in the next three rounds to have any decent RB group. So going RB-WR has dictated your next three picks for you. I hate these spots the most in 12-team drafts.

Advantages

1) Lots of tier three RBs and possibly two of them

2) Good chance of getting a top tier WR in round 2

3) Lots of different starting strategies to employ

Disadvantages

1) Missing out on top two tier RBs

2) Too deep to really box out owners or to use opponent's needs as tools

Draft Spot #10 –

Can go WR or even P. Manning (depends on league) if you do not like the RBs left on the board. You can use owners 11 and 12's rosters to determine whom they will pick in rounds 3 and 4, to your advantage. If you take a RB in round 1, then WR in round 2 gets you a top 3 WR.

Draft Spot #11 –

Much will depend on what pick 10 does. If he does not go with a RB, then maybe the one 3rd tier RB you like will remain. If he goes RB then that will leave P. Manning, a top WR or a lesser RB. You can box out owner #12 later in rounds 3 and 5. The key is to "let the draft come to you" with this pick. Do not walk into the draft with a "RB-RB come hell or high water" mentality. If ten RBs go with the picks in front of you, do not be afraid to go with the top WR and wait on whatever RB owner 12 throws at you.

Draft Spot #12 –

RB-RB; WR-RB, WR-WR or even RB-QB or WR-QB, if Peyton is still available. Your choices are limitless. What you do will determine to a large degree what happens in round 2. If you take Peyton and a WR, then round 2 will be all about WRs and RBs. If you take two WRs, then round 2 may be a mix of QB, WR and RB. If you take two RBs, then round 2 will probably be about a WR run. Again, let the draft come to you. If 11 RBs are off the board then two top WRs can really jumpstart your team; just realize that will dictate your strategy for the rest of the draft as you play RB catch-up with two RBs in the next three picks, at least. If other owners have beat you to the QB or WR "punchbowl," then go with the two best RBs any owner can assemble. The other's picks in round 1 will determine how you can get the best value from the 12th and 13th picks of the draft.

Advantages

1) Two of the first 13 picks

2) Two of top 13 RBs or of top 3 WRs or Top QB

3) Can influence draft

Disadvantages

1) No ability to box anyone out

2) No ability to get value by evaluating other owners needs near you

13th or 14th pick in 14-team league (start 3 WRs , flex pos) –

You have the leftover RBs to mull over. Why are they left over? Because of injury, age or playing time, they have questions. So do you take two of these RBs? If so, one will probably be a bust and the other a stud. If you take two you have a 50% chance of a bust. Why not do some homework and grab the #1 WR who you know will excel and then go with your best choice at RB because you are good at this and can determine the stud from the dud? Or, think about trading up some draft picks. You really have two choices:

Conservative – RB-WR-RB-WR, or

Aggressive – RB-WR-WR-WR-WR-RB-RB-RB or WR-WR-RB-WR-RB-WR. The thing you cannot do with this plan is draft two stud WRs, then ignore the position. You have to keep the pressure on since you start three and possibly four. You need to deplete the WR position since you started the run in rounds 1 and 2. Make WR your solid depth position while getting the best RBs you can.

Any time you go RB-RB or WR-WR in a 14-team league it forces your hand and makes rounds 3 and 4 predictable (draft two players from the other position). Better to start RB-WR or WR-RB; it gives you more flexibility to take advantage of the value opportunities and your opponent's draft.

Table 9.3 – Supply and Demand of Fantasy Positions

Pos	NFL	FF Players(4)	8 Team	10 Team	12 Team	14 Team	16 Team
QB	32	2	16(50%)	20(63%)	24(75%)	28(88%)	32(100%)
RB	36 (1)	3	24(67%)	30(94%)	36(100%)	42(117%)	48(133%)
		4	32(89%)	40(120%	48(133%)	56(156%)	64(178%)
WR	70 (2)	4	32(46%)	40(57%)	48(69%)	56(80%)	64(91%)
		5	40(57%)	50(71%)	60(86%)	70(100%)	80(114%)
TE	32	2	16(50%)	20(63%)	24(75%)	28(88%)	32(100%)
K	32	2	16(50%)	20(63%)	24(75%)	28(88%)	32(100%)
DEF	32	2	16(50%)	20(63%)	24(75%)	28(88%)	32(100%)
DL	124 (3)	4	32(26%)	40(32%)	48(39%)	56(45%)	64(52%)
LB	100 (3)	5	40(40%)	50(50%)	60(60%)	70(70%)	80(80%)
DB	128	4	32(25%)	40(31%)	48(37%)	56(44%)	64(50%)

Notes:

1) 1 primary RB per team plus 4 RBBC teams
2) 2 WRs per team plus 6 WR3s who are good enough to start
3) Based on teams using 3-4 and 4-3
4) 2 RBs + 3 WRs as starters plus a backup at each position is the top number. The bottom number is based on leagues with 2 RBs + 3 WRs, 1 flex position and 1 backup.

What can we gather from this table?

The more teams in the league, the more demand on all positions. (All positions, except IDPs, dry up in 16-team leagues)

The more starters at a position, the higher the demand.

RBs are the most important due to their lack of supply and high demand. Next come WRs who will tend to dry up in larger leagues. On the other hand, IDPs are never depleted to the breaking point, so this table shows that in many cases close to half of IDPs will remain FA after the draft.

What do most NFL rosters look like? Most teams have 3 QBs, 5-6 RBs, 6-7 WRs, 8 OLs, 6 DLs, 8-9 LBs, 7-8 DBs, and 2-3 Ks (usually one punter and one or more kickers).

League-Specific Strategies

1) Leagues that start 3 WRs:

-Need to have at least 6 WRs (8 if in league with flex position)

-3 RBs and 3 WRs by round 6

-Wait on QBs and any TEs other than Top 5 in round 4 or 5

2) PPR Leagues – PPR really affects the 3rd-5th rounds. Loading up on RBs and avoiding the middle WRs is a mistake and much more hazardous than in a non-PPR league. If you do focus exclusively on RBs, your sleeper WRs really need to come through. Grabbing the top WRs is not necessarily a huge advantage, since the price paid may not be worth it when a 3rd-5th round WR can provide so much value with PPR. Do not delay on getting those WRs in rounds 3-5. Consider RB-WR-RB then WR-RB-WR.

3) Smaller leagues, 8- or 10-team leagues – These smaller leagues have less pressure on all positions since less demand (less teams) means more supply. Use your top 100 list for best player available in rounds 1-10 but only get one QB and one TE and make sure you get four RBs.

4) Larger leagues, 14- or 16-team leagues – Having 14 teams each needing two RBs means 28 starting RBs are needed, which is impossible with a 6-team bye week (32 RBs - 6 on bye = 26 serviceable). Someone is going to get hosed at sometime on RB. You will see owners starting M. Alstott in the hope that he gets a goal line TD. This is more advantageous to owners with first draft picks, since there are so few RBs. In this case, having LT is even more of an advantage; not to mention having three picks in the first 30 picks (owners with picks #1 and #2), can make such a big difference, especially if they take RBs. They are almost guaranteed no problems with RB whereas picks 5-14 can give up any hope of having three starting RBs. You must have two RBs after 3 rounds. WR-WR with picks 1.14 and 2.01 rarely works because of the lack of RB production. Not to mention the fact that by the time you draft again, 3.14/4.01 with the 42nd pick, the RB situation will be decimated. Three RBs and three WRs after six rounds is not unrealistic.

5) Drafting players based on being able to trade them later – This happens when you have filled a position and no longer need a player from this position until you get a bye week replacement much later in the draft. In fact, you have a desperate need for another position, but lo and behold, a good player from the position you do not need has slipped to you. Do not draft that second great TE only because you can trade him later. There are three reasons not to do this. First, you have a need elsewhere that can be filled and by drafting an unneeded player you have hurt your team. Second, everyone will know you drafted that player to trade him later and thus his value will diminish since owners know you are desperate to unload the other TE sitting on your bench. Third, you have helped another owner because you have passed on that RB or WR that he was interested in and has now drafted thanks to your grab of a second great TE.

Clock Management

You need to know what the penalty is for exceeding the draft pick time limit. Some leagues simply skip your turn and allow the next owner in line to make his pick and then come back to you. If this is indeed the case, then your only penalty is losing one draft spot (not a whole round). In such leagues there may be times when "passing" is a better tactic. For example, you have the 11th pick of a 12-team draft. In the 5th round with pick 5.11 you have two RBs and two WRs on your draft sheets and you want one of each. You suspect the next owner has the same players in mind. However, if you pick a RB and then the next owner (who has two back-to-back picks) goes with WR-WR, then you lose one of

DRAFT THEORIES/STRATEGIES

those WRs. Instead, "pass" on your 5.11 pick. Either say "pass" or exceed your time limit. Owner 12 then picks a RB with his pick (5.12). Once he picks, you can then choose the other player from the same position with your "passed" pick (5.11). In this case, you would take the other RB. Now he has his 6th round pick (6.01) in which he takes a WR and you can get the remaining player (WR) you wanted with your 6.02 pick.

Conclusions

After all this discussion, the realization should have set in that RB-WR or WR-RB at the end of the 1st round yields the best results. So far we have talked about methods that do not involve comparing players from different positions. We have just focused on drafting methods that were straightforward; grab two RBs or draft two WRs, etc. But eventually in the draft, even if using the above theories, you will find yourself in a situation where you will want to know who to draft: the solid midlevel QB or the up-and-coming young WR? How do you determine who is worth more when examining different positions? That is how the advanced strategies evolved, since they provided a way to evaluate different players at different positions on an equal basis.

Chapter 10 Advanced Draft Theories

Value based drafting (VBD) took drafting (and cheat sheets) to the next level. It was the first of the statistically significant theories to evolve. Two of the more current theories are ZVBD by Rob Zarzycki and the Consistency score (Crank) by Matt Waldman. Information (statistics, who is starting at what positions, etc.) means very little unless it is applied correctly. You may know in your gut that Heath Miller is going to break out this year and score eight TDs; what does that mean to you and your drafting? Where will he rank even if he does produce those kinds of numbers? Is he worth more than Hines Ward or Tony Romo? That is where applications and VBD come in.

VBD – Value Based Drafting

In 1996, Value Based Drafting, as a system for estimating player worth, was introduced into the fantasy football world by Joe Bryant (VBD was originally designed for baseball). VBD determines the value of a player, not by how much he scores, but by how much he outscores the other players at his position. Once that is known, you can compare players at other positions to one another. No longer will you be stuck with the dilemma of who to pick: your #8 QB or #25 RB? VBD gives you the answer. VBD shows why both the Stud RB and the Stud WR theories are good. Why are they, you ask? Because the RBs are so scarce that starters score much more than their backups, and the top WRs score so many more FPs than the rest of the WRs too. It validated these theories using mathematics and statistics. In the case of VBD, a player gets "value" by being better than the player who would take his place if he was lost for the season. So if A. Gates (the #1 TE in a 12-team league) is out for the season, who would take his place (if available on the free agent listing)? The #13 TE since TE2 through TE12 are on other teams. A. Gates should not be valued based on his projected fantasy points total for the upcoming season, but instead should be valued on how many points he will outscore the player who would have to replace him if he got hurt for the year. By using VBD every year, you value every player based on his projected fantasy point total minus the fantasy point total of the player who would replace him (called a baseline player). VBD doesn't encourage you to take the highest scoring player left on your cheat sheets, but the player who is projected to outscore the others at his position by the most points.

To explain VBD, an example is in order. Let's say you are in a two-team league that only starts a QB and a RB and you know in advance how many points each player is going to score this year (you have a time machine and you use it to cheat). You pick first and have a choice between P. Manning (#1 QB) who will score 250 points in your league, T. Brady (#2 QB- 230 points), LT (#1 RB- 200 points) or Steven Jackson (RB#2- 160 points). Who do you pick? Most people would say P. Manning because he scores more points than all the others do. Let us see how your draft goes. You pick P. Manning. I pick LT. I pick T. Brady and you grab S. Jackson with the last pick. How many points will your team score this season?

Team Thumpers	Team Slam
P Manning 250	LT 200
S Jackson 160	T Brady 230
Total Points 410	Total Points 430

Now which team would you rather own? The idea behind VBD is that you need to outscore your opponent by as many points as possible, so you try to draft players that will outscore the others at their positions. If you have more players outscoring your opponents by more points, you should win. If you only wanted the highest scoring players, then your team would be filled with QBs and kickers, who score the most in fantasy leagues.

VBD uses your starting lineup requirements and scoring system to develop cheat sheets. It also helps to avoid players that you may have drafted too early based on their stats, but that are not worth it so early in the draft based on your scoring system and rules. The previous theories discussed (see chapter 9) did not take your starting lineup into account other than to compensate for more RBs if starting more and the same with WRs. VBD does much more. Before VBD, it was next to impossible to compare players at different positions. You could look at your projections for points and pick the player who should score the most (most common thing to do) but that really did not compare a RB to a WR. You were, at best, comparing the scoring of all RBs to all WRs, but not individual worth. VBD provides a method for valuing (hence the name) and comparing individual players from different positions. VBD estimates the relative value and thus draft position of different players at different positions based on the scoring system and the starters involved. Combining VBD with tiering and your opponent's needs can be a powerful drafting tool.

How does it work?

1) Determine the baseline players for each position (see Baselines below). If using worst starter method and 14-team league and start 1 QB, then the FPs for the 14th ranked QB is that position's baseline.
2) Project future performance using historical data (AVT Method) or with forecasts, also known as projections.
3) Calculate the FPs for each player based on the league's scoring system.
4) Calculate the difference between each player's FPs and the baselines value at each position (X-factor).
5) Rank players based on this difference (X-factor) within their position.
6) Rank players overall based on their X-factor, regardless of position. You now have an overall cheat sheet.

In the example above, if the 14th ranked QB is P. Rivers and he is projected to have 180 points, then all QBs would have 180 subtracted from their FP totals. Note that all the numbers should be positive except for the last starter (P. Rivers), who should have 0 FP left. All baseline players will have an X value of 0 points. Players below the baseline player will have negative X values and all players above the baseline should have positive values. The negative values do not mean they are not worth drafting. On the contrary, those negative values are going to help you draft the best backup and reserves on draft day.

Baselines

So what is a baseline? Here is where VBD takes on some different variations. Basically, VBD can branch out into at least six variations based on how you calculate the baseline. The six major baseline theories are discussed below. Remember, they are all variations of how to calculate the baseline that is used in VBD. We will use a 14-team, start 1 QB, 2 RB, 3 WR, 1 TE, 1K and 1 D/ST as an example.

1) Worst Starter

2) Average Starter

3) Worst Starter +1

4) Worst starter plus

5) 100 Pick method

6) RV Method or R Value Method

1) Worst Starter

Let's start with the basic VBD which uses the worst starting player baseline. Sometimes people will confuse the method of calculating the baseline with a new theory, so you may see a theory called the Worst Starting Player theory or the worst starting player version of VBD. The latter is closer to the mark.

The baseline is your reference player for that position. Some players will be above their value but many will be below. Anyone with a positive X value will have more value and anyone with a negative X value will have less value than the baseline player.

Take any player from that same position and subtract the baseline player's total fantasy points projected from the specific player's total fantasy points (TFPs) projected. The difference is his X value. In the case of the worst starting player baseline, it is the **worst starting player** at that position. If you must start 2 RBs in a 14-team league, then the 28th ranked RB will be the worst starter. As an example, if the #14 QB this year is Byron Leftwich, then he is the baseline player for QBs.

How do flex players affect things? Naturally, things get trickier if you have a flex player. Let's say that the same league requires one flex player at either RB, WR or TE. Estimate how many teams will start a RB, WR or TE. Generally, I would go 8 RBs, 5 WRs and 1 TE as their flex and add them in as starters. This number is added to the normal baseline calculations above to determine the baseline with a flex player; so the new baseline with a flex player would be #36 for RB (28+8), #47 for WR (42+5) and #15 for TE (14 +1). The reason is that most will start RBs if available because they score more points on average, but some will have to use a WR due to not enough RBs to go around (2 RB + 1 flex RB x 14 teams=42 RBs, yet only 32 start). And there may be a hot TE that is used in emergencies, so the worst starter baseline of VBD is pretty easy to calculate. The formula would be # starters per team x # of teams + (% using flex at that position x # teams) =Worst Starter Baseline.

2) Average Starter

The next variation is the **average starter** baseline calculation. In this case, instead of calculating the TFP baseline from the player at a certain ranked position, you add all the starter's TFP and divide by the number of starters to determine your baseline TFP. If your league has 12 teams and starts 2 RBs, then you would add the TFP projections for the top 24 RBs (all the assumed starters) and divide this number by 24 (the number of starters) to determine the average starter TFP for that position. This differs from the worst starter baseline method in that your baseline TFP will probably not be exactly the same as any one player so you may not have a player with an X factor of 0. It will also always be higher than the worst starter method since all players above the worst starter are averaged. Thus, this baseline will always have a TFP higher than the worst starter. Another rather crippling disadvantage to the average starter method is it overrates QB, TE and DEF/ST. TE and DEF/ST are two positions that, generally speaking, you only start one player at each and have so much depth and little real difference between them in scoring, that being overrated is very bad for your team. Translation: If you use this baseline you will be drafting TEs and DEF/STs well before anyone else, and to the laughter of all your friends. Even the founder of VBD does not recommend it.

3) Worst Starter +1

Another baseline theory is the **worst +1** method. In this case you take the worst starter and add one because of injuries, byes etc. So in a 12-team league that starts 2 RBs, the RB baseline would be the 25th RB {(2 x 12) +1)}. The result is slightly less TFP for the baseline and is not much different than the worst starter method.

4) Worst Starter Plus

Worst starter plus is based on the fact that the average starter slips a bit due to bye weeks, injuries and the benching of players. When these factors are examined over an entire season, the true average backup tends to be 1.5 x starters, as a baseline. Worst starter plus method uses the number of starters plus 50% as a baseline. Kickers and defenses are treated as worst starter+1 because most teams do not carry an extra kicker or defense and these positions are rarely affected by injuries and such. This makes the formula: #starters x # of teams x 1.5 (except Ks and DEFs which is starters+1)

5) 100 Pick Method

The best baseline may be the **100 pick method.** Joe Bryant and David Dodds, in an article entitled "Value Based Drafting Revisited," state "after years of experimenting; we have found that the best baseline is based on the number of players that will be taken at a given point in the draft." Although100 seems to be the consensus for most leagues, a formula to calculate how many players will be taken by the 100th pick is often used. This formula is based on scoring rules, number of required starters, number of rounds of the draft, number of teams and number of flex positions.

Therefore, other than the complicated formula alluded to above, how do you determine the number of players by position that will be selected, based on the above criteria? There are three simple ways.

1) Use last year's draft as an example.
2) Do mock drafts with the same league setup.
3) Look at an expert's draft of the same type as your league.

Perhaps the best way would be to use the average of two or more of the methods above. In any case you should know how many of each position will be drafted in the 100 overall picks. Using the WCOFF sample draft in Appendix D Sample Drafts, I can see that my baseline using the first 100 picks will be 9th QB, 46th RB, 37th WR and 8th TE. There were no kickers and defenses drafted, thus none should be picked in the first 100 picks. VBD should only be used in the first half of the draft, thus kickers and defenses are not accounted for in this application.

6) RV Method – R Value Method

RV Method (R Value Method) is a customized set of baselines for any kind of league. Rather than using a cookie-cutter method to determine the baseline, a complicated formula based on missing games due to injury, the number of sleepers at that position, depth, etc. is used to calculate the baseline. Robert Zarzycki developed this theory and covers it in his outstanding book, "Drafting to Win."

Projections

What are projections and where do I get them? Projections are nothing more than a prediction of the statistics that a player will produce in the upcoming year. You need projections for every draftable player. Of course, the more accurate your projection, the better your analysis will be and the better your cheat sheets will be. Creating projections on your own is a very time-consuming and tedious chore. Some people love to do it while others delegate it. Many of the available software programs (draft dominator, etc.) or websites will give you projections if you subscribe to their product. You tell the program what the scoring rules are, number of teams, starting position requirements, roster requirements and then either accept their projections or tweak them yourself and let the program calculate your cheat sheets to include an overall sheet based on X values and VBD. A word of caution; VBD is only as good as the projections you use. Garbage in, garbage out. We as humans tend to overestimate and underestimate to extremes. (See Chapter 20 – Psychology of Fantasy Football.)

Always ask yourself – How current are these projections and what is factored into them? It is fine to tweak them yourself (for example, expecting P. Manning to throw 40 TDs rather than the predicted 31), but do not overcompensate for something that your projections have already accounted for. As an example, let's say your purchased (and updated every two days) projections arrive after a starting WR has been released from a team. You need to know if they have moved that player down the rankings because of his release. In other words, has the QB subsequently been lowered, assuming the replacement WR is of lower quality? Have the other WRs been elevated to account for their taking his catches? All of these things would be involved in an updated projections package. If these things have not occurred and you are drafting today, you need to adjust the rankings. If they were already accounted for then any further adjustments by you need to be made only because you did not feel that the adjusted projection sufficiently accounted for the release of that player. If you adjust simply because you did not think they accounted for his release at all (and they did) then you have overcompensated.

How do we predict future performance?

The best way is to use historical data, such as:

1) Last year's numbers; very simple and easily available.

2) The average from several years.

3) The average value of players at that ranking in the past. (see AVT below)

Create forecasts using this information.

4) Projection (guess) based on owners gut.

5) Valuation of other's projections. Take the consensus of several sources.

6) Linear regression of historical data. Lots of math

Combination of historical data and forecasts.

7) Last year's numbers compensated for last year's and this year's events.

Average Value Theory (AVT)

The human predication to over- and underestimate player talent led to the development of the Average Value Theory (AVT) by Wade Iuele. It removes projections completely from the VBD scenario. Rather than use a projection of stats (how many TDs and yards, etc.), AVT uses a historical perspective of the positions based on rankings for that position. Iuele realized that the projections of individual statistics for players were often wrong, but the fantasy points for the ranking of that position were much more consistent. In other words, you know that over the past three years the #2 RB usually scored about the same amount of fantasy points every year. What he suggested was to stop trying to guess how many points an individual would score and concentrate more on where that individual ranked in relationship to his position and then use the historical average for that position's ranking to generate X values. AVT uses two or three seasons of data and averages them based on the positions they were ranked at the end of the season, not by player's name. In this theory, no projections are used just historical (old, factual) data. The knock on this theory, and this has come more recently, is that it is good at getting you the team that will score the most points in your league, but that is not the object in a H2H league. Which would you rather have – Team A that scores 1300 points in the 13-game season but did it by scoring 180 points five times (900 points) and 50 points for the other 8 games; or Team B that scored 1105 points but did it by scoring 85 points consistently every game. Team A scores the most over the season but ends up not making the playoffs with a 7-6 record (they won all the games in which they scored 180 points but lost 6 of their 8 when they scored close to the league minimum of 50 points. Team B made the playoffs with a 9-4 record as they consistently scored more than most teams with 85 points per game. This led to the Consistency Theory (crank scores).

Know when to stop using VBD

1) Abandon strict use of VBD after all the baselines have been drafted (normally from 100-120 picks into the draft). At this point, your overall cheat sheet is no longer used and your positional cheat sheets will be used to get handcuffs, sleepers, bye week fillers, etc.

2) Remember to consider team needs when using VBD (your cheat sheet). If you only start 2 WRs and you already have 3 WRs, a fourth, although recommended by VBD, may not be best for your team.

3) VBD does not consider bye weeks. If you already have 2 RBs on bye week 6 and VBD suggests a RB on bye week 6 also, consider another RB.

4) VBD does not recommend handcuffs, so a decision to handcuff the backup to a key player is your decision.

5) VBD does not take into account players with good SOS to either offset another player on the team or for the playoffs.

What are the Problems with VBD?

1) No one knows what the future will bring for players. No one can predict if LT will score 14, 18 or 30 TDs, so its back to the old "garbage in, garbage out" theory.

2) Value to your team changes every time you make a pick. For example, if you pick two RBs and a QB in round 3 and round 4 comes around, VBD may tell you that another RB or QB is the highest value based player available, but you definitely do not need another QB and may not need another RB yet. Players' value changes as soon as you make your first pick and VBD does not account for team value. If you did draft another QB and he sat on the bench every week except for one (bye week for P. Manning), then how much value would you have gotten with that 4th round pick? True you now have two top 5 QBs and that means another of the other 11 owners does not have a top 12 QB for himself, but that is not much consolation. Utility theory takes this into account.

3) VBD does not account for roster limits. I draft in a local league that has roster limits. This league requires 2 QBs, 2 RBs, 3 WRs, 2 TEs, 2 Ks and 2 DEFs be drafted in the main draft. You must have three RBs – no more, no less at the end of the main draft. Many times in the middle rounds (8 or 9) many of the other 12 owners have maxed out their RBs. That leaves me and one other owner who has yet to get RB#3. If I have two RBs remaining in the same tier, I will pass on the RB position until my last draft pick, even though my VBD board tells me to draft a RB. Why? Because I am happy with either RB that is left after the other RB-deficient owner drafts his RB#3. I will not waste a draft pick on RB#3 until I have to, which will be round 14 when roster limits force me to take a RB. By ignoring VBD I have drafted my RB#3 in the last round of the draft (huge value) and instead picked up more value in the 8th round with a WR.

4) VBD does not account for keeper leagues. If you have a great RB that you are keeping from a previous year then perhaps a stud WR with your first draft pick will be better than another RB. Utility theory accounts for keepers.

Other Strategies or Theories:

Strength of Schedule (SOS) Drafting

Many owners use the strength of schedule on a weekly basis to determine who to start and who to sit but do you use it as a tool to help draft better players? The players have to play against someone and those defenses can determine much of the performance of the players. If your RB plays in a division with three weak run defenses that means he will have at least six games in which his rushing numbers should be high. If your QB or WR plays in a division with the two worst secondaries in the league, there are four games that promise high points. The SOS is less precise with a QB/WR because the score will often influence their production. Falling well behind by the 3rd quarter usually means lots of passing, "prevent" defenses and "garbage" FF points.

Stockpile Theory – (developed by Robert Zarzycki)

Rob Zarzycki says in his book *Drafting to Win* "Stockpile theory specifically supports the following two concepts: 1) it's better to draft a high-potential player or sleeper over a proven, mediocre veteran and 2) it's okay to draft as many of these potential sleepers as you possibly can." In this theory, it is better to go for potential sleepers with more upside potential than players who are valued higher on the VBD scale. In this system if you go for high risk/reward players you are more likely to get a great player than going with middle-of-the-road-but-never-to-be-great players. The theory is that you cannot win championships with middle-of-the-road players. You need to take a chance and go against the statistics, so that when you do get that sleeper it will propel you to the championship. If you load up on high potential players in positions where you start more than one player (RB and WR), you have the best chance of scoring big with them.

Zarzycki's VBD (ZVBD)

In his book Rob points out that "Dynamic drafting involves baselines (or baseline players) that actually change as the draft proceeds, known as dynamic baselines". The variables include your position needs, your opponents' needs, how solid your players are at different positions (if you have P. Manning you do not need to worry too much about QB anymore in this draft) and your questionable players.

Consistency Scores (Crank)-(by Matt Waldman)

The idea of this theory is that scoring the most points at the end of the regular season is not the objective in a H2H league. You do not need to score the most points, but instead need to score the most consistent points week in and week out. Rather than score 100 points in six games and 50 points in the other six games (average 75 points per game), you would want players who consistently gave you 75 points per game or as small a deviation as possible. Adding to my earlier example, I have placed the average weekly score and the deviation (how much fluctuation in scores for the year that a player will have). Which team looks better now, based on consistency?

Team Thumpers	Team Slam
P Manning 250 (15.6 +/- 3)	LT 200 (12.5 +/- 5)
S Jackson 160 (10.0 +/- 2)	T Brady 230 (14.4 +/- 7)
Total Points 410 (25.6 +/- 2)	TFPs 430 (26.9 +/-6)

Thumpers score between 24 and 27 points every week and Slam scores anywhere from 21 to 33 points. In many cases, Thumpers will have a better H2H record because they are more consistent.

The median is a better indication of consistency than the arithmetic mean (average). The median is the absolute middle of the numbers ranked from low to high. Note: If there is an even amount of numbers, then you would take the average of the two middle numbers. Some examples are:

A player scored the following FPs: 0, 0, 10, 7, 13, 7, 2, 1, 7, 7, 8 and 7 through 12 games; which is a total of 69 points. The arithmetic mean is 69/12= 5.75 points per game. The first two games were a slow start but after that he averaged over a TD per game. What is the median?

Ranked from low to high: 0,0,1,2,7,7,7,7,7,8,10,13. The median is seven since this is the middle number when ranked. Therefore, the median shows that he consistently scores a TD for you in FP. This is Maurice Jones-Drew through week 13 of the 2006 season. Lets look at another RB. His totals through week 13 are: 0,8,0,8,1,2,2,7,9,1,30, and 1, thus 69 points for 12 weeks. His arithmetic mean is 69/12=5.75, identical to that of Jones-Drew. However, what is his median? 0,0,1,1,1,2,2,7,8,8,9,30. His median is 2 points per game. Why? He had one great game. Who would you rather have on your team? Which is a better indicator of consistency? The second player is Joseph Addai. Both are rookies with similar numbers, but Addai had one big game with 4 TDs and 171 yards in week 12. Jones-Drew has been more consistent with a TD in 10 of 12 games through week 13. Addai went on to have 23 fantasy points (0 TDs) in the last four games of the season. Jones-Drew finished with 6 TDs and 441 rushing yards, making 70 fantasy points.

Utility Theory

VBD does not account for your team needs, bye weeks, SOS, other owners' picks, keeper picks or roster limits. Other than those limitations, it is great. Obviously, it can use improvement. My utility theory uses AVT for projections of players' performance and VBD based on the 100 picks method of a baseline. Tiers are used to help with gaining value by choosing players from the highest and thinnest tiers. However, where utility theory differs is that it incorporates a formula for choosing positions to be drafted based on how many players you have at that position, how many players you want at that position and most importantly how high up in the rankings the players you have are ranked. In effect, the better players you have the less you need another player there.

Before the draft you will need to rank the positions (QB, RB, WR, and TE) based on importance to your strategy. Start by ignoring kickers and defenses entirely. Before the draft, you determine an estimate for how many "must-have" players from each position you need. For example, in a start 3 WR league, I want eight WRs if roster limits will allow. However, I must have four WRs that start. This is how those roster limits are taken into account by the utility system. You base your "wants" on what the rules allow. If rules only allow six WRs then that is your "utility" number. Let's say it is 8 WRs and 3-4 of them will be starters regularly. You would want 4 good WRs. In our example, we want 1 QB, 3 starting RBs, 4 WRs and 1 TE. You will draft more than this but VBD only works for the first 100 picks or so. So in a 12- or 14-team league, that equates to 7-8 picks.

The focus of this draft theory is to determine when to draft a QB, RB, WR and TE. This positional utility ranking (PUR) will then be used with a "players you want" ranking factor (RF). For example, you may rank RBs #1 for wants and then say you want a Top 10 RB1, Top 20 RB2 and Top 25 RB3. WR is next and you want a Top 10 WR1, Top 15 WR2, Top 25 WR3 and a Top 30 WR4. Next is TE and you want a Top 10 TE1. QB is last with a Top 12 QB1. The PUR combined with the RF determines a Positional Need Ratio (PNR). The PNR decreases every time you draft a player from that position. Other positions' PNR will increase more the longer the draft lasts.

At the start of the draft, you have zero of four WRs. Your PNR is zero. Once you draft a WR you have 25% of your utility (PUR) met but the WRs ranking (RF) must also factor in (PNR). If you start with three great Top 20 WRs then perhaps WR4 can be delayed in order to help satisfy the RB position. In our example, you drafted a Top 5 WR1 so your utility for that player has exceeded expectations. This will decrease the need to draft a WR again and increase the need to draft a RB since there are no players there yet and it stands at 0%. Utility theory considers a player's worth within his position to determine how much "utility" or "want" is fulfilled. The better the player, the more "utility" is fulfilled and the less another player from that position is needed.

The bottom line is the higher ranked a player is at a position, the less you need to get a quality backup. If both starting RBs are great, there is less need for a good backup RB3. You would be better off looking for a starter elsewhere, but the key is to analyze the other player using the utility theory to determine how much "utility or fullness" you get. It may be better to pick a TE1 than a QB1, based on the rankings of players available and the ranking you gave that position. A keeper player can also be analyzed to determine how much utility they provide and how much remaining utility exists at that position if kept.

I am saving a detailed discussion of my theory for my next book. I do not want to give away all my secrets. However, I can give you some hints at utility numbers. The auction percentages for starters are a good place to start. Most auction budgets have at least 80 percent allocated to the top six players (QB1, RB1 and RB2, WRs 1-3). Since the Top 100 players are being used as a baseline, 100 players will be drafted. This is the perfect number for determining percent above or below a want level by referring to a player's overall ranking. If he is ranked 5th overall and you wanted a 10th overall player then he is 5% better than you wanted. Auction values with a $100 salary cap are good approximations of utility values.

Chapter 11 Auction Tips

An auction draft requires much of the same preparation as a redraft league. You need to know where players are ranked within their position and how they are valued amongst other positions. Create your rankings sheet just as you would for a traditional draft, so you know which players to value the highest. You also will need to have tiered the players and have a game plan (go for broke, steady eddy, or cheap chris; see Chapter 12 – Auction Strategies). Just like a redraft, you will need to know your scoring rules and roster spot limits. These will allow you to determine how the top players rank in points compared to others and how deep the position is in skilled players. Highest point value combined with demand for the position equals value.

Use tiers to avoid becoming fixated on a certain individual player. If you really like M. Harrison but see another owner or two bidding on him above his realistic worth and there are several other players still in his tier, then drop out of the bidding war for Harrison and target another player or two from his tier for your team. Tiering helps you avoid reaching too far for individual players and enables you to see other players of similar talent that you can get for better value.

Create a budget and stick to it so that you maximize your spending dollars. With a budget, you have a plan. Of course these budget numbers need to be based on scoring rules, supply vs. demand at positions, number of starting players, depth of roster, and a few corrections based on preference/strategy (avoiding QB early, going with top TE, etc.)

Auctions tend to play out as fast-paced, spending sprees early on (first half of auction) since owners have money in their pockets to spend. After that, it becomes more spendthrifty since some owners have blown their wad (STS). It is the second half of the auction where, if you have a little more cash than everyone else, you can really dominate. Keep in mind that $1 saved for the last half can be worth more than $1 in value.

Nomination strategy:

1) Nominate players you DO NOT WANT but who will go for a high price (Remember you want the other owners to spend their money on players you do not want). If you hate the Dallas Cowboys (come on, America's favorite team?) then nominate T. Owens. Get someone else to pay $40 for him right away.

2) Nominate early those studs you do not want or think will be a bust.

3) Nominate QBs first so that top dollar is paid for them before owners run out of money.

4) Nominate players that you know the Homers will go for.

5) Do not bring up your favorite players until everyone is capped out.

6) Nominate rookies early (except rookie RBs). The earlier in the auction, the more owners tend to overspend, so throw out the hyped rookie WRs and QBs, knowing you do not want them and some other owner will overspend for them.

7) Nominate a top ranked kicker; you may get him sold at top dollar too.

8) Nominate from a position that you have already filled, to burn other's money. If you already have your key RBs, throw out more RBs so others have to spend for them.

9) Nominate the HC of another owner early when others can bid him up.

10) Nominate the #5-8 kickers so you can get one cheap if no one else bids or force them on someone else for more money.

11) Late in the auction, nominate players you intend to buy since you have to start the bidding, especially if the other owners are filled at those positions or have little money left. If 10 defenses are left and all are going to go for league minimum, then nominate the highest ranked one you want.

35 Generic Auction Tips

1) Wait until the end of the draft for kickers and defenses and you can get the ones you want for $1. How, you might ask. Because at the end all of the other teams usually have minimum money left too and no one wants to bid up the price of a player and get stuck with him, so you can usually get your K and DEF for the league minimum at the end of the draft. Don't overbid on a K or DEF. Kickers do not consistently make the top 5 so never bid more than $2 for a kicker or defense.

2) If you have to have a top-ranked kicker or defense, try to nominate them early in the draft and add $1 to the league minimum (top kickers/defenses go for $4-5 in $200, $1 minimum auction leagues). Early on, owners may be reluctant to bid on them since they usually go at the end of the draft and for close to league minimum (and they want to save every precious dollar for the big guys). You may get them cheap.

The same strategy goes for your favorite player, when others are low on cash late in the draft. If you nominate a player and start out at the league minimum, you let another owner come in for $1 more and that may be the max you wanted to spend or could spend (the same may apply to him). Thus, you have let your opponent get in first. If you start at $1 above the minimum, you may scare or force the others away because they would have to bid $1 more. Budget-wise, that is not a good idea at the end of the draft when money is tight.

3) If you spend less than (or more than) budgeted at a certain position, add or (subtract) that money from your budget elsewhere. You do not want to be in the hole at a critical position. After buying three RBs, you do not want to find yourself with only the minimum left for every other position because you overspent.

4) Whom you nominate is important. Have a list of players who you will nominate when it is your turn (unless something else suggests otherwise; for example if an owner grabs a RB in an RBBC situation and you want to throw out the other RB while people have some money to bid him up).

5) Try to bid up other owners' favorite players, but do not bid up a player unless he is going for much less than his fair value. If he is going for 10% or less, bid him up. Stop bidding him up when he gets to 5% of his FMV. You do not want to get stuck with a player while playing this dangerous "bid up" game. If you know that a certain Philly fan has to have Donovan McNabb (and has done so the past 3 years), then there is no reason why you should let him go at 10% below value. In many leagues, some owners fall in love with certain players they have had from season to season. When this occurs, bid up Dante Culpepper because you know "Double Ugly" has to have Dante every year.

***Of course, another tip may be to never bid on someone you do not want. It is oftentimes not worth the frustration of bidding them up to drop on someone then having them dropped on you and ruining your season. Better to let someone have them for a song and watch them perform and either gloat or learn from their stellar performance.

6) The absolute worst thing you can do is have cap money left over at the end of the auction. DO NOT LET THIS HAPPEN TO YOU. Anyone who ends the auction with money has not picked the best team; that extra $2 or $5 could have been used somewhere to get a better player. This means having a plan, using a budget and keeping track of budget surpluses and deficits. Use all of your cap money to obtain the best possible players. Winning teams spend all of their money AND do it wisely. Having $10 as the last team standing and taking your K2 for $10 is spending all your money but is NOT spending it wisely. If you do have money left over, you will be reprimanding yourself all season for not using it to get a better player at some position.

7) Always bid the minimum amount above last bid. Do not get frustrated and raise by $5; that just gives the person you were bidding against the opportunity to unload his least favorite player on you for more than he was willing to raise. I know some think it slows down the auction, but lets face it, you never want to pay more for something than you have to and raising by more than the minimum will inevitably cause you to pay more than needed.

8) Generally, you should try to bid less than, and sometimes equal to, but never over the value of players. A bargain is paying 80-90% of what you thought he should go for. Less than 80% is a steal and 90-98% is good value. The numbers on your cheat sheet are worst-case scenarios; never pay more than 100%, unless he deserves a premium (Top 3 RB, last of the starting RBs, etc). Once one player on a tier goes and there is a run on that position, then the next ones may have a premium attached.

Those who skimp and do nothing but look for bargains end up with money left over at the end of the auction and will regret it (see #6 above).

9) Keep track of what players are going for on your cheat sheet. If you see the #10 RB go for $40 and now the #9 RB is up and going once for $25, bid comfortably, knowing he is a bargain at that price. Track how much players are going for above or below your sheet. If the trend is $2 more or less, then compensate.

10) Track everyone's remaining salary cap, positions filled and the bye weeks associated with them. This is going to require some work and math skills, but believe me some other owners will not do this and you will have a competitive edge over them. Do not track who they bought as this is way too hard and is up on a color-coded draft board (if your league has ventured into the 21st century that is). All you really need to know is how much money owners have left and how many players they need to draft. If they have $40 left and 8 players to draft then the most they can bid ($1 minimum bid) on any one player is $33 ($40-(8-1)=33). That means if they spent the league minimum on the other players ($1 x 7=$7), then they could bid up to $33 now on the player nominated. For those of you who are not math majors, this formula might help:

Maximum Possible Bid = Salary cap remaining – (min bid amount x {# players left on roster to be drafted-1}). Avoid needing the same players as those owners with lots of money left. Try to pick up your players in those positions before the big spenders enter the market.

Assuming a $1 minimum bid amount:

Max. bid = Salary cap remaining – number of empty roster spots + 1.

11) Use a cheat sheet built with league rules and teams in mind. The auction values will change if you have 8 teams in the league versus 14 teams. Likewise, the scoring rules will influence how important each position is and the number of starters can influence the value of players. You should start with a good cheat sheet that represents your league to a tee. How? There is software out there that helps you create auction-specific data. You can also use AAV (Average Auction Values), but be wary because your league specifics can change them. If it is a keeper league, that will affect the sheets. Collect as many other sources of cheat sheet values before the draft; try not to use out-of-date magazines and remember those cheat sheets are for certain league sizes, starters, scoring, etc. Try to compare apples to apples and oranges to oranges.

12) Avoid the last tier player at any position. The last starter at RB is the worst. There will inevitably be a premium paid for these players because of the desperation that sets in with a last tier or starter on the auction block. Two otherwise rational owners will start a bidding war for that last RB or QB, so be ready. Don't wait until the last player comes up. Get a midlevel RB or QB and avoid the cutthroat premium pricing on bottom level players.

13) Know where the tiers are in the players and where the drop-off in talent occurs (large price differentials).

14) Talk up players you do not want, be quiet about players you do. Nominate players you do not want and start them out at a good price (you will not get stuck with them; if you do, you got them at a good price). Stay in the bidding on them until within 5% of their fair value. If you are stuck with them, at least you did not overpay for them. When you throw them out, talk them up. For example: L. Jordan's "11 TDs over 1000 yards and 70 catches last year in 14 games. Imagine those numbers in 16 games with more experience in the system."

Use the media to help you get value at auction. Use the media hype about players that are unrealistic (based on stats) to elevate other owner's expectations. This can be done via e-mail or by sharing the story that says Brett Favre will return to form with 30 TDs in 2006. I did not think he would break 20 (he ended up with 18). However, you do not have to tell others that. Let them make their own conclusions.

15) Don't drink and bid. The two do not mix well. Those who drink usually bid too much late in the draft.

16) Don't overspend too early. Have a plan. Spending $180 on four of the first twenty players and having $1 for the rest of your team may not be the best way to spend the next three hours of the auction.

17) Do not buy the backup and then be locked into spending a lot for the starter.

18) Don't skimp on getting the backup (HC) for your studs. They are your insurance policy. Pay the money and get the insurance that comes with them. In many cases it is just a question of a few dollars for the HC.

19) Holding-out pays off. More money in the middle to late rounds gives you all the power but don't wait too long for the value to come. You need to get a few good players before

the mid-rounds. You can be too frugal and save most of your money for the end but by then no good players will be left.

20) Practice, practice, practice – Do as many mock auction drafts as possible. This lets you try out different strategies and get a better feel for how things should go.

21) Know your opponents. If they are from New York, nominate NYG or NYJ players so they bid on them. Maybe you can start a bidding war on them. If they come from Dallas or like the cowboys then they will be willing to pay more for Dallas players. You can communicate with them via e-mail, phone calls or face-to-face. Do whatever you have to to find out who they like (will overvalue) or don't like (they will avoid these players). Looking at their team roster from last year is a great place to start.

22) Know your league history. Have owners been reluctant to bid high early? If so, take advantage of that by starting out with your favorite player at a higher than normal bid. Maybe the others will not bid him up.

23) In leagues with less teams (8-10) or that allow lots of free agency pickups, the value of the TE, K and DEF are less (minimum value) since you can grab one off waivers for bye weeks/injuries, etc. The same can be said for QBs; value them less in those leagues, as well as their backups.

24) Spend most of your money on RB and WR starters and then use minimums for bench players and others. Success comes from spending on the top skill positions (QB1, RB 1-2, WRs 1-3) since they start. Aim for 80% of your budget on these six players. If the above is changed, go less for QB1 and more for RB or WR. Value comes from getting good players for less money at TE1, K1 and DEF1.

25) The closer the draft date is to regular season, the more you should be willing to spend big bucks on superstars. The further away from regular season you draft, the more things that can happen, namely injuries.

26) Build a tracker before the draft. Write down all roster spots, leaving room for player name, bye week and amount spent. Try to plan ahead (remember that budget) and have a column for budgeted amount beside the player slots. This will help you track your progression, never leave money on the board and get all the right positions. (See Appendix B Table B.2 Auction Budget Tracker)

27) In keeper leagues, calculate what other owners have to spend to keep their keepers. Know your opponent's budget. Subtract this amount from their salary cap to get their new cap.

28) Any player valued at $5 or less can be had for $1 late in the draft if he lasts that long. Be wary of $1 bargains in leagues with 14 or more teams. Since there are fewer to come by, plan on spending $2 minimum for all bench players, etc.

29) Expect to pay a premium for the studs. The top players will go for a premium (usually 5-15% for top players at QB, RB and WR). If you want LT, SA or LJ, you will need to pay top dollar. The same goes for starting RBs in most cases. Don't be afraid to pay full price for good RBs.

30) If you see a couple of owners not spending their money early, think about getting key positions you need before they start a bidding war on those last starting players.

31) Avoid the players that are generally overpriced in auctions. Rookies and players coming off career years are overpriced in many cases.

32) Sometimes the first player auctioned in the draft goes for a little less since some are a little nervous. Go get him if you want him. Then watch out for the run on stud RBs and the premiums you will pay.

33) If a player was just purchased for a price over what you thought they should reasonably go for, then nominate a player from the same position that is as good or better than him. You are trying to get owners to overbid early and deplete their budgets.

34) NEVER get in a bidding war. Once the price exceeds FMV, bow out. Only pay a premium for your Top 10 RB.

35) Adjust players' values during the draft based on money left and whether you are overbidding or underbidding. Keep a plus or minus number somewhere to track if more or less overall is being paid. If players are going for more than you expect early, then the remaining should go for less in the last part of the auction.

Common Auction Mistakes

1) Overvaluing players from your favorite team.

2) Nominating players you want early in the draft.

3) Becoming fixated on one specific player and getting into a bidding war. "I have to have P. Manning."

4) Deviating too far from budget or plan. Auctions can start out great, especially if you grab two stud RBs, but then you find that all your cash is spent and you are unable to bid on who you want. You have to sit back and watch and take the leftovers that no one else wants. M. Alstott anyone?

5) Getting too into the auction and forgetting the basics, like bye weeks.

What if I do not have any Auction Values?

Many auction virgins get hung up on the auction and the values for players. They do not want to calculate values or get caught with the wrong numbers. Not to worry. You really do not need numbers, if you wait and let the draft come to you. First, avoid the first 15 players. All-too-often, they are favorites who are overbid. Wait them out. See what the trends are; let the others have the Top 5 RBs, WRs and QBs. If you use a Top 200 overall list, wait until about 15 players have been picked and note their values beside each name. This should give you some idea of how much the other players near them are worth. If you are using a cheat sheet based on positional rankings, wait until two or three players at the same position are bought and then compare their prices to get a feel for others on that list. Always write the sale price by the player's name. Remember: only buy players who are bargains that you need. If you notice that three WRs have gone for the following:

WR1 $40

WR4 $38

WR7 $32

If WR8 is on the bidding block, what do you expect his price to be? Most likely he will go for $30-$31. If he is "going once for $22, going twice for $22," you need to yell out $23 as you raise your hand. If you get him for $23, great, a bargain was had. If you get bumped, keep bidding until you get into the range where he is not a bargain anymore ($30 and above).

If you are totally lost, then remember this. Determine the smartest owner and outbid him by $1 on who he is bidding on and you may get a decent team.

Auction Situations – What if:

1) You get a few great players early in the draft at a discount. What now? Congratulate yourself, sit back and wait for the bargains later in the draft.

2) If everyone is overpaying and you have no one after 25 players have been drafted, DON'T PANIC! Just make sure you adjust values and don't miss your Top 10 RB or RB2 (Top 15 RB).

3) Its late in the draft and you have more money than the others do. What do you do? Target starters that you want to fill your roster and be willing to pay for them since you saved the money for this. No reason to let the only good WR3 left slip away just to save a few dollars this late in the game.

4) If your salary cap is low (you are almost out of money), then look to $2 and $3 players to fill your roster. Do not spend so much that you only have $1 left for players since there is a big difference between a $1 player and a $2 player at the end of the draft.

5) What happens if Shaun Alexander (because of the Madden curse) is going once for $10 less than the expected price? Don't allow this to happen on your watch. If you can get a value player for much less than expected, grab him and then change your strategy. In this case, bid the minimum amount more and keep on bidding until Shaun comes at a more reasonable price. With a little luck, your bidding has given someone else time to come to their senses and jump into the battle for SA at a reasonable price. If you win him, readjust your strategy. Since you should not pay more than he is worth, you will have gotten a bargain and then can adjust your budget and plan to adapt to this new windfall.

6) What if the first 20 players sell for, on average, $2 over your cheat sheet price? That means there is $40 worth of bargain somewhere else in the draft to come. The opposite is true if most of the players have gone for $2 less than you expected, then later on in the draft some others are going to have to be more expensive than you expected. This knowledge alone can help you get who you want.

7) What if the league is paying more than expected for most players? Who do you nominate? The highest priced bust in your opinion. (Someone you do not want but others will pay top dollar to get.) The reverse is true if you see the league is not paying as much (everyone is keeping their cards close to their vest); possibly throw out the special player you want, hoping to take advantage of this low priced field day. It will not last; eventually you will all pay more for others.

Chapter 12 Auction Strategies

There are many different strategies and this chapter covers the mainstream ones. Just having a strategy is the first step to success. Auctions reward prepared owners and ones that can smartly analyze trends and do some **basic** math. The serpentine draft allows strategies to creep in and rewards smart owners, **but if** you have the 12th pick and go back-to-back, it is very hard to implement any smart techniques. In an auction though, things are very fluid. Even whom you nominate to be auctioned is a strategy. It only takes about 25 players being auctioned to determine who is using which strategy. Look at the budgets left and who has which players; this information will help you figure out who is doing what.

How do you know who wins the auction draft and who performed poorly? Look at the rosters. Add up, according to your cheat sheets, how much each team is worth. Also note how much is starter money and how much is bench money. You will see later how different strategies can affect how much starter and bench money is spent. But for now, the team with the most value according to your cheat sheets did the best and the team with the lowest value did the worst. Of course only time will really tell as the season is played out. Now look at the starter numbers. The team with the higher starter numbers may have an edge assuming injuries do not take their toll. Lets look at some strategies that might influence those starter/bench numbers.

Strategy #1 The Triad or (Studs and Duds)

Objective: Get a Top 5 player at QB, RB and WR.

The first strategy is the "triplets at key positions," "studs or duds" or what I call the "triad" strategy. With this theory you grab the best possible stud at quarterback, running back and wide receiver, perhaps Peyton Manning, LT and T Holt. You may only be able to get the stud RB and WR depending on how much they cost, but you get the idea.

To do this you will pay a high price and then you will have to fill in with marginal backups and hopefuls. You will have an explosive team with a star at each of the key positions. You will need a top 5 player from each of the three positions and this will cost you. For example, you may have to spend anywhere from 70-80% of your cap money on the big three. This will leave you with approximately 25% of your money for your other RBs and WR (s), TE, K, DEF and bench. This will also force you to wait until late in the auction to get those backups since that is when your remaining money will be worth more. When other owners have spent most of their salary cap and are down to a few dollars is when your $40-50 (late in the auction) becomes the most valuable. Your chance now will come in the last third of the auction. Having a dollar more than the other teams means you can get that sleeper that you wanted instead of your opponent. Bargains happen, for the most part, at the end of the draft, so this triad strategy calls for big guns early and then the patience to wait for your opportunity late in the draft.

The thinking behind this theory is that your triad is your base of points and the sleepers and backups are used to find a gem or two to propel you past the other teams. Also, why have multiple studs at one position if you cannot start them every week. (Note: a flex player option defeats some of this argument). For example, lets say I have three top

15 RBs. If I can only start two RBs, then many weeks the extra RB is a wasted asset sitting on my bench until a bye week comes for the other RBs. Better to have fewer but better studs at any one position so they are not wasted.

Some say that the extra quality RB is insurance against injuries. Yes, but they come at too high a price. The bye weeks will mean your RB1 and RB2 will miss two games (one each) and thus RB3 (or backup RB) will only play in two games. Why spend 10-15% of your salary cap on a backup? As far as injuries go, protect yourself with handcuffs as some of your backups. If RB1 and RB2's handcuffs (backups) can be bought for much less (and believe me they can if they are HCs for Top 10 RBs) then go with them, that way an injury to your stud RB is not season ending. Here is an example from a 12-team league, $200 cap:

Thumpers (lots of RBs)		Slammers (one stud)	
Rudi Johnson	$44	Larry Johnson	$74
Kevin Jones	$36	Warrick Dunn	$24
Julius Jones	$23	Deuce McAllister	$10
Marion Barber	$7	Michael Bennett	$2
Total Spent	$110	Total Spent	$110

In both cases the amount spent is the same; but which RBs would you want to root for on Sunday? Larry Johnson, the stud, could beat both Rudi and KJ by himself and if W Dunn just does an average day or if Deuce keeps his job, then Slammers run away with the "championship" (as the NFL fantasy football commercial guy says).

Advantages: High reward; better chance of winning and winning big; lineup decisions are much easier. When you have a stud at each position you never bench them. For example, LJ always starts regardless of the matchups. In the above example, Thumpers will lose sleep each week trying to decide if KJ running against a tough Chicago Bears defense will outscore Julius Jones who is running against the league's worst defensive line. But what if Dallas's coach follows through with his threats of starting Marion Barber? These are the lineup decisions that can drive a fantasy football fan mad. Basically if you have several good choices at a position, you have several good chances to bench someone who will outscore your starters. But if you go with the all or nothing stud, that decision is made for you at draft time. Start every stud and then massage the sleeper/bench to take advantage of matchups.

One key advantage of this theory is that few owners attempt it. Many owners are afraid of failure or do not have the knowledge to really be able to dig out the minimum wage players who can make the difference. This strategy is best for winning it all or losing it all. This may be most useful for winning a high stakes contest because if it works, you have a great team capable of beating the other contestants. On the other hand, another strategy might win you the league championship but not be good enough to win over the other league champions in a high stakes contest.

Disadvantages: High risk; may make you look like you do not know much about fantasy football; need to know more about the lower level players who will make up the bulk of the team.

Injuries can cripple your team when you go all or nothing and one or more of your studs get hurt. You may try to cover yourself with his HC but ultimately the HC may not perform as well as your stud or he may not even start (some hotshot rookie may get the chance and run with it, excuse the pun). Another disadvantage is that the draft may not be as fun since you will be spending a lot of your money in the first quarter or first few minutes of the draft. Then when you have spent 75% of your money you will have to agonizingly wait as player after player gets paraded (auctioned) in front of you while you wait for the late part of the draft to snag bench players on the cheap. Not the best way to spend an auction.

These teams also tend to be top-heavy and need lots of waiver wire/free agent work if your long shots are not panning out. Be careful here if there is a transaction fee or limited number of moves allowed per week or season. You may also find that you do not get three good studs. The studs are usually bought for a premium. In other words, if there are three great RBs, each of them may go for 1-15% more than what their real value is. This is a result of supply and demand; 12 teams are all vying for only three stud RBs, five stud WRs and only one stud QB. You get the idea – you may get a top 10 at each position but not a top 5 at all three positions.

Strategy #2 The Cheapskate

Objective: Get other owners to spend all of their money early and often, leaving lots of bargains for you.

Your mission, should you choose to accept it, is to get as many of the other owners to spend as much of their money as soon as possible. Nominating the highest valued players as soon as you can helps this strategy. Usually the big boys (RBs) get bid up the fastest and for a premium.

Everyone dreams of landing the #1 or #2 RB so the bidding will be hot and heavy and a premium will be paid. Note that both the top RBs and top WRs will usually go for a premium over their value, so start at the top of those two positions and nominate the most expensive based on your cheat sheets. Eventually, most of the owners will have depleted a large amount of their cap. Generally the Top 10 RBs and WRs and Top 3 QBs will take half of the available money off the table. Add in another five RBs and WRs, a few Top TEs and more QBs and you have almost 70% ($1500 of $2200 + your $200, assuming a 12-team $200 league) of the money spent on 40 players. You will still have your $200 but every other team will only have around $65. Now you can swoop in. All of those bargains can be yours. The middle to late rounds is the time to spring your trap. But beware: DO NOT WAIT TOO LONG! If you wait too long there may not be any one left at those positions worth having. Usually after about the #15 RB is when you should get your RB filled. This is also when most teams already have one or two RBs, so their budgets may be filled and they are low on cash too. Now you can grab three bargain (Top 20) RBs for the price of a stud (Top 5). Which team has the biggest threat of busting? The team with one star or the team with three good backs? Which team will be decimated with an injury to their #1 RB?

Quarterbacks are a dime a dozen once you get past the top 3. P. Manning is the king but after that, who knows? So again avoid the stud and get 2-3 serviceable top 20 QBs who you can alternate based on matchups. Wide receivers tend to be the same after the top 15, so you can really wait and pick your sleepers as you want them.

Advantages: Do not overspend so you can enjoy the draft for the entire time; great value picks later in draft are yours for the taking; lots of depth on team to protect from injuries/bye weeks; lots of trade bait to improve team later on. Better to have lots of average to above average players.

Disadvantages: Do not get cream of the crop players; lose some fun by not participating too much early in auction. Easy to wait too long and not get best players and could end up not spending all of cap money. Lineup decisions much tougher because of amount of depth on team.

Strategy #3 NE Patriots style (NEP)

OBJECTIVE: Get lots of depth at every position. Good, not great, players everywhere.

The New England Patriots have won three of the last six Super Bowls and they have done it without any superstars. No studs? That's right; no Top 10 players, just lots of really good ones. This strategy avoids the top 10 big players or the big money guys and instead goes for lots of lower ranked players with upside potential. Why? Year after year many of the big name/big money players fail to live up to their costs; even if they do live up to their costs they rarely exceed them (provide more value) because so much is expected of them in the first place that they are bid up so high. Remember the top RBs and WRs usually end up getting a premium added on to their price tag. Even if you do get Larry Johnson for $72 and he does score 16 TDs and rush for 1800 yards, was he worth it for that price when you could have had two other RBs for the same price who could have been used as flex players, bye week replacements or trade bait?

If he performs (and he might not); if he does not get injured (and he could), then was he worth the price? Maybe, but did he exceed the price with his statistics, thus giving you added value? The top guys will rarely go above and beyond what you paid for them to do. You want to get $240 worth of players (mainly starters not on your bench) for $200 of cap money. If you go for studs and duds, you are taking some long shots at coming up with value even if your studs perform. With the NEP style you have a better chance of exceeding other owners.

As a general ROT you will find that about half of the top 12 picks in any year's draft underperform. In 2005, some say that 9 of the 12 (75%) underperformed. Remember the injuries to Priest Holmes, Daunte Culpepper, Deuce McAllister, Domanick Davis and Julius Jones. In 2006, 7 of the top 12 RBs underachieved. Shaun Alexander, Clinton Portis, Ronnie Brown, Carnell Williams, LaMont Jordan, Edgerrin James and Julius Jones were all predicted to be Top 12 players but finished nowhere near. Let's assume the 50% is right. Why does this happen? The main reason is injuries but also coaching changes, other player injuries, etc. Do you think Chad Johnson will be affected if Carson Palmer's backup (Anthony Wright) starts to throw him the ball? Sure. Football is not as predictable as we think. There are a limited number of games to perform and weather, illness, opponent's strengths and many other unknowns all affect the outcomes.

So 6 of those 12 golden boys (studs) are going to underperform, some will perform up to standard and one might overachieve. Why take a chance on 1 in 12 doing better than expected and providing value? Why risk 6 of 12 not performing up to what you paid for them? Think of it this way: If you pay $72 for LJ based on his being expected to rush for 20 TDs, and he only rushes for 15 TDs, you overpaid for him. Your return on your investment is smaller than if you bought S. Jackson for $47, expected him to get 12 TDs and he scored 15 of them. With him, your ROI (return on investment) increased above the expected amount.

That is why a team with plenty of solid players and a deep bench (like the Patriots) can win championships.

Not only will you be able to handle bye weeks and injuries easier with a team that has many good players, you can also use them as trade bait later in the season. Those same bye weeks and injuries that you have handled so well will be hitting some other owner (a studs and duds strategy team) hard; especially if it is his stud that goes down due to injury. Now you can trade a benched RB who helped you through a bye week (and is no longer going to be used) to another team to help your team get that WR or TE who has blossomed.

Another way to look at it is, "There is no free lunch." If you get a stud, you are probably overpaying for him. No one player is a sure thing, so why overpay? Target RBs and WRs. Get a middle-of-the-road QB and grab your TE, K and DEF at low prices. Get lots of solid RBs and WRs to ride out the rough times.

Advantages: If one key player goes down, your team is not crippled. Another advantage is having more participation in the draft than the cheapskate or studs and duds strategies. You keep everyone else honest and do not allow any steals. Safe and effective strategy, great for beginners.

Disadvantages: Lineup decisions are even harder since you have two or three equally good players for each starter. If you are the kind of person who beats themselves up every Monday morning when you realize that you started the wrong TE and missed out on points, do not use this strategy. You will rarely maximize your points simply because you have so much talent to choose from, but hopefully your season average will be higher than another owner with another strategy. Some call this the "playing to lose" strategy since you are more likely to be middle-of-the-road if players do not pan out, as you have no studs to fall back on.

Strategy #4 The Homer

Build your team around your favorite NFL team or the team that you think is going to be the most explosive. For example, P. Manning ($40), J. Addai ($34), M. Harrison ($40) R. Wayne ($23), D. Clark ($3) A. Vinatieri ($5), IND DEF ($5). For $150 you can have the entire IND team and still have some money left over for RB2, WR3 and backups.

Advantages: Get to root for same team. Always know how they are doing (and you are doing) from their score. If they are your favorite team you can enjoy double the fun.

Disadvantages: On bye week you are dead in the water. If your favorite team fails so does fantasy team. You have a real roller coaster of a season. Nothing is more painful than NFL and fantasy team loss in same week.

Strategy #5 Use no strategy at all

Just wait and let the bargain come to you, but do not be locked into "I have to have a top RB" or "I have to have everyone from the same explosive offense" or "I have to wait till the end of the draft." Just watch the first few players auctioned and if they are at or near their value, let them go; don't bite. See what is happening. If they are going for more than what you think they should, great! That means you will get some bargains later on. If they are going for much less, you should have been bidding and gotten some of these cheap values and now that will determine which way to go.

Strategy #6 Buy one stud and build around him

This is probably the most common strategy employed by owners. This can be a combination of the NEP and the triad. But instead of getting 2-3 studs with the Triad, you get one stud and then try to build lots of depth around the rest of the team.

Advantages: You get to be involved in the entire auction. You can pick which stud to target or not. Lots of bargains at the end of the draft.

Disadvantages: One stud may not be enough to win it all. An injury to your one stud can be crippling.

How do you find the right Strategy?

Weigh the pros and cons of each. Which one is easiest for you to implement? Which one suits your style? Which is better for your lineup decisions? Do you want easy, medium or hard decisions? Try all of them out in mocks. After deciding on a strategy to employ at the auction, determine what players you should be able to fill your roster with and then add up your starter' projected fantasy points and divide by 16 to determine a weekly team score. Is this enough to win the championship? Make the playoffs? Is this the best strategy?

Is there an optimal strategy?

No; auction strategy is part of your own personality (aggressive, balanced or conservative).

Play to Win

Playing to win means taking chances, like you would using the triad strategy. Take chances on WR and QB with either aging talent or up-and-coming players, since that is where the value is and you will not have much money left over after spending 35% on a single RB.

Use Auction Prices to Evaluate Trades

You can compare draft picks or players in trades with auction values. If you are offered overall pick 9 (1.09) for picks 35 (3.11) and 41 (4.05), do you accept it (see Appendix C

Trade Analyzer)? You can look at the worth of the players in your overall auction cheat sheet. Are the two player's values at 35 and 41 worth the ninth player overall? The ninth player is projected to go for \$42. The 35th player is projected at \$22; the 41st player is projected at \$20. So \$42 is a fair price for those two players and the 9th pick is equal to the 35th and 41st picks. The trade analyzer also showed the trades are equal; 288 points to 152+136=288.

What Determines your Dynamic Strategy?

1) Players you have drafted so far
2) Other owners tendencies
3) Players available
4) Your remaining salary cap
5) Your opponents salary cap
6) Amount already bid on a player
7) General value of players left in draft

Auction cheat sheet values do not reflect the needs of your team. The second you win P. Manning as your QB, all of the QBs values should fall in relationship to your team because you do not need another great/good QB (assuming you only start one QB). My utility theory incorporates this and all other dynamics above. You'll have to wait for my next book.

Unique Tactics

1) Raise your bid by more than the minimum. If minimum increments are \$1 raise your bid on the QB from \$5 to \$8. This usually indicates a strong desire to win a player. The rationale is that you want him and want to force other owners out fast or they risk you dumping the player on them. If you use this strategy beware as you may find other owners dumping onto you.

2) Think about position battles. If there are two clear-cut favorites for RB fighting it out; try to get both since they will be discounted due to the position battle. With both, you will have the starter and a HC in case of injury.

3) Unexpected nominations of players with a lower profile will sometimes slip by, especially in leagues with a few inexperienced owners. You can sometimes get a player you want for the minimum bid if others are not paying attention or don't know who he is. An unknown rookie WR who impressed at camp may be such a candidate.

4) If you do get stuck with a player, don't panic. Announce that you are glad to get him cheaper than you thought you would. Note which other owners were in the bidding with you and see if you can trade the unwanted player to them later.

5) If in a league that allows leftover money to go to free agency and that is all the money allowed for FAAB, then budget 20% of your salary cap for that purpose. Don't overspend at auction and end up not able to pick up free agents when injuries or suspensions arise. Unless you are using the triad strategy of getting 2-3 studs then you can forget about saving money for FAAB.

6) Mix it up a bit. If every player you nominate is someone you do not bid on, the other owners will catch on. Throw a curveball every now and pull a "crazy Ivan". The same goes for bidding. Don't have any "tells" such as folding hands over chest, adjusting glasses, etc. On some players bid early and often, on others wait until bids have just about petered out before jumping in at the last second.

7) At the end of the auction it may become more of a snake draft as many teams will have complete rosters or be so low on money that they can only spend the minimum. This is when you nominate or buy your sleepers.

Auction Actions

Reading your opponents (visual and verbal tells):

In an earlier chapter I alluded to the fact that an auction is like combining the fantasy football draft with poker night. Just like in poker where you can tell the situation of your opponents by reading their mannerisms (tells), you can do the same at an auction. There are bluffers, risk takers, and players who will only ride sure things. These characteristics will tip you off to whether or not your opponent is bidding a player up, wants him desperately or is just playing around and feeling you out. One of your strategies is to bid up or bump up the price of players you do not want, think are going to bust or be overpriced. You do this so that they pay more for the player now, leaving you in a better position later in the auction (in case a bidding war breaks out).

For example, a facial expression may give away the fact that you are bidding up the price of a player they really want. A smile or frown may give away that you are hurting their strategy just as a clenched fist or turning red might offer the same non-verbal message. Exasperation or shaking of the head may be an indicator that he is about to abandon the bidding for this player. A good owner never gives these signs away (and sometimes can use them intentionally to decoy his opponents). A verbal indicator may be a growl or a higher voice inflection when bidding. This may indicate a determined owner who can be bumped up on a favorite player.

What about bluffing? It is done in poker but is it also done in the auction draft? You bet. Although it can't happen in an online draft, bluffing occurs quite often during the course of a live auction. How can you tell who is bluffing and who is not? You will never know 100% of the time unless you have some real rookies who wear their NYG E. Manning jerseys to the draft and wear all their other emotions on their sleeve. On the other hand, if an owner appears to look a little too disinterested he may drive the price up as a bluff. A good indicator which is not a visual or verbal tell is the status of his team. Is he close to his max bid? Does he need a player at this position? Does he have more critical spots to fill? These are all indications that a bluff may be perpetrated on you. If so, try to back out and slip the albatross around his neck. Be sure to smile and say "he's yours," and watch his reaction when he realizes he just got his third TE. Ouch! If you really want this player, simply knowing your opponent is bluffing can help you. Try giving some tells of your own when you have outbid him. Act as if you might be losing patience with this player. Act as if you will not go higher. A simple "one more bid" muttered under your breath with a sigh or a shake of your head after you bid, indicating some remorse, may scare him into backing off. Of course, if you have been playing with the guys in your league for years, these indicators will be obvious. Does Matt always drink his beer quickly when nervous? How about John crunching ice loudly when bluffing. You get the idea. I don't want to give away all my local league's secrets. As far as keeping your tells (and you have them, I assure you) a secret, try just staring down at your notes when you bid or hide behind that laptop screen.

Bidding Strategies

There are three main bidding strategies. The first is to only bid on players you want on your team. Never try to bid up a player because on occasion you will get yourself stuck (you will win him when you thought the other owner would go a little higher). The second strategy is to bid up undervalued players so that your opponents do not get a steal. This involves bidding on players if they are undervalued by 10% or more. An example would be Chester Taylor going for $15 when you have him at $25 on your cheat sheet. At $15 he is $10, or 40,% less than what he should be valued at. In this case, before he is sold bid him up and be willing to go to $23 (only an 8% discount). The third strategy is to bid up all players, especially players you think your opponents really want. This is a dangerous game and can involve having a player dropped on you but it is very fun and challenging.

Most bidding eventually comes down to two owners. If three or more owners are bidding (excluding myself) then I am fairly comfortable bidding in this environment, knowing that when it comes down to two others and myself I need to pack it in, if I do not want to get stuck with the player. Look at what the other owners already have. Do they have a great TE? Why would they be bidding on another one? Perhaps (shock) they are trying to drive the price up. Know what the other owners have and need, to determine if they are just bumping the price up as you would do. Finally, check to see what his maximum bid is. Remember the formula: (Maximum Possible Bid = Salary cap remaining—(min bid amount x {# players left on roster to be drafted-1} this will let you know how high he can possibly go.

When bidding, jump in on players you want at the end of the bidding process. Why waste energy bumping someone by $1 every time? Just sit back and feign disinterest until the bid is "going once," then jump in with $1 more. You have just saved yourself some voice and not given away your intentions until the latest possible moment. By the same token, always increase your bid by the minimal amount. Most owners know how much they are willing to pay for a player so if you increase it by anything more than the minimal amount it may put you so far above that you win the player but could have had him for less. Wait to get into the bidding and increase only the minimum amount.

How to calculate your own auction values

1) Calculate how much money is to be spent above the minimum bid. It will be total money to be spent minus minimum bid per player or (# Teams x (Salary cap-Roster size) =money to be spent)

12 Team league, $200 cap, 20-man roster

12 x (200-20)= 12 x 180=$2160 to spend on players above the minimum bid.

2) Determine x values for all baselines consistent for the number of players to be drafted at those positions. Add all X values up. (For example: the Top 24 QB X values plus the Top 50 RB values plus Top 50 WR, etc.)

Divide money to be spent by x values drafted.

$2160/4000 X points =each X point is worth $0.54=X point auction value

3) Multiply a players X value by the X point auction value (determined in step 2)

So LT at 150 XPs is worth $81 (150 x $.54= $81)

Generalizations

– Most owners love RBs (thus more likely to get in a bidding war on them).

– Obtain Average Auction Values (AAV) for all the players who will be drafted. AAV is what value the player is going for in other auctions.

– Many owners will overspend early, so value at middle and end of draft can save you pennies. People do this because the money is burning a hole in their pocket.

– Better teams have a co-manager who calculates what other teams have in their salary cap and what positions they need and have filled.

– Avoid the Top 5 RBs and the premiums they demand. Focus on getting two of the Top 5-15 RBs at a good price. Get one of the Top 10 RBs as your RB1. If RBs are going for a premium, suck it up and pay it to get a Top 10 RB. Without him you will be too far behind and have to make it up with great WRs.

– Nominate the 4th-6th best kicker or defense for the minimum bid. If someone outbids then they paid too much for them. If not, you get your kicker or defense for a good price and can use the $1 saved to bump up another position.

– If league does not require a kicker, don't draft one. Pick one up off waiver wire if there will be plenty to choose from, especially if draft is many weeks before season starts. This is especially good if FAAB is different money than auction salary cap.

– Use cheat sheets to make sure the money adds up. 10-team leagues with $200 cap and 16-man roster means that the Top 160 players should equal $2,000.

– As a rule of thumb, if you have the most money halfway through the auction, you should be in good shape.

– Do at least one, and I suggest several, mock drafts before the real thing. Several Internet sites make this much easier than it used to be. For example, Fantasyauctioneer.com lets you do mocks against 11 online players and lets you join free mock auctions (or snake drafts for that matter). While some participants will make a "mock" of the mock auction because they are not playing for real money, in most cases it will be filled with dedicated owners wanting to practice. Xpertsports.com allows mock drafts to be scheduled and preformed on their website, but I have found them to have fewer auctions than some of the others. Try out any site that will allow you to do mock auctions. It will give you more confidence and let you see what players are going for. Mock AAV will let you know what the average going price is for players in mocks. But mock auctions may be of less utility than a traditional draft, because many times WHO is nominated can have more of an affect on strategy, especially end game strategy.

– Remember that those recommended auction values are just that, <u>recommended</u>. Auctions take on their own shape once started. So don't get excited if Larry Johnson goes for more than what you think he should or if J. Shockey goes for less. Knowing why and taking advantage of it are the keys.

– If you "play to win" you will need to take some chances, such as 75% of cap on three studs, making starting RBs 60% of budget or spending 35% of cap on a stud RB.

– Pay high prices for starters but not for backups, who will ride the bench most of the season. Budget most of your money (90%) to starters. Only about 10% should go to bench players.

– Keep your mouth shut most of the time. Do not give out information that other owners do not know. When B. Roethlisberger is nominated and someone says, "Yeah but he just got in a motorcycle accident;" this is giving free information to others who have not done their homework. They have taken any advantage that others have gained by research and given it away. It is different in a traditional draft since draft position determines who gets drafted, but in an auction it is every man for himself. If you want to prop up a player that you hate by saying something like "I hear J. Jones is the man this year," be my guest, it is a harmless rumor. But providing research for others should not happen at the draft. In fact, that is what makes auctions great. It really is every owner for himself.

– Know your competition; is anyone a Homer? Do they wear their favorite team's shirt to the draft and always take those players, sometimes too early or for too much? Does anyone hate another team so much that they will never draft them? One guy I play with is a diehard Cowboys fan. He would rather die then draft a Redskins player. I know he is not serious when he starts the bidding for a Washington Redskins player.

Budgets

Use table 12.1 for ROT percentages to create your budget. It is based on starting 1 QB, 2 RB, 3 WR, 1 TE, 1 K, 1 DEF and 18 player rosters.

Table 12.1 – Auction Values Based on Strategy

Position	Aggressive	Balanced	Conservative	
QB1	3%	6	10	
RB1	35	30	20	
RB2	25	20	15	
RB3	2	3	5	
RB4	1	1	3	
RB5	.5	1	1	
RB6	.5	.5	1	
WR1	15	15	15	
WR2	7	8	10	
WR3	3	2	2	

WR4	.5	1	1	
WR5	.5	.5	.5	
WR6	.5	.5	.5	
TE1	1.5	5	10	
K1	.5	1	1	
DEF1	.5	2	1	
QB2*	2	3	3	
TE2*	.5	.5	1	

* Some owners will choose not to draft a QB2 or TE2 and this opens up more room for RB or WR sleepers. If you cannot use the waiver wire to add TEs, Ks and defenses to avoid bye weeks then I suggest removing RB6 and WR6 and replacing them with K2 and DEF2 at those same values.

1) If you will only start 2 WRs then decrease the percentage from WR3.

2) If your league has a flex player then bump up the RB3 and WR4 numbers at the expense of something else.

Setting a Budget

RBs will always have the biggest budget (up to 70%), followed by WR and QB. K and DEF generally have the smallest amount budgeted. The typical budget ranges per position are 5-20% (10-15% average) for QB. RB is 30-70% (50-60% is most common). WR is 20-40% (less if you only start two). TEs only warrant 1-10%. Kickers and defenses get even less at 1-4%. Of course, it all depends on how aggressively or conservatively you want to play. A conservative plan says no player should cost more than 20% of your budget (this avoids the superstars who can cost up to 40% of your budget), but it may leave you without a Top 10 RB. A very generic ROT is 10-15% for QB, 50-60% for RB, 25-35% for WRs (less if you only start two, this is for three WRs) and the minimum for TE/K/DEF and bench. Use the following tried and true formula for starters: 1 x QB 5-8%; 2 x RB 60%; 3 x WR 30%; the minimum for all other positions/backups (2-5%).

How do you convert the percentages into dollars?

First calculate your position budget (salary cap x percentage). Two RBs are 60%, thus $200 salary cap x .6=$120. The next step is to allocate that money to every player in that position. This means either two $60 RBs or one more expensive and then you adjust the other to fit in your budget. Some suggest spending 35-40% on a stud ($70-$80) and the remainder on the best RB#2 you can get . The WRs have 30%, so $60. Use 15-20% ($30-$40) on a top WR and then the rest on the other two. Remember your backups will need to be considered too, but many owners will concentrate on starters first, then scrape some money up for bench players.

Building a Budget for an Auction

I include two good methods below for creating a budget. The first starts with a strategic plan and goes from there. The other uses previous data on champions as a starting point. I prefer the second method. Imitation is the highest form of compliment.

A) Strategy Based

Your strategy is trying to get three top players; a triad.

Start with your cheat sheets. Add up the top 10 player's values at each position. For example, the top 10 RB values equal $580. Divide that by 10 and you have a good value for a top 10 pick. In this case 580/10 =$58. Another way would be to look at the #5 RBs value. In both cases add a premium of 10% to the RB and WR value since the top players at each position generally go for 5-15% more than their value. So our $58 RB is now expected to go for $64.

Now the fun begins. Determine how much you want to pay at each position. As mentioned earlier, a good ROT is 50-60% for RB, 10-15% for QB, 25-35% for WRs (less if you only start 2) and the minimum for TE/K/DEF and bench. Tweak those percentages based on your scoring rules (are QBs worth more because TDs are 6 points?) and starting positions. If you have a flex player that can be a WR/TE only, bump up the WR or TE budget. If a flex player is RB/WR only, you might add some to both categories or create a separate flex budget (10%). Also look at how the league auctions have gone in the past. What is the historical money breakdown by positions? This is not something you have to use but it will serve as a guide.

Let's use 10% QB, 55% RB, 30% WR and 5% others/slop.

With a $200 cap league that means $20 QB, $110 RB, $60 WR and $10 others.

We have already determined how many players at each position we need. Total of 20 players: Starters are 1 QB, 2 RB, 3 WR, 1 Flex (RB/WR/TE), TE, K and DEF. So we plan on drafting 2 x QB, 7 x RB, 8 x WR, 1 x TE, 1 x K, 1 x DEF.

Our flex player will come mainly from RB or WR, so the RB budget is 5% higher and we will need a better RB3 and WR4 than normal.

Next subtract the top value, determined above, from your budget and account for backups. So $110 RB–our stud at $64= $46 for RB2, RB3 (flex) and four backups. The four backups will need at least $1 each and probably $1 more for caution, so let's budget $8. We now have $38 (46-8) for RB2 and RB3. Split evenly it would be $19 each, so let's use $22 for RB2 and $16 for RB3.

Now look at your cheat sheet to see who you can get for that kind of money.

Slammers get Steven Jackson ($64 #5 RB overall), Tatum Bell ($20 #24 RB overall) and C. Dillon ($16 #27 overall to fill in during bye weeks and maybe flex a bit). They have spent $100 and that leaves $10 for four backups so we may be able to get a RB4 as a sleeper, like Marion Barber for $6 with upside potential, before getting HCs for RB1 and 2.

Kickers and defenses are usually bought at the end of the draft for league minimums so do not get caught up in the early rush to bid one of the top ones up. I will bid $2 (or $1 over the minimum) for a K or DEF I ranked high, since this is probably what I have earmarked for them anyway and I like going for one of each and not using a backup until I need it for the bye week.

B) Historically based

1) Calculate how much each position is worth. Look at the last few championship teams and determine how many points of their total came from each position. Example; Team A had 1000 points and 150 came from QB, 400 came from 2 RBs, 300 came from 2 WRs, 50 each from TE/K and DEF. So of the 1000 points, 15% came from QB, 40% came from RB, 30% came from WR, and 5% each from TE, K and DEF. Assuming a $200 budget, I now have a rough estimate of $30 for QB, $80 for RB, $60 for WR and $10 for the other three positions.

2) Consider supply versus demand. Adjust your budget based on rookies or retirements, etc. Will there be more clear #1 RBs this year or more RBBC? Are more TEs performing better? RBs are more coveted and have less depth. QBs are a dime a dozen after top 3. Ks and DEFs are crapshoots. Adjust budget so now QB loses $10 since so deep (now at $20). Same goes for K and DEFs as they lose $5 each (now at $5 per position). And the extra $20 goes to RB (now at $100).

3) Plan for backups. Bench players need to be bought too. Figure out how many bench players you will need at each position and then plan a little over the minimum for them, such as $2 (if $1 minimum). I need a QB#2, three RBs, three WRs, a TE2, I will skip K and DEF and use flex scheduling. Then I have eight bench players at $2 each, that is $16. I am going to bump up the QB#2 amount to $5 because I know he will be critical since I am going for a late-round QB to start with.

4) Plan for starters. For positions that have more than one starter, you need to decide how to spend your budget. Do you want to go for the stud and then some cheap fill-ins or do you want to go for more depth? Example: I have budgeted $100 for RBs. I need two starters and one good RB3 as a bye week fill-in or flex player and then another three backups. Planning on $2 each for backups leaves me with $94 for RB1, RB2 and RB3. A stud RB goes for $70 or more so I elect to pass on him and go with a Top 10 RB for $45, leaving me $49 which I allocate to a Top 15 RB for $35. The other $14 is for a RB3, which should get me one of the last starters in the Top 30.

5) Spread money for each position. Look at where you can save some money and where you want to spend a little extra. I have $5 each for K and DEF but if I really do only draft one each and do the add/drop based on matchups then I do not need to spend more than $1 or $2. I can move that money to WRs and now I have $2 for Ks and DEFs and $6 more for WRs.

The result is $200 to spend on 2 QB, 6 RB, 6 WR, 2 TE, 1 K and 1 DEF.

QB1 $15, QB2 $5 (Total $20)

RB1 $45, RB2 $35, RB3 $14, RB4/5/6 $2 each (total $100)

WR1 $30 WR2 $20 WR3 $10 WR4/5/6 $2 each (Total $66)

TE1 $8 TE2 $2 (Total $10)

K1 $2

K2 $2

Grand Total of $200

This budget should get me a good RB and WR, a decent QB, a good TE and a kicker and defense that I want, by raising the minimum bid once. If I wanted to go with a stud RB for $75-$80 then my budget would have to be changed radically, but I could do it, I would just have to realize that my other players are going to be worth less since I have less to spend. By the same token, as the draft goes I will need to adjust prices and budget based on what is spent. If RBs are being overbid I can save money and get great value at WR, QB or TE.

Chapter 13 Start/Bench Strategy

In many of the most competitive leagues, the draft can be a mere formality as owners use all of their tricks to assemble their teams and get sleepers. It is not until the starting lineup decisions are made that the winners and losers are determined. In fact, no one team dominates in a truly competitive league. It is the points scored weekly from submitting lineups that determines who makes the playoffs. Roster management is about making informed decisions. As John Madden said, with regards to start/bench decisions: "It is a lot easier to stand pat than make a change." There is nothing worse in fantasy football than leaving points on your bench that could have won the game.

Bye weeks mean shuffling players from the inactive list to fill gaps left open as your normal starters have to be benched. The problem is, if you have a flex position and you use your flex player as a normal RB, then you still have to find a player to fill the flex position. In 2006, bye weeks meant that weeks 3-9 saw an absence of some players. Most weeks only had four teams on a bye, but weeks 6 and 7 had six teams on a bye. Those weeks, known as "black Sundays," had owners really scrambling to field a team as 6 of the 32 possible starting RBs and QBs stayed home and watched football on TV. So if you were in a 14-team league that started two RBs, somebody did not have a starter. (32-6=26 starting RBs; 2 x 14=28 needed). It gets even worse when you factor in a flex position. There were quite a few teams with WRs as flex players in those weeks.

Quite possibly the best lineup advice is to watch the football games (and the pre-game shows); especially the Sunday early games, Sunday and Monday Night games and any Thursday or Saturday games. Sometimes breaking news is revealed just before kickoff and can affect your lineup decisions. For example, Player B will miss the game due to a death in his family, or suspension, etc. Perhaps you are starting Player B; now you can bench him and start someone else in his place. You can save yourself some missed FPs by staying on top of the action at hand. Perhaps your WR was catching passes from Player B, now Player X will be tossing those passes to him this week. Maybe you will want to rethink your lineup decisions based on Player X at QB.

Missing a game is different than "not starting a game." Do not overreact to news that your player is not starting. Sometimes coaches will not start a player due to their being late for a team meeting or some other infraction. It is the coach's way of installing some discipline. The player will not be announced as the starter and may miss the first series, but if he is a marquee player (and he should be if he is on your team and starting) then he will get his PT (playing time). In fact, he may have a great game trying to impress the coaches that he earlier angered.

Lineup Rules

Rule #1 – Never Bench Your Studs

There are four types of players: studs, quality, fillers and duds. Generally your studs will be your top 2 or 3 draft picks. So they will be your RB1 and WR1 and maybe RB2 and thus a Top 10 RB or WR and maybe a Top 5 QB. The quality players are your RB3 and WR2. The filler players are fairly consistent players who can perform when faced with the correct matchup. The duds are players who you start if you have to, but who you do not count on too much. There is a reason why studs were drafted that high. Larry Johnson and Peyton Manning should never be benched unless they are on a bye week or are hurt and thus doubtful or out for the game (or unless they lose their job; fat chance). Why? Simple – they are your highest scoring players (that is why you drafted them so high in the first place) and thus they will score the most for you over the season. Do not worry about matchups. They are going to provide you big points if you start them week in and week out. Start them and forget about them. The minute you bench one because he is playing against the best defense is the minute he scores three TDs and has a career high day. Trying to time their big games is like trying to time the stock market. DON'T DO IT. Consider your studs your index mutual funds and let them ride. If the stud has a slow start or a game or two below average, rest assured that he will return to the mean eventually. You just do not want to have him on your bench when he does. If you try to time the big games and the bad games you will be burned more times than you win, so start them no matter what. Some experts think this is just advice for the lazy. They proclaim that you should always start the best players for the week based on research. If you dig into the numbers some, you will find out who your stud is and who is not. Do not overanalyze the matchups. You will not lose sleep by starting your studs and them having an off day. You will lose sleep if you bench LT for Reuben Droughns and LT scores four TDs.

Rule #2 – Use Las Vegas odds to help with close calls

Use the Vegas odds for the lesser player (WR, K, DEF) decisions. Let's take kickers. If you have a choice between two kickers, who do you take? First look at the Las Vegas odds for both games they are playing. Jason Elam is one kicker as Denver plays Oakland. The other kicker is David Akers as Philadelphia plays Washington. Look at the over/under and then who is favored in both games.

Den -3 Oak +3 O/U 37

Phil -7 Wash +7 O/U 47

For those unfamiliar with these terms, Denver is favored to win by 3 points. Philadelphia is favored to win by 7 points. The over/under refers to how many total points (TPs) both teams are expected to score in the game. The higher the over/under, the higher scoring is expected. If a player's team is in a higher scoring game and they are favored by a large margin, then Las Vegas expects their team to score a lot.

The bookies expect Denver to win 20-17 and expect Philadelphia to win 27-20. David Akers should have one more extra point than Jason Elam. Obviously the bookies do not know exactly what will happen but they do odds for a living and thus the over/under should be quite accurate. The over/under says that they expect Philadelphia to score more points than Denver because Philadelphia is favored by more points and the over/under is higher for their game. All else being equal, go with Akers today. If you need to decide between two equal players who will just be a bye week fill-in, choose the player scheduled to play in the higher scoring game (higher over/under score). Be sure to look at the amount a favored team is predicted to win by. There may be instances when a lower over/under game will provide a higher team score because of the lopsidedness of the predicted victory margin.

Rule #3 – Matchups (Defenses your players will face)

Look at a defense's rushing yardage allowed; passing yardage allowed and points allowed. If the defense is good versus the run and the offense gets out in front a lot, then opponents will be passing more against that defense and if they run-prevent a lot in the fourth quarter, their passing yardage may be higher than most.

– SOS or FPs allowed per position are two of the more common tools used to determine who to start.

Rule #4 – Field Conditions

This does not address weather conditions. We will get into that later. This is simply the condition of some of the playing fields in the league and their tendencies. For example, Giants Stadium, which hosts both the NY Giants and NY Jets (on differing weeks, of course) is known for cold, strong, nasty swirling winds which tend to hurt QB numbers. Chicago is another place where winds hurt QBs, and to some extent kickers, but the kicking problem is due to proximity to water. The wind and water effect (heavier air) leads to the ball not going as far. Pittsburgh's Heinz Field, Chicago's Soldier Field and Jacksonville's Alltel Stadium are the worst to kick from due to their proximity to water. Heinz Field kickers hate it. Swirling winds, one end enclosed, one end open, a dirt field and the fact that many other football teams use it ensures that it is a rough surface. The cold of Soldier Field does not help either. A football only weighs 1.4 pounds so imagine what a strong wind can do to a kicker's accuracy. Denver is good because the high altitude makes the ball go further. Miami is difficult because it can be windy and, here is the important part, because of the infield dirt. Early in the season if football overlaps with baseball (Florida Marlins), then the infield dirt is a poor surface to have to kick off of. Surprise, surprise; domes are the best places to kick from. Be leery of kickers in Chicago, Pittsburgh, Jacksonville or Miami and QBs in New York or Chicago.

Kickers kick on either grass or an artificial surface.

1) Grass – nature's turf.

2) Field Turf – This is the new generation of synthetic turf. Field Turf is a brand name but has become synonymous with the other turf. To be precise, it is a synthetic earth (ground up rubber) with synthetic grass (polyethylene) (Field Turf and Momentum Turf are similar and can be found in NO or BALT). Opposed to Astroplay and RealGrass which use rubber bits for the earth.

Studies indicate that Momentum Turf is the best for kicking percentages and thus more FPs.

Rule #5 – Weather Conditions

Before you read anymore do yourself a big favor and bookmark the weather channel NFL weather page as a favorite. Go to www.weatherchannel.com and select tab "In Season" and then "National Football League." You can now see the temperatures and weather for game time. If you click on the game, you will see a detailed forecast. Use this as a reference tool. Winds will affect QBs, WRs and kickers. Swirling winds are the worst. If it is a constant wind from the same direction, QBs and kickers can compensate, but when the wind changes direction and speed frequently, all bets are off; unless your defense is playing there, then that is a good thing!!!

Of course, domes neutralize whatever the outside weather is like.

Do not be too worried about snow. Many WRs love snow because they know where they are going and can use it to their advantage. WRs will also slip less. They can adjust a bit. The defensive player will slip more because he is reacting and does not know where he is going. However, be wary of heavy snow since this will affect the ability of the QBs and kickers to put the ball a long way down field. Rain is the most difficult weather condition to take into account. Joe Theisman says that rain affects some quarterbacks and does not affect others. He says he was not bothered by rain because of where he gripped the ball. The balls are taken in and out and dried off after plays and receivers and QBs try to keep their hands dry. The effect it has on vision is probably most dramatic, as a heavy downpour limits down field views. The players have different cleats for differing weather conditions so it does not affect footing as much as it did in the old days. The 5/8 cleat has more traction, therefore is better for a sloppy field, but it does make players slower. Some RBs seem to prefer a wet track, others do not. Last year S. Alexander proved that snow is no problem for him. He returned from injury in week 11 of 2006 and rushed for 37 yards. Then in week 12, in a sleet/snowstorm at SEA on MNF, he rushed for 201 yards on 40 carries. This accounted for more yards than his entire 2006 season up to that point. Cold weather can affect an entire team, especially if it is a dome team or a warm weather team traveling to a road site that has particularly cold weather. This effect usually becomes more prevalent in mid to late November and throughout December. Good examples are Miami and Jacksonville when they go on the road in December. Cold weather (and I mean really cold weather) is great for RBs, especially those who will get many carries in the second half. By then, the RBs are warming up and the defenders are wearing down. Cold is especially good if it is a night game because it gets colder as the game goes on. Defenders start to tackle poorly due to the cold and the RB gets better and better.

WIND = QB, WR and K problems

SNOW = Good for WRs and QBs

COLD = Bad news for dome teams and warm weather teams when on the road, great for RBs

Outdoor stadiums in northern climates: Buffalo, Chicago, Cincinnati, Cleveland, Denver, Green Bay, New England, New York (Giants and Jets), Philadelphia, Pittsburgh, Seattle

Rule # 6 Check the Injury Report

Do not start doubtful or out players; simple straightforward advice. See Chapter 24 – Injuries.

Rule #7 Coaches comments

Ignore 90% of what comes out of any given coach's mouth. These kind, concerned gentlemen will lie to you if you believe everything they say. They do not want to tell you who they will start and who is too hurt to play because that gives the enemy (their opponent) valuable information. If anything, they want to put out as much misinformation as possible to confuse their opponents as to their intentions on game day. That, unfortunately, also affects you.

Rule #8 Division Rivalries

If two teams are meeting for the second time in a season, look back at what happened last meeting. Did one QB explode? Was it high scoring? Did the kickers kick lots of FGs while the offenses struggled? Does a certain player always seem to "get up" for a game versus this opponent? Look at games in the previous year. Kansas City versus Denver always seems to be a high scoring game.

Rule #9 Ride the Streaks

If your WR has scored in four straight games, why take him out? Let him ride until he produces a zero, then evaluate why he did not produce. WRs, especially once they connect with a QB on a TD several games in a row, can have a connection that lasts a long time. Statistical trends will start to break out after the first few weeks (weeks 4-5). Watch QBs and RBs early. If they are off to a slow start after the first two games, they are unlikely to do well for the rest of the season. (Exceptions to this rule are the top studs in QBs and RBs.) Some WRs start slower than others but are usually able to recover. With a QB or RB, if they are well below their average after week 2, you may have reason to panic. Look for trends (hot streaks). QBs like to throw to the same people. If your WR3 has caught a TD the past four games, you might consider moving him into the WR2 position. If a RB fumbles early, he may get the hook. If he does well, a coach will ride him till he cools off.

Rule #10 Avoid players on teams with late games if league uses a "Roster Lockdown" (SD, SF, AZ, DEN, OAK, SEA)

If these players are game-time decisions you will not have enough information to make an informed choice on them.

Rule #11 Tiebreakers for Toss-Ups

Use the following only if you have used other methods (such as Las Vegas odds or weather) to determine who to start and you have two or three players who are all about the same and you do not know who to start. The first discriminator is home field advantage. If they are all equal, the players at home should have a little advantage. That is why the NFL odds-makers give roughly 3 points to the home team in their odds assessments. So go with the home player. He has had better sleep, has not had to travel and is playing in front of his hometown crowd. If he cannot get fired up for that, then why is he on your fantasy team? Don't forget that Dallas, Pittsburgh and Green Bay have lots of fans who travel to games. Sometimes when they are on the road it is hard to tell who is the home team.

If both are at home, neither are, or that was what made them a toss-up to begin with, then go with whichever will be playing on a nationally televised game. Why? Now they get to showcase themselves to the nation. Most players feel a little extra excitement about playing on national TV and this should give them a slight edge over other players. They will be bringing their "A" game for the Sunday or Monday Night viewing audience. If that is not a factor, use the player you will be able to watch on TV where you live. Obviously this does not help that player play any better, but at least you can get the satisfaction of watching him perform. I would much rather watch my kicker kick FGs live than to nervously watch the two-minute ticker and wonder how long each FG was or if the 6 points they scored was a missed extra point or two FGs, when the first was just slow to be reported. Go with the player on your TV set (unless you have Direct TV and NFL Sunday Ticket, where this dilemma becomes a moot point). The last decision is to start the player who plays in the latest game. This gives you the opportunity to have a chance to win the longest (this simply lets you be in the game and delays the fat lady singing). There is nothing worse than having all of your players play in the early game and seeing that you lost after three hours. I would much rather have a player or two in the second Sunday game and know that I still have a chance to win, however feeble. Even better would be players on the Sunday or Monday night game, but they should already have been chosen with the above discriminators. This again is not some magical formula for providing the maximum fantasy points, it is merely a preferred method for extending the joy of fantasy football.

Decision Tree for Toss-Up Starter Decisions

1) Go with home team players first (QBs play slightly better at home)

2) Next, choose those playing in national TV game

3) Choose a player playing in a game you can watch

4) Finally choose a player playing in the latest game (4 p.m. EST or Sunday Night or Monday Night Football)

Assess SOS

Look at the defense your offensive players face. Are they strong, average or weak against the run? Are they strong, average or weak against the pass? You can calculate these ratings yourself since most defenses will move a small amount either up or down the rankings from last year. So use last years numbers with some tweaking for players gained/lost, head coach/defensive coordinator changes and injuries. Then after about week 3, start to merge this years stats with projections. After week 7 or 8, start to rely on this years numbers and look to rushing yards allowed (RYA), rushing TDs allowed (RTA), passing yards allowed (PYA), and passing TDs allowed (PTA). Remember that a strong rushing defense sometimes forces opponents to pass and thus that defense is "weak" against the pass. The opposite is true too; if a team does not defend the rush well, they may look like a strong defense simply because the other teams do not pass for as many yards against them. This is only because the other team finds that they can run against them so easily. So determine which defenses you can run on, which you can pass on, which defenses you can do anything on. Also figure out which defenses you cannot do anything against, which defenses you cannot run on and which you cannot pass on. Then you can start to juggle matchups based on SOS. Start your QB, WR and TE against defenses you can pass on and defenses you can do anything on. Start your RBs against defenses you can rush on or do anything on. Think twice about starting RBs versus defenses you cannot rush on or defenses you cannot do anything on. Think twice about starting your QB, WR or TE against defenses you cannot pass on or defenses that you cannot do anything on.

Lineup Strategies

"The Counter Play" Strategy

This involves trying to neutralize your opponent's players by starting someone on your team who will benefit from his players good performance. Generally, this will involve the QB and WR. If my opponent starts P. Manning (which he will, believe me), then I will start M. Harrison. The theory goes that if Peyton throws four TDs, most will be to Marvin and I will get some of the points advantage. Thus you have improved your player's score simply because your opponent's player did well and thus you have hopefully neutralized any advantage he may have gained from the superior performance. Some say you shouldn't worry about who your opponent starts, just focus on who you start. Normally yes. For regular seasons, yes. But in the playoffs, when it is single elimination, you need to look at the opponent to determine how much, if any, risk to take. Are you playing the team with LT on it? Take some risk if you want to win. Are you playing the last place seed that got lucky last week to advance but has not outscored you all year? Do not take any risks. Just keep doing what you have been doing. Only by analyzing your opponent can you make good risk assessments.

"The rotating player according to matchups"

Often this is with defenses, sometimes with QBs. Based on the matchups each week, you will decide which of two (sometimes three with QBs) players and defenses to start. You will look for the most favorable matchup. Start defenses that are at home, against poor offenses and/or inexperienced QBs. Start QBs against weak passing defenses or teams with strong offenses. The QB will be playing from behind and thus is more likely to throw.

"Lineup moves based on score"

If you can change the lineup for players right up until game time then use this strategy. If you have two players in late games (4 pm or Sunday or Monday night), for example one kicker who is a steady eddy for 6 points every week and one that is boom or bust (10 or 3 every week), then change the starter based on how well you are doing in early games.

"Playoff strategies"

1) Play the best matchups. Do not be afraid to sit someone you have started all year long if they have not produced down the stretch. There is no reason to be loyal to the first RB you drafted back in August if he does not have the juice or the matchup to help you win.

2) Do not take unnecessary risk. Look at your opponent. What has he scored the last few weeks? What is his weekly average? Moreover, what is your weekly average? Are you going to need a big day or can you coast and make him try to do something big? Do not take a risk on a boom or bust player now, unless you feel you need it to have any chance of winning. If your team has consistently outscored his do not take any chances. Stick with the reliable FP providers you have. If you are playing a team with LT and you have no way of winning unless you come up big, then and only then, look for some pickups to help. However, do a risk assessment before taking on that risk. Are your choices for flex Ron Dayne, who has had a few good weeks lately (85 yards and a TD the last two games) but is facing a tough defense, or M. Colston, who had super games when J. Horn was out and zero games when J. Horn was playing and who now faces a J. Horn-questionable situation?

Which kicker do you start?

1) Which one plays for the team that has scored the most points? Which team is favored by odds-makers to score the most this week?

2) Which is playing the worst defense? Which is on the team with the better defense?

3) Which kicker is at home?

4) Is one kicking indoors? This means longer FGs, more accuracy and more chances. If both are playing outdoors, does either have unfavorable weather?

5) Defense facing? When looking at defenses facing the kicker look at FG s allowed and go with the kicker facing the defense allowing the most FGs. If you are making a starting decision between two kickers and both have scored the same FPs, go with the kicker with most FGs if you need to take a risk for higher points. Look at average points per game. Sometimes a tough defense can mean more FGs and less XPs.

Which Defense do you Start?

1) Who are they playing? Weak offense or a high powered offense?

2) Do they face a young QB or a great QB?

3) Is the defense at home? Home defenses have an edge.

4) What is the weather?

Things to Think About

1) Thursday night games tend to be sloppy. Why?

It is possible that they did not yet recover from Sunday's game (many players say it takes till Friday to recover), or because they had less time to prepare. Thus defenses are better plays on Thursday, QBs not as good.

2) A typical rookie owner mistake is not setting a lineup (but it can happen to anyone). This makes the other owners mad because they needed you to beat your opponent. Don't make that mistake. Set your lineup for next week as soon as possible; if nothing else, bench bye week players and make substitutions based on injuries. You can always change it later. Better to have a serviceable lineup in case you get hit by a Guinness truck and miss the deadline. This means you need to know your deadline. Remember Thursday games. Do it on Wednesday at the latest for your initial hack at lineups.

3) Track the number of touches. Touches equal opportunity. The more opportunity the more chances to score.

4) Physical games = turnovers, penalties and low scoring

5) If flex is used, look at the players who score the most points on average. Do not just blindly put in a RB because they are the most valuable. Look at how your other players eligible for the flex position could do.

6) Don't overthink it! Estimate the possible outcomes with each player and try to estimate the probability of each outcome. This will usually point you in the right direction. For example: Do I start M. Bulger or T. Romo? Hmmm… Bulger has the following outcomes: 30% great, 50% good, 10% average, 10% poor. Romo has 25% great, 25% good, 25% average and 25% poor. It makes the choice easier. I have a 50% chance of average or

worse with Romo and an 80% chance of good or better with Bulger. Go with the stud QB, not the up-and-coming rookie.

7) Intangibles – Look for special events that will motivate players or teams to do better. For example, S. McNair returns to face the team that fired him (TENN) as a Baltimore Ravens QB and goes 29-47, three TDs and throws for 373 yards or C. Palmer and Marvin Lewis giving a "put up or shut up" speech and Cincinnati beats New Orleans 31-16 at New Orleans after losing three straight games.

8) Is there a limit to lineup changes? This is the worst rule a league can have. Why would you limit the number of times you can change your mind in setting a lineup? If it is a rule then that will create different strategies for making lineups decisions. Maybe wait until later in the week to make those calls.

Who do you start in week 1?

This is probably as easy as it is going to get. Start the players you drafted first. Because you drafted them higher you must think they are better than those drafted later. Unless an injury or can't-miss match-up occurs in week 1, the first RB drafted goes into RB#1 position, second RB drafted goes into RB#2, and so on.

QB Injuries

What happens to a team when a good QB goes down to injury and is replaced by a generic backup QB (Garcia coming in for McNabb in 2006 is not a generic backup)? Five things in general can happen but not all of them happen every time. The key is to not just assume one of these things will happen but to determine why they will happen. If a coach announces that he will simplify the passing plays, then look for more RB/TE passes. If he announces that they will run the ball more, look for the RB to get more touches. Don't just assume that because Bulger is out with an injury, T. Holt's numbers will drop. One possible outcome is the team's FPs falling due to poor production. Steve Smith is a great example of "watch who is throwing" to WRs. Without Jake at QB in weeks 14-16, Steve Smith had no TDs. In the other 13 games where Jake was QB he had 9 TDs. He averaged .7 TDs per game with Jake. In the three games without him he should have had two TDs on average and he had none. He never went three games in a row without a TD until Jake was not QB.

Another outcome can be the RBs getting more touches because the emphasis is placed more on the running game than the passing game. (If coach says, "QB2 you cannot throw the ball on 3rd and 5.") Or if the passing game is simplified and the QB throws more passes to a RB coming out of the backfield or to TEs closer to the line of scrimmage. (Long bomb passes can be a disaster, while short, safe passes build confidence.) Young, inexperienced QBs tend to dump off to a TE as a safety valve. They are also tough on RBs as defenses put seven, eight or even nine men in the box to contain the run. Perhaps QB2 finds his "go-to guy" in WR1, because he is the best on the field and is the first option on most pass plays, or he throws more to another WR or others since he has practiced with them more on the practice squad.

Chapter 14 Free Agency Upgrade

A typical rookie mistake is not making any moves after the draft. If you do not make any moves, your team will fall behind. Even if you have a successful draft, your work is not over. The best (most successful) owners always try to improve their team, or at best, block their opponent from improving their team via free agency. For every owner that drafts a great team, there is another that has a weak draft but makes some great in-season additions to make the playoffs. We all make mistakes at the draft. Some of them are more obvious than others ("I'll take Ryan Leaf in the second round"). We can fix these mistakes through free agency upgrades. Free agency is easier than trading, but free agency sometimes does not have the talent you need. In those cases a trade may be your only option. (See Chapter 15 – Trades.)

Things will happen that will force you to make some changes. Many owners will not conduct any transactions early in the year because they still have faith in their drafted team. This is a good strategy as it takes a few weeks for trends to develop. Better to wait than be too rash with dropping key players on a slump. Still other owners will rarely make changes unless forced to by injuries. This is to your advantage. Look at the leaders every week statistically and see if any were not drafted. If available, look at them more closely. Are they getting the touches only because the star is hurt but will be back soon, are they coming in and replacing the star because of his nagging injuries, or is it an RBBC and the star is losing the battle? By observing the box score/stat leaderboards and doing some research, you can beat other owners to the punch on these up-and-coming players. Remember: never accept the status quo, always try to improve.

Formats

There is some confusion about free agency, waiver wire and transactions in general. There are two main types of free agency. The first has dropped players going onto waivers, but free agents can be picked up any time. All players not on a roster at any given time are either on the FA list or on the waiver wire. The waiver wire is for players recently dropped and awaiting processing onto the FA list. Usually a player must stay on waivers for a certain amount of time, during which if another owner requests him and wins he can be claimed off waivers. Any player not claimed off waivers will go to the FA list. The free agent listing includes players who are free (hence the name) to be picked up at any time on a first come, first served basis. The second format requires that all players be claimed off waivers. Some leagues use the FA list and waiver wire as the same vehicle. These leagues use a waiver wire priority to determine who can claim a player.

6 ways of dealing with FA/Waiver wire

1) First come, first served (FCFS)

Benefits those who are watching all ten hours of football live on Sunday when the injuries occur. I have been in leagues where the backup who just entered the huddle is picked up, while the starter lies on a stretcher on the field. That is the Sunday NFL Ticket and wireless Internet for you. Usually allows adds/drops at any time. It is a disadvantage to those of us who have to do things on Sunday like cut the grass or go to a child's recital.

2) Weekly FA

This is awarded based on rankings (also known as worst to first format). All adds/drops occur at a set time in the week, usually Wednesday. At this time, any player who has been claimed by more than one team is awarded to the team with the worst record. As a tiebreaker, the player would go to the team with the lowest TFPs scored to date for the current season. The waiver wire ranking is adjusted each week based on record. Advantages: All owners have a chance to get a player who is suddenly now a starter. Thus, it does not reward the 24/7 football addict, it instead helps to promote parity in the league. Disadvantage: It rewards owners who drafted poorly or who do not manage their team. Thus the 0-6 goofus has a great RB fall in his lap through no skill of his own. It also prevents teams from adding replacements right up until game time, based on injuries and other game time developments and penalizes winning teams. Is that American? We're not in Russia, are we?

3) Waiver wire system

Same as #2 above, but the waiver priority starts out based on where you drafted, and once you claim a player you go to the bottom of the priority list. Thus, if you have the last pick in a 10-team draft, you would have the #1 priority for the first claim you made. But once you make a claim, you then fall to #10 on the waiver wire priority list. Advantages: Rewards owners who got worst picks in draft, does not reward bad drafters or bad managers of their teams. Disadvantages: Still does not allow adds up until game time.

4) Blind bidding

Each team starts with 1,000 free agent "dollars" (FAAB) for the season. Teams bid on players weekly. No team knows the other's bids until the winning bids have been awarded. The team with the highest bid is awarded that player. The winning team's FAAB is reduced by the winning bid amount and a player must be dropped to make room for the new acquisition. Once a team's FAAB reaches zero, they cannot bid on players. Advantages: Fairest system. Disadvantages: Complexity in administration.

5) No transactions at any time

These leagues that do not allow FA pickups, but instead have a supplemental draft. In most cases teams must have larger rosters and bench spots to allow for injuries, suspensions, etc.; otherwise owners will find themselves and their teams so far behind by the time the supplemental FA draft comes around that it will do them no good.

6) Limit the number of transactions

This can be a weekly limit (the most common limit is two transactions per week) or a seasonal limit. Trades and FA pickups count toward the transactions. In rare cases, moving a player from starter to the bench (and vice versa) will count.

* Some leagues have a transactions deadline for the season. After this time, no adds/drops or trades can be performed.

**One way to avoid the disadvantage of not allowing add/drop until game time is to make the above processes only applicable from first kickoff until the mid-week deadline. After the Wednesday deadline, when players have been claimed, the process turns into a FCFS process until the first game starts. Once the first game starts the process of claiming a player is frozen until the next week's deadline on Wednesday.

Free Agent Types

Differentiate between short-term FA (STFA) pickups and long-term FA (LTFA) pickups. A STFA pickup is a player who is only going to be on your team for the current week. For example, your TE2 goes on IR and your TE1 has his bye week this week. You place the injured player on IR and have to pick up a replacement TE to fill-in for this week. Next week your TE1 will be starting and you can drop this fill-in TE to pick up a promising RB or WR. Therefore, the point to a STFA is that you don't need to fall in love with them and want them for the remainder of the season. They are just a stopgap solution to get you through the next week. Ignore everything in the future and just determine who the best player will be for this week.

LTFAs will be on your team until they get hurt, benched or replaced by another LTFA. Therefore, there needs to be much more planning going into the decision to add them. Consider their injury history, the team they are playing for, the upcoming schedule, etc.

There are four types of LTFAs. Fast starters are players who explode in week one but who usually fade in the coming weeks. Good starters are consistent players who look to have improved over last year. Backups for the injured are sometimes picked up as a defensive move, to avoid allowing your opponent to get them and sleepers or hunch players that you cannot afford to let sit on the waiver wire.

Before grabbing a player from the waiver wire, ask yourself: why am I doing it? Why do I think he will perform now?

1) Look at past performance. If he flopped as a starter earlier and is just playing because the starting QB is injured, that does not make him a good starter.

2) Be conscious of opportunity; make sure he is going to play. There is no reason to pickup a WR, RB or QB who steps in for one week (while the starter is out) and has a career day, if that backup will never see the field again all season because the main starter is so good. Even if Jim Sorgi plays a great game and does well, do you really think Peyton is going to be benched? No; opportunity is critical. And opportunity comes from the benching of the starter, a return from injury or a trade. Injuries to the starter also create opportunities but those are a little harder to predict. To realize these potential opportunities you need to do long-term thinking, not short-term planning. Look for the little things. Have the snaps with the first team gone up? Have the touches or looks on game day seen an upward trend? If the starter is splitting snaps with the first team with his backup then he is on a short leash. Insiders will start to talk about a change. Now is the time to pull the trigger, not next week when he is named the starter and even my sister knows who he is. By leading, you can get the QB2 for minimal FAAB dollars. Wait until he is named the starter and his price just went up 20%, at least. He is a low risk/high reward so add him one week early. He is an expensive risk the next week. Don't forget contractual issues. If a team has drafted or traded for a player high enough they will want to see him on the field. (Except for Washington and TJ Duckett in 2006 – go figure.)

3) Supporting players are an integral part of a player's game. RBs need good OLs; QBs need good OLs, WRs or TEs to catch the ball; WRs need good QBs throwing to them.

4) Look for players dropped by other owners too early. Is the player in a slump, but is consistent year in and year out? Regression to the mean will dictate that he should put up better numbers the rest of the season. Is it a RB who just faced three of the top 10 rushing defenses? If so, grab the guy.

5) Get players who will benefit your team. If you have four stud WRs and another falls in your lap; ask yourself if there is another player at another position that you need more. Perhaps you should get the stud WR and trade another one of your star WRs to get a better player at another position.

Actions in the Preseason

Look at the position battles (especially QB/RB/WR) at training camp. If a rookie has a chance to beat out a vet at a skill position, grab the rookie (if available) BEFORE he is named a starter. In other words be proactive and grab the player before he wins the job. At worst, you can drop him after week 1 when he does not start. At best you have gazumped (bamboozled) all the other owners and made a big splash in the FA market before the season starts. Rookie RBs have the best chance to succeed if given the opportunity.

Watch for injuries and be ready to grab their backup, even if only for a short time. This gives you potential trade bait; HC material for the other owner whose player is hurt. Don't forget to remind him that his player is hurt now and may have problems all year with the nagging injury, so he should need his HC. It also blocks that owner from replacing his injured player with that backup.

Actions in the first half of the Season

Don't do anything for a week or two unless forced to by significant injuries, player suspensions, retirement, etc. Some players will start slow. There is no reason to drop a 3rd round draft pick simply because he puts up a few goose eggs (zero points) against tough defenses. If you drafted someone in the early or middle rounds you should hold onto them and let them have time to develop. Look at Muhsin Muhammad in 2004. He had 2 TDs in the first six games and 14 TDs in the last ten games, to finish with 16 TDs. Imagine if you dropped him after week 7 when he caught just three passes for 28 yards and no TDs. Do not overreact in the first few weeks. Do not be the owner who says, "DOH! I wish I had just stayed calm and not cut Jamal Lewis too early." Week 4 means the first bye week; now you can start to evaluate your team.

Do not expect much change in NFL starters the first month of the season. Just as you should not have a quick hook on your studs, coaches who have named starters want to give them a chance too. Build your watch list the first few weeks of the season and be ready to go after the first month.

Consider upgrading at kicker if yours is not in the Top 10 by week 5. Kickers are a dime a dozen and some will be in the Top 10 that were not drafted.

Actions after midseason

Look for rookies with pedigree (won in college) who are behind an aging vet. The "win now" mentality of the NFL means rookies are more likely to get a shot on NFL teams out of the playoff hunt who are trying to develop new talent. Look to teams with three or less wins after week 9. Now look at their schedule for weeks 10-13. What will their record be then? Those are the weak teams that will experiment with their starting rosters.

Many leagues stop transactions (trades/waiver wire pickups and add/drops) once the playoffs begin or even a few weeks before the playoffs begin. If this is the case then you need to make some team adjustments before the deadline. If you ran with only one at a position during the year (rotating and adding/dropping based on matchup) then you now need to get a starter to stick with and a backup in case the starter gets hurt. Also, get rid of any players you do not absolutely need as either insurance or starters, and add RB depth. In some years, nearly 50% of the RBs in week 16 may not be the ones from week 1. Why? Injuries, suspensions, trades, rest for playoffs, benchings, coach's decision, etc. So, before the deadline, go with only two QBs not three, only five WR (if start three), two TEs, 2 Ks (in all cases, an extra player in case one gets hurt) and one or two defenses. This will leave some room for more RB sleepers.

After the bye weeks are finished, once you have your main RBs ready for the playoff run, think about taking out some insurance policies (HCs) on them. If their backups are not already taken (by you hopefully) then grab them as a FA pickup just in case. You may even be able to trade away some bench depth and improve another position to make room for the HC. As an example, you have three bench spots with two good RBs and a WR and you would hate to have to drop one (and expose him to a FA pickup by an opponent as well) in order to make room for your HC. Why not try to trade one of the RBs and the WR to another team for a much better WR? Yes, a two for one trade. If executed, you will have upgraded your WR position (or have a much better backup WR) and you can fill the missing bench spot with a HC RB.

Think about playoff matchups when evaluating FA pickups. Whom will he face in weeks 14-16? Use this as a discriminator.

FAAB Notes

Assuming you start with a $1,000 FAAB, expect to pay anywhere from $100-$300 for a week 1 new starter; $300-$700 is the typical range for a good pickup during the season. Rarely do owners spend over $800 (too much of the budget spent on one player). Most of the spending occurs in weeks 3-5 and then it decreases as the weeks go by until the last week before the transaction deadline, where it picks up' presumably because owners know that they can spend all their money then. There is no reason to save money. You may see up to $900 later in the season if a new starter emerges (that is a sure thing) due to a season-ending injury. That, of course, assumes the owner has that much FAAB left.

Strategies

1) Blocking – This is a tactic in which you grab a free agent player your opponent needs even though you do not need them. A perfect example occurs when Shaun Alexander goes

down with an injury. He hurts his hand the previous week and then on Wednesday is declared out for the upcoming week. Your opponent this week is the owner of Shaun Alexander. If he has not handcuffed Shaun Alexander's backup, then you would be wise to grab Maurice Morris off the free agent list. This is beneficial to you in many ways. First, M. Morris may prove to be a good RB to start this week based on his matchup. Secondly, Shaun Alexander may be out for the rest of the season, in which case you just picked up another starting RB. Perhaps best of all, you have BLOCKED this week's opponent from picking up a serviceable RB. He will be cursing you when he sees that you have scooped up his backup even though you do not need him. This can prove to be a very successful strategy. The same thing can happen even if you do not want the backup. Say, for example, that P. Manning goes down for your opponent this week; perhaps J. Sorgi does not appeal to you as a good QB to have regardless of the status of P. Manning. In that case, you can still BLOCK your opponent by grabbing the best QB available on the free agent list. This prevents your opponent from getting the better backup, assuming he does not have a suitable backup on his bench. QB, RB and TE will usually be the positions for which this strategy works best. Other positions (WR and K) are too deep and defenses never have injuries that would force an entire defense to be unusable.

2) One strategy, in leagues with small rosters and real time add/drops (not occurring in a mid-week transaction), is to block your opponent by dropping your kicker(s) and using that roster spot to block his attempt to acquire the RB or QB he needs for the week. Lets say your league starts two QBs. You have a 12-team league with a roster of 14. Each team has two or more QBs. There are only two starting QBs on the FA list. You notice that neither of your opponent's QBs can play this week since one is on a bye and the other is injured. You drop both your kickers and add the only starting QBs to your roster. You have blocked him from getting a starting QB. If you think those QBs would score more than your kicker, you have just saved some points. Even if you feel you need a kicker, you can drop the worst QB in the last minute before the deadline and add a kicker to your roster. You will have a kicker to start and he will be left with no QB; all because there are so many good kickers on the FA list.

3) Caution is the strategy if your league has a severe limit on transactions. As an example, you are only allowed four FA add/drops all year. This should limit your willingness to risk a pick on a currently injured player. If he does not come back from injury, then you will have wasted one of your FA picks (25%) and another on finding his replacement (50%). You should also avoid injury-prone players since a few injuries can deplete your FA transactions quickly. Most owners will be hesitant to add the flavor of the week player (just scored two TDs and 100+ yards out of nowhere) since, if he is a flash in the pan, it would be wasting a FA addition.

Tips

1) Always have a "watch list" of at least three players from each position that you would add if you had an injury. Think about it this way: "If I could keep two more players at each position, who would I draft?" Perhaps they are sleepers that you want to pull the trigger on if they start to perform. Keep up with who is available and who was just released. When a team adds a player, check out who they dropped and evaluate them for potential. Many times these are players drafted who have just not performed lately. Jump on them if there is a reason to expect a rebound. The players which are dropped most often, when a good

FA or waiver wire player becomes available, are K2 and DEF2. Always be on the lookout to snag one of these kickers or defenses if they can help you.

NOTE: Many websites will let you mark players as watch list; this makes it easy to keep tabs on them as the season progresses and allows you to delete players that others have added.

2) Use "Vegas" odds in determining which FA to pick up. You have narrowed down your FA pickups to two WRs. Which one will perform better this week? (Assuming this is just a stopgap substitution for a bye week WR or flex player.) Choices are K. Curtis (STL) or A. Whitted (OAK). The odds-makers say:

Example: STL -3/GB +3 over/under 45 means the Vegas bookies expect St. Louis to win 24-21.

Example: OAK +7/Den -7 over/under 35 means Denver is expected to win 21-14.

All other things being equal, go with Curtis and STL. They are expected to score 10 more points than Oakland, thus a greater chance for a TD for Curtis than Whitted.

3) Use the upcoming schedule for LTFAs. Do they have favorable matchups? If a QB, look for weak pass defenses. If RB, look for weak rush defenses and kickers – poor defenses in general. A favorable DEF/ST would involve playing low scoring offenses, inexperienced QBs, etc.

4) Carry two kickers starting in the middle of November. Get your spare kicker before the end of the free agency period, if there is an end. This makes sure you are covered in case of injury after the FA period ends. There is nothing worse than seeing your kicker pull a hamstring on a fake kick, only to be sidelined for the next 2-3 weeks and your playoff bound team becoming kicker-less. Another reason to do this is to cover yourself when the bad weather starts to affect games. If your K1 is playing outdoors in a swirling snowstorm, with a K2 at least you have other options.

5) Lead, don't follow, in free agent transactions; plan for your bye weeks at least two weeks in advance. Try to be one step ahead of the other owners. They will be thinking one week ahead. If you are looking for a WR or K that has a good matchup in two weeks, you are much more likely to get him than if you wait till one week away and have to compete with every other owner who is also looking for a bye week replacement player from that position.

6) Do not waste roster spots on an extra TE, K, or DEF unless the rules force you to do so. If the rules state that you must carry a certain number of those positions (such as two each) then you have no choice. If the rules do not state how many of each position you must have on your roster, carry only 1 TE, 1 K and 1 DEF. HINT: Try to draft each of those players so that they all have a different bye week; (i.e. TE has bye on week 7, K on week 8, DEF on week 9); if at all possible, try to get later bye weeks versus earlier bye weeks. This will give you more time to figure out if they are any good before the bye week and perhaps an add/drop will be better than picking up a fill-in for that position. Why carry only one from each position? It frees up roster spots for sleeper picks in other, more critical, positions. Simply carrying only one at all three positions will free up three places for sleepers. Then when the first of those players has his bye week (TE in week 7, in above example) then you will need to make a decision to either cut the TE and get a better one off the FA list (hopefully who has already had his bye) or drop one of the sleeper picks

who has not panned out and pick up a fill-in TE for this week only. (See STFA.) TEs, Ks and DEFs with a bye week in week 9 or 10 are like gold if they are good, since they can be drafted and held almost until the playoffs, before needing to make a decision on the sleepers you drafted in the extra spots. "All will be revealed shortly."

7) Handcuff your RB if he starts to get gimpy or if the head coach indicates a change may be forthcoming. You should handcuff him in the draft (like we discussed earlier), but if you didn't then, definitely HC him if your starter begins to come up a little lame at times. Nagging little injuries late in the game can be an indicator of problems ahead. The head coach making statements like "Rex Grossman is our man for now," may be an indication of things to change in the future. Read between the lines.

8) Look at touches as a stat. Look at yardage and receptions. Both are indicators of TDs to come, unless the WR is a possession WR.

9) If looking for a bye week pickup, make sure he has a great matchup in the week you are going to use him. For example, you select P. Manning as your #1 QB and do not draft another QB due to Peyton's never having missed a game. Peyton has his bye week in week 6 so you need to add a QB in week 4 (two weeks early; think ahead, beat the rest) that has a favorable matchup in week 6.

10) A starter's injury can be your ticket to the acquisition of a great player. Look for injuries and grab the backup to the injured player, especially if it is a starting RB. What about an injury to your player? Your preparedness will determine the champs from the pretenders. Do you have the HC? Do you have a backup RB #3 to fill in? Can you trade away some bench depth to recover? If you do not have the HC, grab him immediately if your starter is out. Some will hesitate and begin to over analyze. "What if he does not start?" "What if he is not any good?" GRAB HIM NOW. If you wait, someone else will grab him to block you. He will definitely do better than your injured player who is out. If he does not start, then try to grab the guy who did start or make other plans for next week. But having a plan (grab his backup) is better than no plan at all.

Don't forget to look to the M*A*S*H unit for stars who have injured themselves and are off the radar screen. Always keep in mind when they are scheduled to return. You may have to add them a week earlier to keep the other owners out. Remember to be cautious with them when returning from injuries, but many times a pickup in week 10 or 11 can turn into a jewel come playoff time. This is even more important in keeper leagues as other owners drop them once hurt and forget they can be kept for next year.

11) Avoid 1-week wonders. There are some owners who will jump on a RB or WR who has a 100-yard game. Evaluate him but also look critically at his performance. Was he a first week wonder? Did he play because the star was banged up and could not play? Is he a new player on the team and this was just the beginning? Is he a RB who had three carries for 101 yards but one of those carries was a fourth quarter dash for 93 yards as the game ended?

12) Analyze game history. You can usually use websites to sort players based on their stats. Look at FP scored, then look at TDs and yardage. Look at catches for WR and carries for RB. A player with lots of catches/carries but few yards may mean less TDs down the road, but someone with lots of catches/carries and yards may be just around the corner from scoring on those big plays. Rookies who are getting more and more touches should be considered sleeper material. The longer you go into the season the more you will

need to look at game-by-game performances. As an example, it is week 10 and you are looking at a WR to replace an injured WR#2. A WR with four TDs, but all of them in week 2, is not as good a WR with only three TDs, one each from the last 3 games. What have you done for me lately?

Chapter 15 Trades

You can control three of four things that win championships; your draft, your lineup decisions and your waiver wire/free agent transactions. All of these are within your control. The other aspect to winning, which you do not control completely, is trading. It involves another human being. That other person is what makes it so tricky. Some owners love to trade, some are afraid to trade and some tolerate it as a necessary evil to improve one's team. Many owners fear trades because they are afraid of losing. If the trade backfires they will look like a loser.

Trading is allowed in some leagues, in others it is forbidden. The high stakes leagues usually prohibit it in order to eliminate the possibility of collusion. In lesser stake leagues ($100 or less) trading may be allowed. If allowed, trading can be a fun and interactive way of playing the game. Participating in leagues that allow FF trades should improve your evaluation and negotiation skills at work. Once you negotiate a 3-team, 6 player trade, negotiating a promotion will seem easy. Some say that trading spices things up. It can really help a league or it can hurt a league, and more arguments come from trades than any other issue. Trades that are unfair or bad (or perceived to be either) can create bad feelings among the owners and toward the commissioner. They can cause teams to quit trying or drop out of the league altogether. Some leagues use a trading deadline to prevent collusion. But if so, the deadline must be early enough to stop teams that are out of contention from dumping but late enough to allow teams to navigate the bye weeks. Week 11 seems like a great choice.

Make sure any trade you accept benefits you. Do not accept a trade just to be trading. You can go the entire season without trading. You can offer, counteroffer, accept or reject trades. No one is putting a gun to your head and making you do any of these. No reply after a certain time is a reject. But be respectful and reply to all trade offers. You do not have to accept a trade. I have been in leagues where not one trade was executed and the league had parity and playoff entrants were not determined until the last week. The playoffs were just as close. I am amazed at people that say they really try to get one good trade in a year. Trading just to trade isn't a good reason. So why trade? Because the chances are high that at some point in the season your team will be affected by injuries, coaching start/bench decisions, other players playing better or your players playing poorly, all of which can lead your team to be deficient in one area or another. Bye weeks also may force you to trade and the need to make a playoff push may nudge a trade here and there. Trades can be good, bad, stupid or unfair. Ultimately you are the one who pulls a trigger on the trade. If you have to ask if you won or lost, you probably lost because you do not know why you made the trade; make trades that benefit your team. You need to know how and why they will benefit you. Either build depth (get a better RB#3), improve a starter (QB#1 is now much better) or buy some insurance (HC RB#1) to improve your deficiencies.

Trades are more likely to occur in dynasty leagues or leagues with large rosters and less likely to happen as much in redraft leagues with smaller roster sizes. Many times in a redraft league with a small roster, in order to meet a need, the other owner will want a little something extra to get the deal done. With a smaller pool of players it is hard to create something as a little extra. Often the only way to get the trade done is to give too much. So it is either a deal that is costly or no deal at all. In leagues with large rosters (typically dynasty leagues), owners have future draft picks, young up-and-coming stars and rookies with potential, all of which can help make a deal. **The more options you have, the easier it is to get a trade done.**

Trading is a game of give and take. Think of trading like being a used car salesman. You do not want to tell the other guy exactly why you want to trade (or what the car's condition really is) because that may scare him away. On the other hand, you need to be as honest as possible so that he does business with you again or at least does not tarnish your reputation with other owners (customers). RBs will always be a desired trading commodity simply because of the law of supply and demand. You will rarely have problems getting takers for a trade involving a RB. The key is to make it worth it for you and the other owners.

Some terms before we proceed:

Proposed Trade – a trade that has been offered to another owner for acceptance. The owner considering it can accept, reject or counteroffer.

Accepted Trade – a trade that has been agreed to by two or more owners and that has been put to the league for approval.

Approved trade – a trade that has been approved by the league as official. Usually approval is given by the commissioner, a vote by owners or by no protest from a set amount of owners.

Types of Trades

1) Players at same position – You trade a RB to Team A and he trades you a RB back. Hopefully both players are of similar value. Then why trade? Maybe one owner likes the other RB better because he is on his favorite team or comes from his alma mater. Perhaps one of the players is on the same bye week as his other RBs. Perhaps one has a weak playoff schedule or a strong remaining schedule, etc.

2) Multiple Player deal – this involves trading multiple players from each team. Usually it will involve one big player from each team. In other words the player you have to move off your roster anyway, to make room for the main player, can be packaged as part of the trade. For example, you want to upgrade at TE and you have lots of WR depth. You offer A. Boldin for A. Gates. You also offer to give Team A your TE1, H. Miller, for one of his WRs, M. Booker, who looks promising in the FF playoffs. You get two players, a TE and WR and he gets two players, a TE and WR. You both improve your teams.

3) Two for one – You trade two good players for a stud player. This often happens in keeper leagues where the two lesser players are up-and-coming players who are traded for the current stud. Keep in mind that if you get two players for one player you will have to drop one from your roster to make room for the additional player.

4) Players for draft picks – discussed elsewhere in this chapter.

5) Players for salary cap money – How much are those salary cap dollars worth? Look at your previous auctions. How much was $1 worth in terms of X points in a VBD system? For example, if 6 XP =1% of value of cap in a $200 auction league,

then $2=6 XP and $1=3 XP. That also happens to be the rule of thumb for money value in a $200 cap league.

Trade Partners

There are five types of traders

1) The ones looking to swindle

2) Those looking to give and get fairly

3) Those looking to trade only if they get the clear upper hand in some way. For example, owners trying to get rid of someone whom they are going to drop in 2-3 weeks anyway; in many cases they are rarely willing to give away good for good.

4) Those who like to talk trades but never pull the trigger. You know who you are.

5) Suckers – those who will accept any trade

Get to know the other owner's tendencies in your league. Give them what they want, not necessarily what is good for them.

1) Does one owner jump on any chance to trade for the first rookie that has a big game?

2) Which owner never pulls the trigger on a trade?

3) Which owner values his own draft picks (or free agency adds) so much that he can never agree to a trade?

4) Which owner does not care about where a player was drafted?

5) Which owner always wants the stud from (insert his college here)?

Focus on owners who want to trade. Do not waste your time or energy with owners who have anti-trading tendencies as noted above. Anytime you find teams with two good players but who can only start one you have a possible trading partner. Some teams are co-owned and use the good owner/bad owner trick to get you to trade but then use the other owner as the guy who says "NO."

Steps to execute a Trade

1) Identify what you need (your weaknesses). You are weak at TE. You have two of the league's worst and every time you add/drop one he turns into a stinker too.

2) Identify what you have to offer (your strengths). Your teams strength may lie in the fact that you have four starting RBs and only start two per week (no flex). Thus you would like to have three starting RBs (one for bye weeks and weak matchups) so you have an extra starting RB to trade.

3) Look for what you need from other owner's teams. Determine which players in the league, on other teams, will fix your weakness. Have the names ready. You must have some objective in order to know when to proceed. Do not have just one name. "I must have A. Gates," is not a need but a want. "I need a top three TE," is a much better objective.

4) Determine what that owner needs

5) Make an offer, utilizing your own personal strengths and weaknesses in the trade. Maybe your own strength is a good history of trading and your weakness is giving away too much right before the deadline, to get a playoff push player.

Trade Do's (Steps to a successful trade)

1) Compromise or overcome objections when they do not hurt your team. Sometimes a kicker or defense can sweeten the deal enough to get it approved. If your league allows trading draft picks, think about that to increase value for your trading partner. Also avoid too much compromise. There is a saying, "better no trade than a bad trade." Do not be so wrapped up in getting a trade done that you lose sight of the objective. "Okay, instead of T. Heap I will take A. Crumpler and give you my RB#3 instead of RB#4." Compromising too much just to get a trade done is the worst thing you can do. If the trade is not going to happen, then move on to the next owner who can help you and start talking to him.

2) Try to make the trade look like his idea. If you can get the other owner to suggest the trade, you have a higher chance of getting the deal done. For example, he has two TEs that will be an improvement to your team. One is A. Gates, the #1 TE in the league, and the other is A. Crumpler, who is having a good season and has a favorable SOS remaining including a dream week 16 matchup. Start by asking how much for A. Gates. He suggests a price and you comment that you cannot afford that much, although you agree that A. Gates is the best TE in the league and worth it. You come back with a lowball offer for Crumpler. He raises the stakes on Crumpler and you counter by adding in your TE2 as a deal sweetener since he will need a TE as a backup anyway. He counters with his own offer that includes Crumpler and his RB4 (who is on both his and the NFL's bench) and him getting your TE2 and RB4. You accept because you get your TE and a RB who has potential to be a starter versus some FA back who has nothing going for him. By letting him suggest the final trade offer, now there is no way he can back out of it since he suggested it. You get what you wanted all along and he feels better about it since it was his idea.

3) State the obvious. Imply everything else. Minimize talking about why a trade is needed. In trades, less talk is more if you can get the other guy to jump to conclusions. If you tell your trading partner that you need to get a RB for a bye week replacement that is coming up, that is the obvious. If you trade him a RB that has fumbled the last four weeks and is about to get benched but he does not know it, that is tactical.

4) Use the "us versus them" mentality to build allies. This is especially helpful in leagues with divisions or where one team has dominated for several years. Try to build up a rapport with other teams in the other division that are fighting a "bully" or dominating team. The same applies if your league has been dominated by the same owner for several years. Try to convince the other owner in the trade that it will help both of you to combat the "bully" or end his dominance. When trading with an owner from another division, a simple "You need this to beat Team A this year. Do it and I will see you in the Super Bowl," can work miracles. Next thing you know, a trade acceptance note has appeared in your e-mail box.

5) Avoid trading with division rivals that can beat you for a title or playoff spot. Trading with them after you have played them and have a comfortable lead over them is acceptable, especially if they have yet to play your division rival. "My enemies' enemies are my friends."

Trade Don'ts (Steps to an unsuccessful trade)

1) Don't congratulate the other owner on the trade. This will naturally make him suspicious of why you are so smug at making the trade. He is a big boy; once he hits the accept button there is no need to hold his hand anymore.

2) Don't gloat or rub a trade in the face of anyone. Keep your mouth shut and enjoy whatever success you had without alerting all the owners that you are a "slick willy."

3) Don't get personal or emotional. Never attack an owner's intelligence, personality or family. If the owner you are discussing a trade with begins to get personal or emotional, just sit back and listen and then try to steer the conversation back to facts and statistics. If you have to walk away, then do so; but do it with dignity. Always say "thanks for the offer but I am going to decline. Maybe we can come to something next time." Always end negotiations on a friendly note to keep them open to future trade talks.

4) Do not make a trade offer without looking at the other owner's roster. You look foolish trading a RB to a team that has RB as their strength.

5) Never try to trade an injured or demoted player. If you want to move him, let the other owner know the player's situation; doing this one time will ruin any reputation you had as a fair trader.

6) If you constantly try to pull off the monster trade that is unfair, eventually other owners will not trust you when you do bring a good trade to the table.

7) Do not try to trade a player who you are going to drop anyway. This is the worst type of owner. He will e-mail or call several owners and tout a player who he likes but is willing to trade now. A few days later, when no one bites on his offer of trade bait, he drops the player. What do you think the other owners he contacted about a trade think now? They think "That $%%^ must think I am stupid to try and trade me his trash like that." The owner who does this poisons any relationship they have with those owners. The next time he brings up any trade talks, legitimate or not, they will turn away. Talk about burning bridges.

8) Do not lie or make up stats or quotes. This will lead to other owners finding out and quickly labeling you as untrustworthy. However, if you state that C. Portis is on track to score 14 TDs, after he has scored 7 by the mid way point; that is a valid tactic. The fact that Washington played the easiest schedule in the first half of the season is something the other owner should evaluate.

9) Do not assume that your trading partners rank players the same as you. If you think R. Brown is worth more than B. Westbrook, try to get a straight up trade. Do not sweeten the deal until asked. Always start with your lowest (yet not insulting) offer.

10) Do not lie or knowingly give bad advice. If you intentionally lie (notice the words intentionally) or give bad advice then other owners will distrust you from then on and you will find yourself with few, if any, trading partners. Instead of saying "C. Portis will rush

for 15 TDs, I promise," say "C. Portis has rushed for 12 or more TDs in two of his three years as a pro, and Washington has Al Saunders at OC now." State the facts and let the other owner jump to conclusions. Statistics do not lie; others interpretations of statistics is where the lying comes in. Remember there are lies, damned lies and statistics.

Trade Communication

1) Communication is the key. Always keep the lines of communication open. Start with an innocent "What would it take to get Marvin Harrison?" Even if he says, "Nothing on your team," now you have established some communications and can go from there. Always ask the selling price first, it may surprise you at how low it really is. If you start with an offer, you may pay too much. Start out by asking "how much?"

2) Open-ended offers allow you to start the dialogue without tipping your hand about which player you want. As an example, "I am not happy with my TE play. Is there any way for me to get one of yours?" or "My WRs suck! I see you have lots of depth at that position. What will it take to get a WR in trade?" Don't forget the open-ended counteroffer. "I cannot let M. Harrison go right now, he is in a groove. But I might be willing to let someone else go for a RB."

3) Bounce the trade idea off a neutral party or a trusted friend. "Do you think this is a good trade? Why or why not?" You might post it on another website message board for feedback. Be careful about posting it on your league website without the permission of the other owner. It is sometimes bad form to announce other's trade offers. In general, the more points of view you receive, the better the analysis. Remember to note as many league specifics as possible in the post so that others can evaluate accurately.

4) If trade talks hit a snag, find out what is causing the holdup. "Why can't we get this trade done? What do I need to do to make this a win-win deal for you? Is there anything we can do to get this done; time is running out for my team!"

5) Downplay your trades and your ability to get trades. Always keep your mouth shut. If you think you got the better end of the deal, for heavens sake do not brag about it. A simple "You never know. All will be revealed," is much better than constantly reminding a beaten owner how you bested them. Please do not send out a mass e-mail reminding every owner how you got the steal of the century. That just reminds them not to trade with you in the future or to keep a wary eye on your activities.

6) It is up to the other owner to evaluate players in a trade. Focus on the positives of players you are trading. Concentrate on their potential (estimate year-end results calculated on performance to date but ignoring SOS or teammate injuries). When trading away, help seduce them with words like "proven" if an aging vet and "tremendous rewards" if an untested younger player. If trying to trade for a vet, emphasize their injuries and decreasing stats and skills. If trying to acquire younger players, do not forget to stress their "unproven" history and the track record of many years to blossom in the NFL. Accentuate the positive and diminish the negative. Cut and paste quotes or news reports that improve your case, "C. Portis is well on his way to 1000 yards this season," or hurt his case, "Steve Smith appears to be sharing catches with K. Johnson."

7) Always announce to the entire league when you are shopping around a player or a draft pick. This allows you to get the best offer on the open market. If you accept the first offer, you never know if you could have gotten a better deal.

8) Good vibes – If you are on the message board (MB) most of the time and are the voice of reason when things get too heated as far as owners and disagreements, then you will be seen as the "wise" owner and thus more approachable about trades.

9) If a trade really works out well for my partner, I remind of it subtly. "Nice to see you win big last week with S. Jackson leading the way with two scores." I want him to remember that he got a fair trade from me and it was a good trade for him too. Be careful with this if the player you received has done much better or you may get a "Thanks, but R. Brown's ten TDs in five weeks looks much better to me. I am regretting that trade every day."

Responses to Trade Offers

Always respond to offers in a timely manner. Nothing turns off an owner more quickly than no response to a trade offer. I hate having my offers just hanging in the wind while the rest of the league moves rapidly forward. If you only check the website twice a week, tell everyone this. If you are going on vacation for a week, tell everyone so they will know you cannot communicate in a timely manner about trades.

For every trade accomplished there are ten trades that could not be worked out. Trading is a skill. Have dignity in trading and rejecting trades. When you make an offer, stand by it. Live by your word. Do not bad mouth another owner simply because he does not want to do your trade. Remember that you will want to trade with him again. If you bad mouth him at any time, you will probably lose a trading partner or at least a potential trading partner. Not to mention a voting member of the trade approval committee (if all owners can veto trades). It is in your best interest to be the most honest salesman you can be. Do not insult other owners for any reason, especially not over a trade. Trades are like some people's babies, they take great offense when their children are revealed in a bad light.

What do you do when you get a totally one-sided trade offer? Do you get angry? Are you disappointed? Do you think the owner is wasting your time and you promise yourself to never trade with him again? All are normal reactions and things you need to remember when crafting YOUR deals with others. Remember those emotions and strive not to arouse them in others. On the other hand, as a potential trade partner, do not dismiss others out of hand. Some owners start low and like the art of haggling. Anyone who has been to the markets and bazaars of many European or Middle Eastern countries can relate to this tactic. They expect you to bargain and hope you will accept less than they are willing to part with. Counter their lopsided offer with your own reasonable offer (but not your best offer or that will remove some of your own wiggle room). Play their game but with less movement of positions. An offer of trade (even a bad one) is better than no offer at all. At the very least you get to see who the other owner likes or values on your team and you have opened up some communications with them. If the trade is totally unacceptable, explain why and move on. My worst reply is "Would you accept this trade if you were in my shoes?"

8 Rules of Trading

1) Select trading partners based on need and personality. Look at all the rosters in your league and identify who is strongest where your need is. Now look at those teams and determine where their needs are. A great trading partner is strong where you are weak and weak where you are strong. It is a match made in heaven. You can help him and for this he will help you. Don't forget personality too. Remember the trading types. Never give up on any one owner but also do not waste too much time or energy on an owner that obviously does not or will not trade. Many times new owners will make friends with a few owners and develop close ties to them and subsequently trade exclusively with them. This is natural; people we know and trust are more likely to become trading partners. Just do not eliminate the other owners simply because you do not know them as well. Always have the trading door open.

2) **Criticize in private, praise in public**. My dad always told me that and it applies to the players on your team too. Never communicate your displeasure with a player openly. That just allows other owners to know how you feel and gives them the chance to lowball you during future trade negotiations about that player. If you have any criticisms, keep it private. Don't talk bad about your own players. On the other hand, always pump up and promote your players. Use stats to brag about them or use other's "expert" commentary. Other owners will soon covet your players and trade offers will come flooding in when others realize what great players you have.

3) Always do your homework. How will this trade affect my team? How will it affect his team? Like playing monopoly, buying the railroads and finding out you can not build hotels there, you need to know the rules. Is it a keeper league? Will I be getting a player who is an aging vet or retiring? What does his remaining SOS look like? What is his fantasy playoff schedule? What is his NFL team doing? What is the status of his injuries or his teammate's injuries? Is there any competition for his job? What about his contract for next year?

4) Know your deal breaker. These are players who you will not trade. Better to know these up-front and maybe even announce them to the other owner as "off the table." No reason to waste time with offers for them.

5) Present your case. If the trade really is win-win, you may have to sell his "win" portion. This could be because he does not see that he has a weakness at a certain position. Point out this flaw to him (diplomatically, of course) so that he can identify his needs.

7) Once the trade is a done deal; forget it ever happened and move on. No reason to gloat that you got a great deal. No reason to treat that owner more favorably in the future just because you got a trade accomplished with him. Now focus back on your team and continue to seek out strengths and weaknesses.

8) Establish relationships. Get to know ALL of the other owners. Ask them questions about their lives, philosophies and successes. Once you know the other owners, you can begin to get a better feel for how to handle trade negotiations with them.

Trade Tips

1) The two easiest positions to get thrown into a trade for some extra value are the kicker and defense.

2) Sell High. Buy low. Trade away (sell) players coming off a season high week or if the next stretch of schedule is against them. Trade for (buy) players coming off a tough schedule (they should do better) or who have not performed as expected.

3) Always check the health status and team website for demotions after a trade is offered.

4) Look for add-ons. If you are going to drop the backup TE you have been carrying anyway once you acquire your trading partner's stud TE, then offer that TE as part of the trade. Some owners actually think that more players are a better trade, even though they will have to ultimately drop a player from their team if they get more players than they traded. Look for players he will have to drop to make room on his roster. If there is someone on his bench that you would rather have than allow going to the waiver wire, ask for them.

5) Trading is an art. Always evaluate a trade and make sure, in your opinion, that you get more than what you trade away. Note that some owners will look at things differently. Some owners will only look at FP per games played. Some will look at the future schedule and use that. Still others may look at playoff matchups, etc.

6) Very simple but often unheeded advice. Watch out for bye weeks coming up and account for them in player value. Players A and B are equal in value. Player A has had his bye week, player B has his bye week coming up. Who would be the most valuable? Player A since he has all the games remaining as an asset whereas player B will miss one week of the remaining games due to his bye week. Also look at upcoming scheduled matchups and playoff matchups.

7) Will you face your trading partner in an upcoming game? Will your helping him in this trade help him to beat you in a regular season matchup?

Common Reasons for a Trade to be Rejected

1) The offer is too lopsided in your favor.

2) The offer helps your team (of course) but does nothing for his team or does not help his weaknesses. Strengthening strength is not necessarily improvement on his part.

3) Your team is strong as it is and your trading partners do not want to make you more powerful.

4) Your trading partner does not know what he is doing.

5) You have a reputation, either as getting the advantage in trades or not being a good trading partner.

6) You are new to the league or trading and other owners do not trust you yet.

How do you fix the reasons listed above? First, make fair, intelligent, win–win trade offers. This should remedy reasons one, two and five above. As for being new to the league, you just need to build some rapport with other owners. Try to get some dialogue going.

Trade Strategy

1) Two for one – Many times you can package a two for one deal so it looks as if you are giving away the farm. However, the other owner must drop another player to make room for your two players so you may get a package deal that is better than you expected. He only sees the two for one aspect though. Remember that even if the player he gives up (in addition to the stud you want) is no good; you can drop him and pick someone up off the FA list. Many times I will find a FA that I want first, then work out the two for one so that I can get a better player and another chance at a sleeper.

2) Playoff push trades – these involve a little sacrifice now (after you have clinched a playoff spot), in order to get a better player for the playoffs. For example, you have two good RBs. One faces an easy week 12 and 13 but then a terrible playoff stretch (weeks 14-16). You trade him for a slightly lesser RB who faces an easy week 14-16 schedule. The trade looks a little like you lost but it may provide a big boost in the playoffs.

3) Target players with significant changes late in the season. These players will be overvalued on draft day but their new system, coach or team will require half the season to make the adjustment and thus they will underperform early in the season. Target these players beginning with the second half of the season for trades. Do take advantage of other owners who WILL overreact to the underperformance and will drop or trade good players early.

4) Trade depth. Can you have too much of a good thing (depth)? Yes; if you have four great RBs but can only start two, then every week after their byes you will be faced with tough lineup decisions and may be losing points at other weaker positions because you have not traded some of your depth to strengthen the other weaker positions. Trade your least favorite RB and a WR2 or WR3 to get a better WR2 if you are weak at WR.

Evaluating Trades

The best evaluation is always ask yourself: "Would I accept this trade if I was in his shoes?"

Trade value is determined by players involved, number of teams in the league and the scoring system and rules involved. The number of teams will determine position demand.

– Trades can be good, bad, stupid or unfair.

1) Good trades are win-win situations. Good trades occur when both teams get something they need, thus improving their team. An example would be Team A trading their backup RB for Team B's backup WR. If both players were not being used, but were better than the starters the other team had, both teams gained (improved) on a starting position while sacrificing some bench depth to acquire a starter. Many times the ultimate trade winner or loser will not be determined until the season is over. Anytime there is no loser, only a better winner, then that is a good trade. For example. if my new WR2 did better than your new QB1, but your QB was better than no QB. You should strive for all win-win trades,

that way the owner will keep coming back for trades. Who would you rather trade with? The owner who swindled you or the one who gave you a win-win trade?

2) Bad Trade – The trade is not even but the owner on the losing side is doing so for a reason. Perhaps he is taking a chance to make a playoff push. Then again, maybe the other owner knows more than you and is trading the better player before he is traded in the NFL, the nagging injury he has is revealed or he is benched for another starter.

3) Stupid Trade – Trade where one team gets a player that is far more valuable than he trades away. This is a trade where you, as the owner, would never execute the trade, but it does not involve collusion; simply another owner who is desperate or unknowing. The losing owner just is not smart enough to know it is a losing trade, or does not know how bad it is or made it by mistake. In all three cases, he has not colluded with the other owner. Stupidity is no excuse but in trades it can be a reason.

4) Unfair Trade – An unfair trade involves an obvious disparity in trade values and thus may suggest collusion.

Mathematical evaluations: Three primary methods of evaluating trades.

1)   Use a trade (draft pick) chart (See Appendix C Trade Analyzer). If you are offered the 5th best player in the league for the 15th and 25th best players in the league, that is pretty much equal. The 5th overall pick of the draft is comparable to both the 15th and 25th picks. Try to put the players in terms of overall player worth and compare them like they were draft picks (see below – trading draft picks).

2)   Another method is to use a draft spot cheat sheet as a rough guide using current player positions. If you use the 3-year AVT method, keep the sheets with players (RB#5, etc.) to use as reference. If offered the 5th best RB in the league, then you can compare which other QBs or WRs would be equal in value, based on AVT FP projections. For example, if you want C. Taylor (RB#10, AVT 100 FPs), which WR would be fair? WR#4 (AVT 98 FP's) would be the closest choice. Notice, in the methods mentioned above, that where the player was drafted is of no consequence. It is all based on what his rank is based on this years stats. Once the draft is over and the season starts, a players value should not be based on his draft position but rather on how he has performed, how he is expected to perform and the scoring system under which he will perform.

3)   Use auction values. If offered a player for two other players, look to see if the values are close (adjusted for, if they have over or underperformed to date). If you are offered draft picks, this can be a quick and easy way to evaluate them (see Trading Draft Picks below).

Trading Draft Picks

How do you calculate the value of draft picks in a redraft league? Once the season starts in a redraft league all you need to determine is how the player will help you in the remaining games of the season (through week 16/17, if you make the playoffs). But what if you can trade draft picks for the upcoming draft? In a redraft league, draft picks are more valuable the closer you get to the #1 pick. By this I mean that the difference between the 1st pick and the 6th pick in the draft is higher than the difference between the 31st and 36th picks. There is a huge difference in value between 1.01 and 1.06. There is not as much difference in value between 3.07 and 3.12. Although both have five picks between them, the early picks are more significant. Thus the closer you come to picking first, the more valuable the picks. The rounds are not as important as the number within that round (think overall pick). The 3.12 pick is just a little better than a 4.01 pick, but not by much. The more teams in the league, the more important a different round pick becomes. So if you hear "I will give you a third rounder for him," make sure you know where in that round it falls and how many teams are in the league (or drafting in that round if a keeper league). The NFL Draft Pick Chart can prove a useful tool as well. For example, it shows that the 1st pick of the draft is worth 3000 units. The 4th pick and the 12th pick overall would be worth the 1st pick. The problem with the NFL Draft Pick Chart is that it takes into account other things such as offensive linemen, etc. You need to have a draft pick chart that accounts for your league and the skill positions you use. I have provided a portion of my own trade analyzer in Appendix C. Note that it is for a redraft league not a dynasty league. In a dynasty league, you are trying to determine worth over a period of years.

1) Trades in which you get more points than you are trading away are favorable to you. Trades in which you get the same or close (within 1%) should be considered fair deals. Trades in which you get between 1 and 5% less should be evaluated carefully; even though you are getting less, do you have other reasons for the trade?

2) Trades in which you lose 5% or more would seem to be BAD TRADES. As an example, you give up the 2nd and 23rd overall picks and get the 12th and 13th in return. You give away 559 points of value and get 516 in return. A 43-point difference is over 7% less. Not a good trade unless you think all of the RB studs will bust this year.

3) You can use this to evaluate players too, as long as you think of them in an overall value context. See mathematical evaluations, earlier in this chapter.

**Use AUCTION prices to compare draft picks or players in trades. If you are offered pick 9 (1.09) for picks 35 (3.11) and 41 (4.05), do you accept it? (See Appendix C Trade Analyzer). You can also look at the worth of players in your overall auction cheat sheet. Are the two player's values at 35 and 41 worth the ninth player overall? The ninth player is projected to go for $42. The 35th player is projected at $22 and the 41st player is projected at $20. So $42 is a fair price for those two players and the 9th pick is equal to the 35th and 41st picks. The trade analyzer also showed the trades equal 288 points; 152+136=288.

TRADING DRAFT PICKS: If you know that you have the 4th pick of the draft but do not really care for the three or four RBs that will be around at that point, then try to trade down and get a lower first round pick (say 9th when you will be picking a RB that you really wanted anyway) and then get a higher 2nd round pick (or even more if you can negotiate it and the league will allow it). The opposite is also true. Let's say you have the 10th pick of a 12-team league and you really do not like what will be left over at RB (based on mock drafts and ADP) by the time your name comes up. In this case, try to trade up for an earlier pick so that you can get Mr. Dependable no matter what the cost. Another advantage of a draft day trade of picks is the confusion it bestows to other owners. Now it makes the draft harder to track (who you have drafted or need) because you have changed a few of your pick positions. This alone is worth trading picks, especially if it gets you away from some of the tougher owners.

Timing of Trades

Before the season begins, when a player is purchased through the auction (or drafted), his value is set at about face value (or what price in dollars or draft pick that you paid for him). Then as the season starts he enters the secondary market. If he does well (or is desired), his price will go up and supply and demand will balance out. His price will go up the more people want (demand) him. His supply is fixed at one individual. At some point his price will peak and begin to decline as you get closer to the trading deadline. Economists call this the declining-price anomaly. You are more likely to get the best price for him right before the deadline as his owner worries about not being able to trade him.

Most owners will come out of the draft thinking they have had a perfect draft and a perfect team. There is little to be gained by trading then unless a team has obvious flaws, such as both QBs on the same bye week. But even then the owner may want some time to see how things develop. Trades usually happen after week 3 and not before. Why? Week 4 is the first bye week and it takes a few weeks of frustrating performance before some owners give up the ship early. No one gives up on a player after week 1 anymore. If they do, let me know I want to play in that league too. Injuries can be another reason for trades and they tend to start to pile up after a few weeks. Look for some activity after week 3 due to byes but most activity will occur from week 5 up until the deadline. A dip in trades may occur just before the deadline because some owners give up on getting a deal done close to a deadline.

Timing can be the trading deadline, the big game versus a rival or any chance of making the playoffs. Being the first to realize an owner needs something (his RB1 is now out for the season) can be a form of timing too. Look for key events. An owner loses his star WR to an injury. Now your bench WR who is starting and making ESPN highlight reels looks pretty good as trade bait. Did your opponent's RB just produce another goose egg in week 7; time to get him some help. Two weeks before the trade deadline look at who is in the hunt and who needs help to stay in the hunt. Sometimes these owners are so playoff-obsessed that they will make a desperate trade to secure that player needed for the playoff push. Injuries and time of the season can determine trade likelihood.

Take advantage of these critical times:

1) Loss of a starter - He loses his WR1; your WR3 can fill the void if packaged right and if he panics enough.

2) Slow start – If an owner starts slow and loses a few games or sees poor performance from a good player, now is the time to strike a deal.

3) Owner has bye week blues – easiest and most likely reason to get a trade done. Do you hate the bye week because it forces you to make some lineup adjustments that do not seem fair? You bench your RB1 but your opponent does not have to bench him this week; that kind of thing. No worries mate! Start to use it to your advantage by preying on the weak during their bye weeks. Look at your opponents. Do any of them have multiple players at the same position off on the same bye week? Both starting RBs off week 6 and only one serviceable replacement RB? POUNCE. Offer a trade to get the RB that you want and offer him, as a lifeline, another RB who has a bye week coming up when he can platoon him. You get the RB you wanted in the draft (but he stole) and also get to dump a

RB with his bye week coming up anyway. Now assuming you have the backup RB for this week (you inherited a RB with this week's bye), you have your dream team. Many times an owner will overreact to finding a bye week hole that needs to be filled and you can trade a less than equal player to "help" him out.

4) After about week 6 or 7, most owners have a good feel for which players are producing and which are not. Trades after this period will tend to be equal since some of the unknown that was around at the start of the season is eliminated.

5) Teams that are winning appear to be easier to get trades done with than teams that are losing. Winning teams have better players and thus are afforded higher prestige. Losing teams are assumed to have no players of value and have to "shake things up."

6) Teams needing to win badly – Either on the bubble of playoffs or playing a rival and needing a win for seeding purposes or bragging rights. These teams may be willing to let a good player go who has great upcoming matchups, because they are desperate for a win now.

7) Right before the deadline (a week before to give you time to communicate back and forth), look at teams that are making a push and teams that are in danger of coming in last place. Both will be motivated to shake things up a bit. Read: desperate. Especially if they have just suffered an injury, suspension or benching at a major position.

Trade Disputes (Is it a Fair Trade?)

What is a fair trade? Trades are subjective and different advantages are seen by different owners. As the old saying goes, "beauty is in the eye of the beholder." What is good to one owner may be bad to another and unfair to a third. Basically, a trade should improve both teams in some manner. Some believe that there is no such thing as an unfair trade (both owners agreed to it). In other words, they feel that no owner would intentionally collude thus all trades must be allowed. This is the Mary Poppins theory of trades. They will never veto a trade simply on the principle that all parties agreed to it. Other owners say most are okay but some trades are unfair and need to be vetoed. Many times the ones protesting the loudest about a lopsided trade are dead wrong. It takes a long time to determine the winner and many times it is not the team everyone thought was getting a steal. When we try to evaluate a trade as fair or unfair, we run the risk of imposing our own opinions on other's trades. You need to evaluate it from their perspective, not your perspective, and perhaps giving owners the benefit of the doubt is best in all but the obvious circumstances. Just look at any trade offer that is posted on a MB. There will be many differing opinions on whether it is a good, bad, stupid or unfair trade. You may not agree with their reasons but you may agree that their reasoning was not unfair. What is fair to one owner may be unfair to others (that is why we have the draft; opinions differ).

Some leagues rely on the commissioner's approval of trades; others rely on owners to vote to approve trades or veto trades (certain number vetoing =trade not put through); other leagues have an early trading deadline to prevent collusion for a playoff push. A commissioner's duty is not to evaluate trades but to stop teams from cheating. If you had to evaluate trades you would be biased based on your own thinking. Cheating means they knowingly are attempting to pervert the league through a trade. I have never seen this in any of my leagues, although I have protested a trade or two as an owner (Steven Davis for Jamal Lewis preseason in 2005). S. Davis turned out to be the steal there, although I thought otherwise at the time. See, I do make mistakes. So I have vetoed a few trades and regretted it every time after watching those players involved. I prefer the commissioner be left out of the equation and only league owners vote. Trades in a redraft are different than in a keeper league. Keeper trades must be evaluated in the long-term and are harder to evaluate. It will always take longer to determine a winner and a loser. Commissioners are important in keeper leagues because a lopsided trade can hurt a keeper league for several years.

What can be done if the trade seems unfair? First, post a message stating your objections and asking both owners to explain why they think the trade is good for both teams. Both owners should easily be able to explain why it is a fair trade to them. One person's perception of fair is another's perception of bad. Secondly, if you still have doubts, protest or veto the trade, if able.

What is collusion? Collusion is a conspiracy between two or more teams where they intentionally try to improve one team at the expense of another. An example of this would be a one-sided trade. If Team A traded LT to Team B for Team B's out-for-the-season kicker, then collusion could reasonably be suspected. Are the teams intentionally trading players to improve one team? The best way to deal with a uneven trade is to have the league rules prevent them with a detailed procedure for protesting collusion. However, many leagues do not have such a written policy because it is hard work and seems a little too hard-core for the fun, friendly league they are involved in. However, mark my words; some time in the future you will wish you had these written guidelines in place.

Chapter 16 WCOFF, NFFC and AFFL

Mention high stakes fantasy football and most people think of the World Championship of Fantasy Football (WCOFF) or the National Fantasy Football Championship (NFFC). However, there is a third event that deserves recognition too, the American Fantasy Football League (AFFL). The AFFL is different from the other two in that it does not have a draft location. It is entirely a "live online" draft. There may be some other leagues that satisfy this requirement but these three high stakes leagues get the most attention and will be the focus of this chapter.

None of the big three allows trading in order to prohibit collusion. In fact, Greg Ambrosius, Founder, National Fantasy Football Championship and Editor, Fantasy Sports Magazine told me "People are tired of losing their league due to a trade. NFFC is the next challenge beyond the local league. We are not taking players away from their local leagues, but instead giving them other options".

They all use Free Agent Acquisition Budget (FAAB) systems, involving a blind bidding arrangement with a fixed amount of bidding dollars. Both WCOFF and NFFC have a $1,000 FAAB (AFFL uses a $2,000 FAAB). Both WCOFF and the NFFC have the same starter requirements. AFFL allows an extra flex position and one less WR. The scoring rules are similar but with a few nuances. All have similar rules about draft protocol with the exception of the NFFC, which uses the Kentucky Derby style system. In 2007, the NFFC will use 3RR. (See below for a discussion on each).

What is the definition of a "high stakes" league? Some say it is a $1,000 or greater entry fee. Most define it as a league with a $50,000 or greater grand prize. Early attempts at these high stakes leagues often ended in failure because the "championships" did not get the required number of entrants. Therefore, the prize money was less and teams that did win felt "cheated." Imagine competing for a chance at $100,000 only to find out that you won $27,000 since only 25% of the needed teams signed up. Skepticism became the buzzword of these championships. Enter the World Championship of Fantasy Football (WCOFF) in 2002. They held a high stakes tournament and ran it right.

WCOFF started in 2002 when Lenny Pappano (who runs Draftsharks.com, a fantasy football information site) and Emil Kadlec (who is the President of Fantasy Sports Publications, Inc.) joined forces to launch a high stakes fantasy football competition. Before 2002, there were trade shows with lots of industry types promoting their individual products but nothing for the fantasy football competitor to attend and enjoy. "Enjoy" being the key word. Previously, fantasy football fans would watch "the experts" draft, but they could not participate themselves. To quote Lenny, "If you're the average FF enthusiast, how exciting is a trade show?" The same 50 executives would come to these trade shows, and there would be some experts and discussions, but no event for the average fan to compete in and try to be the best.

As it turns out, the World Series of Poker (WSOP) was the inspiration for these two founders. They came up with the idea of a championship fantasy football event in Las Vegas from WSOP. The crucial point in the creation of the event was their decision-making process. They designed WCOFF with only one thing in mind. Lenny says, "We started with the phrase, 'If we could compete in this event, we would want to...' and then we filled in the blanks." What do we want to do in Las Vegas, the fun capital of the world?

We want to have a chance at a very big prize. Say $200,000. We would want autographed giveaways. In addition, we would want a party in the ESPN Zone after the draft. The only thing missing from the ultimate guy weekend would be a golf tournament and a poker night. Do not worry, those have been incorporated too, unofficially. Ultimately, WCOFF was and is built around the principle of producing a product where people say, "This is great… who would not want to do this?"

Many people do not realize that these two built the WCOFF with a "if you build it, they will come" mentality. At some point, when the applications with entrance fees were not coming in fast enough, Lenny told his wife that they might have to mortgage their house, but that was not necessary. Build it they did, and people came. The great part is the evolution of this event over its five-year history (2006 was its 5th year). The participants have a message board (MB) and their suggestions and constructive criticisms have helped shape the direction the WCOFF has taken.

Interview with WCOFF co-Founder Lenny Pappano

Sam: Do you have any amusing anecdotes from your five years of running WCOFF?

Lenny: "One of the first people we met with in Vegas was Andrea Rice – then the manager of the ESPN Zone. We told her about what we wanted to do, and that we wanted to rent out the entire ESPN Zone to hold a party for 1,000 WCOFFers. She was very polite and handed us a contract that committed us to about $80,000 for the party. We took the contract home, sniffed it, gave it to the attorney, and then sent it back signed. So the night of the very first WCOFF party at the ESPN Zone, as people are streaming in, Emil looks at Andrea and asks: "Did you ever think this night would happen, when we first met with you?" And without breaking stride, Andrea says in her Texas accent, "Nope; no way." I have to confess, I was shocked by her answer. I chimed in with, "You DIDN'T?!" And Andrea says, "Oh Lenny, if I had a dime for every dreamer who has come in here wanting to rent out the whole place for a party…" As we found out later from her, that WCOFF party marked the first time the entire Las Vegas ESPN Zone had been rented out for an event. And we signed our names on that contract like it was nothing. Maybe we were too ignorant to know how ignorant we were, and it wound up being a blessing in disguise."

Sam: How would you best describe WCOFF?

Lenny: "It's the Super Bowl and Mardi Gras of fantasy football all wrapped into a four-day weekend!"

Sam: Can you give a little history? Like the number of participants?

Lenny: "We started out at 552 teams in year one and had 840 last year (2006), on our 5th anniversary. We're not sure yet on how many we'll have in 2007."

Sam: Some outside and inside WCOFF have complained that the prize money for the winner ($200,000) has not gone up as the number of contestants has grown. Why?

Lenny: "We've polled our folks and they overwhelmingly have expressed the opinion of wanting more money going into league winners as opposed to increasing the top prize. Nonetheless, I suspect that the grand prize will begin to creep upward in the next few years."

Sam: Any hints for the future of WCOFF?

Lenny: "We'd like to continue growing the event to accommodate more fantasy football enthusiasts, while still keeping the event's intimacy and sense of community."

Lenny Pappano is President of Fantasy Football Draft Sharks, Inc. (draftsharks.com), and has been published and quoted extensively in a variety of fantasy football magazines.

WCOFF

WCOFF is fantasy football's premier event. It is the highest of the high stakes championships. Ask any fantasy footballer to pick the event of the year and inevitably, most would nominate WCOFF. No other league has hundreds of fantasy footballers competing for a $200,000 first prize and the title of World Champion of Fantasy Football.

On September 8th, 2007, entrants will attend a live draft in either Las Vegas, Atlantic City (started in 2006) or Orlando (started in 2007). WCOFF joined NFFC as a multi-city high stakes league in 2006. All of the drafts occur simultaneously, and each team is placed in a 12-team league. The entry fee is $1,495 plus a $165 event fee. The Grand Prize is $200,000. Second place gets $45,000 and third place pulls in $25,000. League champs win $6,000, second place in the league gets $1,800 and third place gets $500. WCOFF has more prize money spread out among more players. They also have a consolation competition for teams not making the fantasy playoffs. Another event is a playoff competition called the "one and done contest," both of which are nice touches to keep the fantasy football fan going, even when he is out of main event contention. They also have prizes for all members of the league that score the most points in the 11-week regular season, just to keep owners fighting all the way.

There are 70 leagues of 12 teams each, so 840 competitors in WCOFF in 2006 (Although rumors say that 900 may be the number for 2007). The regular season is 11 weeks long (so that all 12 teams in a league can play each other once). Week 12 is the LCG, in which the top W/L team faces the highest point scoring team that remains. There is also a consolation game for third place between two other teams. All of the league champions (70) plus 27 wild card teams will advance to the overall playoffs, held during weeks 13 through 16.

The main event for WCOFF is the Saturday live draft, but the fun does not start or end there. WCOFF also has a viewing party on Thursday night for the NFL kickoff game. Friday is auction drafts, Hall of Fame drafts and draft masters drafts. Saturday after the main draft, WCOFF hosts a kickoff party that night at the ESPN Zone restaurant in Las Vegas. On Sunday is a viewing party for Sunday games. I enjoy WCOFF tremendously. I will participate in WCOFF again this year. It is a great feeling to stand in a room with hundreds of other fantasy football fans, competing with them in simultaneous drafts. Lenny and Emil care about the hobby and have done a great job promoting fantasy football and WCOFF.

WCOFF has an online version of their tournament called the WCOFF satellite leagues. The entry fee is $220. First prize is a trip to the following year's WCOFF (including entry fee and events fee) and airfare and hotel room for two nights; or you can take an approximate cash payment of $2,000. The league format is 12-team leagues. The starters are the same and the roster is the same as WCOFF. The time limit for the online draft is two minutes per pick. The scoring rules are the same. The major difference is that it is a 14-game regular season and there are no H2H games. It is a total points league, with the top four scoring teams advancing to the playoffs. The playoffs are single elimination with the winner of week 15 playing in week 16 for the championship.

WCOFF Scoring

The following are some of the rules for WCOFF:

Rosters are 20 players. Starting lineups are as follows:

1 Quarterback

2 Running Backs

3 Wide Receivers

1 Tight End

1 Flex Player (RB, WR or TE)

1 Kicker

1 Team Defense/Specials Team

Scoring: An individual offensive player on any active WCOFF starting roster will be credited points for scoring in the following manner, unless otherwise noted:

a. Passing:
Yards passing divided by 20 (e.g. 215 passing yards = 10.75 fantasy points).
4 points for every passing TD.
Minus one point (-1) for every interception thrown.
2 points for every two-point conversion.

b. Rushing:
Yards rushing divided by 10 (e.g. 89 rushing yards = 8.9 fantasy points).
6 points for every rushing TD.
2 points for every two-point conversion.

c. Receiving:
Yards receiving divided by 10 (e.g. 112 receiving yards = 11.2 fantasy points)
6 points for every receiving TD.
1 point for every catch.
2 points for every two-point conversion

d. All Other TDs:
6 points for any TD scored by recovered or returned fumbles, laterals, or any other means by which a skill position player (QB, RB, WR, TE or K) is awarded an individual TD, except kickoff and punt returns. No rushing or receiving yardage is awarded for a TD returned on a fumble.

Placekicking:
1 point for every extra point
3 points for every FG of 1–30 yards plus .1 point for every yard thereafter.
Example: a 43-yard FG would be worth 4.3 points.

f. Team Scoring (Defense/Special Teams):
1 point for every sack
2 points for every team takeaway (interception or fumble recovery)**
6 points for every TD (via interception return, fumble return, punt or kickoff return, blocked FG return, missed FG return, blocked punt return)*
2 points for every safety
5 points for every shutout ***
2 points for allowing between 1-5 points ***
1 point for allowing between 6-10 points ***

* TDs scored on "fake" FGs or "fake" punts do NOT count as defense/special teams scoring. TDs scored by the offensive team after a blocked FG or blocked punt do NOT count as a defense/special teams score. TDs scored on a double-turnover only count for the individual player who scored the TD, not for the team.

** A double turnover is considered points for the recovering team's defense and ST. For example, team A's offense fumbles and team B's defense recovers, but then fumbles the ball back to team A's offense. In that scenario, team A's defense and special teams (along with team B's defense and special teams) are both awarded a fumble recovery.

*** Any and all points scored against a team are considered points scored against the special teams and defense. Thus, as an example, a turnover by the offense that is returned for a TD is considered as points scored against the special teams and defense.

Note that WCOFF only awards 4 points for a passing TD (NFFC gives 6 points). WCOFF does not subtract a point for fumbles and awards a full point to RBs for PPR (NFFC awards .5 points to RBs, all other skill positions get 1 point). WCOFF awards fewer points to a defense for holding the other team to a shutout or reduced points.

NFFC

Greg Ambrosius, Founder, National Fantasy Football Championship and Editor, Fantasy Sports Magazine told of how NFFC started in 2004 in three cities: Las Vegas, New York and Chicago with 224 participants. That year the NFFC awarded over $280,000 in prizes. 2005 brought 280 players and over $350,000 in prize money. 322 teams took part in NFFC in 2006 and competed for over $425,000 in prize money.

NFFC owns the distinction of being fantasy football's first multi-city, high stakes competition. On Saturday, September 1, 2007, they will conduct drafts at the Flamingo Las Vegas, the Oakbrook Marriott in Chicago, the New York Hilton in New York and the Tampa Convention Center. In their competition, first prize is $100,000. The entry fee is $1,300. League prizes are $2,500 for W/L champ, $2,500 for TFPs champ and third place (total points) gets $1,000. Another $2,500 goes to overall champion in a contest between the W/L champ and the TFPs champ.

The NFFC will consist of 26-32 leagues, each with 14 teams, so anywhere from 364 up to 448 competitors. This differs from WCOFF in that they only have 12-team leagues, but with a much larger total entry pool (840). Regular season for NFFC is weeks 1-13. Each team will play each other once. (This differs from WCOFF's regular season of 11 games). Roster size is 18 and the draft is serpentine but will have a 3RR, a third round reversal. NFFC draft leagues will use 3RR in 2007, meaning that the draft order will begin with team 14 to start round 3 and then continue in serpentine fashion after that. The NFFC is using 3RR to balance the talent pool throughout these 14-team leagues. Therefore, an owner with the 14th pick will get 1.14, 2.01 and 3.01. Players may be drafted at any position at any time in the draft, but each team must have at least one player for each of the designated starting positions by the end of the draft.

Starters are the same as WCOFF.

NFFC Scoring

Scoring: Players can accumulate points in a number of ways:

a. Passing:

.05 points for every yard passing (works out to 1 point every 20 yards).

6 points for every passing touchdown

2 points for every two-point conversion

minus 1 point for every interception and lost fumble

b. Rushing:

.10 points for every yard rushing (works out to 1 point every 10 yards).

6 points for every rushing TD

2 points for every two-point conversion

minus 1 point for every lost fumble

6 points for a recovered offensive fumble for a touchdown (RB, QB, WR, TE)

c. Receiving::

.10 points for every yard receiving (works out to 1 point every 10 yards).

6 points for every receiving TD

1 point for every reception for WRs, TEs and QBs

0.5 points for every reception for RBs

2 points for every two-point conversion

minus 1 point for every lost fumble

d. Kicking:

1 point for every extra point

3 points for every field goal from 1-30 yards

3 points for every field goal plus .10 points for every yard after 30 yards (i.e. a 47-yard field goal would be worth 4.7 points)

e. Defense/Special Teams

1 point for every sack

2 points for every interception or opponents' fumble recovery

6 points for every touchdown (interception return, defensive fumble return, punt or kickoff return, blocked field goal return, blocked punt return). All special teams and defensive points are awarded to the team responsible, not the individual player. Should a kicker, punter or field goal holder throw a pass off a fake attempt, however, the offensive output for that offensive play would go toward the individual player, not the special teams. Also, any lost fumble or "muff" on a special team play does not result in negative points for that individual player.

2 points for every safety

12 points for a shutout by the entire team

8 points for allowing 2-7 points by the entire team

4 points for allowing 8-12 points by the entire team

2 points for allowing 13-17 points by the entire team

Another unique aspect is that the W/L leader and the total points leader for the league each get the top prize of $2,500. These two teams then compete in weeks 14-16, with the highest scoring team earning another $2,500 in prize money. Therefore, there is no LCG. If the same team is the W/L leader and the TFPs leader, then he is awarded $7,500. Both the W/L champ and the TFPs champ advance to the three-week playoff, where their week 1-13 average goes with them. Additionally, any team that scores in the top 10 overall in TFPs, but does not make the playoffs, based on the above scenario is added to the playoffs.

The NFFC uses a KDS (Kentucky Derby Style) system, which allows owners to pick a draft spot preference in advance of the random selection of leagues. NFFC participants will get to rank their draft spot preference before leagues are formed. The theory is that some input is better than none. Undoubtedly, all players will list spots 1-3 in that order, but after that some may prefer to move down in the draft to secure higher picks around the turn. Still others may prefer a lower pick to the middle so that they can use predictions on what the owners ahead of them will do so that they can get value. As an example, picks 1-7 will be ranked 1st through 7th but then perhaps 10th and 11th get higher preference than 8th and 9th. The NFFC will use each team's preference within a league to determine draft spots after the order of preferences are determined.

Another important difference in 2007 is the 3RR used in the draft. Why introduce this? In 2005, 43% of the league champions picked in spots 1-3 and it became more pronounced in 2006, as 18 of the Top 32 teams (over 56%) drafted from picks 1-3. Thus the decision to try 3RR.

In this case, round 3 will have a reversal so that the first pick in round 3 will be team 14 and then it will go back down to team 1, who will get the last pick in round 3 (unlike a true serpentine draft where team 1 would get the first pick). This is designed to even the playing field a bit. Rounds 4-18 will then be serpentine (round 4 will have team 1 pick first, round 5 will have team 14 pick first, and so on).

The format will look like this:

Round 1	1-14
Round 2	14-1
Round 3	14-1

Round 4   1-14

Round 5   14-1

Round 6   1-14

And so on, doubling back every round from here on out through round 18.

NFFC satellite leagues will consist of 14-team leagues. There will be no overall prizes for competition between leagues. Entry fees vary from $75 all the way up to $1,000. The scoring and roster rules are the same for the satellite leagues as the NFFC main event. The differences occur in the playoffs. The top W/L team and the next three highest scoring teams make the playoffs. They will carry their 13-week regular season average into the three-week playoff competition. In leagues with a $250 or greater entry fee, the regular season W/L champion and TFPs champ (weeks 1-13) will win their entry fee as prizes.

The NFFC also has an Ultimate League with a $5,000 entry fee where 14 teams compete for a $40,000 league first place prize. This league has an 89% payout ratio.

AFFL

AFFL is a $75,000 contest with an entry fee of $500 for 250 entrants or a $100,000 contest with an entry fee of $1,200 for 300 players. Of course, the real difference between AFFL and WCOFF and NFFC is the **live online draft format**. Now you no longer have to leave the comfort of your own home and travel to a city to participate. Instead, stay at home and play online. The format is 12 teams per league with a maximum of 50 leagues for the $75,000 and $100,000 prizes. The regular season includes weeks 1-11. The LCG is in week 12 and overall playoffs are in weeks 13-16. The team with the best W/L and the other team with the highest points total will meet in week 12 in the LCG. Sixty-two teams (50 league champions plus 12 wild card teams with the highest week 1-11 points) advance to the overall playoffs. In the playoffs, your average score from weeks 1-12 (different than WCOFF) will be included. The top 5 win prizes.

Rosters consist of 20 players. Starters are 1 QB, 2 RBs, 2 WRs, 1 TE, 1 K, 1 DEF, and 2 Flex (RB, WR or TE). This is different from WCOFF and NFFC in that AFFL has an extra flex and one less WR. The scoring system is similar to WCOFF but any TD over 51 yards gets a 2-point bonus and turnovers are -2 points. QBs also get 1 point for every 10 yards over 300.

Neil Wickam, Commissioner of the AFFL, spoke to me about the league history. "The league started in 2004, the same year as the NFFC. 2006 saw 84 teams participate in Platinum with the winner receiving over $47,000" (a total payout of $90,720 or 90%). He estimates 200 players in 2007 for the Platinum Leagues. Of course, AFFL has no "bricks and mortar" business costs so their payouts can be higher. But that is not all; in the words of Neil, "We pride ourselves on having the best customer service".

Other Tournaments

1) Fantasy Football Tournament of Champions, FFTOC, is a fantasy football contest unlike any of the ones above. This contest has no draft or roster management. You can play any player you want, but only once. It is often called a "one and done contest." You start 1 QB, 2 RBs, 3 WRs, 1 TE, 1K, and 1 DEF. It has a typical performance system based on 1 point per 20 pass yards, 10 rushing yards and 10 receiving yards. The regular season is weeks 1-12. The 2006 winner won over $17,000.

Since some of the other contests also include some form of a "one and done" contest, here are some considerations if you find yourself participating in one:

1) Do you start the studs up front to make the playoffs?
2) On the other hand, do you save some of the studs who you think will have great playoff matchups, so that if you make the playoffs, you can have a chance at the championship?
3) There are no shortages of good QBs to choose from based on matchups. I suggest go for broke on them in regular season (don't save Peyton for the finals).
4) Start RBs based on their matchups. (i.e. the defenses they play influence their performances more than at QB). In fact, weak rush defenses help average RBs more than the studs, so consider saving the studs for other matchups (vs. average defenses) and use an average RB against a poor rush defense.
5) Stud RBs produce much more than the rest of the RBs, so they give you a huge advantage in the playoffs; if you can, save them for the playoffs, and try to get in using other RBs during the regular season.
6) You need 36 WRs in regular season and another 12 in postseason. That is 48 WRs to go through. If you can save the better WRs for postseason, you will be in a better position to win the championship, and if you need to go through 48 WRs all season, you may as well get some of the deeper WRs while they are hot.
7) Normally two WRs from the same team will not put up good enough numbers together, so avoid starting R. Wayne and M. Harrison on the same week.

Suggestion for a High Stake League (HSL)

Have a HSL based on auctioning draft picks. Determine draft order by bidding for the draft spots (takes away all complaints or questions about who drafts first). For draft picks in rounds one and two, each spot is auctioned off starting with pick #1. Teams bid real money to acquire the draft pick. If a team bids $900 and wins, then he pays the league $900. Next, pick #2 is auctioned off and so on until pick #14 in a 14-team league. Each team can only buy one pick per round. The last pick will go for the minimum bid of $1. Then round 2 picks are auctioned off the same way, with pick 2.01 going first, all the way until pick 2.14, which is the last pick and will go for $1. Rounds 3-20 will be serpentine, with the draft order based on the round 1 and 2 draft picks. FAAB would be blind bidding with owners putting in their real money equal to the FAAB budget. For example, $1,000 paid if $1,000 budget or $200 paid if $200 budget. Money left over at the end of the year returns back to owners (or not) depending on the rules. Prize money for 1st through 3rd place comes from entry fees. Weekly prize money for the team scoring the most points that week comes from draft spot bidding and FA money divided by 17. If the entry fee was $5,000 and FAAB was $1,000, you would have to pay $6,000 to play. If you decided to play it cheap and get 1.14 and 2.14, then it would cost you $2 more to play. If you went with 1.01 and 2.01, it could cost $1,500 or more to play, above the entry and FAAB fees.

Payouts

When discussing a HSL, the topic of conversation normally turns to "What is the payout?" Alternatively, "How much return do I get for my investment"? The cash returned is a ratio of prize money to cash collected to play. To calculate it, first determine the cost of the event. Entry fees multiplied by the number of teams participating will give you the amount the organizers receive. Next, add up all the prize money paid out. If there is only a prize for first place then that will be the cash returned; if there is a prize for 1st and 2nd place then both added together is the cash returned. Divide the prize money by the fees collected to get the cash returned (the higher the percentage the more money returned to the winners). If a league charges $100, has 12 teams and pays $1000 for first place, that league's percentage of cash returned is 1000/1200=83.33%. **Prize money/fees charged=cash returned.**

WCOFF is sometimes compared unfairly based on just their league payouts, but WCOFF's critics conveniently leave the other contests and other giveaways (autographed memorabilia for example) out of the total payouts. Once these additional payouts are considered, their payouts are on par with the other contests. In the WCOFF satellite leagues a 12-team league will take in $2,640 in entry fees and payout $2,000, for a payout ratio of 76%. This may be misleading too since the trip to WCOFF could add up to a value of over $2,300, if you opt for that, which makes the payout ratio closer to 87%. NFFC satellite leagues have 14 teams in a $250 league, equaling $3,500 in entry fees. The payout for that league is $2,900 ($500 each to the regular season W/L Champ and TFPs team, plus $1,650 for first place, $500 for second place and $250 for third place in playoffs). The payout is 2900/3500=83%. The $100 entry fee league (which is a winner-take-all 16-week TFPs league with a $1,300 entry fee to the next NFFC as a prize) pays out nearly (1300/1400) 93% of the entry fee. I am assuming you can get a cash equivalent, but I am not sure.

There are other considerations besides total payout. How many competitors will you face in your league? How many teams from each league advance to the playoffs? How many will you compete with if you make the playoffs? How good is the customer service of the HSL? Do they provide any freebies (prize drawings, raffles, goodie bags at the draft)? One other factor may be what I call the "Fame Factor". How much recognition do you get by doing well in the HSL?

The number of teams in your league and the number who advance to the playoffs will determine your initial chances. If it is a 12-team league and two teams advance to the playoffs then all things being equal you have a 2 in 12 (17%) chance of making the playoffs. If the league has 14 teams but only two advance, the odds are tougher (14%) to make the playoffs. Once in the playoffs, how many will you face? If you face 96 other teams in the playoffs then you have roughly a 1% chance of finishing in first place. Of course, these odds do not consider your previous TFP's that are carried over into the playoffs or the quality of your team and the ones you will face. However, if you only had to face 50 other teams then your odds have doubled of winning the Championship.

Another factor to consider is how many places win prizes. In some leagues, prize money is awarded to the top three finishers, in others only the champion wins prize money. I like to see the top three earn something, that way if an injury strikes my team in the playoffs at least I get something.

Chapter 17 WCOFF Preparations

* The following preparation advice will work for most leagues, especially leagues that start 1 QB, 2 RBs, 3 WRs, 1 Flex (R/W/T), 1 TE, 1 K and 1 DEF.

The draft is the most important factor in success at WCOFF*. Large rosters (20 players or more; starting nine or less) give you plenty of room to stockpile players. WCOFF is about drafting smart, because the leftovers at the skill positions (after 240 players are gone) are non-existent. Once you have your team, your start/bench decisions will mean the difference between first, second or third place (and no championship game) and your FA bidding can be the extra points that get you into the money of the playoffs.

Steps for Preparing for WCOFF

1) Know the rules. (See Chapter 16 – WCOFF)

2) Participate in as many mock drafts as possible, with WCOFF rules and players and from your draft position.

3) Create cheat sheets using VBD and your own baselines. I prefer the 100 pick baseline with the AVT method for my projections.

4) Check message boards at WCOFF and other places every day for gossip, words of wisdom, etc.

5) Once the leagues are released, find your draft spot and start to formulate a game plan based on your draft spot and the first 100 picks.

6) Scout your opponents. Determine their WCOFF experience and drafting and FAAB tendencies. Establish contact via the MB.

WCOFF ADMIN: 12 teams, 20-man rosters, start 1 QB, 2 RBs, 3 WRs, 1 Flex (RB/WR/TE), 1 TE, 1 K, 1 DEF/ST

Scoring is 1 PPR, 1 point per 10 yards rushing/receiving; 1 point for 20 yards passing, -1 for INTs.

What to expect

Different studies show a draft history of approximately:

– 29 QBs on average (1st one in round 2)

– 71 RBs

– 82 WRs

– 22 TEs (1st in round 3)

– 17 Ks (1st in round 11)

– 19 DEFs (1st in round 10)

Of course, each league will be different, but the averages above are close to what you can expect in the draft.

Table 17.1 is a sample of several 2006 WCOFF drafts that I noted on the floor after the main event. It will help you determine when positions are more likely to be drafted.

Table 17.1 WCOFF Sample Draft

Rd	1	2	3	4	5	6	7	8	9	10	11	12
1	R	R	R	R	R	R	R	R	R	R	W	W
2	Q	R	R	W	R	W	W	W	W	R	W	R
3	W	R	W	R	W	T	W	R	R	R	R	W
4	R	Q	W	W	W	R	R	W	R	W	R	R
5	W	W	W	T	R	R	T	W	R	W	T	R
6	T	W	Q	R	R	W	R	R	W	Q	W	W
7	W	T	R	Q	Q	W	W	Q	T	W	R	Q
8	R	Q	R	W	W	R	W	R	R	R	W	W
9	R	R	T	R	W	Q	R	W	W	W	R	T
10	W	R	W	W	W	W	W	T	W	W	W	R
11	R	W	R	W	T	W	Q	W	R	T	W	W
12	R	W	D	R	Q	Q	R	R	Q	Q	Q	R
13	R	D	R	W	R	D	R	W	R	R	R	W
14	W	W	W	W	W	T	W	R	W	R	R	T
15	Q	R	W	T	D	W	Q	D	Q	K	T	Q
16	T	W	T	Q	D	R	R	Q	K	R	Q	R
17	D	Q	K	D	T	K	W	D	W	W	R	D
18	D	K	Q	K	R	W	K	W	W	K	D	R
19	K	T	W	W	K	W	D	Q	D	D	K	K
20	K	R	D	D	W	D	W	K	W	T	K	R

What does this analysis reveal? Not only does it tell you where the runs will be, but also how many players from each position you can expect to be drafted, and thus the depth needed.

In the first six rounds, 35 RBs and 28 WRs were drafted. Of the remaining 9 picks, 4 were QBs and 5 were TEs. Overall, 26 QBs were drafted as most teams went with two QBs. P. Manning went in round 2 in many cases and the last QB1 went in round 12 (two teams did this). Of the 26 QBs drafted, most are starters (maybe two sleepers), meaning that eight starters are left in free agency. Expect a QB run in rounds 5 and 9. RBs were the second most-common draft choice behind WRs, as 77 RBs went off the board and most teams drafted seven RBs. No team drafted more than seven RBs; two drafted only five RBs. All the RB starters, backups and any third stringers with potential are drafted. Yes, one team (each draft) started WR-WR and did not draft their RB1 until round 3. Starting 3 WRs, a flex position and PPR, combined to place much more importance on the WR position. In all 83 WRs were chosen, with teams carrying seven or eight WRs on average. With that many WRs drafted, both starters from every team and all WR3s with potential are gone. WR runs happen in rounds 2, 3, 4, 6, 8, 9 and 11.

One team, on average, would go RB-RB-RB and draft a WR in the 4th or 5th round, at the latest. Of the teams, 75% went with 2 TEs. A. Gates went in the third round in most cases; the last TE1 went in round 11 for two teams. There are 11 TE starters with limited potential available in free agency. Expect a TE run in round 7. Also, 75% of the teams went with one kicker and they were drafted in the 15th-20th rounds. This leaves over half of the kickers on the free agency list. Half of the teams went with one defense and they were drafted as early as the 12th round. Nearly half of the defenses will be available for free agency. Again, the above data represents a small sample of the total 2006 WCOFF drafts but should give you a great starting point for strategies.

A realistic overall 100 list should last until the 8th round and include 10 QBs, 40-45 RBs, 40 WRs, 10 TEs and no kickers or defenses, because that is how the draft should fall out. After that, owners are OBE (overcome by events) drafting HC, considering bye weeks, shortages and their own strategies such as boxing other owners out.

10 Tips for WCOFF (and most high stakes games)

1) Get to Las Vegas or Atlantic City the day before your draft. There is nothing worse than not being able to get the updates you need, worrying about missing the draft or rushing to get there beforehand. Save yourself some stress and arrive the day before. Use this time to check out where you are going for the draft. Do not bring your wife or kids. No distractions.

2) Rest the night before. Staying out until 5 a.m. at the casinos playing cards, chasing women (or playing women and chasing cards) does not a great draft make. Treat this like your draft at home but without the booze.

3) Thursday's kickoff game occurs before the Saturday draft. The points from Thursday count. Use Thursday's game, but do not go overboard; if they did well, factor it in. Some owners took C. Batch (who played for Ben Roethlisberger and had a great game) in the last rounds simply to get his 24.15 points in week 1 that were already known. Hey, a win is a win. If a stud has a bad game on that Thursday, do not be afraid to draft him, just realize he may not be your starter for week 1.

4) Check out the auctions and other drafts on Thursday (high stakes league) and Friday. Use that extra data to find sleepers, adjust ADP, and finalize round 1 picks. Do not use DRAFT Masters, as that is a different format (no transaction leagues).

5) If you want a player, draft him; ADP be damned. Half the battle of any draft is knowing when to draft a player before someone else snatches him. WCOFF rules make WR3 spots more valuable, on average, than ADP data that is not customized for WCOFF rules.

6) Do not get caught up in the hype. Relax, enjoy it and do not be intimidated. Granted, that is easier said than done. Remember WCOFF is just like any other draft you have done, except your opponents will be more prepared. But most are not "experts" in the field. They are people just like you. Of the 12 at your draft, two have so much money they don't know

what to do with it, so they came to Vegas to have some fun. They are gamblers with no FF base. Three or four are veterans but their draft position and strategy may be their downfall. To win the big prize you need to take chances and many times they do not pan out, so it is boom or bust for these players. They either look smart or stupid depending on how things go. Two or three will be newbies like you, some of whom will be intimidated or hung over. Advantage you. Of course, there is always one team at the draft without a clue. Just hope it is not you (one team asked me during the draft how many WRs they needed to start each week!). Usually 2-3 players will be FF fanatics like you who have played WCOFF several years but have nothing to show for it. You can win this thing; especially if your draft spot is 1-6. LOL!

7) Grab RBs or WRs with the first seven picks unless P. Manning is available after round 3. Last three picks should be DEF1, K1 and TE2, in that order. Then use waiver wire for K and DEF if needed later.

8) You have plenty of time to make picks (90 seconds), so be prepared and have 4-5 players ready so when it gets to you, you are ready to pick.

9) Remember that there are no trades, so stockpiling at any position other than RB or WR is not advisable. WRs are easier to add from the waiver wire.

10) Finally, **remember the key is pass receptions!** The more passes a player catches, the more points your team earns (1 PPR). More touches also means more chances at TDs and yards. RBs with lots of catches are a gold mine. RBs that catch many passes out of the backfield can be serviceable late round additions.

11 Strategies

1) QBs have less value in the league since RBs, WRs and TEs get 1 PPR. The difference between QB8 B. Favre and QB16 C. Pennington was 28 points; between QB7 T. Brady and QB19 T. Romo, the difference was 55 points (and Romo did not play every game). Not much difference for the picks you sacrifice. You can wait a long time before drafting your QB1 in round 8 or 9. It's a good idea to follow this up with QB2 in rounds 10-14.

2) The key is depth at RB and WR. Bye weeks, RBBC, game time decisions and injuries will drive you nuts when you are trying to fill a starting roster with 2 RBs, 3 WRs and a flex, if you do not have bench depth at those positions. I highly recommend 1 RB and 1 WR after round 2 (this more than likely means WR1 in round 2). After round 4, having 2 RBs and 2 WRs is a must, and 3 RBs and 3 WRs after round 6 is a pretty good strategy too. Seriously consider a WR3 with pick 5 and if not, then with pick 6.

3) WCOFF scoring (PPR combined with requiring 3 WRs to start and having a flex position) does a great job of elevating WRs value relative to RBs. WRs are more important because with three good RBs you can expect each to have a bye week and one game out with injury. That means starting a 4th WR as a flex player for 6 weeks, or almost half of the regular season. Plan on starting a 4th WR as a strategy, and if you have three good RBs some weeks, you are that much better off. In 2006 there was a dropoff between the Top 14 WRs and the other WRs. Another dropoff occurred after the Top 25. Get your WRs early and often; 7-9 WRs are a must. Try to get 2 WRs in the first 4 rounds and then 6 more in rounds 5-17.

4) Be flexible with your roster but plan on 2 QBs, 6 RBs, 8 WRs, 2 TEs, 1 K and 1 DEF. If your QB position is shaky then go 3 QB and 1 TE, but think of TE2 as your drop player to pick up a bye week replacement for K1 or DEF1 later in the year. Your sleepers should be RBs and WRs.

5) Wait on a kicker till after the 12th round and close to the end. If other teams are waiting then grab your K1 after the 12th if you can get the one you want (and he has a late bye week). Usually the 5th or 6th ranked kicker can be had 3 rounds after the first kicker went (15th round). Only draft one kicker and use the other spot for your sleeper. You cannot predict Top 5 kickers. The difference between the 6th and 12th kickers, in 2006, was a mere 6 points. The 6th and the 19th kicker were separated by 17 points. That is less than 1 point per game, where teams typically score 120 in a week. Hmmm.

6) Wait on defenses too. Many owners rank defenses differently. I have found that simply by waiting (letting five defenses be drafted before you get concerned), I can get one of my Top 10 defenses very late in the draft. Only draft 1 defense and save a spot for a sleeper. Play matchups with the waiver wire until bye weeks are over and you need to get your team ready for a playoff push. The 2006 difference between the 5th and 13th defense was 16 points. Again, this is 1 point per game in a league where teams average 120 a week.

7) Winning teams select 2 RBs and 2 WRs in the first 4 rounds (probably RB-WR-RB-WR). Why not QB or TE? Because you start 6 at RB or WR every week (2 RB, 3 WR and a flex). So ignore QB and TE and focus on WR and RB. Notice I said WR first there!

8) If you have the 11th or 12th pick consider WR-WR. You will have to go RB with the 3rd and 4th picks, but you are going against the flow and can find lots of value. It is tough to win a league without one of the stud RBs, but will a good enough RB fall to 11th? Why not take two Top WRs? Statistically the 11th draft spot has done better than the other bottom spots. Perhaps that is because of this strategy.

9) Use wavier wire and make sure you have 2 QBs, TEs and kickers before the transaction deadline of week 11.

10) Winning teams average 140-150 points per week. Practice different strategies in your mock drafts and see if you can get that kind of production from your results.

11) TEs do not get much love either. They make a terrible flex player and do not catch enough, (Top 5 excepted), to really take advantage of PPR. If tempted by the 2nd -5th Top TE expect to grab one in the 4th or 5th round. 12 TEs scored over 130 points in 2006. The difference between TE2 and TE12 was 64 points. Wait on the TEs but possibly get a Top 10 TE before your QB1 (round 9-12). Get TE2 with the 20th pick, since he will probably be dropped for bye week help later.

Table 17.2 Draft Strategy by Round

Rd	Position	Comments
1	RB1	This could change if late round draft pick
2	WR1	Must have WR1 by end of round 2
3	VBD	RB or WR

4	RB/WR	Must have 2 RBs and 2 WRs
5	VBD	WR3 versus RB3
6	RB/WR	Should have 3 RBs and 3 WRs
7	RB/WR	Depends on team need
8	TE1 or QB1	What have other owners done at QB?
9	QB1 or TE1	Need Top 10 TE
10	QB2?	
11	RB1 HC or WR	Use ADP to decide if round 11 or 13
12	VBD WR	2 QBs, 4-6 RBs, 4-6 WRs, 1 TE by now
13	RB1 HC or WR	If HC taken in round 11, then go WR
14	WR	How many of 8 WRs do you have?
15	DEF or Sleeper	
16	Sleeper 2	Looking for 8 WRs by now
17	VBD	RB6 or WR8
18	DEF or Sleeper	Avoid TE1s bye week if picking DEF1
19	K	Avoid TE1/DEF1 bye weeks
20	TE2	Avoid TE1 bye week if going with TE2

WCOFF Draft Strategy

Use Table 17.2 for an overview of a WCOFF strategy.

If you have three starting RBs by the 7th round then focus on WR4. If you have two starting RBs and a prayer for RB3, get your RB4 here. If a RBBC, this is a great chance to get the other RB in the same RBBC, or a goal line vulture.

NOTE: You should have 4 RBs and 3 WRs or vice versa after round 7 (maybe with a TE, 3 RBs and 3 WRs).

Rounds 8-10: QB x 2 and a TE. Check bye weeks for QB1 and 2; think about HC RB1, if needed, and get best TE1 you can with the latest bye week. Maybe get two QBs with picks 8+9 or 9+10. This may start a run on QB2s and can buy you some time.

Rounds 11-13: Handcuffs, catch-up with RB or WR (by now should have 2 QBs, 4-6 RBs, 4-6 WRs, and 1 TE)

Round 14: You need to have 8 WRs. How many do you have by now? Of your next seven picks, three are spoken for (DEF1, K1 and TE2), so with this pick and three others you need to get to 8 WRs and 6 RBs. RBs are probably taken care of with three starters, RB4 and RB5 as HC, leaving RB6 as a sleeper.

Round 15: Defenses, at least the top ones, tend to stick around a few years, so I think this position, more than kickers, will provide value if you can get a top one. That's why I say

DEF before K. Is it a little early? Maybe. Some advise going DEF-K as early as round 12, but I think round 15 is just right. It might even start a run since if it's a round or two before the experts pick theirs in the last rounds (18-20). Try to get a K1 with the latest bye week and not on the same bye as your TE1.

Round 18: K or DEF if you are going to go with more than one at these positions or your DEF1 if not already taken.

Round 19: Grab a kicker who does not have the same bye week as TE1 or DEF1 and has a late bye week if possible (especially if you are going to forgo the K2).

Round 20: Pick up the missing TE2, who will be dropped to pick up a bye week replacement for K1 or DEF1 later in the season.

Auctions (Budget and Strategies)

Master Plan for WCOFF Auction ($200)

7% QB ($14)	QB1	$10
	QB2	$ 4
51% RB ($102)	RB1	$ 55
	RB2	$ 33
	RB3	$10
	RB4	$2
	RB5	$2
38% WR ($76)	WR1	$30
	WR2	$20
	WR3	$14
	WR4	$6
	WR5	$2
	WR6	$2
	WR7	$2
2% TE ($4)	TE1	$3
	TE2	$1
1% K ($2)	K1	$2
1% Def ($2)	Def1	$2

Starting Allocation = $179, assuming RB3 starts as Flex (90%).

1) I move more money to RB and WR at the expense of QB and TE because with an extra starter (the flex) I need a better RB3 and WR4. If you can get a K and DEF for $1 each, that will be even more money that can be used on the TE1 position. A serviceable QB is all you need. Most of your budget should be at RB where there is less depth, and search for your bargains/sleepers at WR.

2) If you go for a stud at RB for $75, you may have to change your game plan for RBs 2, 3, 4 and 5. Notice that my WCOFF budget cannot be adjusted much downward in TE, K or DEF. I therefore know that any changes must come from the big three (QB/RB/WR).

3) In my 2006 WCOFF auction I actually spent $10 QB, $120 RB, $65 WR, $2 TE, $2 K, $1 DEF. Yes, only 1 defense at $1 and 1 kicker for $2. Of course, getting A. Brooks and D. Culpepper may have been my downfall in 2006.

FAAB Strategy

Just because you have a great draft and know who to start does not guarantee victory. As mentioned earlier in the book, circumstances will conspire for you to need to work the waiver wire. Whether it is your own need or to block another rival team from acquiring that great new RB; you will need to know how to bid using your budget.

Free agent pickups other than TE, K and DEF will be slim to none. There will be a few QB and WR gems to pick up, but do not expect much RB help. Good teams do not have to pay early; instead they use their budgets in weeks 3-5 after the one hit wonders have proven themselves or flopped. Winning teams tend to spend less in the early weeks and more as the season progresses (including weeks 9-11 when getting ready for the playoffs).

By week 4, over half of the WCOFF teams have spent over 40% of their FAAB budgets. By week 7, one-third of the owners have spent 90% of their budget. The best teams are not afraid to put in higher bids ($300-700) for a player. They tend to pay more but get more from the few players they target. So get those gems early and be prepared to spend for them. Don't forget to save some money for bye week pickups and injuries later in the season.

You need to be quick to grab a RB who has a potential to move into a significant role and you will have to bid high for him. A RB who is the starter due to a significant injury can go for the max of $1000 (assuming the owner has that much cash). Many potential RBs will go for an average of $600 or more but prices will vary from league to league. That is why it pays to know who has spent what.

Owners should aggressively attempt to improve their team through FA early, because with an 11-game regular season, money or great players late in the season does you no good if you are not in a playoff hunt. Winning teams spent all their remaining money in week 11, trying to improve the team for the playoffs.

WCOFF Blind Bidding Tips

1) Never bid round numbers (200, 230, 250), instead bid 201, 231, 251
2) Remember, the first couple of weeks are critical to getting new people but weeks 3-5 are best to allow time for them to prove themselves worthy of your cash.
3) Watch how bids go the first couple of weeks. Look for information such as bid amounts, who has been dropped, how much everyone has left, etc.
4) Always have some money for end of season. You may need it for injuries or a playoff push.
5) On a bye week K/DEF may go for $20-$30 ($1-15 normally).
6) Always submit enough bids to win a player at the position if he is needed to replace a bye week player. As an example, your only kicker has a bye week

coming up. Put in contingency bids for multiple kickers so that if you do not get your first few bids you will get a kicker in any case. I have put in 10 bids for 10 kickers so that I get one.

Chapter 18 Rule Variations

This chapter lists the different types of rules that you can use in your league. Some are better than others. Commentary has been added to accentuate the obvious advantages and disadvantages of some of the rule variations. Later in the chapter we will focus even more on rule clarifications and how certain plays are scored. Finally, the chapter ends with a review of some of the latest draft rules that can be used to offset the advantage of an early draft pick.

Unique Rules

IR Rule: If a player is listed by his NFL team as on IR (this would be annotated on your league website), then an owner can declare him as IR (move him to IR status versus starter or bench) and have an open spot on his roster for another player. So in effect you keep him without him taking a roster spot. This allows you to pick up a replacement for him while he is hurt. However, any player declared as IR cannot start unless they come off of IR, in which case they count toward normal roster requirements. The number of IR spots available per team can be unlimited or limited. Normally one or two is the limit. Some leagues allow any player to be placed on IR (really just two more roster spots), but you cannot have 2 players from the same position on IR and IR players do not count for points in tiebreakers. Other leagues put some stipulation that an IR player must go to the bench for a week before he can start. Still other leagues insist that only doubtful or "out" players can be placed on IR. Usually holdouts and bye week players cannot be on IR but check the rules as some leagues allow any two players to be on IR (you cannot use them, so that would be the place for holdouts, etc.). IR can cause some controversy unless the rules are very specific and even then NFL teams and coaches play fast and loose with IR descriptors. Many leagues have chosen to eliminate IR rules and just expand their rosters by two more players to not have to deal with injuries. A keeper league may make a more convincing argument for having IR spots. Not having an IR system forces the owner to make hard choices of whether or not to keep an injured player. These decisions are especially difficult in keeper leagues.

AFC or NFC rule: Only players from the specific conference can be drafted. In an AFC-only league, only AFC players can be drafted. NFC players would be prohibited from playing in the league. Now you have 50% less players to choose from for the draft; talk about limited supply.

No (insert NFL team here) allowed: This prevents any player or DEF/ST from that team to be drafted. As an example, in a "No Dallas Cowboys league," no player from Dallas nor the Dallas defense would be available for use in the league. This rule is usually seen in areas where there is a deep rivalry, as in GB vs. MINN or WASH vs. DALLAS.

Points Allowed by Defense: In most instances, points scored against the offensive unit (for example: Baltimore is the defense started, therefore points scored by Baltimore's opponent while Baltimore's offense is on the field) do not count as points scored against defenses. So safeties, interceptions, fumble recoveries returned for TDs, and FGs blocked and returned for TDs would not count as points scored against Baltimore's defense. The variation would simply be that all points scored are against the defense.

Points for categories can only be scored by those positional players: In these leagues QBs only get points for passing. RBs only get points for rushing, receivers only get points for receiving and kickers only get points for kicking. In this case, RBs cannot score points for passing yards/TDs, receiving yards/TDs or kicking. Likewise, a kicker cannot score points for throwing a TD pass on a fake FG. Therefore, in this league, LT would not get points for throwing or receiving TDs as he has done in the past. This is very restrictive and it is hard to understand why this is a good rule.

IDP Leagues: See Chapter 21 – Individual Defensive Players (IDP) and Defenses.

Points for yardage on fumble/interception returns: IDPs may be awarded 1 point for every 10 yards of a turnover recovery. Therefore, a 51 yard FR for a TD would mean 6 points for the TD, 2 points for the FR and 5.1 points for yardage on the play.

"Team Positions": With this rule, you draft all of the team's players at that position. For example, instead of drafting P. Manning QB IND the individual, you would draft all of the IND QBs (P. Manning being the most important of those). This rule helps when a QB for a team gets hurt, or benched, for any reason. Now, instead of missing out on fantasy points because P. Manning is groggy on the sidelines, you earn whatever points his replacement does as well. Nothing can be more frustrating than seeing your QB come out of the game in the first quarter never to be seen again that day. The Team QB rule alleviates that dilemma. In the real world, if someone gets hurt you put in their backup from the bench. In this fantasy football league, you would own the team's backup QB. The problem is that it limits the number of QBs that can be drafted. Since in effect you are drafting the team's QB and there are only 32 teams; in a 16-team league with a requirement of two QBs there would be no QBs on the FA list. But you would never be without a QB because you would always have your two team QBs (ex. Minnesota and Dallas). This rule removes some of the sleeper pick aspects because it does not allow teams to have access to as many QBs. For example, many in 2006 took a chance on Vince Young or Matt Leinart as sleepers, hoping they would eventually start. In a team QB league, whoever picked TENN QB or AZ QB received these players as well. So the sleeper aspect gets factored into your overall choice of Team QB. Someone who thought M. Leinart would be great if started might have wanted to grab AZ QB knowing that they got K. Warner or M. Leinart, whoever started. Generally, this team rule will only apply for QBs, TEs or kickers; although some IDP leagues use it for DL, LB and DB. The problem with this is that you remove some of the strategy from the draft. If an owner gets both M. Leinart and K. Warner with one pick, then some other owner does not have a chance at drafting Leinart as his sleeper. Some owners hate this rule with a passion. They explain that when you draft your fantasy football team, you draft backups. They are on the bench, ready to step in when needed. All of the players on your team wear the same jersey as your fantasy team, so getting another player to play on your team does not make sense to the diehard. You should have drafted his backup at the draft if you wanted him.

Bye Week carryover: This rule allows the average points a player has scored per week to be carried over and used the week the player is on a bye. Advantages are that no player ever has a bye week. Owners cannot claim the luck factor because they did not play Team A when LT was on a bye. The disadvantage is that players with an earlier bye week can have averages distorted in either direction. For example, Chad Johnson has a bye in week 3 after scoring 5 TDs and 356 yards the previous two games. He will have a 2.5 TD and 178 yard bye week; probably an inflated average. On the other hand, if he was hurt and missed games 1 and 2, his bye week average will be zero and thus he probably will not be started. In effect, owners have the knowledge of how well that player will do on his bye week and can decide whether to start or bench him with that knowledge, which is not fair.

Doubleheaders (DH) Schedule: In these leagues you will play two teams some weeks, instead of one. This helps to eliminate some of the whining about unfair scheduling. Some leagues want to have a 16-game regular season, so they schedule doubleheader games (games in which you play two fantasy teams, not just one) in enough of the non-bye weeks to give them a 16-game record for the regular season. As an example, 12-team league, two divisions of 6; 6 teams make playoffs, which are held in weeks 15 and 16 (week 17 skipped). The 14-week season would include two doubleheader weeks to give a 16-game season. DH weeks need to be on non-bye weeks and preferably as late in the season or early in the season (depends on your thinking) as possible. If doubleheader week is week 1, then after week 1 you will have either a 2-0, 1-1 or 0-2 record since you played H2H two different teams. Some leagues play doubleheaders every week as a way to prevent the "I scored the second most points and still lost" whining. With a DH every week, if you scored the second most points, the worst you can be is 1-1 for that week. It also allows having more teams in the playoffs and starting the playoffs earlier, to allow for byes for top seeds. Opponents of this method say that if you are going to play two teams a week, wouldn't it be more fair to play every team each week (see All Play League below), in which case it should not be a H2H league but a points league (saving you the hassles of having teams with 100+ wins or losses a year). DH games are a great way to make the season more equitable so that all division teams play twice, or so that every team plays the other teams the same number of times. As an example, with a 12-team league, you could have a 13-game regular season and nine DH games, so that your season is 22 games (2 versus each team), or have one DH game so that each division team plays each other twice in addition to eight games versus all the other teams.

All Play League: This is where all of the teams in the league play all of the other teams every week. If you have a 10-team league and a 14-game season, you would play 126 games in the regular season (9 games a week x 14 weeks=126). Your record might be 84-42. This eliminates any whining about playing Team A when their key player was on a bye week, because everybody plays everyone else every week. This also eliminates the "I played every team when they had their best week" excuse. But then again, why not just do a TFPs league? It is the same thing only with more consistency.

Draft order determined by record: Leagues have the draft order (for the following year) in reverse order of the finish for the prior season. If you are in a 12-team league and finish in 12th place, you would get the 1st draft pick next year. This is more appropriate for keeper leagues that attempt to let owners build a team, versus redraft leagues where you start from scratch every season.

Allowing the higher scoring team to make last playoff spot: Only suggested if a few teams make the playoffs; if 50% of teams make the playoffs, then this is a moot point to some degree. Some leagues allow the last playoff spot to go to the highest scoring team left that is not in the playoffs (WCOFF has a similar type rule). If 4 out of a 14-team league are to make the playoffs, then the first three make it based on winning percentage, and the last spot is for the highest scoring team not already in the playoffs. This prevents the "I played against everyone on their best week" whine. Of course, there have been times when the 6-7 team makes the playoffs and the team with the 2nd highest scoring does not make it.

However, I hate to see a 5-8 team make the playoffs and possibly win the Super Bowl with a losing record.

Minimum # of Position Requirements: This rule forces owners to own a certain number of each position at all times. For example, all teams must have a minimum of two of each position on their roster at all times. This makes the draft easier for beginners. "Okay, I have to have two kickers and two TEs, etc". It also makes it easier to use strategy in the draft if every team has to draft a certain number of each position. In the later rounds if teams have not met their minimum, you know they will have to draft players from those positions. It also makes creating cheat sheets easier since you know how many at each position will be drafted. (2 TE x 12 teams=24 TEs drafted) Generally, if any limits are used then they will be used at all positions but in rare cases you may find a minimum number of QBs but no limit at TE or DEF, or something similar.

Maximum # of Players at Each Position: This rule prevents owners from hoarding players at a certain position. The maximum number is designed to prevent one or more teams from drafting/acquiring a monopoly on a position. If five teams had five QBs each in a 14-team league, then two of the remaining teams would not have a QB. For example, 32—(5 x 5) =7 QBs left for nine teams.

All starting positions must have a player/team in them: This is the so-called Monday night negative points rule. You must have a player active at each position. It can even be a bye week player or an injured player; you just cannot have an empty spot. This is only applicable in leagues that allow a position to score negative points and allows changes to lineups right up until game time. Team A has a 1 point lead over Team B going into Monday night. Team B has no players left to play so Team A has won the H2H match as long as his players on MNF do not score negative points. Team A sees this and benches his QB, who is playing on MNF, so that he cannot get negative points for his interceptions (leaving his QB starter position empty). If this rule were in effect, then he would have to start his MNF QB. And take his chances. It comes down to ethics, since the rules allow the owner to bench the QB before Monday night's game. I think an owner should have this added (albeit very rare) strategy option. It just adds one more facet to the game. Thus, I am against this rule. The other side of it is this: in the NFL you have to start a player even if you think he is going to throw picks, or fumble, or give up lots of points as a defense. Another way to limit this (much less desired) would be to make all roster changes effective five minutes before the first game of the week is played. But as discussed elsewhere, this is not a good option.

Method to Lower Scores: Divide all teams' total scores by a number (example: 4) to arrive at the score posted. This is more for leagues that have added PPR and yardage, yet still want to see a box score of 42-30.

No Decimal Rule: No points are awarded unless it is a whole number; so 9 yards in a 1 point per 10 yards league is zero points, not .9 points. Still other leagues will round the final score either up or down, so that it is a whole number. Instead of: Team A wins 58.7 to 43.1, it is 59-43. Of course TFPs scored in the season can still be tabulated with decimals if TP is a category for tiebreakers or the like.

Allow Formations: Teams always must have five total RB/WR/TEs and a minimum of one (and no more than 2 RBs or TEs) plus QB, K and DEF/ST, of course. For example, the one back formation (1 RB, 3 WRs, and 1 TE), the standard two back set (2 RBs, 2 WRs, 1

TE) or TE formation (1 RB, 2WRs, 2 TEs).This is just another variation of the flex player, but it does require some thought by the owner about whether he wants 2 TEs or can pull a RB out and add a WR. The 2 TE concept can help if you draft a great sleeper that comes on strong. This is a clever variation of allowing a flex player at RB/WR/TE.

Allow Draft Picks to be Traded: This has two variants. Allowing only current year draft picks to be traded. (You want the #1 pick this year, 1.1. I will trade you my 4th pick in the first round and we can swap picks in the 3rd round.) The other variant allows teams to trade future draft picks. I will give you C. Portis and my third round draft pick next year for LT. This allows teams to give up on this season and trade away players for next seasons draft picks. It provides more strategy. (See Appendix A for websites that allow you to compare trading picks.) Be careful; what if the team doing the trading does not return for next year? Best idea is to only allow teams to trade future draft picks if they have paid those years dues in advance. For example, Team A wants to trade Team C a player and a draft pick in 2008. He can only do so if he has paid his dues for that year (thus preventing him from trading something that he may not have otherwise). This prevents owners from trading a draft pick in the future but then not being around to payoff that pick. If he decides not to play, his entry fee pays for the owner who takes over his team and has lost a draft pick.

No ties: Leagues will not have ties as an outcome. They will break ties by allowing teams to nominate a bench player as a tiebreaker or use player positions to break ties. Whichever team's QB scored the most, if still tied then RB, etc. Or perhaps it is whichever team's bench scored the most. Or whichever team had the most TDs. See Chapter 19 – Commissioner Information, for more insight into breaking ties.

Points for rushing attempts, receptions (see PPR) or pass completions: You might allocate 1 point for every 10 rushes, receptions or completions. Why award for rushing attempts; if he carried 10 times for 12 yards, who cares? Receptions (see PPR discussion later) and completions as a stat? Most QBs throw 15-20 completions per game, so I don't think this is much of a factor, other than giving more points to QBs, but they will all get about 2 points per game for this.

Start a Head Coach: You have to start a head coach each week. If his team wins, you get points (typically three) added to your fantasy team. This is seen more in salary cap contests than in serious FF leagues.

Groundhog day/"What if" rule: Allows owners to change one lineup decision after the games have been played. If you should have started Randy Moss who caught 2 TDs, but instead started H. Ward who had none, then in this type of league, your one groundhog day change for the week would be to start Moss instead of Ward and your team would get 12 more points. Of course, your opponent can do the same thing and perhaps his change is to start M. Harrison from his bench instead of T. Holt, with a net gain of 18 points. It can be a double-edged sword. Nevertheless, the rule is unique.

Defense affects your opponent's fantasy score: If your defense ranks in the top 5 (based on total yards allowed) for the week played, your fantasy opponent's score is reduced by a certain amount. Some leagues use points (based on how much scoring is in your league; for example, 6 points normally subtracted for a Top 5 defense); others use a percentage (20%). If your defense finishes in top 6-10, then 3 points are subtracted, or 10%. The same applies if a defense finishes in the bottom 5 (add 6 to opponent's score or multiply his score by 20%) or bottom 6-10 (3 points or 10%). Defenses in the middle, 11-22 ranking, would have no effect. Your defense does not score points as such, just modifies your opponent's score based on their performance. Problems with this occur when your opponent's players end up playing your defense in real life. Now he is doubly penalized. For example, when his offensive skill players play against CHI DEF in week 12, their fantasy production is low (his QB gets no TDs) and then his fantasy team loses points too (because of the modifier from CHI DEF ranking in the Top 5). So some of his players end up with lower points simply because they happened to play a tough CHI DEF and then his TFPs for the week are reduced because you started CHI DEF and they finished in the Top 5. Another problem is the delay in getting scores until after the MNF game. Some leagues allow your defense to score only when they score (safeties and TDs but not TOs or sacks). Not recommended.

Points per reception (PPR): Give one point (or sometimes .5 points) per reception. This makes WRs and TEs more valuable. Some advocate only giving PPR to WRs and TEs (i.e. no RBs would get this). Others say to limit RBs by making it two catches equal one point versus one catch equals one point for WR/TE. Advocates of the no-RB PPR say that PPR gives the WR/TE a better chance of equality in the draft and that giving PPR just helps those RBs who catch many balls, out of the backfield, attain superiority. Like LT needs any more help! Those against PPR point out that it is not something easily reported in the media or in sound bites on ESPN. So the "guess my team's score" from the headlines factor means PPR is not as desirable. PPR is a big favorite in leagues with 3 WRs and flex positions.

Points per Dropped Pass: Hard to track and even harder to follow on TV. Nevertheless, it would perhaps placate the no-PPR people. Then again, who would track catchable passes versus non-catchable versus tipped; this is a nightmare. QBs get points or WRs lose points in these leagues based on dropped passes.

Restricted Trading: A variation that allows trading after the deadline but only between teams that are within one spot of you in the rankings. Therefore, if you are 4th in a 12-team league, you can trade with the 3rd, 4th or 5th ranked teams. If in a two division league and you are in first place, you could only trade with the first place team in the other division or either 2nd place team in the divisions.

Rules to beef up defenses

Change rules to give more emphasis on Points Allowed (PA).

0 PA = 20 points

1-9 PA = 15 points

10-16 PA = 10 points

17-20 PA = 5 points

Safeties would be increased to 5 points. Turnovers and sacks stay at 1 point and DEF/ST TDs are 6 points. Blocked kicks are 2 points. This tends to weigh the DEF higher on draft day.

A scoring system where QB, RB and TE are all relatively equal in value

Starting 2 QBs helps QBs and starting 3 WRs helps WRs. Awarding points to WRs and TEs only for receptions helps both. Making passing yards (1 point per 15 passing yards) closer to rushing and receiving yards (1 point per 10 rushing/receiving yard) helps QBs.

So Start 2 QBs, 2 RBs, 3 WRs, 1 Flex RB/WR/TE, 1 TE, 1 K and 1 DEF/ST

1 point per 15 Passing yards

1 point per 10 Rushing/Receiving Yards

4 points for TD passes; 6 points for rushing and receiving TDs. -2 for INTs and 1 PPR for WR and TE.

Rule Clarifications:

NOTE: Many problems arising from TD questions can be eliminated by stating in the rules that all TDs scored by a player are counted.

1) Double turnovers where the offense fumbles (or throws an INT) and then tackles the defender, making them fumble, and then the offense scores a TD, do not count as a defensive score. Your defense/ST has to be on the field to score a DEF/ST TD. The argument will be that if the QB throws an INT, he and the other offensive players then turn into poorly trained defensive players trying to tackle the defender who intercepted. Sorry, your defense has to be on the field for your DEF to score. The TD is not given to any of the offense since they lost possession and the subsequent TD is not a rush, pass or receiving TD, but a FR for a TD. Unless your rules state that FR TDs count or you have the catchall phrase "All TDs scored," the TD will not count for the offensive player.

2) Points against the defenses/ST: Some leagues do not count points scored by the opponent's defense (INT returned for a TD), but do count points on a KR and PR, since these were scored against your special teams unit. The easiest way is to say that all points scored count against the defense. Your rules need to state otherwise. For example, points versus DEF are only scored while the DEF/ST is on the field.

3) What if the kicker scores on a fake FG? Does he get the TD credit? What about a kicker throwing a two-point conversion pass on a botched XP attempt? If the kicker scores, he should get credit, since he is an offensive skill player.

4) Is a score on a fake kick or punt a special team's play? No. Unless the rules specifically state that scores on fake kicks are to be counted then these scores do not count. Why? ST means punt and KO returns, so only points related to those events should be credited to a ST. Punts and FGs occur on fourth down, when the offense is still on the field. In many cases the QB is the holder (remember T. Romo hmmm…) for FGs. The ball has to be kicked across the line of scrimmage for a change of possession. At that time the defense is no longer on the field, instead it is the special teams unit.

5) Is a blocked kick returned for a TD credited to the defense or the special teams? See the answer to #4 above. Once the ball crosses the line of scrimmage, the defense becomes a ST unit. If the kick is blocked it is blocked by the defense, since it has not crossed the line of scrimmage. If it never crosses the scrimmage line and is returned for a TD, then it is the

defense that gets the credit. If it ever crosses the line of scrimmage then is returned for a TD, the credit goes to the ST unit. Note: In many leagues the defense and the ST unit are combined.

6) If any offensive player plays on defense should he get defensive points? D. Branch (or Mike Furrey) is playing safety and intercepts a pass and scores a TD; does he get the points? No, their team's defense gets the points because to award them to the player would be awarding double points. This is another reason for IDP; in this case you could award the points to the player since you would not have a team defense playing.

7) If a player that normally plays on defense scores as an offensive player should he or the defense get those points? This is also a great reason why IDP should be used. In that format, players can get points for offensive or defensive categories. If W. Sapp scores a TD on a TE pass, should the defense get the TD? No, the defense was not on the field.

8) The QB throws a pass to a player who catches it and then laterals to another player who then scores. Who gets what? The Dante to Randy to Moe conundrum. The QB gets credit for all the yardage and the outcome, since it was a passing play. The receiver gets a catch and yardage until the lateral occurs. The player receiving the lateral gets receiving yards for as long as he has the ball. If another lateral subsequently occurs on the play, the next player gets receiving yardage from where he caught the lateral until he relinquishes the ball or the play stops. Note: Only the first receiver gets credit for a reception. The other players receiving the lateral do not get PPR.

9) What happens if a RB carries the ball, then laterals to another player who scores a TD? Who gets what? Just like in #8, the RB gets a carry and rushing yards until he laterals the ball, then the other player gets rushing yards (but no carries) until he relinquishes the ball (fumbles or laterals) or the play ends.

10) A player retires or is suspended. Can he go on injured reserve? That depends on the league rules. Generally, the IR is just that; a reserve place for players who are injured. How your league interprets "injured" should be spelled out in your rules. Many rules state he has to be out or questionable by Wednesday's injury report. Then he has to be moved from the IR to the bench for a week before he can be started.

Draft Position Inequality

There is a large problem (or perceived problem) in the high stakes leagues (WCOFF, NFFC, etc.) and it can affect every fantasy football league. It is the "superstar effect" or the early draft pick effect. Every year two or three players seem to excel and deliver much more than everyone else. These are the top RBs. Getting LT in 2006 made it almost impossible to lose. The problem occurs when a large number of teams with the first, second or third pick make it to the championship. Research shows that in 2005 in the NFFC, 43% of the league champions picked in spots 1-3. (In WCOFF, over 50% of the league champs from the past three years have come from picks 1-3). In 2006, 18 of the Top 32 NFFC teams (over 56%) drafted from picks 1-3. In 2006 at WCOFF, 55% of the Top 20 teams had LT on their roster. The Top 3 (and 9 of the Top 15) WCOFF finishers all had LT. In 2006, 50 of 70 (71%) LT owners made it into the LCG. Statistically only 16.6% should have been there. The top 3 picks at WCOFF made their championship games over 50% of the time. Statistically only 25% of picks 1-3 should have been there.

Some have said that 80% of the LCG came from the first 6 picks in 2006. That should have been 50%. In 2006, 35 of the Top 50 WCOFF teams came from picks 1-3 (70%). It seems that the serpentine draft as we know it favors the top picks much more than the bottom half. For those who scoff at such talk, simply ask an owner in NFFC or WCOFF who has a Top 6 pick if he would trade it for a bottom half pick. I doubt if anyone would take that trade. The knowledge of the owners should determine who wins the title, not where you were randomly selected to draft.

How do you fix it? What can a league do to even the playing field?

High stakes bidding for draft position may solve some of this problem (see Chapter 16 – WCOFF, NFFC and AFFL). In this scenario, you bid real money for the first and second round draft spots. The last spot in round 1 goes for the minimum bid of $1. Then you bid for picks in round 2. Again, the last pick in round 2 will go for $1. The remaining rounds will be serpentine based on the order from rounds 1 and 2. This way everyone gets a chance to have the #1 pick for a price. Nevertheless, is there another solution for our friendly leagues?

A better way may be the addition by subtraction method, or Slam's rule. In this case, the top three players are simply removed from eligibility to be drafted. No team can draft them thus they (the superstars) are not allowed to influence the league. They are out of play for the season. But how do you determine who the top three players are going to be? Simple, let democracy decide. The teams who do not get the first three draft picks each select three players to exclude from the draft. These teams have no incentive to NOT list the three best players in the league and whom they would pick with the first three draft picks, if they had them. Why? Because they want to get those three superstars off the market and away from the three teams lucky enough to have the first three picks. You could even allow draft spot #3 to nominate two players for elimination, because he does not want the drafters in front of him (#1 and #2 picks) to get the superstars. Drafter #2 could be allowed to nominate one player for exclusion; he would nominate the best player available so that the #1 pick would not get him. Thus, after all those ballots are cast, 9 x 3+2+1=30 votes. The top three vote-getters would be eliminated from the draft and the league. That way no one could claim that they won the league since they had the #1 or #2 draft spot. Those draft positions (1-3) are still more valuable (possibly) but the SUPERSTAR that everyone agreed was the instant ticket to the Super Bowl is eliminated from the equation. After 2006 this may be renamed the LT rule. If this rule had been in effect in 2006, most leagues would have taken LT, LJ and S. Alexander off the draft board before the draft started. This also will mean three less starting RBs available for the draft.

Two other options deal with changing the traditional serpentine draft structure.

3rd Round Reversal (3RR)-

The first two rounds of the draft are serpentine and then round 3 is reversed. So instead of team 1 getting the first pick of round 3, team 12 (or the last team) gets the first pick and then round 3 continues with team 1 getting the last pick. Round 4 starts with team 1 getting the first pick and the serpentine method begins for the rest of the draft. 3RR gives owners picking after the top three a stronger chance to compete and not have their competitors, who picked first, at an insurmountable advantage. Now with the first pick (presumably LT) and 24th pick you get the 36th pick and 37th pick instead of the 25th and 48th picks.

The format will look like this:

Round 1   1-12

Round 2   12-1

Round 3   12-1

Round 4   1-12

Round 5   12-1

Round 6   1-12

And so on, doubling back every round from here on out, through the last round.

Double Serpentine Draft (DSD)

This is where a draft reverses order after every even round. For example: 1-12, then 12-1, then 12-1, then 1-12, then 1-12, then 12-1, then 12-1, then 1-12 and so on and so on. WCOFF may be considering this since NFFC went 3RR.

The format for DSD looks like this:

Round 1   1-12

Round 2   12-1

Round 3   12-1

Round 4   1-12

Round 5   1-12

Round 6   12-1

Round 7   12-1

Round 8   1-12

Round 9   1-12

Round 10   12-1

Round 11   12-1

Round 12   1-12

The main disadvantage is that it gets a little complicated as far as figuring out who drafts next after the reverse each time. It also will play some havoc with the strategies of wrapping around the corner and taking advantage of what the owners next to you do for the 1-3 and 9-12 picks; because now 9-12 gets to play off of what 1-3 have picked and vice versa.

Chapter 19 Commissioner Information

The following advice is based on personal experience as I have had the honor and pleasure of being a commissioner in one or more leagues for the past 11 years (starting in 1996). I have run leagues on three continents (North America, Europe and the Middle East). The best advice is to follow the KISS principle; Keep It Simple Stupid. If the league can afford a management service, purchase it. It makes the commissioner's job that much easier. The next best advice is to keep track of the money and pay owners on time. Under no circumstances should you spend their money on other things and not be able to pay off winnings. If this happens, your tenure as commissioner will be a short one, I assure you. Commissioners need to be dictators on occasion and presidents on others. Ask for feedback from the other owners and make changes based on their (and your) needs. However, be ready to stand your ground for the betterment of the league. Unpopular formats will lead to negative owners and that can mean losing interest from one or more owners. Lack of interest is never good for a league.

Commissioners must be ethical and honest. Set the standard. Be the best commissioner you can be and your owners will respond with their own high standards, as well. I remember an article that said "always elect as your commissioner a guy you would want to date your sister." That is the right attitude to have. Try to do everything on time. Do not coach other owners on how to run their team (this leads to resentment and is unfair to other owners) but you must try to cajole inactive owners to participate. Above all else, remember everything you do must be aboveboard and fair to all owners.

Some suggest rotating the commissioner duties every year. I disagree completely. The commissioner job is a labor of love that involves a newsletter and all the other little things that keep a league afloat. Some other owners may do just as good a job, but some would not. Stick with the commish that likes to do it and does it well. However, paying half of his entry fees is a nice gesture to show the league appreciates his hard work (paying the entire fee might promote laziness).

How you handle the unexpected events (and there will be one every year) will determine how good you are as commissioner. Remember every action you take as commissioner sets a precedent for the future of the league. Do what is right for the league first, even if it means going against your team or your friends. You will know in your heart what is right for the league. The league must come first. And if at any time a commissioner's integrity is called into question, he must be willing to step down. Always have an assistant commissioner to review your trades, handle league duties while you are on vacation and to step in if you do step down.

You will find many interesting ideas in the next few pages. Some may be for your league, some may be scoffed at and still others may spur some discussion and lead to a change later. The ideas may come with some discussion here as well, as to their merits. Do not change for change's sake but instead strive to make the league a better, more enjoyable hobby. And remember the commissioner's job does not receive any awards and the best you can hope for is to do a good job, in which case no one will notice. It is only when something gets screwed up that everyone takes notice of the commissioner. Suffice it to say it is a "labor of love" and a thankless job.

Different Types of Owners

Recognize the different kinds of owners and apply the right management skills to each.

1) Terrible Tony: These guys are the real problem children of fantasy football. They may start out fine but when they get a grudge they hold onto it and then stir up problems. Usually they will feel wronged by either another owner or the commish. They tend to have constant e-mail bashing, MB bickering and attempts to destroy their enemy. These owners are the ones most likely to collude. Ban them if collusion is discovered.

2) Fantasy Fred: This is the best owner anyone could ever ask for. He acts and thinks like you in that he is dedicated to the league and the hobby. He always gives it his best and rolls with the punches when he loses. Supports the commish in almost every aspect. If he questions something, it may need to be addressed.

3) Know-it-all Ken: He thinks he is the expert. He comes to the draft and belittles everyone else's picks without being funny. He brags incessantly about his great picks. He constantly questions league rules and why they exist. He pushes the limits of the rules and beyond. He cannot stand losing (who can?) and will blame anything and everyone but himself for losses. He will stir the pot of controversy just for fun and may make bad, one-sided trades at the end of the season when he is out, just to influence outcomes.

4) Quitter Quinn: He plays to win and talks a great game, but when he feels things are not going his way he threatens to quit midseason and ruin the league's competitiveness. If a trade occurs that he does not like, or if a trade of his is stopped, he threatens to quit. He can also be a fairweather owner who quits after being eliminated from playoff contention. The league is usually better off without Quitter Quinns.

5) Humble Hank: He plays because everyone else in the office plays or because a good friend roped him into joining. He never complains, but also rarely does anything. He is a mouse on the MB and his team is on autopilot. He misses bye weeks and injuries. He is the dependable doormat of the league. You need to try to pull him out of his shell and get him into the game. Ask him questions about his team; berate him for losing or making bonehead non-decisions. My favorite is to give out weekly "What were they thinking" awards. Make him trade offers to get him thinking and involved. These are the Fantasy Freds of the future; we just need to draw them out and introduce them to the excitement of the hobby.

Fines, Fees or Penalties

1) New owner initiation – Pizza and beer at draft or designated driver on Hooters road trip.

2) If the draft position for next year is determined by the standings from the year before, be careful about teams that will throw a late season game in order to finish last and get a better draft spot. A severe penalty for coming in last place prevents this phenomenon, such as having to host the SB party, serve everyone at the next draft or wear a dress and wash the SB winner's car. All of these things make the late season games more competitive. This is another reason to have a "toilet" bowl.

3) Have a transaction fee (pay to add/drop/trade), but use the money for the end-of-year party instead of adding it back into the prize money. Possibly $0.25 per transaction? Why penalize or make people pay to do smart things like try to improve their teams or fix

injuries that have befallen them? I like one fee that includes everything. Kind of like a cruise.

4) If owners want to trade future draft picks, they have to be paid up for that year's entry fee.

5) If an owner has not paid his entry fee, then do not allow the team to make any transactions until the entry fee is paid.

6) Late-to-draft fine or penalty. Case of beer if within 30 minutes late. Later than that, have someone else draft their team for them.

Draft Suggestions

1) Be prepared for late owners. Have a fine or skip over them until they arrive.

2) Offer free food and booze to anyone who wants to help you with the draft, whether it is traditional or an auction.

3) Have the draft in Las Vegas. Have some "ladies" help with the draft. These "helpers" will come to owners and take their hand-written draft slips back to the draft board and post them.

4) Review the rules before the draft and hand out a sheet with the rules, payouts, deadlines and owners data (phone numbers and e-mail addresses).

Payouts

Age-old question: Do you give all the money to the champion or spread it out so more owners win something, or are competing for something and thus having more fun? Is it a fun league or a cutthroat league? Which sounds better: one hundred percent to SB winner or fifty percent to SB winner and fifty percent in other prizes? The best suggestion is 50% to the champion and 20-30% to 2nd place and the entry fee back to the winner of 3rd place. This gives two more teams a reason to care about week 16 games as they fight for third place.

Trophies: Have a "traveling trophy" (like the Stanley Cup or Claret Jug). This gives the champion something to really show off, brag about, and bring to the draft next year. The "traveling trophy" should have a plate with previous winners names engraved and the year they won. Also, have an individual trophy for the champion to keep forever. In addition, have a trophy for the worst team too. The worst team trophy should be suitably embarrassing and must be displayed until the owner presents it to next years winner.

Weekly prizes for high score keep all teams competitive and prevents them from "dumping" players at the end of the season.

Super Bowl rule – whichever teams scores the fewest points for the year has to wash the Super Bowl champion's car. This keeps every team fighting for points. The alternative is to have the lowest-points owner host the SB party.

Playoffs

Consolation Bracket (also known as the Toilet Bowl): Teams not in the playoffs go here to play. The loser of the games advances each week until the ultimate loser is crowned. He must pay some price for being the worst team in the league; for example, buy the beer for the SB party and serve it, wash champ's car, etc.

Miscellaneous Roster Information

Establish who decides player positions. Is it the stat management service and their positions assigned, or will it be some other source? Can a player play multiple positions or does the owner have to declare his primary position for the season? For example, in 2007 was M. Colston a WR or TE for New Orleans? Is M. Sellers a RB or TE for Washington?

Different Roster Deadlines:

1) Roster Lockdown – All lineups are to be in five minutes before the first game of the week. This "locks" in all players from then on for that week. In other words, you could not change your starting RBs after the Thursday games on Thanksgiving. Therefore, you are forcing owners to make decisions on Thursday, in some cases, for Sunday's games. If your entire lineup must be in before the first game, it hurts the owners who are on top of things and are watching the games live. If there are any questions surrounding a player playing in the afternoon (4 p.m.) or Sunday or Monday night games, then you will have to make decisions on them before all of the information is in. This amounts to luck to me and I do not like these formats. I think start/bench decisions are best left to owners right up until game time. That way if Mike Shanahan wants to bench Mike Bell, or deactivate him for the game due to injury, then owners who know where to look or are watching can find this out in time to make other arrangements. The worst case is on Thursday games (which in 2006 started in week 12, with Thanksgiving, and occurred every week through 16). If you have to make all start/bench decisions on Thursday, that puts too much luck into the equation.

2) Game Time Decisions – All players involved in those games must be submitted five minutes before their kickoff. This allows you to change other players if their games are played later that day or on another day. As an example, I have two RBs playing on Monday Night Football. I can wait to choose the one I want to start five minutes before the MNF game starts. Note: This should only be used as an option if online lineup services are used. It will drive a commissioner crazy having to keep up with all the changes if not done by a service.

3) Sunday Lockdown – All lineups for early games must be set before that game starts; other lineup decisions must be set before the first Sunday game. This gives you flexibility for early games (Thursday and Saturday) but still requires all lineups be finalized before the first game on Sunday.

Establish rules for lineup changes for owners away from a computer or without one. Allow them to phone in lineups to the commissioner up to five minutes before kickoff. The commissioner must always have an answering machine with a date/time stamp for verifying lineups submitted this way, to make sure they are on time.

Lineup Submissions – If a team does not submit a roster then the previous week's lineup is used. The first players drafted will be used to fill an initial week 1 lineup.

Commissioner Tips

#1 Use a software program or, better yet, a website that does all of the calculations for you. Yahoo, ESPN and CBSSPORTSLINE all offer free league hosting. They will allow you to draft online, manage your league and run your playoffs without ever lifting a finger to load stats or crunch numbers. The scoring can be customized to some degree. The rules also have some flexibility as far as starters, "Can't Cut Lists," etc. If you do not use a website then you will have to run the stats, and you will have to be the one everyone calls for lineups and add/drops. This was fine in the old days when there was no other way. Now with the advent of the Internet, there is no reason why you should not use a website to host your league.

#2 Print and publish the rules well in advance of the draft. Many of the rules will be on the website if you use Yahoo, etc. However, internal rules, like your maximum and minimum positions in the draft, draft time limits and other specialized rules, need to be published and available at least a month before draft day. The rules should be easy to read, not like some contract a lawyer wrote. (See League Constitution later in this chapter.)

#3 Buy a draft kit each year if having a live draft. It costs about $20 but it is well worth it. The draft will look and feel more professional. It will be easier to read and easier to load the data into the computer than everyone's handwritten scrawl. The draft kits come with all of the players names on color coded labels based on their positions (ex: yellow for QBs, blue for RBs, white for WRs, etc.). These labels are easy to peel off and then stick on the board in the spot reserved for your team and the pick you just made. Many have online support so that you can print out the fantasy team names in advance. The draft board is just a large piece of sturdy paper with columns and rows for team names and labels with the player's name and team. The draft board should be large enough to handle all the teams and the players they will draft. It is a must!

#4 Send out everyone's e-mail address and phone number (for trade communications, etc.). Most of the websites will have a list of owner's e-mail addresses, but the phone numbers posted on the message board just after the draft is a nice touch. Be careful with some site's message boards, as they drop old posts if too many get on during the season. For example, Yahoo dropped a league's rules (which had been posted at the beginning of the season) midway through the season because there were lots of posts (mainly trash talking), and the memory could not support keeping that many.

#5 Require that lineups be in a minute before the website deadline, that way people who wait till the last minute and find the website will not let them on cannot claim they did not have a chance. Yahoo requires lineups be in five minutes before kickoff. I recommend you set the limit for the league at six minutes before. That gives an owner a minute to get it in after the league deadline, but before the Yahoo deadline. Consider it slop time. Also, if an owner cannot use the website (to set lineup or perform add/drop), have them post a message on the message board to that effect. This will let all the other owners know that he wanted to do that action and it will give that action a common time/date stamp. If the MB is not working then have (based on the rules) that owner e-mail the commissioner and all other teams, or at the least the other team he is playing that week.

#6 Always collect the entry fee before the draft starts. Preferably a week before the draft, so you have time to find a substitute if someone cannot come up with the money. Of course, if it is a local league with a $10 entry fee, then these are not hard and fast rules. But if it is a $100 entry, well, SHOW ME THE MONEY! If you have the money then that owner can draft. That is the rule. If you allow a team to draft without paying first, you run the risk of them bailing out after the draft because the draft did not go well or their player was hurt before they paid you the money, so they quit. This can become an ugly situation in higher stakes leagues. By the same token, as commish, you need to make the payouts as soon as possible after the outcome is decided. Everyone likes a little cash during the holidays. "Look what I won, honey" may make playing a little easier next year, with the significant other.

#7 Have a trade deadline. This is the latest that trades between teams can be conducted for the year. This rule prevents teams from colluding via trades to improve one team's chances at the expense of the other team and the league. Three weeks before the playoffs is a good rule of thumb. This way team A, which is out of playoff contention in week 12 (playoffs start week 14), cannot trade all of his good players to team B so that team B beats team C. Having a weekly high scoring team prize could also prevent collusion.

#8 Penalties for dead teams? What is a dead team? If an owner ignores his team and does not make any roster changes for several weeks, that is a dead team. How do you penalize that team? Charge a fee for last place? Have to wear a dress for or host the SB party if in last place? Another option is fines for owners who start bye week or injured players, with the contributions funding the end-of-year party.

How to avoid the "autopilot" or "ghost" teams. These are the teams that are managed by owners who do not change their lineup all year. They join so that they can score some brownie points with the boss or be able to have a conversation at work from August to December. But they are the ones who start the same lineup week after week. They do not account for bye weeks, injuries, suspensions or even deaths. They are the deadbeat owners who lose to every team but yours, since they always have one fluky week of high points and it always comes against you. How do you prevent this from happening? Threaten to ban them next year? Yeah right. Perhaps penalties for starting players who are "OUT" or on a bye week? Make these large monetary penalties. You could also have a vote the following year to determine which owners are worthy enough to return. This makes for a very interesting rule. It is hard to enforce as excuses will come hot and heavy.

#9 Start early. Canvas owners right after the fantasy football Super Bowl and see who is planning on coming back. I hope that every owner will be back, but some drops do occur for various reasons (two biggest being moving away or baby on the way). Send follow up e-mails to all returning owners in May announcing the start of the season and the anticipated draft date. It is never too early to get that on the books. I have found the weekend before Labor Day is best, since many people travel out of town for the long Labor Day weekend. Of course, the NFL ruined some of the best guy weekends, which centered on drafting, partying and then watching some football when they moved the NFL season opening one week later than Labor Day weekend. Thanks NFL.

Try to get replacements lined up by the end of June. Start with friends of owners currently playing now. If they enjoy watching football, they are prime candidates. Next, try co-workers, college or high school friends. It is a great way to stay in touch. Look to local sports bars as they may sponsor a league or two. Just make sure they are committed. Once the league is full, do not stop there; always have a few owners on the waiting list, in case someone cancels at the last minute.

#10 Be creative. There are many leagues out there that are TD-only and have a starting lineup of QB, 2 RBs, 2 WRs, TE, K and DEF/ST. Try going with an auction if everyone will be present. Add a flex position. Try IDP. Do a minimal keeper to keep interest in the league from year to year. Do whatever it takes to make it FUN! (See 8 Ways to Improve League, below)

#11 Have a SB party and awards presentation. And hand out the money.

#12 Remind all owners that scores are not official until _____. This prevents the "I went to bed last night a winner and woke up a loser. What gives?" There are usually a few scoring corrections every year. Someone does a shuffle pass or fumbles and someone else takes it in. Now the league reviews and rescores the play as far as stats are concerned. Tell all your owners to count their own scores separate from the web scoring stat counter and if there is ever a problem, have a way of correcting it.

League Constitution

Make sure you have written rules that cover everything. If taking over an existing league, read the rules carefully and look for anything that might have been left out. Refer to Chapter 4 – Types of Leagues, for help with setting one up. A sample outline for a league's constitution is:

Section 1 – Objective: Is it to have fun and learn more about football or is it to reward the best footballer with a trophy or money?

Section 2 – Teams and rosters: How many teams in the league? How many players on a team (roster size), how many starters; players from all of NFL or AFC or NFC only; limits by positions (min/max), IR spots?

Section 3 – Fees: Entry fee, other fees (fines or transaction costs; amount charged whenever a player is activated, traded, added or dropped). Some leagues will not have a charge for all of these actions.

Section 4 – Prizes (money, trophies and parties): Overall, weekly, TFPs, regular season, trophies, last place prize?

Section 5 – Draft Process: Draft order, serpentine or not; auction considerations such as who gets honor of bidding first; does bid go from last winning bidder or go around table; number of rounds, time limit for picks, penalties, breaks? The draft date and location can be TBD.

Section 6 – Standings and Scoring rules: to include examples of valid and invalid plays.

Section 7 – Stats: Who will provide it? What if there is a disagreement with it?

Section 8 – Free Agency: Free agency deadline, FCFS, bidding or priority system; limits on number of FA transactions, FAAB? Deadline is very important here.

Section 9 – Waivers: deadlines, length of time on waivers, waiver priority listing, limits?

Section 10 – Trades: deadline, limits?

Section 11 – Miscellaneous rules: keepers, salary caps, schedule, playoff structure, tiebreakers?

Section 12 – Governance: who has right to veto trade, owners or commissioner; conflict resolution? Submitting protests and rules to cover anything not in the rules. Ethics, as in, what will happen if collusion occurs; expelling owners?

Conflict Resolution/Changes to League

Have a system in place for dealing with things that come up that are not covered in the rules for this season (then change the rules for next season). Consider not only the letter of the law, but also the "spirit of the law." There are three ways to deal with such an issue: commissioner, committee or let the league decide. If the rules state that decisions by the commissioner concerning issues not covered in the rules are final, then the commissioner is the final approving source. I feel that this puts too much power into one man's hands; not to mention, others may feel alienated. This is the least popular method of dealing with controversy. A committee can also meet and decide. Committee members are decided upon prior to the season. The positions may rotate from year to year. The committee can reach consensus either by a majority or unanimous decision. It is best to have an odd number of members (three as a minimum, five as maximum). Too many members make this committee unwieldy but have enough so that if two of the commissioners are involved in the dispute they can excuse themselves and still have a functioning committee. Finally, the commish could propose a solution and have the league vote on it. A simple majority will carry the decision. This takes time because all owners must be given enough time to respond. The league rules should state whether it is an open vote (who casts what is seen by all) or a secret ballot, in which case the commissioner may know who voted for what (unless the management software can handle it). ESPN has a voting section on their league's websites.

In some leagues a Competition (Rules) Committee has been set up (like in the NFL) to decide on what rule changes to approve or bring to the other owner's attention. This committee could be a trifecta of the commish and two other owners who vote on rule changes for the upcoming season. If a 3-person committee is used then a unanimous decision would be required to approve a change so that only the worthy changes are carried out. Owners can nominate any rule changes after the season ends, then it is taken to the competition committee. Another way is to e-mail all owners and a majority or 75% voting yes will pass it. Write down anything you think of or see as a problem during the season and fix it before the next season starts, but save all rule changes for the off-season. Never change the rules after the draft has occurred. Owners draft based on rules in effect at the time of the draft. Changing the rules is unfair. Rules that are changed need to be changed well enough in advance to allow owners to adapt to the new rules. A good ROT is at least 2-weeks advance notice and preferably a month before the draft. If you only get together on draft day, that is too late to change the rules. Try the leagues MB, an e-mail campaign or form a competition committee and then get their decisions out in a timely manner.

8 Ways to Improve your League

You are in charge of running a league. Perhaps this is the first time you have done it, or the tenth time. As with most things, there are easy ways to run a league and there are hard ways. If it is your first year maybe you can make some good choices now to help you in future years. The following tips can be used or ignored, your choice.

1) Have a "Toilet Bowl" that coincides with your fantasy football playoffs. Teams not making the playoffs face off in a "Toilet Bowl" with losers advancing. In week 16, as the Super Bowl is going on, the two loser teams from the "Toilet Bowl" will face-off. The loser has to either, a) buy food or beer for next year's draft, b) "slap a little leather" and add a monetary penalty to the Super Bowl party fund, c) wear a dress to the next draft or d) wash the SB winner's car, etc. In addition, the "Toilet Bowl" will determine draft order if draft order is based on previous year's finish. By having a Toilet Bowl "winner," you can encourage active participation by all owners throughout the entire season due to motivation not to be in and lose the "Toilet Bowl."

2) Make the draft special.

a) Hold it in a special place. Some draft venues may include a local sports bar, hotel, or restaurant. Buffalo Wild Wings restaurants have connections with CBS Sports line and encourage customers to hold their fantasy football drafts at their establishments. The bar electronic games now have FF-type games on them for looking at your team.

b) Use a draft clock. Finally someone has marketed a clock for a reasonable price. It will cost you about $45, but it is a one-time fee. It is remote-controlled and you can set warning and end-of-time alarms.

3) Have a newsletter or website with quotes, articles, a draft review, game recaps, predictions for next week's games, rule highlights, records (best W/L, highest points ever, etc.), guest articles, Q+A, etc.

4) Improve free agency with a different system than FCFS, or as I like to call it, "Those who have no life get to take advantage of the rest of us." Free agency can be any of the systems listed in Chapter 14 – Free Agency Upgrades, except FCFS.

5) Turn into a minimal keeper league. (See Chapter 22 – Keeper Leagues.)

6) Have a dedicated spot on the roster for only a rookie. This forces teams to draft a rookie and groom him for future years. To start the process, add one spot on each roster that has to be a rookie. The following year, the owners must keep that rookie (now a second year player) on their team for the next two years. So draft him and keep him for three years. Every year you would have a rookie spot that can only be filled with a rookie and in subsequent years, your rosters will increase by the rookies from previous years. After the third year, the first rookie drafted will have to be let go and his spot replaced by another rookie. So three total roster spots are added (one each year for the first three years) eventually to the league; this is kind of like a "minor" contract addition.

7) League Pro Bowl between divisions on Super Bowl day or week 17 (if Super Bowl is on week 16). In this case, one division will face the other division in a "Pro Bowl." The losing division buys lunch for the winning division; if there are three divisions, then the loser will buy lunch for the other two divisions as they compete in a three-way matchup. The "coach" of the Pro Bowl teams can either be, a) losing or winning owner from

division playoff game or b) voted "coach of the year" by other division owners. The coaches then pick a pro bowl lineup from players within their division. All owners must have at least one player on the division pro bowl team.

Make week 17 fun even though your league is not using it. Have a "Dream Team Contest." Every owner can submit a lineup of any NFL players he wants and see who scores the most points in week 17 for a prize. He can pick any players he wants as long as each starting position is filled. It keeps everyone involved. It saves the fantasy football SB for week 16 when fewer players are resting for the playoff push. And it adds a little fun to week 17.

Allow in week 17 for all teams to turn in their normal roster and the team with the highest score gets his entry fee back. This also helps prevent trades that might be colluding. Collusive trades occur in leagues where no incentive is provided to be competitive all year long.

8) Determine the draft order well in advance. Have a draft order party (or do it at the Super Bowl party) to determine what the draft order will be for the upcoming year. By knowing in advance what your draft spot will be, you make trading draft picks easier and it allows practice mock drafts to determine what kind of players will be available at the draft. It will heighten the excitement of next year's season if you know for 6+ months what your draft spot will be. The flip side is the disappointment of whoever has the last draft spot.

Stat Sources

Many leagues (and thus commissioners) will state in the rules that the online management system is solely responsible for stats and their decisions are final. The league is using the management service for scoring, so why go somewhere else for stats when you are paying for this service? It is the best and easiest way. The league hosting service is the most impartial way to track stats. They do not have a stake in who wins your league and thus should handle appeals quickly and fairly. There will be a bad stat or two on occasion, but it prevents the headaches associated with appeals within the league. If there are too many stat errors (or some not corrected to everyone's satisfaction) then use a different service next year.

However, if using an online management system for stats is not how you want to handle it; what else can you do? The rules can be written to allow for a commissioner judgment on a stat/scoring protest. Many leagues will designate a source other than their league management software (for example, www.nfl.com or Stats Inc.) as the league's official scoring source. This allows owners to appeal in the case of an error that the management software decided not to fix. Some online management software will allow the commissioner to make manual adjustments to the scoring if the need arises. Also keep in mind that the NFL makes scoring changes the day after the games.

If you allow an appeals process:

a) Make sure the appeal deadline is shortly after the week's games (such as Wed. at midnight).

b) Make sure the process is completed before the first game of the next week.

c) Notify the other teams of the protested stat.

d) Make sure there is a process to correct the error.

Do not have a league vote on the protest. Submitting a scoring revision to the league for a vote becomes a popularity contest in some cases, or some owners vote against enemies and for friends, rather than what is just for the parties involved and the league. This is where a commissioner earns his pay, in making a decision that is best for the league and fair for all owners.

Ties (or How to Avoid Them)

There are two primary types of ties in fantasy football. There are weekly ties in H2H leagues when both competing team's starters score exactly the same amount of points and ties in the standings for playoff spots or waiver wire priority, etc.

Game Tiebreakers

Someone once said a tie is like kissing your sister. Enough said. How do you avoid them? How many ties can you expect? If in a 12-team league with basic scoring, then perhaps anywhere from 3-6 ties in a year; if you are in a performance-based league then possibly 2-4 ties. The more stats you score, the less likely you are to have a tie. Inclusion of fractions also decreases the likelihood of a tie. Of course in H2H leagues weekly ties can be counted as ties just like in the NFL. But if you do not want the hassle (or for single elimination playoffs where you need a team to advance), you can use the following to break a tie.

1) Compare bench player's scores – This may lead to a strategy of carrying more kickers and QBs than normal since they tend to score more points than the other positions backups. In terms of scoring, the team that wins the tiebreaker can be given an extra point.

2) Bench players compared one at a time to break the tie – Nominated in order before game time. In this manner, teams will designate the order of their bench players for comparison for the tiebreaker. In other words, if teams are tied, then team A will have his first bench player compared to team B's first bench player. If still tied, it goes to the next player nominated, and so on. This method is less likely to see extra QBs and Ks hoarded since coaches only get one player to win the tie.

3) Highest scoring bench player – The team with the single highest scoring bench player wins the tie. For example, team A's highest scoring bench player has 12 points and team B has a player who scored 14 points. Team B wins the game.

4) Compare individual bench players starting at top or bottom – This list usually starts from either the top or bottom of the bench and goes further through positions if a tie continues. For example, if you start at the top of the bench, then compare bench QBs for each team. The QB with the higher point total wins the game. If still tied, compare RBs next. Continue until out of bench players. Problems occur when players are on bye week. It would suck to have a tie and then you lose the tiebreaker because your QB is on a bye.

5) Team that scored most TDs wins.

6)   Home team wins ties – The problem with this is that some leagues play an odd number of games so some teams will have a better advantage in tie situations. Many leagues do not use home or away scheduling.

7)   Coin flip – This is hard to do in leagues where owners are not located near each other. It will depend on the trustworthiness of the commish or you can find some sites that will do a random coin flip for you.

NOTE: Many management software services do not support ranking bench players; so option 3 may be easiest to implement.

*Another alternative is to say that the team who has started the least number of bye week players wins the tie. If neither has started any bye week players (as it should be), then you use another tiebreaker method.

What if you allow ties in the regular season; how do you break a tie in the playoffs?

Some use the H2H feature. Whichever team beat the other in the regular season gets the win. Some other leagues use the team with the highest points in regular season or the best record. This seems silly if the whole point of the playoffs is for everyone to start from scratch, but it does reward a team that did well in the regular season, which may be another point altogether. If you do not want to use the past to break ties, then use any of the above "game tiebreakers" for playoffs.

Some leagues suggest that both teams advance or push into the next round, with the higher score in the next round advancing and facing the expected opponent, but this push of two teams is unfair to their opponent because now he really faces two teams instead of one. As an example, teams A and B tied in round 1 and are pushed into round 2 versus team C. Team A scores 34 in round 2, team B scores 58 and thus advances to play team C, who scores 43 in round 2. If team A had won in round 1's tiebreaker, team C would have won in round 2, but as it is he has to face the team that scored more in round 2 also. Not fair.

Ties in Standings

You have played 13 or more games and now two or more teams are tied for that last wild card spot into the playoffs. Who will advance and who goes home crying? Use whatever tiebreaker everyone can agree on. However, start with the NFL's tiebreakers since we are trying to mimic that league somewhat. Also don't forget that these tiebreakers may affect the draft order for next year if your league uses standings or regular season finishes for that. And they must be written into the rules.

For a simple set of divisional tiebreakers, a league can use this:

- Regular Season Record

- Head-to-Head Record (some leagues prefer TFPs for the season)

- Record in the Division (makes for rivalries and makes those division games more important)

- Total Points for the Season

- Most Points Against (strength of schedule)

- Coin Toss

For wild card, teams use the same formula after the divisional winners are determined. The only difference will be that "Record in the Division" will not apply unless all are in the same division.

Most ties will involve two teams and are easy to handle. It is when three or more teams are tied that it begins to require some thought. Some leagues place TFPs scored as the second tiebreaker. The reason is that H2H records can be misleading if every team has not played the same number of games against the other teams. If a team is involved in a three way tie and has swept all the other teams then it is easy, they should advance; but what if they won two of the three? What if one of the three teams only played two against the others and split (won one, lost one)? What if one team only played one game against the others but won; is 1-0 really better than 2-1 or 3-1? Another reason comes from the fact that W/L is influenced by bye weeks. This creates the old "You played team A when LT was on a bye week, that's why you have more wins than me" whine. TFPs scored during the regular season is a better measure of team versus team for determining tiebreakers because it is not influenced by the schedule or other factors. That fact that you played him when his RBs were hurt has no bearing on how many points you scored during the season.

Do as the NFL does with tiebreakers and multiple teams. Once a clear winner emerges, the other teams go back to the beginning, as if that advancing team was no longer competing. For example, three teams fighting for two places:

Team A (8-6, 1-1 Beat B, lost to C, FP 560)

Team B (8-6, 1-1 Beat C, lost to A, FP 593)

Team C (8-6, 1-1 Beat A, lost to B, FP 537)

All three teams have the same regular season records (8-6) and H2H records (1-1) so the first team to advance as a wild card team is team B, based on his scoring the most TFPs in the regular season (FP 593). We are assuming they are all in one conference for this discussion. Now the process starts all over again, with team B out of the mix.

Team A (8-6, 0-1, Lost to C, FP 560)

Team C (8-6, 1-0, Beat A, FP 537)

Now team C advances as wild card team #2 since they beat team A in their H2H matchup.

Trades

There are several ways to handle trades. One is to allow the commissioner total authority to veto any trade he feels is unfair; but allowing the commissioner to decide places too much power in his hands. Another method is to make owners vote on trades. If the required number of "no" votes do not come in, the trade is approved. The problem with this is the length of time to vote and the state of interest by the owners. If most owners check the league website on Saturday or Sunday before kickoff, then a trade may slip through the cracks. Still another method is to have a trade put up for approval, and if a certain number of owners protest it then it is either rejected or goes for review by the commissioner or a committee. Rejecting it is fine, but why have a democratic vote to protest it and then send it to another body for rejection? This seems like two processes combined. Either leave it to the commissioner or let the owners vote it down.

Judging trade fairness is one of the hardest choices you will make as commissioner. If the commissioner reviews the trades, then have an alternative method for reviewing his trades, such as taking it to two neutral owners. How are they determined? Should they be in or outside his division? You could have his assistant review the commissioner trades and a backup review any trades between the commissioner and the assistant. You can start to see some of the many problems with the "commissioner has all the power" solution. Allowing owners to protest trades avoids having the commissioner take on these duties. Some leagues use a system where if a certain amount of owners protest, then the trade will not go through. How many owners must protest before a trade is rejected? 50 percent? 25 percent? I think 50 percent is too much in a large league and 25 percent is too little in a small league. Usually, 25 percent in 12-team or greater leagues works best; two of the owners will be in the trade in any case, leaving 4 of 10 (12-team league) to protest it if it is to be rejected. Too low a percentage (or number of owners) results in a few owners with grudges vetoing. You do not want two or three owners having all the power to stop trades. If you have a small league (8-10 teams), then require a 50 percent majority to overturn. It is hard to get all the owners to vote on anything, much less all agree, so avoid a requirement of over 50 percent. Some leagues simply state that if two or more owners protest then it goes to a league vote. Another problem with voting on trades is that it can become a popularity contest.

Evaluating trades for fairness has to be the hardest commissioner duty. Look at talent, but also at needs, motivations and circumstances. I would also look at the motivations of the owner(s) protesting the trade. Look at needs for the traders. Many times a lopsided trade occurs because a team has a need in one area and great strengths in another area. In this case a lopsided trade is okay. Don't ask "Is it a fair trade?" Ask instead, "Is it an unfair trade" (i.e. is it fair enough)? Trades do not have to be fair (both teams may think they got the best deal of the trade) but they do need to be reasonable. Did both teams get something out of the trade? If yes, it was a good trade. Perhaps the most important rule of all is "innocent until proven guilty." If there is any doubt about collusion then you must let the trade go through. Be very careful about reversing a trade; a reversed trade has long-term effects. It can make owners resentful as if punished. Some owner's will feel like their "steals" have been singled out. The "hard-core" may think the league is no longer worth playing in if they are being restricted or held back.

At some point an owner will threaten to quit and go home if he does not get his way. IGNORE this poor sport. He does not have the league at heart and you are better off without him if he does quit. Next year, consider not inviting him back due to his behavior disrupting the league's flow. He is probably bluffing, but if he does quit either give everyone a win against him (go back and adjust previous games so that no team lost to him), find another owner to take over his team, or run his team by the league (kind of like the Montreal Expos with baseball) by starting his highest ranked players, regardless of matchups, unless the player is doubtful or out, in which case they should be benched. By the same token, if one owner is always involved (either in shady trades or protesting every trade), consider whether or not he is an asset to the league.

Do not just say in the rules that unfair trades will not be allowed. Define the entire process for protesting a trade; define what an unfair trade is and give examples. Also include whether trades can involve cash, future picks, etc., or if they must be current players traded now. Some leagues have a deadline of 2-3 weeks before the end of the regular season or rules that state once a team is eliminated from playoff contention they cannot trade. The time it takes you to create a written policy could save you many problems down the road and the next commissioner will no doubt thank you.

Below are some thoughts on creating your trading rules.

The process should include:

1) Types of trades that could potentially require a veto vote. Give an example.

    a. Team A trades his two starting RBs for team B's backup kicker. Use a common sense test on this one. If the majority of owners think it is unfair, then... if it smells like a rat and looks like a rat it is probably a rat.

    b. Team A trades his only QB (#1 in league) for team B's worst WR (#55 in league).

    c. Team A trades the same players back from an earlier trade. This is called player borrowing and helps teams prevent bye week blues. Team A has a RB on week 6 bye, so he trades for team B's RB who has a week 7 bye. Team B sends his backup that can play on week 6 for Team A, while team A sends his backup that can play in week 7 for team B. After week 7 is over (week 8 if they were smart) then the two teams trade the same players back. This "trading players for a limited amount of use" should be prohibited in the rules.

2) The process for a trade to be reviewed (one protest, 20% of owners protest or commissioner initiative). Time limit for protest to be filed; investigations and outcomes.

3) Things to be investigated and who does the investigating; needs, motivation, value of players (or picks or both), commissioner or a committee? Committee members-random or pre-selected and excused if in the trade?

4) Possible outcomes and how they occur.

Arguments that should not work for protesting a trade:

1) It makes team A too strong. That is the point in trades, to make your team better.

2) It makes team B too weak. Trading involves giving up something to get something. As long as team B improves his team elsewhere, then it is reasonable to expect his team to weaken where he traded a player away.

3) Team A has a much better record than team B. It may mean a little more scrutiny, but the fact that a team with a 6-1 record is trading with a 1-6 team means that the winning team does not fear the losing team can come back to hurt him.

4) They are good friends or they trade often. The amount of trades or the relationship of the trading partners should have no influence on a veto decision.

5) Both teams are not getting the same in return. It does not have to be an equal trade. Some trades may be 3 RBs for 1 WR. Some may be 2 RBs and a WR for a QB. Some owners will accept less in order to fill a need. Team A cannot get anyone to

trade him a RB to fill his injured RB2 position. He is desperate and trades his two best WRs (WR1 and WR2) for a RB2 and WR3, simply because he feels that he needs a RB2 to get him into the playoffs and his backup WRs (WR3 and WR4) are good enough. If both teams got what they needed, it is hard to veto the trade.

Investigating a protested trade:

1) Contact the team that is getting the weakest part of the deal first. Inform him that a protest has been made and ask him to explain the reasoning behind the trade.

2) Next contact the other party in the trade. Inform him that a protest has been made and ask him to explain the reasoning behind the trade.

3) Consider all the facts.

Making your ruling:

1) First, if you decide to veto it, get both owners involved and explain that it is going to be vetoed by you and give them a chance to annul it and try another trade. This eliminates some of the hard feelings of having a trade vetoed officially.

2) If they refuse and you have to make a ruling, make it fast and authoritative (indecisiveness is a weakness.)

3) Return the traded players back to the original owners and explain that the trade was vetoed because it threatened the competitive balance of the league. If the trade was deemed collusion then you must consider their punishment (commissioner or a committee may decide this). Punishment for collusion should be banishment from the league forever. Obviously, this is a last step.

4) If veto is appealed (if you offer appeals), explain why you ruled the way you did, then put it to a league vote. If a majority votes to overturn your ruling, the trade will go through. If not, then matter is settled for good. Some leagues allow trading partners to vote; I disagree. Let their peers vote on your decision. The owners involved are biased in their own favor. Do not let them vote.

Types of Trades

The "future considerations" trade – This will involve FAAB money, salary cap money or future draft picks. Do your rules prohibit trading of cash or future draft picks? If not, it will be hard to veto these trades. Create a constitution or add it into the existing one next year, if league does not want to allow it.

A "collusion" trade – This will be very lopsided and may involve owners who are good friends. These are not typical, but may occur in pay Internet leagues where they have teams in other leagues too. If collusion is involved, immediate expulsion of both owners is customary. Be advised that these types of rulings can tear apart a league as the other owners tend to take sides.

A "lame horse" trade – This involves Team A trading team B a great player who just happens to be hurt and is out for a long time. "Uh, gee commish, I didn't know he was banged up." Sure… If you are in a new league with beginners, you may want to void the trade and remind owners not to take advantage of one another like this. If you are in a big boy league, then the trade will stand because it is buyer beware! The other owner should have done his homework before consummating the deal. Note: "If it is too good to be true, it probably is." Some leagues will allow a 24-hour money back guarantee. If either party changes their mind within the 24 hours, they can void the deal.

A "bad" trade – Here, one owner is swindled, or so he or others think, and now he wants it reversed. This may be because he has buyer's remorse or others have convinced him he was taken. Again, if in a big boy league, you hit "accept" and the deal is done. If others say it is unfair, remember many times the end of the season sheds a different light on a trade's value. Unless it was collusion, let it stand.

Rules to spice up a league

1) Punishment for each loss – This can be in the form of a fine ($1 every time you lose) or a progressive fine (doubles each time you lose or only if you lose back-to-back, if you want to take it easy). Say you have a progressive fine for losing. If you lost two in a row, the second fine would be $2 (first was $1) and if you lost your third game in a row you would owe $4. If the fine is progressive for losses, then a losing season can sting the wallet. A maximum loss of $50 is a good rule to implement. This rule helps motivate everyone to be competitive, and on draft day you will find much more attentive, informed owners. If you do implement this, I recommend everyone put in $50 extra fine money, held by the commish, and owners get the remaining balance back after the regular season ends. This prevents the bad sport owner who has dropped 6 of 8 games and is going to quit and stiff the league.

2) Player misconduct fines – If any player on your team gets arrested, suspended or (insert the bad deed of your choice here), then the owner has to pay a fine. This could be progressive or just a flat $5 fee each time. This makes drafting some players less desirable and makes free agency a little more complicated too.

3) Everyone must play rule – If a player has not started by a certain week then he will be cut from the team. This is more of an issue in keeper leagues where rookies have been drafted for future years.

4) Award bonuses for performance of the week – In this case, a bonus (usually 3 points) is awarded to the longest pass, rush, reception for a TD and FG. So even though you are up by 2 points and your opponent's players are done, you still may have to watch MNF because his QB is looking at a passing performance bonus for his 41-yard TD pass, and that will defeat you. Now you find yourself rooting for Eli Manning or J. Campbell to throw a 41+ yard TD pass.

5) Lowest scoring team for the week hosts the next week's Monday Night Football party. Losing can become a family affair. Your wife may start to make lineup decisions after you host MNF parties three weeks in a row.

6) Play a bye week player and he gets dropped – Big penalty for a huge mistake. If you start a bye week player, then that player is dropped the following week. Another corollary is that the dropped player is banned from the league for the rest of the season. You do not want another team to luck into him on the waiver wire.

7) Popular Player Fine – If a player appears on the cover of SI, or any other designated magazine, there is an imposed fine.

8) Bonus points for playing injured guys – Give 1 point for playing a questionable player, 2 points for playing a doubtful player and 3 points for starting a player designated as out. Of course, the player has to actually play at least one play to earn the bonus. If T. Heap perpetually plays with a doubtful tag, that's 2 points almost every week.

9) A "Homer" League – You own the NFL team you desire. You get all the points from your Team QB and Team kicker. You have to keep the QB, #1 RB and #1 WR, TE, kicker and DEF/ST from your chosen NFL team. You then draft other players to fill in your roster.

10) The team that comes in last place has to accept a team name (for the following season) conferred to them by the other owners. Some good ones are: corvette cowgirls, burp-slurping gutter wenches, my wife's team or I play like a girl.

11) Award a home field advantage bonus of a certain number of points. It helps if you have an even number of games in the regular season. Have the schedule determine who is home and who is away; then award the home team bonus points. I would suggest 3 points if your league is primarily a TD-based basic scoring league; 5 points if yardage performance is used and more if your scoring is accelerated (PPR league, 11 IDP players start, etc.) So the home team would start the games already ahead by 3 points in the TD-only league.

12) Start an offensive line – This team OL gets points for allowing fewer sacks, allowing rushing yards or passing yards. They can also get negative points for a poor performance.

13) The M*A*S*H rule – If your starting player gets a season-ending injury, you are given first priority to pick up his backup next week, if available on the FA list. If B. Favre goes down on Sunday and no one drafted (or picked up previous to the injury) A. Rodgers, then you (as Favre's owner) get the first chance at his replacement if you drop the injured player. However, if some other owner drafted Rodgers, you are out of luck. The rationale is that it takes some of the luck (bad luck, that is) out of the equation. There is a time limit of one week to this "right of refusal" rule, so that the bad luck owner does not keep the potential player off the market for a prolonged period of time. Some leagues just say in the rules that an owner has three days after the injury to pick up his backup. In the case of RBs and WRs, there may be multiple players who could potentially backup. With kickers and QBs it is a little more cut-and-dried.

14) Pillaging rule – The winning team gets to take one player from the losing team. (This is minimized by prohibiting any top 6 draft picks from being pillaged). Sometimes used in playoffs in that you get to pillage a player from losing playoff team. Strange but unique.

15) Déjà vu rule – Each owner can change one starter after the games are over for that week. If you started S. McNair and he got hurt in the first quarter, giving you zero points, bench him and put in P. Rivers, who at least got 9 points. Or if L. Betts exploded for three TDs while on your bench, put him as your starter. But you could not do both, only one "do over" per week. Can be frustrating to win and then end up losing due to the mulligan, but it could also help you too.

16) Allow college players to be drafted? Realize that college football's schedule does not match well with the FF playoffs but may be good for keeper leagues where you can really cultivate some talent further out.

Miscellaneous League Suggestions

Multiple divisions versus one big division – First, how do you determine who is in what division? Two fair ways are a random draw or by draft picks. If by random draw after the draft, you would pick teams to go in one division at random. If the draft pick method is used, then if there are two divisions, every odd draft pick in the first round goes into one division and every even pick goes into the other division. If there are three divisions; picks 1, 4, 7 and 10 go in one division, 2, 5, 8 and 11 in another division and 3, 6, 9 and 12 go in the last division. Why have divisions? It is more like the NFL, makes for easier scheduling, creates rivalries, etc. The argument against it is, "But usually one division will be stronger than another. Why should a weaker team from another division beat out a stronger team that just happened to be in a strong division?" For example, the north division winner is 8-6 with 500 FP, and goes to the playoffs for winning the division. Yet the 9-5 team who was in a three-way tie for first does not make the playoffs because he lost the tiebreaker to both teams in the other division? Use of wild cards can help but will not totally eliminate the problem.

Arrange divisions based on fantasy football parity. Have 50 percent of teams make the playoffs based on division winners and wild cards. In a divisional format, the same number of teams from each division will go to the playoffs (i.e. the #2 WC from one division will advance even if his record is not as good as the #4 team in the other division). Every year have two divisions: the "champs" and the "chumps." Those teams not making the playoffs from last year go into the "chumps" division. Those who made the postseason last year go into the "champs" division. There are big-time bragging rights playing in the champ division; you take a rash of shit playing in the chump division. This guarantees that 50% of the playoff teams will be different each year, since 50% of the playoff teams will come from the chump division. Those in the champ division will have to fight and scrape to remain in champ year after year. The teams that return to the chump division will be humiliated as a repeat offender.

Another suggestion is to have three receivers (versus 2 WR and 1 TE), but they can be either WR or TE. So one owner may start 3 WRs, another may start 1 WR and 2 TEs, still another could start 2 WRs and a TE. This flexibility adds more scoring to a league. Allows TEs to be used, but not mandatory, so more 3 WR sets will be seen. This does deplete the WR core more since most teams will skip TE unless they can get a Top 5.

Maximum roster limits – The maximum number of players at certain positions is limited. For example, the limit may be five RBs (max) per team. This prevents hoarding (when one team tries to get as many RBs as possible to prevent other teams from having any) to get trade bait and, if no one else has RBs then that trade bait is more valuable. Another example may be a team in a 16-team league that drafts 3 QBs or defenses, thus eliminating a backup for a team. The problem with maximums is that it takes one more skill or technique away from the owner. It is best for beginning leagues or those with a large number of teams (16) to simplify the draft and regular season moves. The basic roster limits are 3 QBs, 5 RBs, 6 WRs, 2 TEs, 2 Ks and 2 DEFs. The opposite is minimum roster limits, usually 2 QBs, 3 RBs, 3 WRs, 2 TEs, 2 Ks and 2 DEFs. This forces teams to draft players at the weaker positions and guarantees that there is some FA depth at the RB and QB positions.

If you are in 10-team league but want less free agents and more of a big league feel, then try adding a flex position or two. Add flex 1 (RB/WR/TE) and/or flex 2 (QB/WR/TE) and increase the rosters sizes to accommodate them. Your league will feel like a 14-team league that does not have a flex spot. Less is more when thinking about starter requirements. Some leagues require 2 RBs or 3 WRs. With a 12-team league, 24 RBs will be started. On weeks with six teams on a bye and some hurting or in RBBC situations, that can mean that some owners are starting substandard players at those positions. Consider starting only 1 RB or 2 WRs to eliminate the poor performances and loss of interest that weak starting players can cause. This may be more of a factor in dynasty leagues where roster depth is deep. The WR position may be the only position where multiple starters should be considered in large team leagues.

In the playoffs, have teams retain average points scored per game from regular season. Therefore, if team A had an average of 110 points per game and faces team B with a 100 point average per game, then team A will start with a 10-point lead in their playoff game.

"Can't cut" list – This is a list of the top 20-50 players and you cannot drop them from your roster during the season. The reason is to prevent an owner from quitting on a stud player too early in the season and allowing some lucky owner to pick him off the waiver wire. The "can't cut" list should be updated weekly so that injured players out for the season are removed from the list. It would be unfair to have them stay on the list after being out for the season since the owner could not drop (cut) him and pick up a replacement. Just because they are a stud does not mean they can never be cut. If injuries or suspensions force them out for the season then the owner should have the option of cutting them from the squad. Unless it is a keeper league, in which case he may not be allowed to cut him if that allows another team to pick up a stud for next year. Another option is a "If cut, not available to other teams for rest of the season" list.

For leagues with more than 16 teams, (up to 32 teams), create two separate leagues with champs from each league meeting in SB.

League Administration

16-Week Season

4-team league – One division, 15-game regular season (5 games against every other team) and top two make SB in week 16

6-team league – One division, 15-game regular season (3 games against other teams) and top two make SB in week 16

8-team league – Two divisions of four teams, 14-game regular aeason (2 games against other teams) and four teams make playoffs in week 15, SB in week 16

10-team league – Two divisions of five teams, 13-game regular season (play division teams twice, others once) and four teams make playoffs (the highest scoring two teams in weeks 14 and 15 combined advance to the SB), SB week 16 or four teams make single elimination playoffs, 14-game season

12-team league – Three divisions of four teams, 13-game regular season, (play 2 of 3 division rivals twice, everyone else once) six teams make playoffs (top 2 get byes in week 14) SB in week 16 or a 14-game regular season with only 4 playoff teams

14-team league – One division of fourteen teams, 13-game regular season (everyone plays once), six playoff teams with top 2 getting bye in week 14

16-team league – Two divisions of eight, 15-game regular season, two division winners meet in Super Bowl; or 13-game regular season with two DH weeks to give a 15-game schedule, eight teams make playoffs

17-Week Season

4-team league – One division, 16-game regular season (5 games against two teams, 6 versus the other team) and then top two teams meet in Super Bowl

6-team league – One division, 15-game regular season (3 games against other teams), top 3 make playoffs with #1 team getting bye and going directly to Super Bowl in week 17

8-team league – Two divisions of four teams, 15-game regular season (3 games versus one team, 2 games against other teams), four teams make playoffs in week 16, SB in week 17

10-team league – Two divisions of five teams, 15-game regular season (play division teams and two others twice and 3 non-division teams once), four teams make playoffs in week 16, SB week 17

12-team league – Three divisions of four teams, 14-game regular season, (play division rivals twice, everyone else once), six teams make playoffs (top 2 get byes in week 15), SB in week 17

14-team league – One division of fourteen, 14-game regular season (everyone plays once, play one team twice), six playoff teams with top 2 getting bye in week 15, SB in week 17

16-team league – Two divisions of eight, 15-game regular season, four teams make playoffs in week 16, SB in week 17

Chapter 20 Psychology of Fantasy Football

"Psychology of perception" – Why things look the way they do.

Fantasy football owners misinterpret information all the time. We think we know more than we really do and we tend to overreact to performances, both good and bad. Do you know how little you know? We tend to take the wrong chances. We hate to lose so we play things conservatively. On the other hand, biases make us think certain events are more likely to occur when they are not. This leads to riskier choices. The key is knowing what you do not know.

It is always easier to accept defeat when the person who beat you goes on to win the championship. You can rationalize that you were second best when in fact you lost in the first round of a 3-round playoff. This rationalization is just one example of psychological issues that affect every fantasy football owner.

Winning at fantasy football is not about beating someone else, but about controlling your own performance. You cannot control team C and how they do; you can control how your team performs. You can take risks to try to improve your performance, or not take those risks and go with an average performance. The choice is yours.

I am going to ask you to examine everything you think you know about fantasy football. We will discuss how people make decisions and how you can make better (more rational) decisions. Today, with the Internet and fantasy football information services available, you have limitless amounts of information at your fingertips. Anyone can, with a little work, find just about everything they wanted to know right before game time. And yet we still make the wrong decisions, start the wrong players; add the star backup who does not get on the field, etc. All that information is useless if we let our emotions (or human biases) get in the way. If we misinterpret the information (or let our emotions hurt our judgment) then the good information has not done us any good. I will tell you how to save yourself from these loser mentalities and increase your "luck" factor.

Fantasy football players (like most humans) use mental shortcuts to estimate probabilities and predict risk. These shortcuts or "biases" can be harmful. Some of the more prevalent ones are described below:

Fantasy Football Biases

1) Owners base broad predictions on narrow samples of data (the law of small numbers) when, in fact, they should use the law of large numbers. The law of large numbers states that only a large sampling of data can give an accurate picture of the information it is drawn from. When we add a player who has scored two TDs in the last three games, even though he is the #2 WR (on a team that does not pass well, and history shows has not done well at the WR#2 positions) we are using the law of small numbers. Another example might be if you look at defensive TDs from last year. That is a narrow sample. On the other hand, defensive TDs from 2000 through the present is a very large sample of data.

Of course it depends on if you are looking for team performances or overall performances. Data can get old very fast. By this I mean changes to the NFL rules can skew the statistics from previous years. Recent performance is a better predictor of a team's defenses than how they did in 1993. But don't just trust recent performance, look at the big picture. It does not take much to think you have a trend. Several TDs at home versus away. Do I now start that defense based on their scoring all three of their defensive TDs at home this year, based on 5 games? No, this is too short of a data field to make those kinds of assumptions.

2) If something is easy to remember, we tend to think it happens more often. Like hitting that sleeper pick, the rookie RB, or our boom/bust player's great games (versus his bust games).When we think of rookie superstars, everyone remembers Reggie Bush and Edgerrin James. Both came into the league and started out on fire (Edge had 13 TDs in his rookie season and Reggie had 8, plus 2 in the playoffs). Therefore, they are easy to remember because of how well they did. However, that does not mean that many rookies do well in their first year, rather it is quite the opposite. Therefore, the easily remembered event leads us to take risky chances on rookies when in fact only rookie RBs tend to do well and even then only 33 percent of the top rookie RBs perform well.

3) When estimating future values, we anchor our projections on any number that happens to be handy. Any suggestion of an outside number is enough to distort our view of that future value (such as fantasy football magazine covers with 20 TDs for RBs, etc). A perfect example is estimating P. Manning's TDs in 2005 after his 49 TDs in 2004. Due to the fact that he was in the news with 49 TDs, that number biased most predictions for him in 2005. I saw anywhere from 30-50 for him. In fact, he had averaged 28 TDs for 4 of his past 6 seasons, if 2004 was thrown out as an anomaly. A realistic estimate for him would have been 28 TDs, well under what most suggested. He threw 28 TDs that year (31 in 2006, his Super Bowl year). Whenever you read an article by a guru before the season or hear a talking head proclaim a number of TDs for a player, that is an anchor that sticks in your mind, which you will use unless you fight this bias.

When pundits predict big years for studs, they anchor everyone's perception of those players future performances. Maybe that is why over 50% of the Top 10 picks in many drafts disappoint. Don't let the experts anchor your expectations of the player's performance. They are making educated guesses at best (at worst they are just trying to get you to spend money buying their service or magazine). Armed with enough data you can do the same, if not better.

4) Losing feels worse than winning and we will do almost anything to prevent losing. Losing can mean a game or a player. Owners tend to hold on to poor performing players too long and trade/drop good players too soon. Why? We hate to admit a loss when we drop a player we drafted. If we drop a player we hand-picked, we are admitting that we did not know what we were doing when we drafted, traded or added him. Likewise, if one of our players has done well lately we have a tendency to trade him too soon so that we can acknowledge his accomplishments and bask in his glory.

How much do we hate losing? Imagine a coin toss where if it is heads you lose 50 fantasy points but if it is tails you win whatever you wagered in fantasy points. How much would you be willing to bet? Many owners insist on twice (100 points) as many points to be willing to take the risk of losing 50 of them. Losing feels twice as bad as winning, so we want to avoid losing by not taking as many risks. Losing feels twice as painful as winning feels pleasant.

We hate to lose so much that we make inconsistent gambles to avoid losing. Mentally, we would rather lose a close game but look to be in control than take a calculated risk that could pay off big but if it does not we end up looking like a loser. For example, in many leagues if the payout is only for the top team then it makes sense to try to be the extraordinary team and not a middle-of-the-road team. Most owners can draft a middle-of-the-road team that is competitive but does not win the big prize. To win the big prize in some of the money contests you have to be extraordinary. I am not talking about local Yahoo or Sporting News leagues, but the advanced giveaway leagues where the top 10 in 20,000 get a prize. Above-average means taking more risks on some sleepers and outside shots. This "risk it all" technique, if it pays off, will catapult you not only to your league championship but also into the top rankings for the overall competition. If it fails, your team will look like a lovable loser hanging out at the bottom. Nevertheless, realistically, to win the HD TV or the trip to the Pro Bowl (or whatever they are offering), you need to be head and shoulders above the rest and that means reaching for sleepers and hoping they come through; and if they don't, you *will* look a little stupid.

5) We see trends where there are no trends. We don't realize regression to the mean. Chance alone dictates that an unusually good or bad event is usually followed by a more ordinary one. If a player has scored 10 TDs most of his career and is in the middle of the season with only 1 TD, unless he has been injured or has lost a key component to the offense (QB, RB, etc.), then that player should regress to the mean. By this I mean he should rebound with a higher than average number of TDs for the remainder of the season. Likewise, if a player has 6 TDs on average for the past four years and this year has 5 TDs in eight games, regression to the mean dictates that he will probably have less than the average number of TDs the remainder of the season. He may finish with seven or even eight TDs but he probably will not continue with five more TDs in the next eight games. He may do just that, but the odds are against him due to regression to the mean, assuming all other variables (injuries, systems changes) stay the same. We tend to see trends and believe them (for example, 5 TDs in eight games, above) when there are no trends.

6) Group think – Do not believe everything everyone else takes for granted. This is where you can uncover a gem. For example, every pundit says Stephen Davis is over the hill and will be replaced by the new rookie DeShaun Foster. Davis remains and becomes the goal line vulture in 2005, grabbing 12 TDs. If you were a lemming like everyone else, you would have missed his potential. Think for yourself.

7) Laziness in assigning value – Many people will avoid choice if given the opportunity due to their unwillingness (laziness) to research the options and their fear of the consequences of choosing poorly. If an owner has his draft pick and there are three real choices RB A, WR B or WR C, many times the owner will take RB A without hesitation because he does not want to decide between WR B and C. However, if he already has three other RBs and can only start two, is he really getting value with that pick or is he just making things easier on himself (settling) with the pick? Value is sometimes not just related to importance but how much energy or prestige we can get from a thing. "If I pick that new rookie QB and he does well, everyone will know I am a football god." That is a harder choice. Do not be lazy. Know why you choose.

8) Familiarity bias – Players on "Homers" teams or players held by owners in previous years and that did well will be drafted a round earlier than predicted. We have something in our subconscious that makes us hold onto them since we know them. Many owners will only remember the good or great performances by players on their team last year and thus

overvalue them. Subjective memories lead us to overinflate known players. We know them like family and do anything to get them back.

9) Sunk costs – Once we invest in a player or a theory we tend to talk ourselves out of abandoning it because of the time or capital we have invested in it. The best reason not to draft a kicker early is that if he gets off to a slow start you feel obligated to stick with him rather than cutting him and going with a better option from FA. If you are not heavily invested in your kicker (high draft pick), then you are more likely to look at improving that position. The same goes for any highly drafted player. Owners will say " I can't bench him, I drafted him too high."

10) Most owners will overreact to both good and bad player news. This means they will sell a good player when he has had a few bad games and they will buy an average player after he has had a few good games. Take advantage of that. Know why you drafted a player and why you are dropping a player. Has anything changed with your initial analysis?

How can you fight these biases?

1) Keep your hunches where they belong, as sleeper picks in the later draft rounds. Avoid the temptation to grab that rookie early. Let the other suckers follow the crowd and grab him too early.

2) Step back and look at the big picture. Don't panic because your #1 RB has not scored any TDs in the first four weeks. Look at your entire team, look at the league, and look at his NFL team. Maybe the first four weeks were low scoring statistically throughout the NFL. Maybe he played the toughest defenses on their schedule; maybe the key OT that helps make the holes for him was out and will be back soon. Don't rush to conclusions before looking at as much data as possible.

3) Think long-term not short-term – Don't worry about every yard or TD every week obsessively if you drafted them long-term (either for the entire year or several years if keeper league). Focus on how they have done at midseason or end of the season. You do not ask how much your house is worth every day, so don't worry about players every week. Studies show that owners who get wrapped up in analyzing their team each day get too consumed in the short-term statistics and miss the forest for the trees. (I think I'll bench LT this week since he plays at Baltimore. Instead I will start Reuben Droughns at home versus Indianapolis?) At a minimum, wait for the first three weeks to unfold.

4) Use autopilot – Plug in the studs and leave them there. They are the studs because they will deliver stud-like returns. If you try to "time" the league and move studs in and out based on matchups, you are more likely to have your stud on the bench when he has a breakthrough day and vice versa. Constant tinkering produces poor results. Many teams would be better off without as many roster changes and add/drops. I have seen many owners who draft well and then only make changes to replace injured/suspended players; they do well because they avoid trying to time their performance and accept a good performance versus a great performance (with the risk of a below-average performance). Some say that picking a defense or kicker and starting them all season long is what gets the most from average players. Trying to play the matchups defeats the "all kickers are the same" mentality.

5) Do not let other owners see you get mad when they steal a pick from you. It helps their confidence and makes it harder to trade for him later. In fact, when I hear another owner exclaim, "Rats, I wanted him," I make a little asterisk by the players name and put an abbreviation for that owners name there to remind me later that he values him highly.

Fantasy Football Addiction

I am obsessed with fantasy football. My mood swings are based on whether I won or lost. I am either a great happy employee that everyone wants to be around or a mean old miser who people keep avoiding.

If you ask my wife she will say that I have dual personalities. From mid-February through June, I am a devoted husband and worker bee. In June I start to get the "craving". I start to have football withdrawal signs. Then in July I get a fix of fantasy football information (magazines, websites, league setups and sign ups) and all is well for a month. In fact, I'm as giddy as a teenage girl at a Justin Timberlake concert. Woohoo! Then in August, I turn into a completely different person. Schedules have to be arranged based on football games. Vacations are put on hold through February. Notice that I said *through* February. Just because I won the fantasy league trophy in late December does not mean that football or fantasy football are over. No, there is the week 17 mini-tourney and then the playoff format and of course, Super Bowl Sunday with a football pool, etc. No, I am not a fairweather football fan, as some are. I enjoy the greatest game in the history of mankind until it ends on Super Sunday. Sometimes I watch the Pro Bowl, but not as much as I would care to admit. It has no meaning to me other than to make sure my keepers do not get hurt.

I spend hours on the computer (an hour here, 20 minutes at lunch there, and two hours on Sunday mornings) every week looking for insight into who I should start, who to drop and who to trade. Finally, my wife suggested tactfully that we get a laptop computer so that I would stop wearing out the carpet as I made the trek from the living room to the computer room every 15 minutes on Sunday afternoons. Only later did I realize this was a great move for her too; now she could have a computer to use herself (as if two hours a day, from 1:30-3:30 a.m., was not good enough for her on the family computer). Our friends ask us why we never had children and I instantly answer that they would take time away from my Sunday football viewing and they would want to use "my" computer. My motto is now "Cats – not kids." My cat Samantha watches the football games on my lap and enjoys sleeping on my computer table as I pour over links and favorites and new sights of hundreds of web pages.

Anyone who knows me knows not to call after 1 p.m. on Sunday or after 8 p.m. on Monday night during "the season." Violators get one more chance; if they blow it, our friendship is over. Okay, I did give my Mom one more chance. She is still on probation.

So I am addicted. What can I do? This game we love is an addiction, plain and simple. The sooner you admit you have a problem the quicker we can start to solve your problem. Here are my 12 steps to recovery:

1) Admit you are obsessed with fantasy football (at least July-Feb).

2) Share the computer equally with others in your home.

3) Spend equal amounts of time with your family and the other owners in your league.

4) Do not get angry when other people get phones calls too.

5) Do not set a time limit for their calls but not yours.

6) Stop going into every book store and buying each new fantasy football magazine you see.

7) Spend more time on Sunday mornings with your family, having quality time (watching the pre-game does not count as quality time).

8) Go to church more often during the football season (especially if they have an early morning service).

9) Go outside on Sunday afternoons for an hour or two (use TIVO or a DVD recorder to tape the late game and then watch it without commercials when you get home).

10) Work 95 pecent of the time when at work, versus your usual 5 percent.

11) Get a fantasy football "buddy" to help you with your recovery.

12) Avoid temptation – move to the Caribbean.

Luck Factor

Is there luck in professional football? Sure. How do I know that? Have you ever taken a look at the shape of a football? There is no doubt that the pigskin can bounce in many different directions on a fumble. Have you seen the NFL films of fumbles? That is just one aspect of luck. I could go on and on; weather conditions, star player injuries (how many sports hernias have QBs had lately). Okay, so luck is involved in the NFL. Does it apply to fantasy football? You bet. Any owner who has started a Denver RB only to find M. Shanahan benching him at the last second knows this. Nevertheless, some owners use the "luck" excuse to be lazy at this hobby. Do not let that happen to you.

Everyone will agree that some luck does play a part in fantasy football. Some believe that the entire thing is "nothing but luck." The majority of these owners are usually the lovable losers who never make it to the playoffs. Others feel like it is a combination of skill, knowledge and good luck. These are the owners who always make it to the "big dance." There has to be some element of luck to it, as anyone who has ever seen their stud RB hurt in the first week of the fantasy playoffs can attest. But how much of this great game is luck and how can you be luckier?

First, what is lucky in fantasy football? Luck is watching your opponent start a no-name #3 WR due to injuries and his bye weeks and then that WR scores two TDs in a lopsided 45-17 loss; or scoring the second highest points only to lose to the weakest team on their best week ever. Or you start a FB due to mismanagement, only to see him rush for two TDs in place of the RB who got the team down to the 1-yard line. All are examples of luck; some good, some bad, but all are short-term luck. In the long run, the better prepared and more skilled owner should prevail.

Injuries are luck to some degree. No one can predict who will be hurt and who will stay healthy during the season, but you can help yourself with that luck too. Avoid RBs over 30 years old. Avoid players returning from previous injuries that are hard to come back from. Avoid QBs who run a lot and/or take lots of sacks due to a weak offensive line. These are all steps to prevent the "bad luck" of an injury.

Your draft position is luck if drawn at random (bidding for draft position or awarding it based on previous year's performance negates this), but this too can be negated to some degree by drafting skill and use of wrap-around picks, etc., to improve choices. Believe it or not, there are some owners who would rather not have the #1 draft spot, instead preferring to have #2 or #3 so that they can take advantage of some draft strategies and have a quicker 2nd pick. I am one of those owners, depending on the players available. Others want the #1 pick any day of the week and control their own destiny.

Studies have shown that when you score more points than the average in a single game, you win more times than not, but not all the time (60% of the time you should win, an 8-5 record in a 13-game regular season, which will make the playoffs, I assure you). When you look at W/L records compared with the season point totals, it shows an even higher correlation between scoring more than everyone else and having a better W/L record. So simply scoring more than average every week may not get you into the playoffs but scoring more than average over the entire season will get you a better W/L percentage and into those playoffs more often. If you look at owners who have played in leagues for long periods of time, you will see that the correlation between luck and winning decrease, but those same owners may skew the numbers some because they will have their own learning curve over the period in question. There can be no doubt that the longer you play, the less luck will affect your ability to make the playoffs.

Clearly, game by game, there has to be some luck involved because some players have great games while others have bad games. In 2006, Joseph Addai had four TDs in week 12. The rookie had done little until then. That same week Tony Romo threw for 5 TDs. Having both of them on your team that day has to be more luck (desperation) than skill at that point in the season, as Romo was only named the starter a few weeks earlier. Even throughout your career there may be an occasional year when season-ending injuries force a better owner to miss the playoffs in favor of that "lucky" owner. But, in the long run, I believe the good owners make the playoffs due to their superior drafting, free agent pickups, trades and start/bench decisions. I have been the commissioner of a league that has an 11-year history (the league name and location changed but I still ran it with the same rules) and I have only missed the playoffs once in those 11 years. That is consistency and that means skill. Of course, the one year I did not make it is the one where I had a few too many drinks at the draft. I like to think I have a perfect sober record. Over time the better players will have more success while the weaker players will see less playoffs. Sure, on a weekly basis another team can beat any other team because of some luck, but if the league is designed correctly, then skill should win out season to season. On any given weekend, 40% of the wins come from luck; over a season maybe 25% of the wins are luck; but over the long-term only about 10% of the Super Bowl trophies on my mantle can be attributed to luck.

In every league there are probably a few owners who "consistently get lucky" and have a great draft, then make good trades (sometimes with those great draft picks that panned out) and wind up competing in the playoffs each year. The average owner calls many things luck, but a great owner plans and anticipates these things so that luck, good or bad does not interrupt his great season. Thomas Jefferson is quoted as saying "I'm a great believer in luck, and I find the harder I work, the more I have of it."

What are some characteristics of lucky owners?

1) Lucky owners like to experiment. They explore new draft theories. They take chances on sleepers. If you take chances you are more likely to find a sleeper and have a great player that no one expected. If you prefer to sit back and go with only tried and true draft strategies and stock deep backups at every position then you will not have room for any sleepers.

2) Lucky owners are more extroverted. They like to meet people and discuss different things. They are more likely to be in a chat room or MB and to pickup a tip that they can then evaluate. This extroverted side also allows them to meet/discuss with other owners about trades and other fantasy football issues. Thus a lucky owner may have better rapport with other owners and is more likely to get a trade completed (and more likely to take a chance on a trade offer from another owner, too).

3) Lucky owners listen to their gut. Many times other owners come down with decision paralysis, where they cannot make a decision for fear of making the wrong ONE. This leads to "action by inertia," not making a decision, which will, in fact, be a decision. Though not a good one. Or they will waste valuable time trying to evaluate every aspect of a trade, add/drop or start/bench decision. Lucky owners listen to their gut, make intuitive decisions and then spend more time researching other things for their next decision. How do you feel about the decision or course of action you have chosen? Will it keep you up at night? Probably best not to take that action. Are you giddy with joy? Sounds like the right choice.

4) Lucky owners never quit. Even when all looks hopeless, they fight on. Unlucky owners who experience a three game losing streak and are almost mathematically eliminated from the playoffs, will shut down and collapse under their own problems. Lucky owners will fight for one more win and keep trying till the season is over. Even in defeat, lucky owners learn from their mistakes and vow to never repeat them.

5) Lucky owners look at the big picture. You are not going to have the top player in each category but you can try to improve your players in each category. Take stock of who you have, who/what areas can be improved and how to do it. Lucky owners take positive action when needed.

6) Lucky owners are optimists. Imagine that two fantasy owners are watching an NFL game together and both of their players collide in a wicked hit and are injured and out for the season. The unlucky owner exclaims "I just lost my player for the entire season. I have lost." The lucky owner shrugs and says "At least I know for sure I can drop him and pick up someone else. It could have been a lingering injury and his status could have been up in the air for weeks, tying down a roster spot." The lucky owner sees the glass as being half-full and his mood for the rest of the week is fairly upbeat. The unlucky owner is mad at the world for his bad luck and makes some poor/hasty decisions to try and address his wrongful luck. Who would you rather have as a co-manager?

7) Lucky owners avoid group think. If all the experts are saying WR A will have a great year then his value will go up and up, he will rise up the draft boards and his

ADP will rise. If you do not think he will do as well as others say, then he will be overvalued for you, but that might make his teammates undervalued and thus a steal for you in the middle rounds. Then WR B becomes very valuable as a round 8 pick. Sell high and buy low. The best time to buy is when everyone else is selling a player because someone else is being bought. The best time to sell is when everyone else is buying the hype of a player.

8) Lucky owners make their own luck by being in the right place at the right time; watching the NFL games on Thursday, Sunday and Monday night and staying up on the news (injuries, benchings, etc.) and then going to the league site and taking advantage of that news. For example, you see a stat tracker that says A. Thomas rushes for 66 yards and a TD instead of Willis McGahee. You go to use the Internet (before the halftime highlights, because then everyone will know what happened) to see how many carries A. Thomas has and see that he has all of the rushes since the 1st quarter and McGahee went out with a broken foot. You then drop a scrub from your bench and add Thomas to use next week or in subsequent weeks. Is that lucky or was that destiny?

Sanity and Fantasy Football

What is your personality and does your team show it? Are you a gambler or the steady eddy? The gambler will have lots of sleepers and "chance takers" and will usually score lots of points or the fewest points. The steady eddy goes the safe route; he can rely on his team to score the average (maybe more, maybe less), week in and week out. Do you have steady performers who have few highs and lows or do you have high-octane performers who can leave you high and dry or skyrocketing to the win? Which do you like better? Draft for that personality. Who is best for you? What is your risk tolerance? Can you handle a few zero-point performances by the riskier player or would you rather score some points at the risk of not being high scorer? Emotions must be kept out of the decision-making process.

There are emotional dangers in going with the high-reward/high-risk players. In many cases, these players are inconsistent; they will score a large majority of their points in one bunch. They inspire greed in an owner and in turn you will manage your lineup poorly. You run the risk of watching them score a ton one week on your bench, so you start them the next three weeks regardless and see them put up goose eggs. So you trade them shortly thereafter and they score big again. These are all preseason things to consider.

Do you hate to lose by the end of the 1 p.m. games? If so, then pick someone from San Diego, San Francisco or Denver because all of their home games are at 4 p.m. and thus you should always have some hope in those late games.

Does your team have players you want to root for or loathe to root for? If you cannot stand T.O. then don't pick him. You will not enjoy him on your team. If you like to root for the underdog then go with underdogs at DEF or K.

Do injuries drive you crazy? Then don't take any chances with injury-prone players. Does Mike Shanahan and his RBBC make you want to break something? Stay away from the two RB sets or the RBBC players. By doing this you may take the emotion out of bad decisions and turn them into rational decisions. Just remember you may also be sacrificing some production for all these "I will not draft XX" decisions. However, you may also be building more peace of mind with a team that fits your personality.

Other Biases

1) Winning teams have better players and thus are afforded higher prestige. Losing teams are assumed to have no players of value and have to "shake things up." These biases can occur when another owner is seeking a trading partner.

2) Many owners will "out think" themselves. They will bench the stud RB who is playing a tough defense and start the up-and-coming new star RB. Who gets more points? Usually the stud RB performs and the rising star falls back to earth.

There is nothing worse than knowing that you cost yourself a win or some money by changing your mind and benching someone in favor of someone else. You tinkered with the players who got you to the dance. Dance with the girl you brought to the dance.

3) Always look at the stats. Do not let your emotions cloud your judgment about players. "He's a bum. Why would I want to draft him?" Because he had 22 TDs and only 9 INTs in 2006.

4) Owners tend to do more harm than good to themselves when they tinker with their team's lineup. Don't get me wrong, if you are doing it for the right reasons (bye week, injuries, playoff push, HC, etc.), great. But many times owners are trading to trade and tinkering with lineups just because they can. Trying to time two kicker's performances or two defenses may be a lost cause.

5) When owners experience a powerful emotional event (big game or big zero performance), our brains do not work the way they are when we are calm. Unfortunately the analytical part of the brain stops working in these times and we think irrationally (sell the bad player, keep the great player).

Chapter 21 Individual Defensive Players (IDPs) and Defenses

Many leagues have defensive/special teams (DEF/ST also seen as DT/ST or D/ST) as one of their starting positions. In these cases, you draft the entire defense and special team of one NFL team. This is called a team defense. Whenever that team plays, your DEF/ST plays. For example, if you have Baltimore's defense then whenever Baltimore plays a game you would get any defensive/special team statistics from Baltimore. If they have three sacks, an interception and hold their opponents to zero points (a shutout), then you would get fantasy points for those events based on your league scoring. Team defenses are the easiest way to incorporate defenses into a league. With team defenses you do not have to worry about demotions, suspensions or injuries making your defense not available for play. The defense will always play (except on its bye week). Demotions, suspensions and injuries will affect how the team defense plays and these situations should be considered, but in general a team defense is an easy play week in and week out.

Strategy: Some owners pick one defense and let them play throughout the season based on the assumption that most defenses are the same statistically and if you play them every week (except for their bye week) then their scoring should average out. Some owners pick up two defenses and alternate them based on their matchups, hoping to optimize their fantasy points This is called "defense by committee (DBC)." The theory behind DBC is that you can save a draft pick early on (i.e. not drafting one of the top 5 DEF/ST) and instead grab a couple of average defenses in later rounds because the two average defenses have great matchups on different weeks that will provide the same fantasy points as the better defense drafted much earlier. It does not make sense to draft a top defense and use this method to draft a middle-of-the-road defense. You will be drafting both defenses earlier than you need. The objective is to find two middle-of-the-road DEF/STs (based on ADP) that will compliment each other when one faces a touch offense or is on a bye week. Things to look for: easy combined schedule based on last year's opponents and some tweaking of last year's offense based on this years expectations for those offenses, and defenses not in the top 10 ADP ranking (so other owners do not grab one early, thus ruining your strategy). Note: You should not go into the draft expecting to get exactly these two defenses, instead have several committee pairs of defenses and go with whichever pair is still on the board when it is your time to draft a defense. For example, if your pairs are MIA+NE, MIN+DET and IND+SF, but NE has already been drafted and you suspect that a Homer will grab MINN next round, then take IND with your pick and grab SF before they should go, according to ADP. It may not have been your first choice for a defense pair but it is still a pair that will work in the DBC approach. Even better is to have IND and several other choices to choose from to match up with their defense.

Still other owners draft a good defense that has a late bye week and play them until their bye week before analyzing the defense's scoring trends. Another technique is to simply add/drop a defense every week based on matchups. This can only be done in leagues that do not limit your weekly/yearly transactions (no reason to use one of your two allowed transactions every week on getting a new defense). If you do decide to add a defense weekly based on the matchups, it could free up another roster spot (the other spot that a DEF/ST2 may have held) for a sleeper pick. Also be aware of the league rules, as you may have to pick a permanent defense or two before any free agency deadline for the season.

So far we have not mentioned special teams much. The special teams are the kickoff and punt return teams. If your DEF/ST scores a TD on a kickoff or punt return then they are awarded those points. St. Louis special teams with Dante Hall will provide some extra points when he runs a KR/PR for a TD. Generally, you do not want to pick a defense solely for its KR/PR record, nor do you want to pick a defense only for it defense. Look at both aspects when analyzing this position.

There are opponents of the DEF/ST. They claim that DEF/ST is too basic. Sure it is good for the casual fan since it requires little involvement, but there is too much luck involved. There is no consistency from year to year, and lets face it, most leagues draft them with the last picks, so they are boring. If you want to expand your fantasy football playing experience and get more detailed in the defensive realm then individual defensive players (IDPs) may be for you. With IDP you do not draft entire defensive teams but instead draft (like the name implies) individual defensive players. How many you draft is up to you. If the league wants to start slow then maybe just draft one defensive player. Remember these IDPs will be replacing the points provided by your DEF/ST. Some leagues say any defensive player can be drafted; others specify certain positions within the defense. For example, defensive lineman (DL), linebackers (LB) and defensive backs (DB). DL can be broken down into defensive ends (DE) or defensive tackles (DT). Linebackers can be broken down into middle linebackers (MLB) and outside linebackers (OLB), also known as strong side linebackers (SLB) or weak side linebackers (WLB). The TE will determine the strong side. The strong side LB will line up on the same side and usually cover the TE. These positions (DL and LB) make up the front seven of the defensive team (DT). The two types of front they will employ are the 3-4 and the 4-3. The remaining four players are the DBs and they can be broken down into safeties (S) and cornerbacks (CB).

Some "ceremonial" or "token" IDP leagues start only one IDP or one IDP at each of the three overall lines (DE, LB and DB). Most leagues will have between 3 and 6 IDPs. Many IDP leagues will allow you to draft the same amount of IDP players as offensive players (seven). So in a typical 1 QB, 2 RB, 2 WR, 1 TE, 1K league, you will also have 7 IDPs consisting of 2 DL, 2 LB and 3 DBs. Allowing this many IDPs also forces the IDPs to be valued on par with offensive position players and thus prevents the drafting of all offensive players then IDPs as an afterthought. Still other leagues use flex IDPs. The ultimate IDP is to allow the same NFL formations of IDPs. So teams would start 3-4-4 or 4-3-4 at those positions. Remember, the more starting IDPs you have, the more bench IDPs you will need and the more players needed to be on your roster. Think longer drafts!

Why use IDPs? Well if the purpose of fantasy football is to bring NFL football to you in a realistic manner, then picking your own defensive players (versus being handed an entire team with one draft pick) is more realistic. This sense of "ownership" at building your own "purple people eaters" is another reason why many IDP leagues are also keeper leagues. The sense of controlling your team's destiny from year to year and building a legacy is enhanced by individual defensive players. Once you have played IDP, you will not go back to a simple team defense. Note that in the IDP keeper leagues most owners do not keep IDPs unless it is a dynasty league. The scarcity of RBs usually drives this decision.

Another advantage of an IDP league is the ability to counter a weak offense with a strong defense and vice versa. These two sides of a team introduce a greater chance of parity. Rookies will also have a greater impact in a IDP league. They will start more and thus be more of a factor to draft and play. The NFL draft becomes more of an event in an IDP league. Now instead of only caring about the offensive skill players taken, you can concentrate on everyone taken on the first day (except for offensive linemen). With three IDPs starting on each team, that is possibly six more games that you have a stake in watching intently.

What are the disadvantages of IDP leagues? The draft will be longer since there will be more players drafted. If you remove the DEF/ST and add 6 IDPs plus backups, that is 10 more players than you had before. Another knock on IDPs is that you may lose owners or find it hard to attract new owners due to the uniqueness of IDP. Some disadvantages are more whines than worries. Some say it allows defensive players to determine the winner of games instead of the offensive players. Yet another hit is it takes away from your ability to tell how well you did by watching the highlights, since defensive stats are rarely mentioned.

Adding IDPs will help you understand the game of football better and learn more about the defensive side of the game. For example, who is the best LB or DB in the game? If you just use DEF/ST you probably know some of the bigger names such as Michael Strahan, John Lynch and Julius Peppers, but do not know too many past the big names. Just like when you started playing fantasy football and your offensive player knowledge grew, if you add IDPs, your knowledge base will grow on the defensive side of the ball too. Remember this though: great IDPs in fantasy football do not always mean big name defensive players from TV. The scoring categories will determine which IDPs are more valuable, not their name recognition. Some say that IDPs are more luck than skill. Hog wash. It all comes down to research and knowledge and the more you know, the better you can coach. IDP leagues are the PhDs of fantasy football. They are slowly becoming more popular but to date the majority of leagues are still team defense or no defense oriented. Bottom line is you should try an IDP league to see if you like it or not.

Team Defenses

Watch scoring rules as some leagues are starting to give more points to defenses making them worth more than the casual look. Look for yardage allowed (careful more passing yards will occur if they are a good run defense) and turnovers. These both generate low scores for opposing teams and opportunities for scores from your defense. However, teams do not tend to move in large directions from season to season. Therefore, a great team will stay good and a bad team will stay somewhat bad. Some defenses are consistent (Balt, NE, TB) but that depends on how your defense earns points. For team defense scoring see Chapter 5 Scoring Systems.

Scoring

Tackles and the big play (sacks, safeties, turnovers, etc.) are the main scoring components of IDP. Scoring categories for IDPs can consist of touchdowns, solo tackles, assisted tackles, fumbles forced, fumbles recovered, interceptions, passes defended, sacks, safeties and blocked kicks. Tackles occur the most and thus bring in lots of scoring. Tackles are as plentiful as yards are to offensive players. In essence, one tackle is equal to 10 yards in many IDP leagues. Big play events like sacks and takeaways are the equivalent of a TD for an offensive position player. Most leagues do not award points for forced fumbles, instead awarding for the fumble recovery.

A typical scoring system using IDPs may be as follows:

Tackle/Assist	1 point
Sack/Interception/Fumble recovery/Safety/Blocked kick	2 points
Defensive TD	6 points

Much like the different scoring systems discussed in chapter 5, IDP leagues can have different scoring systems too.

Tackle systems account for the basics but do not award for assists, safeties or blocked kicks.

Tackle	1 point
Sack	3 points
Interception	4 points
Forced fumble	2 points
Recovered fumble	3 points
Pass defended	1 point
Defensive TD	6 points

Big Play Systems account for the basics and add more emphasis on big plays (sacks and takeaways).

Tackle	1 point
Assist	0.5 points
Sack	7 points
Takeaways (Interception or Fumble Recovery)	10 points

Combination – as the name suggests, this is a combination of Basic and Big Play with a tweaking of points awarded.

Tackle	1 point
Assist	0.5 points
Sack	4 points
Interception	5 points
Forced fumble	2 points

Recovered fumble	2 points
Pass defended	1 point
Defensive TD	6 points

*Take a careful look at the sack-to-tackle ratio in scoring. If sacks are worth 4 points and tackles are worth 1 point, then the ratio is 4-1. Many say that a 4-1 ratio is the highest you should go (and some say even that is too high).

**LBs will dominate an IDP league if the scoring is the same for all IDP players since LBs are involved in all the categories on a consistent basis. Some leagues have weighted some of the categories for a more equal distribution of fantasy points. (Much like a QB is only given 3 or 4 points for TDs in most leagues and PPR to help WRs and TEs.)

***Fumble Recovery (FR) is a crap shoot as anyone around can and will fall on a fumble and recover it. Fumbles forced (FF) is a better category because it awards IDPs who do something on their own.

NFL Defensive Schemes

Do you know enough about how the game is played? Maybe you played some football in high school or college. Maybe you are a student of defensive schemes. Owners who understand the schemes' strengths and weaknesses will be in a better position to find those players in the middle to late rounds who will produce.

Defenses react to the offense. Defenses must read the offensive formation and the players on the field and then react by using certain members of their own personnel or schemes that are best suited for what the offense is going to do on that play. But of course, you do not have the individual plays to make choices (perhaps future fantasy footballers will have this option), you have to determine your IDP starters before game time.

What do offenses tend to do and how does it affect IDPs?

1) Offenses that spread the defenders over the field with a wide open passing attack will use three and four receiver sets on most plays. This will drive defenses to employ a 4-2-5 or nickel defense. If they normally play a 4-3, then one of their linebackers will see much less time as they start an extra DB the entire game for the nickel. The nickel back will also probably lead the team in tackles since he falls into the MLB role only in a deeper starting position. A great run-stuffing MLB, who is poor against the pass, is in for a long day if he plays since he will be defending a lot more passes with these pass-oriented offenses. The offense will spread the ball around to everyone including RBs out of the backfield. So the RB will rush less and catch more, another reason the MLB does not perform as well.

2) Primary rushing teams – Here the starting RB gets all the work and the MLB gets all the tackles. These teams try to manage the clock with rush after rush after rush and then hope their defense is strong enough when they are forced to punt. The slot WR (WR3) never sees much action, as what little passes do occur go to WR1 and WR2. These offenses typically have two TE sets or a TE and FB. A CB who does not handle the run well will not get much stat production. On the other hand, LBs and SSs who tackle well can have a field day.

What is a Strong Side?

As soon as the offense breaks the huddle and moves toward the line of scrimmage the captain of the defense (usually MLB) must call out the strong side of the formation so that the seven up-front defenders (DL and LB) can position themselves appropriately. Whichever side the TE is on is the strong side. Hence, the strong side is the side with the most blockers and thus is the biggest danger to the defense on a running play. But what if there are no TEs or two TEs? In either case it is a balanced offensive line so the side with the single RB is the strong side (or the side with emphasis from the defense). If there are two backs and the FB is on one side while the TB is behind the QB, then the side with the FB becomes the strong side. However, instances with 2 RBs can also be a pro formation (backs are split behind the QB) or an I Formation (backs in a straight line behind the QB). In these cases look to the WRs; anytime the line and backfield are balanced (pro or I formations, double TE or no TEs with balanced RB), strong side will have a WR or TE behind and outside (or split wide). If the line, backfield and WRs are balanced, then use the wide side of the field as strong side. Whew!

Defensive Systems

Some teams will use either the 4-3 or the 3-4, depending on who they face, but for the most part teams pick one scheme and adapt it for their defense. Baltimore runs a 4-6 but this really is just a variation of the 4-3. Teams with strong LB talent may switch to a 3-4. Be wary when your IDP moves to another team with a different system or his own team changes systems. His stats may change dramatically.

What scheme are they playing in? The base formation or scheme is the one used most often on the field. Usually this is a base of 3-4 or 4-3. The first number is the number of linemen and the second number is the number of LBs. If you hear a team has changed into a dime or nickel package, that just means it is an obvious passing down and that the team has brought in 5 DBs (in nickel package) versus the normal 4 (or 6 DBs in a dime package; don't ask me why it is called a dime). Just for your own knowledge, the quarter defense is when a seventh DB is added (at the expense of a DT), thus the idea is to give up 4-8 yards rushing or short passes but to not give up the long ball.

Often you will hear defenses referred to as "bend but don't break" defenses. The idea is to give up only a small amount of yardage on any play, limit the big yardage plays, force the offense to run many plays and hope that the offense, in executing all of these plays, makes a mistake somewhere and turns the ball over. This is also sometimes called a finesse or "read and react" defense because they look for keys as the play occurs and react to them. On the other hand, an aggressive defense does not look for what the offense is doing at the snap. Instead they attack the offensive formation at weak points in an attempt to disrupt the play before it can get going. The aggressive style may get more sacks and negative yardage plays as the defenders break into the backfield, but they are also more likely to get burnt on their blitzes (and single man coverage) and give up the big plays. Aggressive defenses try to determine the outcome of the play based on their movements versus the other way around. The key to a good aggressive defense is a good CB who can handle single man or "bump and run" coverage.

4-3-4 (RDE, RDT, LDT, LDE; WLB, MLB, SLB) – The most common defensive scheme.

This is the best way to stop the run or blitz the QB because you have more defensive players up front. DTs are usually for stopping or blocking the run while faster DEs are used for rushing QBs (more sacks) and stopping RBs (tackles). The MLB is crucial to this scheme because it funnels the RB to him (so he is very valuable). He needs to be quick and smart, making plays from sideline to sideline (think Brian Urlacher). The WLB will blitz the most and get the most sacks. This scheme needs five good outside men and two big run-stuffers in the middle at DT.

Cover 2 – The Cover 2 is named for the position of the safeties that play back and are responsible for their half of the deep zone coverage. The two deep safeties divide the field in half (a large area to cover for sure); the CBs need to jam or interfere with the WRs off the line to help the safeties adjust. This defensive scheme is designed to slow the speedy outside deep threat (Steve Smith, T. Owens, etc.), by playing the safeties wider. The three LBs and two CBs divide the short and middle part of the field underneath the safeties and each takes a fifth. The four DLs are expected to create the pass rush (a good pass rush is critical) and thus blitzes are rare in this scheme. The Cover 2 has weaknesses that can be exploited in the deep middle between the safeties and over the CBs, but underneath the safeties. For this reason, the Tampa 2 was designed. The Tampa 2 is really a 4-4-3 form of Cover 2.

Tampa 2 – (used by TB, IND, CHI, MIN, BUF and DET); A form of 4-3 but has some notable differences. The MLB is dropped back into zone coverage to fill the deep center between the safeties. This allows the safeties to play more toward the CBs and help them, thus eliminating that weakness. The CBs and safeties divide the outside into fourths. The Tampa 2 depends on great DEs and DTs to create a solid pass rush since they will not get a MLB's help. The LBs need to be quick and smart and be able to play the pass coverage; the CBs need to be strong enough to stop the run if it gets to the outside. The Tampa 2 "under tackle" is the player assigned to penetrate his gap and get to the QB. He can be very productive in this scheme. The WLB can be just as productive as the MLB in these schemes as well. CBs who are willing to stop the run in this scheme can see great production (Ronde Barber and tackles). They need to be physical and have good ball skills. MLB, DE and S still have value in this scheme and do not overlook a great player at DT, WLB and CB. With almost 20% of the league using this in 2006, more DTs, WLBs and CBs will be making a name for themselves.

4-6 – (really a 4-4); Not seen much today other than Baltimore Ravens. Four DLs and Four LBs, so eight in the box. Designed to collapse the pocket, rush the QB and limit rushing. The problem with eight in the box is that the CBs are forced into man-to-man coverage and a good QB with enough protection can pick it apart.

3-4-4 – (RDE, NT, LDE; LOLB, LILB, RILB, ROLB); This is a flexible system where you can blitz with five or drop eight into pass coverage, but it needs a great NT and physical OLB. OLBs get more sacks from blitzes. In a 3-4, the DL are playing a 2-gap scheme, trying to fill the gaps and let the faster LB roam, which means they (LBs) will have better stats. In a 3-4 there are two inside linebackers (ILBs) and two OLBs. This scheme is less common but many are beginning to turn to it (PIT, SD, NE, HOU, DAL, CLE & SF), since New England won their three Super Bowls. Miami, Denver and Oakland have thought about transitioning to it.

Positions within each scheme

DE in 4-3 – They have to stop the run by preventing the RB from getting around them and they also provide the pass rush. They have to have vision and quickness to avoid all the offensive tricks to block them (double-teams, pulling guards, etc.). DEs who play every down and do well are your ideal players. Think Julius Peppers. The more powerful DEs are on the right side, opposite the left tackle who protects the QBs blind side.

DE in 3-4 – He has less pass rushing and containment duties (these fall to the OLB). Instead he needs to stop the run and or take up space or blockers so that his LBs can make the tackles. This position generally has less production due to their reduced roles.

DT in 4-3 – His job is to fill his gap and then pursue the ball carrier. As for pass rush, many times they will push their offensive opponent back into the QB or flush the QB out but they are not as quick to make tackles. They are hole-fillers not tackling machines.

DT in 3-4 – Even less of a fantasy football threat. They get double-teamed on most plays and rarely produce stats that you should care about.

LB/DL – A new type of player who is listed as DL but can line up at LB too. They get to rush the passer but also can drop back and get tackles at LB. Think Shawne Merriman.

SLB 4-3 – Why does a strong side LB not get more production since he is on the side the offense is normally rushing to? The answer lies in why they are rushing to that side; because they have more blockers on that side. Those extra blockers are usually targeted at the SLB. Either a TE, FB or pulling guard is determined to take him out. The SLB will try to force the runner to change course while he takes on these blockers but alas he himself rarely makes the tackles. On pass plays he is responsible for the TE or FB. If there are no TEs or FBs then the defense will be in a nickel defense and the SLB may be on the bench.

WLB 4-3 – He is the second best FF option. Many times he will be left free to roam. Since he is on the weak side he will not have a blocker assigned to him thus freeing him to make the plays. Some teams (AZ, NO, SEA, SF) have gone to a right side OLB and left side OLB. In this regard they do not change positions based on strong or weak side. If so, draft the right OLB since most QBs are right-handed.

MLB 4-3 – The ultimate IDP player. Every defensive scheme is designed to funnel plays down the middle of the field and into the jaws of the MLB. The DTs take out the OL, leaving the MLB free to make the tackles; these players flow to the play and are always near the mix. The MLB will read the offense to determine if it is a run or a pass. He watches the offensive line at the start of the play; pass blockers tend to stand up immediately, while to run block they fire out to engage defenders.

OLB 3-4 – He functions much like a DE in 4-3 scheme (he is a pass rusher at heart). If your league has sacks weighed heavily then he may be a good player to have, but his tackle opportunities are limited.

ILB 3-4 – All of the top IDPs play RILB because most QBs are right-handed.

CB – They play either man-to-man, zone or bump and run. They are inconsistent in FPs. If they cheat up to help the run they are more likely to let a WR get behind them for the deep ball. Some teams will use the Cover 2 scheme a lot. In the Cover 2, the safeties will play deep and the CBs will play more to support the run and cover underneath. Otherwise, only a few are in the Top 20 in tackles because they are reluctant to take on that charging RB.

And their inconsistent interceptions do not make up for the lack of tackles. The best CBs are the worst fantasy IDPs because no one ever throws to a "Shut Down" corner. CBs in Cover-2 schemes seem to do best at FPs.

FS – He is free to roam and try to make the big plays. He backs up everyone on the field which means keeping everyone in front of him. Since he is often the last line of defense, he must be a good tackler. Look for a FS on teams with a weak LB group.

SS (Strong Safety) – These guys are the tacklers of the secondary, especially if they have a great SLB in front of them to clear out the blockers and force the runner around and into the SS. Their first job is run defense and in passing downs may provide double-team help.

Conclusions – Draft MLB, WLB, DE (4-3), SS and FS. These are the positions that are going to score FPs for you. There are other players at other positions who are exceptional IDPs but they are rare and are proven commodities. Do not take a risk on an unknown player at any of the other positions because chances are he will not get the opportunities to score for you. The top 10 DBs are good fantasy draft picks, but after that – who knows. Watch out for corners that were great last year but not the year before. Inconsistency is their middle name. A simple way to remember IDPs is to give them an offensive player equivalent. LBs are like RBs, DBs are like WRs and DLs are like TEs.

Tips for a First-Year IDP Owner

Read your rules and determine the following:

1) How many IDPs do you start? (3, 6, 8, 10+?) Having three IDPs mean they have little value. Rank them between TEs and kickers. Build up bench depth and get IDPs late since there will be so many to choose from. With six IDPs they are increasing in value but are worth the same as a TE. Once you hit eight starters, IDPs become on par with the Top 30 WRs. Once you get into 10 or more, you are more than likely in a dynasty league and IDPs outnumber the offensive skill players, so IDP is king; or just as important as WRs. But do not get carried away. Expect the stud IDPs to go in the 3rd to 4th rounds. No sooner; as RBs are still the moneymakers and have much less depth.

2) What is the scoring system? Do tackles count? Assist tackles? Is return yardage counted? Do passes defended count? Fumbles forced? IMPORTANT: Even if your league does have an IDP-friendly scoring system, that will not make the individual IDP positions more important. It will just place more emphasis on the studs at that position. For example, what if you increased points for yardage from 1 point per 10 yards to 10 points per 10? It would not mean that WRs were more valuable than TEs or RBs, because both TEs and RBs get the bump up in points. It would make the top RBs, WRs and TEs worth more based on the drop-offs at those positions. The key is to know which IDP positions are the most valuable based on your scoring system.

3) What are your lineup options? Can you use a flex option or is it scheme dependent? Some common flex options are: the 3-4 (3 DL, 4 LB, 4 DB), the 4-3 (4 DL, 3 LB, 4 DB) and nickel defense (3 DL, 3 LB, 5 DB).

4) Are the IDP positions defined? DL becomes DE and DT. DB becomes S and CB.

5) What is the wavier wire/FA situation? Are you limited in some way or is it unlimited? Unlimited or a large limit plus a deep free agent pool means less emphasis on drafting.

IDPs become less valuable in the draft if you can pick up serviceable ones any week with a transaction. Use your roster on RB and WR sleepers and use FA/waivers to fill in IDP bye weeks. On the other hand, if league waiver policy is restricted you will need to cover yourself for injuries and bye weeks with IDP depth, thus making them more valuable in the draft.

6) Avoid the common owner mistakes with IDP, such as:

a) Ignoring positions until late in draft.

b) Not analyzing the situation: nagging injury, faced double-teams due to other DEF injuries, different schemes.

c) Not looking at tackles; looking at big names.

7) Generally it will be LB-DE-DB with CBs and DTs further back. IDP players are more middle to late round picks. The stud offensive skill players go in the early rounds. Rookies rarely have much impact. DE and CB are the toughest for rookies to jump right into. The 2-3 year veterans are more likely to be productive.

Strategies

– Look for a CB or two or three to establish themselves in the first few weeks of the season. Typically it is a 2-3 year player who plays opposite a talented CB. These are the up-and-coming CBs who can make a big difference when added to your team. Also keep an eye out for the new Cover-2 corners as some will begin to show their worth after the first few games. Do not rely on just one or two games as some teams they face may not present them with as many opportunities. Get CBs that are getting "picked on" after the season starts. The key is that they need to be good enough not to get benched but bad enough not to be a shut down CB. Supporting talent will influence this too.

– After the middle of the season, look for DLs who have stepped in due to injuries and are making a name for themselves. Their less-used bodies should give them an advantage as the season grinds to its conclusion (think playoffs for you). Another player to look for is the high draft pick who has been let go by his drafted team and picked up by another team. Grab him in keeper leagues and see if he makes the starter list next year.

– Know what the scoring rules are. Go through last year's stats and see which positions are more valuable, IDP-wise. Certain stats benefit certain positions. How much value (FPs) is the average LB to average WR to average RB to average DE? For example:

1) DEs will have the best shot at FPs consistently as they come into the backfield for the sack (and try to knock the ball out of the QBs hand). Scoring (fumbles returned for a TD) is too luck-oriented to predict.

2) Passes defended help the DB position. If it is not used, their value drops considerably (DLs more valuable than CBs). Usually a CB will get anywhere from 10-16 passes defended per season or average about 1 per game. The LB will have five or six passes defended. Bear that in mind when looking at the scoring system.

3) Leagues that award greater than 3x for sacks and 4x for interceptions as compared to tackles are skewed in favor of the big, unpredictable plays. For example: tackles = 1 point, sacks = 4 points, interceptions = 5 points is a big play league.

4) CB value depends on points for INT and passes defended.

5) Don't target sack guys (DLs) more than the reliable LBs. Big sack guys can disappoint. LBs are the RBs of IDP. LB, then DL(DE), then DB.

– Don't draft a shut down corner (big name is usually a good indication of a SD corner) because QBs will not throw to him. Rookie CBs or CBs replacing a vet will get thrown to a lot and thus have more chances for INTs and passes defended.

– IDP redraft league vs. IDP keepers. In a redraft league you can wait longer (after round 6) before going with IDPs because there is lots of depth, but in a keeper league you need to get the young, good talent earlier. In a rookie-only dynasty draft, a mid 1st round pick on the "can't miss IDP stud" may be realistic.

– One technique is to go basic with DEF players and load up on offensive talent. Do not have DEF depth but instead use the waiver wire to get bye week/injury pick ups. Use extra roster room for offensive sleepers.

Think of DLs as TEs. There are not that many so once the top few are gone the position really flatlines. If sacks are not emphasized as much and your rules allow it, focus on drafting LBs (the RBs of IDP) as opposed to DLs.

– LBs get the most tackles, so if tackles are important get an LB. Normally they do everything so getting a LB is good general advice. Tackles are the easiest to predict from year to year also. The more the league awards tackles the more you should draft LBs. In teams with weak front sevens in rushing, usually the safeties get more tackles (SS). "Everydown" lineman (versus lighter, smaller DL used for pass rushing) are better since they play more. More PT = more tackles, baby. Be wary of sack leaders from the previous year. Sacks are harder to predict and there is no guarantee that he will get the same sacks this year.

– If league splits IDPs into individual positions:

1) Grab a DT who produces since most do not.

2) MLB and ILB get lots of tackles so target them first if tackles are rewarded.

3) SLBs tend to have weaker production, WLBs generally have good production if they are fast and stay in for passing downs.

4) OLBs in 3-4 should see some sacks but may get less tackles. LBs tend to get pulled in passing downs so look for the ones that will stay on the field no matter what down it is.

If you have a choice of starting a formation, for example the 4-3, 3-4 or nickel, always go with 3-4 as this gets you more LBs starting. Rarely will you want to use the nickel since this starts five CBs and they are the least valuable IDP in most standard scoring systems.

Sacks occur more often than turnovers and safeties but less frequently than tackles so sacks are the second most important scoring category. Sacks usually go to DL and DE in particular. OLBs in 3-4 get more sacks and LBs in 4-3 can too, if given the go-ahead by the coaching staff. The prediction of sacks becomes easier as the season progresses and as OL quality is determined. QB replacements (especially young QB replacements) also make start/bench decisions easier.

Pre-Draft Tips

1) Use VBD to determine when to start drafting IDP.

2) There are lots of IDP on the waiver wire, so do not forget to factor in supply and demand into VBD.

3) Look for "bend but don't break" defenses, not great defenses. The great defenses (example BALT) force so many "three downs and a punt" scenarios that they do not get lots of chances for tackles and turnovers. NE, on the other hand, has a "bend but don't break" attitude and they stay on the field more often. On the field, more means more chances for an IDP to score points. Another factor will be an offense that is not good, thus giving the ball back and putting their defense on the field again. In fact, having a great rush defense actually hurts the defense since that will force the other team to pass, in which case they usually move quickly or kick it away. Great defenses (especially great rush defenses) are a hindrance to great IDPs.

4) Forget the hype. The media loves to focus on the sack leaders but many times those guys are behind in FPs because of poor tackling opportunities. Know your FP projections and do not bite off on the big names but little IDP producers. (If your league does not require DL then go with LBs almost exclusively). The guy who tackles well is the one you want, not the one that show boats after a sack or INT and gets all the ESPN highlight time.

5) Ignore the INT and fumbles recovered stat. They are hard to predict and there is not much difference between the leader and the #25 guy. Look at solo tackles. They are the bread and butter of IDP scoring.

6) Some leagues allow 1 point for every 20 return yards. If so, note which DBs are return men since this is a nice chance for more points.

Draft Strategies

Where would you draft an IDP? The answer, as with many things, is "it depends." In this case it depends on your scoring system. Does it award points for tackles, assists, turnovers and sacks? If so, then IDPs are going to be more valuable than if they were only awarded points based on sacks and turnovers. Remember there are lots of tackles and assists in every game. Tackles are the equivalent of yardage for IDPs. As a ROT, the less yardage rewarded to skill players, the more valuable IDPs become; if your league awards 1 point for every 10 yards and 1 point for every tackle, then IDPs are worth about the same as TEs and Ks. If your league only gives 1 point for every 25 yards and 1 point for tackle, then IDPs become more valuable; on par with WRs. In this case, the top DL or LB may go as early as the 4th round. Most owners usually give them some thought after the starting RBs and WRs are gone. IDPs will fight with backup RBs and WRs for draft slots; usually rounds 6-8 if tackles and assists are rewarded. The problem with IDPs is there are so many of them compared with RBs and WRs.

If your league has no scoring for assists and a minimal reward for tackles, then IDPs will start to be drafted toward the end of the WRs, but before K and most of the TEs (note there will be no DEF/ST to draft in an IDP league). IDPs will not supplant the offensive skill players except most TEs and they will be more valuable than the dreaded kicker. Know the defensive schemes employed by the defensive units and the role the players will have in that scheme. **However, because there is so much depth at IDP and the differences between #10 and #40 at any position is less than the offensive skill positions, generally it will pay off to wait before drafting an IDP.** Get both starting RBs and WRs (if 3, get 3); then and only then think about IDPs. If the Top 5 at all the IDPs are gone (especially LB) then wait some more. Get your backup RB, WR and starting QB and TE; then in round 10 or 11 start to look at IDPs. Think TEs and kickers here. If you don't get a top one then don't bother early.

Why are IDPs so undervalued? What can be done to improve their worth? IDP does not become more important even if you increase the scoring emphasis, because there is so much depth. They are like QBs in that even if you give them more points for passing yards, every one of the QBs get it and there are so many middle-of-the-road QBs that it does not make the position itself more valuable. The same applies to IDP, as all the players are still making sacks, tackles and INTs. No, to increase the value (or when they will be targeted in the draft), you need to increase the number of IDP players started. If 6-8 IDPs started, now the positions start to look like WRs in that there are still lots out there but you need more; the differences at the positions are significant.

Once you start to lessen the number of IDPs remaining after the draft then those drafted will become more valuable. So the more IDP players, the more valuable they will be, but even in leagues that start 10 or more IDP players, offense will still be king. Why? Say you are in a 12-team IDP league that starts 11 IDP players (4 DL, 3LB, 4 DB) just like the NFL. Having 11 starters plus 11 backups equals 22 IDP players per team, times 12 teams=264 players drafted. But remember, there are 11 players on 32 teams that start (not counting part-time players), so 352 IDPs (see Table 9.3 Supply and Demand of Fantasy Positions) in the NFL are available. That means 88 players are still on the FA list after the draft is over.

Many owners are unfamiliar with IDPs. This may be because more TV highlights are offensive scoring plays or simply because your league only recently went to IDPs. In any case, many owners have a bias to offensive players and/or defensive stars and thus they do not do their homework when it comes to IDPs. Your knowledge of them can be where you set yourself apart from the rest of the pack. Drafting starting IDPs while others are getting QB and WR backups can give you a significant advantage.

1) Go with offensive players (starters) first since they are less deep in players.

2) Top IDPs at each position will probably go in the middle rounds; other IDPs in the late rounds and the kicker will still go with the last pick.

3) Save room on the bench for backup offensive players since they are less available on the waiver wire.

4) Grab LBs, and lots of them, if your league does not weigh IDP stats against them.

5) Once you get a good IDP at a position, move on to the next position or get depth at offensive positions. Depth is not a must at IDP because of supply and demand.

Who to Start Basics

LBs – Go with MLB over WLB and WLB over SLB. If you have to go with a SLB choose the one that is facing the stronger TE. More passes will come his way.

DBs – Pick the DB facing a passing offense and preferably a QB that throws lots of INTs.

DL – Go with the DL that is facing the most sackable QB (i.e. not M. Vick or Peyton Manning). The right side DE usually faces the best offensive lineman because this is the QBs blindside. Look to exploit injuries on the OL too.

1) Avoid shut down corners (Champ Bailey, Charles Woodson) because they do not get as many chances at tackles or INTs as the average CB.

2) SS are better at tackles; FS are more like CBs, helping in pass coverage (INTs).

3) Time of Possession – An IDP who plays on a team with a poor offense will see more plays because his offense has less time of possession. More time on the field equals more sacks, tackles and assists. Just make sure the rules do not penalize for passes beaten on.

4) You want IDPs who are on the field every play. If he is a specialty or package player he will have less stats. On nickel and dime packages (passing downs), if players are off the field they cannot tackle, sack or intercept.

5) Bad teams (poor offenses or bad teams in general) or teams playing tough schedules will produce more tackles. The bad teams will be behind and their defense will face lots of rushes trying to burn time off the clock. Result – lots of tackles for the defense. Same goes for playing a tough schedule. They may be a good team but if they face lots of hard teams, the defense will be on the field more and tackling more.

6) Good teams with easy schedules may produce more big plays. If your team is comfortably ahead, the opponent will have to take chances and pass a lot so your DLs (sacks) and DBs (Int's) may have better stats.

Chapter 22 Keeper/Dynasty Leagues

Leagues can be classified as either redraft or holdover (also called rollover) in terms of ownership. Redraft leagues are also known as seasonal leagues. In a redraft league, each year the owner starts from scratch. No players from previous years are kept. In a holdover league, owners can "keep" or retain any number of players for the next season. The number of players, number of years they can be kept, and the exact circumstances are based on the league rules and can differ from league to league. Holdover leagues can be further broken down by the number of players that are kept. If a league keeps less than half of the players (usually anywhere from 1-5 players) from the previous year (in order to prevent one team from becoming too dominant), then it is referred to as simply a keeper league. The less players that can be kept, the more a keeper league resembles a redraft league However, if more than half of the roster is kept (including in many cases all of the roster) then that league is called a dynasty league. For the remainder of this discussion holdover leagues will be broken down into keeper leagues or dynasty leagues.

Some of the advantages are:

1) It can help to individualize a team more. "Oh yeah, that's the Vince Young team;" since Vince was drafted in 2006 and held for several seasons, thus illustrating the owner's great vision.

2) It can help bring owners back for the next season since they have a connection to their team and the league (versus an entire redraft each year or a complete do over).

3) A good draft (especially the first one) can benefit you for many years.

4) You can "grow" younger players and watch them develop and reward your team.

5) Ability to plan for the future (next season) by trading good veterans this year for younger players or draft picks next year.

6) It is more realistic than a redraft league.

7) Encourages more participation even if out of the running for playoffs because you can build for next year through free agency and trades.

8) Allows the owners to stay involved in the off-season because they have to make decisions on whom to keep, if any, before next years draft. So they will track others players and possible keepers and have to factor that into the draft (less supply, more demand).

Some point out that holdover leagues might have a weakened draft in future years, and consider it a disadvantage. After the inaugural draft, the other drafts are not as fun; since there will be fewer players to draft from, so it is less of an experience. This is particularly true in dynasty leagues where future drafts are just rookies or disregarded players. However, in keeper leagues where only a small number can be kept, the drafts are just as fun but with more strategy. Pundits also point out that you cannot have your favorite player for a long time if you do not draft him first. Another problem with dynasty leagues is the initial draft will take much longer since you will probably draft more players than a redraft league. But the following years drafts will be much shorter since many players will be kept from previous years. Other disadvantages are the difficulties that occur with the administration of holdover aspects. While they are exciting, they may not be for beginners due to the long-term planning that is involved. So it may be difficult to get owners to play initially and especially to join once keepers are established.

In general, holdover leagues provide more of the real feel of managing a team. They also add to the enjoyment of fantasy football. Holdover leagues also tend to use more auction drafts. This may be to allow all owners the chance to draft any player, especially if they can keep that player for future years. Owners should be dedicated and thus a more established league may consider moving to a "keeper/dynasty" format in order to spice things up. This chapter will examine both keeper and dynasty leagues and highlight the strategies, rules and trades that they use. Finally, you will find a step-by-step guide to turning a redraft league into a holdover league.

General Rules

I suggest you set entry fees for the first year high enough to give next year's new owner (if needed) a free entry. For example, if you want to charge $50 a year to play for 10 teams, then charge $55, so that each team pays 1/10 of the new owner's entry fee. That way, if someone bails, you can tell the new owner that since he will be taking over a team that he did not draft, his first entry fee is free, half off, or something along those lines. Another way is to always have all owners pay for the current year and next year in advance. If they quit, the entry fee for the person taking over their team is paid for one year. Note: You probably should make the replacement pay something to play or else he will just quit at the end of his first year. Consider charging him half what all the other owners are paying or give him half off for his first two seasons.

Keeper Leagues

Keeper leagues allow less than half of the roster to be kept. Keeper leagues are referred to as "Keeper-X"; for example, Keeper-2. The "X" is the number of players owners are allowed to keep from year to year. Keeper-2 would be a league in which you kept two players from year to year. Some leagues allow a certain number of players to be kept (you keep four players in Keeper-4); still others allow a certain number at each position to be kept (ex. 1 QB, 1 RB and 1 WR) or a combination of styles (1 TE, 1 K, 1 DEF and 3 other players). There are two main types of keeper leagues: normal keeper and minimal (or partial) keeper.

Normal keeper leagues allow any player to be kept. Normal keeper leagues also reward the strategically thinking owners by allowing them to keep some of their better picks from the previous season. It can have a detrimental effect if teams become too dominant. For example, we call one team in our league "the LT team" since LT is responsible for the majority of the points and success for that team. Any other owner not so fortunate to have an LT (or LJ) can feel as if the league is tilted against him. Therefore a minimal keeper league may be better to prevent the domination of your keeper league. Minimal keeper leagues allow only players drafted after a certain round to be kept (thus preventing the better "stud" players from being kept). Some leagues will also limit the number of years you can keep a player.

Normal keeper formats:

A) Keep and pay a top draft pick – Each team can keep up to a certain number of players each year. For every player kept, a draft pick must be paid. If you only keep one player, then you pay with your first round draft pick; if you keep two, then you lose your first two draft picks. If you keep three players, you forfeit your first three picks and thus have your first pick of the new year's draft in round 4.

B) Free Keeper – No penalty (draft picks lost) to keep players (but usually limited to 1 or 2 keeper players).

C) Keep and forfeit the round they were drafted in – You can keep a certain number (three seems the most common) and have to forfeit a pick from the round you drafted them in last year. If you keep your 2nd and 5th round picks then that is who you draft again in the 2nd and 5th rounds of this years draft.

Minimal (Partial) keeper formats:

A) Minimal Keeper – Limited number of players can be kept (1-3) and only if drafted in middle or later rounds (9th round or later, as an example).

B) Minimal Keeper with penalty – Same as minimal keeper except you you must pay a certain number of rounds as a penalty (example: 4 rounds) and give up the draft pick next year that corresponds with a pick X rounds earlier than where you drafted him. For example, you draft V. Young with the 14th pick in 2006. If you keep him in 2007 you give up a 10th round pick (V. Young is automatically drafted by you again in 10th round in 2007). If you kept him again in 2008, you would have to give up a 6th round pick and he then would not be eligible for keeping in 2009 because he was drafted before the 9th round. This forces teams to try to draft a sleeper or rookie as late as possible (thus increasing their value in the following years if keeping). It also prevents teams from keeping the big stars and thus eliminating interest of others to join a league where there is no one left to draft.

*The minimal (or partial) keeper leagues are the best of both worlds. By minimizing the number of keepers to one or two, you still get the same competitiveness of trying to find a real sleeper for the next year but you maintain your league's integrity and fullness of the draft year in and year out. Only allowing players picked after the early rounds to be keepers assures that the studs are not kept and ensures that true sleepers will be tried.

Keeper Rules

1) FA pickups during the season are considered drafted in the last round of the draft (some leagues say 10th round so that they are not a steal) or you can only keep players drafted and held for the entire year. This eliminates any waiver wire/FA add or trade problems since none of these players can be kept.

2) Trading deadline is probably still the best way to go, since some teams can unload players they will not be keeping.

3) Some leagues use a "progressive" keeper pick penalty. In this case, after the season is over, if you keep a player you must pay a 1 round penalty for the first year you keep them. The next year you keep them, you pay a 2 round penalty. The penalty gets progressively higher for every year you keep the same player. To keep the same player from year to year involves a sliding scaled penalty, not to mention that you paid a penalty to keep him originally, so it gets progressively worse.

4) What is fair concerning declaring keepers? Do you do it right before the draft or a week prior? If it is done prior to the draft, posting on the league website presents an unfair advantage to those who have yet to declare their keepers. Perhaps have owners send an e-mail to the commish. If so, send it with "read receipt request." That way if he looks at it early (cheating) then you will know. If the commish got to look at everyone's keepers before declaring his that would not be fair. Best to do it well in advance of the draft, so all know how to account for the players.

Keeper Strategy

Most strategies will depend on how many players you can keep and the penalties involved. Imagine in 2005 when T.O. was out for the season; or in 2006 when R. Williams was suspended for the year. A team could pick him up and hold him on their roster for the year with a late round draft pick, then keep him for the next year as long as the penalty was not too large. A great strategy unless the keepers are given up for first round draft picks, and even then it may be worth it, depending on the player.

Try to win this year. In a keeper league, only a limited number can be kept, so focus on winning this year and not as much on building a dynasty (that would be a dynasty strategy). Win now, rebuild later. Rookies may take years to develop. Be smart about who you keep and make choices about whether you want to win now or later.

Keeper leagues also make auction league values change based on the players kept and their value. If an owner keeps a player, it affects two things. First, that player is no longer available, thus the player potential at that position is drained and the owner who kept him will have less money to bid with, thus affecting the remaining player's values. You need to find out who is being kept and at what cost. Then remove these players from your rankings. Finally, adjust the money in the total pot to bid on the remaining players and use that value to recalculate the auction values for the remaining players that will be drafted. (See Chapter 12 – Auction Strategies.)

Always evaluate long-term before dropping a player. This sounds obvious, but you need to make decisions based on if you are playing for this year or next. If you have a shot at the playoffs and need to drop a keeper for a fill-in that will give you a chance at the playoffs, you make the call. Keep in mind that once you drop them you probably can't keep them. Trade draft picks for next year to get studs for this year or trade studs this year who you will not keep next year for draft picks next year. The trick is knowing when to realistically start planning for the next year. You are not going to win every year, but you can have a middle-of-the-road team if you focus on winning every year. WRs generally play longer and with less injuries, so base most of your keepers around WR studs, especially in minimal keeper leagues. However, do not do this at the expense of great RBs.

Age is a huge factor with keeper players. Youth has advantages; if the RB is 32, he may not have many years left to produce for your team. If he is a 24-year-old second year RB then his future is bright and so is your team's. Choose youth over older players. This is more of a factor if you are in a dynasty league or a league where there is never a penalty for keeping a player. If the player is not likely to be kept for long periods, then this is less of a factor. It is a non-factor in redraft leagues. The longer you can keep players, the more this is a factor. Do not focus on age and future possibilities for every player you draft. If you can only keep two players from year to year then use these criteria for the first few rounds (your top players) but do not use them for every player. M. Stover in round 13 will not be a keeper and thus you do not need to pass him up just because he will not be around for you in another five years. Then again, maybe he will.

Keeper drafts and redraft drafts are very similar in the early rounds. Great players are great no matter what and you want them on your team. The middle and late rounds are where keepers become more of a factor (and it also depends on the rules; if you can only keep players drafted in or after the 9th round then that is when things will change a bit). In a redraft league, you need to get starters, even before sleepers, for the most part. In a keeper league, you can cultivate some players who will not play this year but you know will start eventually. You cannot wait forever but your time horizon in a keeper league is much longer than in a redraft. Rookies and inexperienced but talented players will fit this category. You always want to draft talent, and if it takes a year or two for that talent to start, then so be it, as long as you have the roster spots to wait it out.

Keeper Trades

Rule #1: Get value. Look at VBD ranking versus a good ADP for your league. Remember that you are not giving up a draft pick in a redraft league though. Keeper draft picks are usually worth a round less for every one keeper allowed, if first round picks are sacrificed. So if four keepers per team are allowed, a 1st round pick would be worth a 5th round pick in a redraft league and you should expect the same level of players available. But don't forget rule #2 below.

Rule #2: The top picks in a keeper rookie/free agent draft are worth far more than in a redraft league. The closer you get to the #1 pick the more valuable the differences in picks. Why? Let's assume you are in a 12-team keeper league that allows you to keep three players. That means 36 players are kept, but not necessarily the top 36 players. Some teams will have drafted four or perhaps five players from the top 36 ranked players for this coming season. Other teams will have only one or two players from the top 36 for this season (due to retirements, career injuries, suspensions, etc.). Now the team with five of the top 36 players can only keep three, so two of the top 36 players will go back into the draft available for all teams. The team with only two top players may be allowed to keep only two and get a supplemental draft pick, or may be forced to keep three players regardless, in which case they kept their two top 36 players and one other player. So, whichever team has the first pick of the draft will have several key players to choose from (assuming a small keeper number); the larger the number of players to keep, the smaller the amount of non-keepers to choose from. Note: There will not be many of these top players available in the draft, so there will be a big drop off in talent after they are gone. The rookies will help to balance this effect but in general you will want the first pick, if possible, so that you can grab the best available top player that had to be jettisoned by a player-rich team.

Rule #3: Evaluate players in trades differently. Are you trading to get another keeper? If so, is he better than who you planned to keep? Are you trading to get someone whom you cannot keep because of restrictions? If so, his value may be less to you than a redraft trade of the same players.

Rule #4: When trading draft picks, try to determine what you may be losing. Estimate what the pick is worth and who you may be giving up with that pick. If you are trading next year's 1st round pick and you are 1-8 and two games worse than anyone else, then you may be giving up pick 1.01. This would mean the first shot at the top rookie or FA. Look to see who may be coming to the NFL next year. Any super once-in-a-lifetime rookies? Say P. Manning or R. Bush? Hard to pass them up unless the deal is a really good one.

Rule #5: Off-season trades will get you less value than in-season trades, in most cases. The reason you are trading is more than likely to get some value for a player that you cannot keep. Let's say you can keep two players, but you have three top 10 RBs. In this case, rather than give away (drop) one of those three RBs you can try to trade him. Unfortunately, you may not get a top draft pick for him, even though he will probably go in the first round of the R/FA draft. Why? Other teams do not want to give up their chance at other unknown possibilities. A 2nd round pick may be your best offer. In which case, trade him since it is better to get something for nothing. If you have to drop him you will get nothing in return for him. If you do drop him you are building up the depth of players available in the draft and this means you may be able to draft him then or at the very least, you will get a player who may not have been available had you not dropped him. Some suggest you do not accept lowball offers because this will condition other owners to think you can be lowballed. I say play the market, and, if the offer is too low, do not be afraid to dump him back into the FA market. Who knows, maybe you can get him again next year.

Rule #6: Do not trade the stud mentioned above to just anyone, if you can help it. Make sure it is a team near the bottom. Do not trade him to the top team, especially if he has room for another keeper.

Who to Keep

1) Which players are projected to do the best in the upcoming year? First calculate your player projections and do whichever analysis you prefer to come with your cheat sheets. For example, AVT to come up with rankings and X points.

2) Next, weed out and eliminate some players based on eligibility requirements. For example, if you can only keep rookies from last year or those drafted in round 9 or later. Come up with a list of those you can possibly keep.

3) How many can you keep? Are you limited to a certain number of keepers? If so (say 2), then add one to that number (2+1=3) and use that to take the top players. So, I would only look at the top 3 ranked players from my team based on my cheat sheet.

4) Which positions have the most value? Normally this will be RBs, then a top tier WR, then QB, then TE; kind of like the order in which you draft them. So a top RB is a no-brainer to keep. Rarely would you keep a K or DEF unless you paid no penalty to keep them.

5) What is the draft order? This will help you determine who to keep and who others will keep as you evaluate ADP.

6) What years are left on their contracts? Are there anchors or bridges available? (See contracts at the end of this chapter)

7) If you are paying a penalty, ask yourself this very important question: If I do not keep him, will I be able to draft him later than the penalty I face? In other words, if you keep S. McNair but give up a 4th round pick, could you have drafted him in the 5th round or later and saved the 4th round pick? If the answer is yes, you can get him in the 5th round or later, then DO NOT KEEP HIM. If you want him you can grab him in the 5th round and you will have gotten value from not keeping him. Obvious value occurs when a player will go in an earlier round and you are giving up a later round pick as a penalty. A no-brainer for me was C. Taylor in 2006. I drafted him in 2005 in the 16th round and to keep him in 2006 all I had to do was pay a four round penalty. Therefore I got C. Taylor in the 12th round of my keeper league draft. On most draft boards he was going in the 3rd round. That is value. But I had to hold him all of 2005 while he was Jamal Lewis' backup. Project each player's EDP. Using his overall position (say 45th) and the number of teams in your league (accounting for their own keepers), what round would you expect him to be drafted 45th overall? With 12 teams, no one giving up a 1-3 round pick means 45/12=3.09 EDP; thus giving up a 4th round pick would be fine.

8) Repeat the same process with the other owner's teams to determine their keepers. If a player can be kept at the same or even one round earlier than anticipated, mark them as questionable (not everyone ranks player alike). If the penalty would be at least 2 rounds too early, then mark him as not a keeper. If the player can be kept for a penalty of at least 1 round later than his anticipated draft spot, count on him as a keeper.

9) Other considerations are who other teams will keep, what your team will look like and supply and demand. If all 11 other teams keep two RBs each, you may be forced to keep your RBs even though they are not that good, just because of the lack of RBs. If faced with two equal players, go with the RB over all the other positions. RBs are scarce and in a keep-2 or keep-3 league they are very scarce. Most owners will keep RBs so they will be a rare commodity on draft day. That is why you need to hoard players at this position too.

10) I drafted in one keeper league last year that allows a team to keep two players but also has a maximum player position limit in the main draft (each team can only draft three RBs). There is a supplemental draft after the main draft with no restrictions. I had three keeper possibilities, but only two could be kept. My choices were Carson Palmer (but I would have to give up a 4th round pick), Chester Taylor (give up a 12th round pick) or Kevin Barlow (give up a 10th round pick). I went with Palmer and Taylor, even though Barlow and Taylor returned the most value. My reasoning was, if I took both those RBs then I could only draft one more RB in the draft. I wanted to get two good RBs to go with Taylor. I did not want to be stuck with L. Jordan and Taylor and Barlow. So I kept C. Palmer, even though I had his ADP in the 4th round. I did not get additional value by taking him. Instead, I got peace of mind knowing before the draft that my QB and RB2 were a lock. This allowed me to come up with a draft strategy, knowing two of my

players in advance and what position they played. I drew the 2nd pick and took L. Johnson with pick 1.2. In the 2nd and 3rd rounds, I could target WRs R. Wayne and A. Boldin. Of course, C. Palmer was my 4th (keeper) pick and I finished off the 5th round with F. Gore. So by keeping Palmer and Taylor, I knew I could get a RB in round 1 and two WRs before Palmer, and then RB#3 in round 5.

11) Always consider trading draft picks or players to get something. If you have no one worth keeping, consider trading some of your draft picks to another stronger team that has "extra" keeper players. By the same token, if your league only allows you to keep two players but you have three keepers worthy of a 1st or 2nd round pick, then try to trade the third player to another team for some of his draft picks. If you have good players but cannot keep them all, try to trade them for something.

12) Consider the scarcity at other positions and what keeping a player can do to help your draft strategy. If you hate TEs and have to decide between two mediocre ones and you have a chance to keep A. Gates, then do so. He may be worth far more to you that way than his VBD ranking.

13) Look at the future. How many more years can you keep this player? If faced with a choice between two equal players and one can only be kept for one more year and the other can be kept for three more years, go with the player who can be kept the longest.

14) Youth vs. Age – All things being equal, go with youth over aging vets. The aging vet is more likely to break down, retire, etc.

15) Consider posting a note on the MB trying to get some insight into which way owners are leaning. This is the time to be honest (somewhat) because no one can steal those keepers away from you before you get the chance to make a decision.

There is a simple way to determine who is available to keep. Eliminate all Ks and DEFs and all but the Top 5 QBs and TEs (but look at all RBs), if the sacrifice is an early round draft pick. If you can keep but pay no price, then the best players based on VBD will be kept (usually RBs). If the price you pay is to forfeit the round they were drafted or pay a round or two penalty, look at each players cost and compare that with his ADP to determine if he should be kept.

First Draft/Rookie Draft

Keeper leagues are those most likely to use the NFL's way of determining draft picks for the following year based on standings from this year. Keeper leagues generally set the draft order for the rookie/free agent (R/FA) draft in the reverse order of finish and do not serpentine the order between rounds for the same number of rounds that players are kept. In other words, the worst team drafts first and the champion drafts last in every round for four rounds, if you can keep four players. Then round 5 reverts to a serpentine draft.

Preparation will be close to the same as a redraft unless you can keep a lot of players, in which case refer to dynasty strategy. Keepers in most keeper leagues will be the stud players, those drafted in your first several rounds. For example, in a keeper-2 league, expect to keep two of your first three players drafted.

Focus on this year and the next in a keeper league. Leave any planning for beyond two years to a dynasty league unless you can keep more than two and are not limited to how long you can keep them. Another scenario that allows longer planning is if you are forced to keep rookies.

How do you expand a keeper league or bring in new owners?

To become a keeper league, have an expansion draft, just like in the NFL. In this case, allow each original team to protect two players, then have the new teams (assuming two) draft who they want from the other teams. If a player is picked from team A, then that team gets to protect one additional player (so that great teams are not raided from too much). The expansion teams would also get the first picks in the rookie draft for that year. By protecting two players, teams do not lose their top 2 picks, which is the equivalent of their first two draft picks. The expansion teams then get to choose a few players from other teams that are the equivalent of 3rd or 4th round picks. By having more choices to get these 3rd and 4th round picks, the expansion teams will have more depth and their early picks in the rookie draft will give them a fighting chance in later years.

Dynasty Leagues

What is a dynasty league? You keep most, if not all, of the players on your team from year to year. You have a chance to build an empire. You not only want to win your league championship, you want to win it three or four years in a row. You want owners using the term "3-peat" with your team name like it is a natural extension. You want owners threatening to quit the league if the commissioner does not do something about the all-powerful Slam's Slammers.

The main advantage of a dynasty league is that you can keep your favorite players or players from your favorite NFL team forever. It also creates a better format to showcase knowledge of players through trades and drafting, thus your research pays off more. Not to mention the format reflects the NFL in a more realistic manner, as there is no off-season since your team is affected by things that happen 365 days a year. Those same advantages can be disadvantages; such as, if you do not draft your favorite players it will be many years before they become available to you. Probably the biggest knock on dynasty leagues is that it is hard to recover from a really bad initial draft. Not to mention that you miss out on one of the best parts of fantasy football, the draft. In a dynasty league there is a R/FA draft but it does not last many rounds and is much smaller than even a keeper draft. The last distraction of a dynasty league is that they are the hardest (of all types of leagues) in which to find someone to replace owners. New ones will need to take over a team they did not draft (kind of like the real NFL though).

Usually these leagues have bigger rosters (22+ or can be up to 40 if IDP is used), because you will be drafting some players based on their future potential. They may take a few years to develop. Think roster deep, waiver wire thin when you think of dynasty leagues. It is probably best to say how long the league will last upfront so that each owner knows how much (and long) of a commitment he is making. A penalty for leaving early or being booted out (by a majority of owners voting, of course) may deter the less dedicated from joining. I suggest you have owners pay entry fees at least two years in advance and up to five years, if possible. This also allows those owners to trade draft picks for any years they have pre-paid.

You must have dedicated owners; those willing to ride out a bad draft and take pride in bringing a down-and-out team from the cellar to contention in the shortest amount of time. You need owners who like to take on a challenge; owners who are committed for the long-term to the league. The more owners you have, the greater the chance someone will fall out. Have two alternates just in case.

Dynasty Rules

1) The first rule of a dynasty league is that changes to scoring or rules are forbidden because owners drafted their players based on the rules at that time. Changing rules after the initial draft hurts everyone and should be avoided at all costs unless all owners unanimously agree to it.

2) If an owner leaves the league, look for another owner to take over the team and offer him a discounted entry fee to take over an existing team. (That is why you have owners pay for a year in advance or all pay a little over the fee to cover for a new owner to join).

3) Roster size – Triple the number of starters plus add a few for rookies. For example, if you start 13 (1 QB, 2 RBs, 2WRs, 1 TE, 1 K, 2 DLs, 2 LBs, 2 DBs), then 42 (3 x 13=39+3 rookies=42) would be a good roster size. Rosters need to be big enough to accommodate starting lineups, bye weeks, injuries, cultivate developmental players and deal with suspensions, retirements, etc. Dynasty leagues are all about the draft and trades and not about waiver wire moves every week. Owners should NOT be able to save themselves every week by grabbing a waiver wire player who is a stopgap replacement for a bad draft.

4) No need for a trading deadline because of the ability to keep players. This should prevent teams from unloading good players when not in contention for playoffs.

5) Subsequent drafts should be in order from worst team to best team and not serpentine. This will help with parity in the league. So, the worst team in the league will get the first pick of the draft in each round. Of course, in a dynasty league you are just drafting rookies and FA leftovers.

6) Some leagues will allow teams to draft more players than roster requirements and then have a cut down day (just like the NFL) where teams must reduce their roster to a required number.

Dynasty Strategy

1) Hold onto IDP studs until they breakdown. IDP studs are too hard to replace and hold their value longer than offensive players. By studs, I mean Top 10 LBs and Top 5 DEs.

2) Three components make up a good team:

    a)   Depth at every position (in case of injury, bye weeks, etc.)

    b)   Balanced team of young up-and-coming players and proven vets.

    c)   Future potential studs: players with 3-year potential; youth for youth's sake is wrong, they must be quality players.

Too many young players who have yet to produce or too many old players who are peaking may also mean trouble in future years. The older your roster is, the more likely it is to be adversely affected by injury, retirement and benching. Try to find one of the three areas above that you have in abundance. Maybe you have five good WRs but only start two. Even with one for depth, that leaves two to trade. Maybe you have four potential studs and can trade one for a vet that will give you more balance. The preferred trade is when you can trade a vet, who is having a career year, to another team, for a younger player who is doing just as well. Now you do not sacrifice FP and instead get rid of an older player who may have seen his best years and get youth on your team for many years to come. Remember that future draft considerations, if allowed, can be used to sweeten any deal or maybe the deal itself.

Three main strategies:

1) Short-term view – Play for today, use redraft cheat cheats, never pass up a good thing now.

2) Balanced view – Mix it up between the aging vets and the young players. Draft to win this year, but with an eye to next year's plan with 2-4 roster spots.

3) Long-term view – Stay away from the over 30 RBs, hoard draft picks, jettison aging vets who start to slip, grab rookies and ride them until they get to be 30. Too often this mentality leads to a "win next year" attitude, instead of a "win this year" fight. You may not be around next year! Try to win it this year, stop waiting for the dynasty team that may never come!!!!

Miscellaneous

Rookies and young players tend to be overvalued in dynasty leagues, especially by long-term strategists.

Veteran players tend to be undervalued in dynasty leagues, especially by long-term strategists.

There are more long-term strategists than short-term strategists in dynasty leagues, thus demand is high for rookies and younger players and lower for vets.

Owners with a long-term strategy will trade to get future draft picks, but these players tend to be boom or bust and are unproven. Rookies have a 50 percent production rate.

Long-term strategies do not account for the chaos that is the NFL. Players get injured, suspended, benched, retire early, etc. all the time. To say that your RB is going to last for the next four years is a pipe dream. Thus plan 2-3 years in advance, but no more. Expect chaos.

Stop trying to build a grand dynasty and have all the other owners look up to you in awe as you sweep three championships in a row with great draft picks, super rookie picks and FA pickups that make everyone envious. It is not going to happen. Remember the chaos theory.

Draft for potential. If you draft only veterans then the production will inevitably decline from these players. Draft for some upside (2-3 year veteran WRs, QBs who will start in near future and be good).

If in a dynasty league, who you cut will have to be evaluated to determine if he is worth cutting or not. Do not cut unless you feel you can gain when you conduct the yearly draft. (i.e Will there be some rookies or FAs who are better than the player(s) you cut?)

Be careful of QBBC or RBBC situations. If you draft them you just get two roster spots wasted and neither player will probably do as well. The NFL team they play on will trade or draft to fix the weakness in the subsequent year and you end up with two mediocre players.

Short-term solution (aging veterans who may shine this year but are on the way down), or long-term investment; (rookies and up-and-coming players with potential) or win now or win later? A mixture of both types of players (replenished during each year's draft) can keep a team competitive. You can always trade future prospects (draft picks or players on a team with potential) to try and win this year. But many times you are cutting off your nose to spite your face. To win, and win consistently, you need to cultivate younger players and get rid of aging players before their value plummets.

The time to start rebuilding is the day after you are eliminated for this year's playoffs. Don't give up the ship too soon. Injuries and other factors can have huge ripples through the league. Just because you need to win five of the last six games does not mean you won't.

The best rosters have star players for this season, backups to fill in during bye weeks and a few promising stars for future years.

Rebuilding your team takes patience and thought. The good news is that if you stunk last year, you will get a top pick in the upcoming draft of rookies. You should be able to get a rookie RB who may start this year, and if not, then definitely next year. Rebuilding takes time. Be patient. Also, you may get offers of trades for that draft pick. Do not get suckered into giving away your future for an aging old veteran who may or may not produce this year.

An injured or underperforming player still has value in future years. Do not get the itch to trade away your studs simply because they underperformed in one year.

The New England Patriots dynasty was not created over night. It takes years and years of crafting (excuse the pun) to get to a position of dominance and then great drafting and trading to stay there.

For a RB size matters and smaller is not better for long-term durability (downgrade as appropriate).

Trade away RBs at a certain age (28 or 29). This ensures that you get value for them before they start to fall apart or retire on you.

In dynasty leagues you are less concerned with what other teams are drafting and more concerned with creating your team. If another owner starts a run on TEs you should not panic. Do not jump on the bandwagon because you plan on taking T. Scheffler, the Denver TE who will not start but should be a star down the road. So wait, grab a serviceable TE for this year and also get Scheffler for the future.

Once the starters are filled in and you have a few critical backups then you need to think about the future. Young players with upside are the name of the game. They may not start this year or even next year, being a benchwarmer for a year or more, but if he pays off later and you have him versus some other owner, you made the right move. Maybe he's a rookie QB who will not start for two years. Do you take a chance or pass him up for the WR who is entering his 3rd year and came on strong the last half of the season? Maybe you have to decide between the rookie QB and the #2 RB, with the knowledge that the #1 RB is in the final year of his contract. You need to evaluate talent, opportunity and value to make a decision that will be beneficial to your team.

How Long Should I Hold my Rookies in a Dynasty League?

1) Studies show that for QBs, those drafted in the first four rounds (primarily 1st and 2nd rounds), are most likely to succeed in the NFL and, if so, within their first four years. The 1st round QBs tend to be the best and start to produce from their 2nd year onward. If he has been around for more than six years and not been in the top 5, chances are he never will.

2) RBs can contribute early in their career, but will not last as long. Rarely do RBs have stud years after seven years in the league (Tiki Barber is one notable exception). After ten years, most RBs are done. You need to grab the NFL's 1st round rookie RBs because they have a greater chance of success than the RBs drafted in other rounds. But do not ignore 2nd and 3rd round RBs, as they generally do better than later drafted RBs.

3) It is no surprise that 1st round WRs succeed more often (they last the longest and produce the most). They can also achieve "stud status" in the later years of their career (such as the 9th and 10th years). That said, they are most likely to be a stud in years 2-7 (with the 3rd year more prevalent for Top 10 WRs). There are good WRs from the NFL 2nd and 3rd round draft, you just to need to find them. Hint: They may be from the schools who do not get the most publicity.

4) TEs who are drafted in the first round of the NFL draft tend to have the most success. They tend to produce immediately or in the 2nd year, after learning the systems, etc. TEs drafted after the 1st round tend to be more blocking TEs and thus not as successful, fantasy-wise.

The higher the player is drafted in the NFL, the better his chance of succeeding in the NFL. First round draft choices correlate to the highest FF rankings and the most stud years. The scouts know what they are doing.

Keep rookies at least three years to see if they develop. If he has not done anything after 3 years, you can drop him with confidence. However, the earlier he was drafted in the NFL, the more leash you may want to give him

On average, 1 of the Top 3 RBs will become a stud, one will be average and one will be a bust. The problem is figuring out which will be the good ones and which will be a bust. Because only 1 in 3 rookie early round RBs become stars, do not give up on proven talent to chase after a would-be star.

Most rookies (other than RBs) do not help your team in their first year. You have to give them time to develop. If they have not turned up after four years, they probably will not. Drop them.

So grab a rookie if he is a 1st rounder and expect good things in a few years (or second half of the season if a RB). But do not give up the ranch for pick 1.01 because it is very hard to determine which 1st round RB will succeed, be average or bust.

Dynasty Trades

A bad trade is more dangerous in a dynasty league since it will affect you for years to come, versus a redraft league where everything starts over the next year. In order to evaluate trade potential, you need an idea of how long the player's career may last. Other factors include: How many teams are in your league? How long will it run (hopefully indefinitely but some have time limits)? What is the roster size? How many starters (and thus how many bench players)? Finally, how many starters are at each position? A league with 3 WRs and a flex position makes WRs more valuable than a league where you only start 2 WRs.

Dynasty R/FA Draft Pick Value:

Roster Size – The larger the roster, the less valuable a pick is. Why? The larger the roster, the less players that are available in the R/FA draft. In this case it is because there are less FA. The bigger the roster the greater the chance of having better players than those acquired in later round draft picks.

Number of teams in the league – The more teams in the league, the more valuable a draft pick becomes. This occurs because there will be more rookies taken on rookie draft day, so getting an extra pick can mean more in terms of getting better rookies.

Number of Starters – As the number of starters goes up, the value of a draft pick increases. This is because you need more players to start, so getting rookies who can start when your other players retire or have a season-ending injury is more important. Why? Because you have a greater chance of losing a player to injury or retirement, the more players you need to start.

Position of Starters – If you start more RBs, that makes your draft picks worth more since the RB position sees the shortest career. If you start 2 QBs, that position has the longest career, so that would lessen the value of a draft pick. WRs tend to have longer careers than RBs, so starting 3 WRs and a flex may also decrease the value of a draft pick.

Years in the future – The more years you have to wait on the pick occurring, the less value it has.

Draft Round – In a dynasty league, the value of the draft picks drop off rapidly since there are less skill position players available than in a redraft league. If all players are allowed to be kept, then less players will be available from FA. Draft picks are worth less.

First draft

There is no more important event in fantasy football than the initial dynasty draft. Mess this up and you will be paying for it for many seasons to come. You must have a plan of attack. Ask yourself; do I want to win this year at all costs, do I want to try to build a dynasty team that will kick butt for years to come or do I want to build a balanced team that can go either way? There is no right or wrong answer, only a plan of attack that will keep you on track. But if you focus on the long-term, your dynasty league team will be better served. Make no mistake, you will be tempted to drift away from your plan. If you are trying to win this year, undoubtedly a young rookie prospect will slip to you in one of the rounds. You will then be faced with the decision of taking the rookie, who will probably not produce for a few years, or going with the needed vet player at another position. It is okay to abandon the plan for an unexpected gift, just make sure you get back on the wagon next round.

Focus the early rounds on talented players who are just entering the prime of their careers. Do not take risks early on because if they fail you will be paying for them for years to come. What do I mean by this? Randy Moss, in Oakland but not doing much. In 2006 he was hyped up some with A. Brooks at QB. If you spent a 2nd round pick on him in 2006 in an initial dynasty draft, you are kicking yourself now.

Do not worry too much about finding that rookie who will be the foundation of your dynasty team. If you reach too far for that rookie sensation, you are sacrificing too much this year. Wait and get him later in the draft or use your prowess to pick up another "impact player" in next year's R/FA draft. Do not pass on good older players just to get young, unproven talent. Good, young, proven talent is always better than good, old talent, but they both are proven commodities. Remember that rookies are just that, unknown. Look for players with proven ability (two years under their belt) but that are not past their prime either (how many years so far in their career – RB-5 max, WR-6, QB-7?).

In middle to late rounds, start to look for sleepers (young, promising talent) that can help now as a fill-in and years down the road as a starter. You will be tempted to grab the old vet who will give you a few points as a bye week backup. DON'T! He may help you a little this season. And I do mean a little; he will not help you in 2-3 years when you need the most help because everyone else has their young promising players and you do not. After you have your starters, sacrifice some bench depth and grab some players who will need a year to two to develop. It will pay off in the long run. Look for rookies or second year players who were drafted in the 1st round of the NFL draft. Let the NFL scouts do the work for you. An NFL 2nd round WR who shows flashes of brilliance may be a good bet too.

Rookie Draft dynasty -

You are looking for talent with opportunity. Watch for stud potential and keep an eye on those operating in the best schemes (thus most potential). The first RB drafted in the NFL draft is more likely to be successful than the others after him. WRs are all over the place. QBs have a 75% chance of becoming a stud if they were the first QB selected in the NFL draft. RBs taken in the 4th or later round of the NFL draft rarely end up as starters. First round NFL RBs have a 50% chance of getting and holding a starting RB job. Do not be afraid to trade draft picks since only the top draft picks (usually RBs) tend to pan out. WRs take time to develop and, even then, may not. You are better off with a 1st round NFL WR, but there are no guarantees.

Using a rookie draft pick on a QB is a waiting game as they usually do not take the field for a few years, thus burning a hole on your bench. Not only do you have to wait for them to start, but even then it may take a while for them to become good (hmm… see Eli Manning). They are late round rookie picks at best and assume at least two years of bench time. If there is a franchise QB who has a good chance to start in his rookie season (M. Leinart and V. Young come to mind from 2006), then they should go in the middle of the first round, because if not another owner will pick them.

Usually RBs flood the rookie draft first round just like in the redraft leagues. Expect them to be picked exclusively in the first half of round one. Why? RB is the key to any team and that rule does not change with the rookie draft.

WRs get more love in the rookie draft, as every owner tries to find the stud WR who will break the Top 20 in his rookie year. Look for the top WRs to go in the 2nd half of the first round. Late round WRs will end up taking just as long to develop as QBs (two years), and thus may not make the team for the duration of the season.

A good quality TE can easily be picked in the 2nd and 3rd rounds after all the RBs and stud-to-be QBs and WRs are grabbed. Look for great value here, as TEs on the waiver wire that produce are few and far between. A stud TE will go in the first round after all the RBs are gone but before the stud WRs, since they take a little longer to develop.

Before you target rookie WRs and QBs who will take 2-3 years to develop, consider an IDP with great potential but limited current opportunity. These players will get their chance sooner, rather than later, and you will know if they are valuable well before the WR or QB comes of age. If your IDPs flop, you can always draft some more rookies the following year. If they impress, you can keep them because they will start in year two. In other words, these IDPs with potential should breakout or bust early, thus giving you trade bait or an empty slot for the following year; as opposed to carrying a WR or QB for three years before knowing if it was the right move or not.

IDPs

Rookie IDPs will usually start to fall around the 3rd or 4th round of the rookie draft. Do not be afraid to improve your draft position in these rounds to be in a better position to get the highly coveted IDP.

Rookies DLs – Target a DE who can play in a 4-3. Look for bulk, but not too much (260-280 lbs). You want a player who is quick with the first step but big enough to stand up against an oncoming RB. He needs to be able to control the blockers so he can get to the QB for the all-important sack. You need size, speed, quickness and strength. Usually they will start to be picked in the 5th round or later, after all of the offensive skill positions are gone.

Rookie LBs – Look for ones who will play MLB or WLB. Look for athletes who are quick off the ball and who can tackle. Speed is a plus but at MLB the plays will come to him and as long as he is quick and can tackle he will get his fair share of stats. Angles and quick reactions are more important than speed here. This is where the value occurs. They have tremendous upside and can have the same value as a WR or TE. They are mainly 2nd and 3rd round picks, along with those WRs and TEs.

Rookie DBs – Hard to predict because more depends on other factors (scheme, supporting cast) than skill. Target safeties first, look again for good tacklers and those safeties with good recovery speed. About the same as DE, but really good rookie DBs can go in 2nd round.

How to convert to a Dynasty League

1) Start from day one as a dynasty league or convert after a redraft season, so essentially it is like starting from scratch.

2) Converting a keeper league into a dynasty league is the more common approach because often redraft leagues progress to a minimal keeper (dipping their toes in the keeper format), then progress to full keeper and on to dynasty. The advantage here is that players you love are already on your team as keepers and can now be kept forever. The disadvantage is that teams with poor rosters are now at a disadvantage because they get to keep all of them, but maybe do not want any of them. In fairness, they may have drafted differently had they known the league was going to turn into a dynasty league the following year. Instead of drafting all of the old vets who looked promising last year, maybe a few more rookies or younger players would have made the squad. So, I suggest you start from the beginning with a new draft... and make it an auction draft. Auctions and dynasty leagues go together like peanut butter and jelly. In the auction, everyone has the same chance at LT, as long as they are willing to pay for him.

IDPs in Dynasty Leagues

IDPs are the vital element to winning in dynasty leagues that have large IDP starters. IDPs' usually take less time to develop and you can tell if they are a stud or a dud much quicker, so target them as sleepers or rookies more than other QBs or WRs. Learning a system or finding a spot may take a while and the impatient owner will drop or trade him cheaply; you can take advantage of this. IDPs will retain their skills longer into their career than offensive players, but will quickly lose their skills once their demise begins. So IDPs, especially your stud IDPs, should be kept as long as possible. Most owners are weak at IDP; take advantage of that. Look for players who have moved to different teams and schemes and that have more opportunities. Late in the season is the perfect chance to steal an up-and-coming player before he makes it to next year's draft. Look for players with great skill playing behind a vet whose contract is up after this year, or behind a vet with a big contract extension decision forthcoming (especially on a team with salary cap problems).

Salary Caps/Contracts

Salary caps and contracts are two ways to spice up a league and give the owners more of a management role in either a keeper or dynasty league system. The best draft format for salary caps is an auction, because it sets initial salaries based on what was paid for a player. Contracts can easily be used with either a traditional draft or an auction draft. Salary caps can be a tool in promoting player movement within keeper/dynasty leagues to prevent teams from becoming too dominant. There are many ways to run a salary cap or contract keeper league. The more common formats are:

Salary Cap Keeper – This is an auction league where the auction values from last year increase by some amount (for example 5%) for the current year. Any player on your team the previous year can be kept; however, their salary goes up by 5%. Your salary cap stays the same (for example, $200), therefore you cannot keep everyone from last year or you would pay $210 and be over budget by $10. Last year I bid and won LT for $80. I can keep him this year for $84 ($80 x 105%=$84). If I do keep LT, then I will have $4 less to bid on other players; the 5% premium is the price for being able to keep him absolutely. Usually players are kept for a maximum of four or five years in salary cap leagues.

Player Salaries – A player's salary will be what was paid for him at the auction. If a player is coming off waivers or added through free agency, then his salary is $1.

Some leagues use an automatic salary increase from year to year. This ensures that no player remains dirt cheap for too long.

Methods of automatic salary increases:

1) Percentage increase from last year's salary. All players will see their salaries increase by 5% each year. This works great for the big players but is horrible for the sleepers that were chosen and broke out last year. They will still be a tremendous bargain even after their salary is increased by 5%. Their salary should be commensurate with other skill players of their caliber. For this reason, the performance-based salary system was designed.

2) Performance-based increase/decrease. This takes into account where a player ranked in relation to others at his position. For example, if a WR is drafted for $10 in 2006 and finishes ranked in the top 10 then his salary should be at least equal to the salary of the 10th best WR. In other words, if at the end of the season your player is not being paid within 25% of what he should be, then he needs to be adjusted up or down. Remember to discount injuries that can affect performance. So the number of games played will have an effect. If our WR had a salary of $10 and now the nearest WR has a salary of $28 (use last year's values for each position based on monetary value), then this year he is worth $28. The 10th highest paid WR went for $28 so that will be the new salary for your WR. By the same token, if you paid $28 for the 10th highest paid WR but he performed like the 20th WR, then his salary may decrease to $12.

Contract Years

Tool used to keep parity in keeper/dynasty leagues while keeping everyone interested in the league. Best used in leagues that do not want to have the hassle of managing a salary cap and the procedures of increasing or decreasing those from year to year. It still creates more work for the commissioner who takes on the administration of keeping up with contracts (track where all players were taken in the draft, if they were added as FA, and in what contract year they are in). Advantages: 1) More of a GM 2) You must plan strategically with LT contracts. Do you give the three-year contract to the quality vet or the up-and-coming youngster? 3) Teams will draft for need based on contracted players. 4) Makes players available after three years, so that all owners get an eventual chance at favorites. 5) Limits player dumping as they are yours for the next season.

There are several formats for contract keeper leagues:

1) All contracts are the same length – Assign all players drafted a 3-year contract, thus after three years they go back into the player pool to be drafted. Owners get a "franchise tag," where every year each owner can extend one expiring contract for another year (at which point the player has to go back to the FA pool).

2) Contracts of differing lengths – Each owner is given a number of contracts to assign to players after the draft is over (for example, two 3-year contracts, three 2-year contracts, and two 3-year rookie contracts). Once a contract on a player expires, that player enters the

draft pool for next season. Each succeeding year, a team will get two 3-year rookie contracts. Like in the pros, you cannot drop contract players so you have to take the good with the bad from the players you decide to sign to a contract. The different lengths of contracts make owners decide whom to give long contracts to. Rookie contracts make teams draft at least two rookies every year. An "anchor" or "bridge" is a way to sign a player that comes off one contract to another contract without having him go to FA and being vulnerable to getting snatched out from under you. Anchors or bridges are awarded to teams that perform well during the season. To get an anchor or bridge, you need to win the championship or score the most regular season points. Only one anchor or bridge can be awarded to a team in any year. They are transferrable from one year to the next. If you have M. Harrison and his 3-year contract ended in 2006, and you have an anchor/bridge from last year for winning the SB, then you could use it to assign M. Harrison to any contract that is open. This will probably be the 3-year contract he just left.

For example:

First year – After the draft, each owner is awarded two 3-year contracts and two 2-year contracts. After the draft and before the season starts (or some deadline established by the league), each owner assigns one player to each of his contracts. Any player not given a contract is on a 1-year contract and will go back into the draft pool at the end of the season. The two players given 2-year contracts will be on the team this year and kept for next year. The two players awarded 3-year contracts will play this year and the next two years. So in effect you have a keeper league with four players as keepers, but with more strategy needed in deciding who to keep and for how long.

Second year – All of the players under contract are ineligible for the draft since they are already on a team. At the end of the draft, each owner is given two 3-year contracts. Teams who have gained or lost contracts, due to trades, will have more or less draft picks, which will be made up at the end of the draft. For example, team A trades a player with a 3-year contract and gets one back with a 1-year contract. At the end of the year, he will have one less returning player and thus get to draft an extra player after all the other owners have established their rosters. The team gaining the player loses his draft pick in the last round, since he has an extra player.

Third year – At the end of the second season, all players on 2-year contracts from the first year go back into the draft pool because their contracts have expired. After the draft each owner is given another set of two 3-year contracts. If he has not traded, the owner has two players on 3-year contracts that expire after this third year; two players on 3-year contracts that expire in two years and two players who just signed 3-year contracts. Every season a team will get two 3-year contracts and probably have two contracts that are expiring.

3) Progressive forfeit – All players drafted have 2-year guaranteed contracts with options for a third and fourth year. Allow keepers in the same round for next year then add a one round penalty when kept in the third year and a two round penalty when kept in the fourth and final year of their contract.

4) Contracts and option years – When a player is acquired through the auction, he is given a 3-year contract, with each subsequent year being at the same auction price. After two years (the player's third year), he enters his "option year." At this point, he can be dropped, resigned for one more year at the current price (thus fulfilling his contract) or signed to a guaranteed long-term contract. The decision must be made prior to the draft. If he is dropped, he becomes available for the upcoming draft. If he is signed to a 1-year

contract then he becomes available for the draft the following year. If he is signed to a long-term contract, a "signing bonus" must be paid, which is equal to half the total value of the long-term deal ($5 minimum signing bonus). Also, the player's new salary will be his current salary plus $5 (assumes a $200 auction league) for every year on his contract. As an example, lets say you signed S. Jackson in 2004 for $20 and you had him again in 2005 for $20. Then in 2006, you gave him a three-year contract in which you agreed to give a salary of $25 in 2006, $30 in 2007 and $35 in 2008. Your signing bonus to him would be (25+30+35=$90/2=45) $45.

5) Unlimited contracts but at an increase of 20% (from auction price) each year. All amounts are rounded up to the next whole dollar amount. After his contract is over, he can be resigned with the added cost of a 50% signing bonus. Here, the longer the contract, the cheaper it will be to keep him, but the more costly if you have to drop him.

As an example, I won Joseph Addai, RB Ind, in 2006 for $10. I then had three days after the draft to decide what kind of contract to give him. See Table 22.1 below.

Table 22.1 Contract examples

	LT Contract for 6 years	2006 for 3 years, then 2009 for 3 years
2006	10	10
2007	12 (10+20%)	12
2008	14 (10+40%)	14
2009	16 (10+60%)	48 (17+signing bonus 50% next contract)
2010	18 (10+80%)	21
2011	20 (10+100%)	24

Special Rules for Contracts

1) Do you allow an owner to drop a player that has been cut by the NFL? Some leagues do, others do not. I am in the "do not" camp. If you allow a team to drop a player that has been cut you are excusing his poor decision in signing an overvalued player to his team. By allowing the player to be dropped, you free up cap room (player's salary prorated of course) for that owner to get away with a bad decision. I prefer all contracts be guaranteed. You sign him; you have him for the year. Unless you trade him or drop him, in which case you still have lost that money, but now you have an open roster spot that you can use to get another FA, assuming you have money in your FAAB.

2) Contracts must be filled with players by a certain time limit for resigning (usually two weeks after the real SB) and before the first game for newly drafted players.

3) Contract bonuses are additional contracts awarded based on merit. For example,

winning the league or scoring the most regular season points would be another 2- or 3-year contract.

4) Anchors – Players at the end of their contract must be released back into FA, unless you have an anchor (awarded based on performance, such as: #1 in regular season, scored most points in regular season, won SB, etc.), in which case you can sign them to any available contract. As an example, you have LT who is coming off his 3-year contract, but you have one anchor for scoring the most points last year. So instead of dropping LT, you sign him to a one-year contract, which is now free, since that contract expired at the end of the season.

5) Franchise tag – Allows owner to keep that player indefinitely without a contract. Only one player can have the tag at any one time. Once the player is traded, he loses any franchise tag. (i.e. the tag is not transferable, although the player is tradable.)

6) Rookie contracts – In order to encourage owners to take a risk on rookies, their contracts get an automatic one-year extension. So if you give a rookie a 3-year contract it would automatically be four years. Other leagues call certain contracts "rookie contracts," which can only be filled by rookies to encourage drafting and signing them.

7) Limits placed on maximum time you can have a player. After that time he would enter the FA pool.

8) Some leagues allow contracts to go to the trading teams, other do not. If you do not, then the player will go to the other team but only under contract for the current year. He will then have to be given another contract or go into FA.

Chapter 23 Offensive Skill Positions (QB, RB, WR and TE) – How to find the sleepers or breakout players

Different studies use different definitions of stud, breakout player, sleeper, etc., so it is hard to determine the best method for finding one of these players. Some studies looked at 1st round NFL picks only, others looked at just 1st and 2nd round picks, still others looked at all rounds. Some studies for sleeper analysis called sleepers "any player who performed better than last year," still others said the player had to be unknown. Breakout definitions were even more all over the place. Five TDs for WRs were breakout criteria in one study, still another used 1200 yards. The differences between just those two is Top 5 to Top 25. So your definition of stud, sleeper and breakout player will have a lot to do with how well you find them. Below are some generalizations on the terms and how best to find the players. The chapter ends with some generalizations on the starters and some nice-to-know information on them.

Who is a Stud?

Different people have different definitions. Some say they must have two or more Top 5 seasons or one Top 5 season and two or more Top 10 seasons. This prevents the one-year-wonders from making the lists. The point is that a stud should be a top 5 player, or at least a Top 5 player who may occasionally slip into the top 10. I prefer to define a stud as someone with three Top 5 seasons, with two Top 5 Seasons and 2 Top 10 seasons or with 5 Top 10 seasons. This prevents the two-year-wonders from making the list, as with QBs Jeff Blake and Kurt Warner. Some say a stud is anyone in the top 25% of starters. So if 12 QBs and 12 TEs start then the top 3 are studs. If 24 RBs start then the top 6 are studs. If 36 WRs start then the top 9 are studs. Why do you care? Never bench a stud unless he is hurt or benched. That advice makes owners ask: Who is a stud? So the Top 3 QBs and TEs, Top 5 RBs and the Top 10 WRs are all studs. I would expand the RBs to Top 10 as studs, simply due to scarcity. Another way to look at it is the first two draft picks you made are studs. Maybe the top three draft picks, depending on how well you drafted or how many teams are in the league.

Who is a sleeper?

A sleeper is someone who is relatively unknown and who performs much better than their draft position. So what defines "performs much better?" A QB in the middle of the pack who finishes in the Top 5. A WR drafted in the last half of the draft who finishes in the Top 10. I say to be a sleeper he has to be drafted in the bottom half of the fantasy starters and finish in the top 40%. Some say sleepers are usually found as a late round draft pick or a waiver wire pickup? I disagree with the waiver wire candidate being a sleeper. If you thought he was going to break out then why not draft him? I am sorry but picking up a player that does well early on does not give you the bragging rights to call him your "sleeper pick." Some say that a veteran who has fallen out of favor can be a sleeper as long as no one really expects him to do well in the first place, so the relatively unknown part of the definition may need to be replaced too.

The key is to have at least ten sleeper picks ranked in order of expected draft position. That way when someone steals a sleeper or two it will not destroy your whole sleeper plan. Having just two or three sleepers and seeing them taken before you can pull the trigger is a bit demoralizing. Of course, the later the round you take a sleeper the more the payoff if he performs (because hopefully you picked someone with value ahead of him, rather than grabbing your sleeper a round earlier).

Sleepers give you a chance to break away from the other teams. This sets you apart and gives you a better chance of winning a championship. I do not know how many times I have seen an owner draft well but never gamble on a sleeper or two. This owner only makes the playoffs half of the time and never understands why I always make the playoffs. It is because I take a few gambles and when they payout it means I have a great player that no one expected. He usually gives me the extra edge I need to make the playoffs. The trick is finding the sleepers.

Tips for picking sleepers

1) Look for a window of opportunity. Does the starter have injury problems, contractual issues, off-the-field problems, fumbling problems? Is there a new coach or system to be used? Did the team add/lose another player (add stud RB/ lose WR#1) who can help? OL additions?

2) Avoid listening to the pundits. If everyone is saying player X is a sleeper then everyone will move him up their draft boards and he will not be a sleeper. Watch out for bandwagons and anointed sleepers, that is always a bad sign.

3) Use trends – WRs breaking out in third year, tall TE, etc.

4) Look for improving teams or teams with an easy SOS. Give end of season performance some credit. Did the player have a great second half last year? This might be a good indicator of things to come. Many teams will let some of their backups get some PT (playing time) in order to evaluate their talent. Perfect example, "Fast" Willie Parker played on week 17 in 2004 as a replacement for Jerome Bettis. The following year he became the starting RB.

5) More sleepers are of the young variety than the old variety. Look at 2nd or 3rd year players simply because they have had time to learn their systems and make the rookie mistakes. You are more likely to find a sleeper in someone who has not been in the league more than four or five years. If they have been playing longer they have had their chance and it probably has passed them by. There are exceptions to this, but for the most part go with youth for sleepers.

6) Trust your instincts. If you have played this game long enough and watched NFL football long enough you will develop your own gut reactions to certain things. Trust them.

Draft Steals and Busts

What is a "steal" in the draft? I like to think it is any player drafted two or more rounds below where he finished in the end of season rankings based on total fantasy points. If I drafted a WR in the 9th round with the 117th pick and he finishes 28 places higher or more, then he was a steal (89th overall in points scored; 7th round, 5th pick). Of course, the later you go in the draft the less VBD is used and the harder it is to use this method to validate draft picks.

A player who performs one round better than where he was picked would be considered a good pick. Again, in a 14-team league that would be a player who finishes 14 spots higher in the rankings than his pick.

An early (reach) pick would be a player who finishes a round further down the rankings.

A bust would be a player who finishes more than two rounds lower than he was drafted.

What is a "Breakout" Year?

Again, you have to determine what your definition of breakout is before you can really analyze who does what.

Some studies use 1000 yards and eight or more TDs. I think this is a good benchmark. That would put them roughly as a Top 15 RB or WR in most leagues, with 100 points for the yardage (1 point per 10 yards) and 48 more point for the TDs. History will show that 4-6 WRs are new to the Top 15 WRs from year to year. What about QBs? At least 20 TDs and 3200 yards is a Top 12 QB.

How do you find a breakout player?

QBs

1) QBs are most likely to break out in their 3rd and 4th years of play.

2) QBs who hold the clipboard for 1-2 years do better in a starting role.

RBs

1) RBs only need two things; talent and opportunity. Opportunity comes from having a good OL too.

2) Youth is everything to a RB. One of the three top drafted rookie RBs will break out. Most will break out in their 2nd-4th year, depending on opportunity. The first RB drafted in the NFL draft is a stud 80% of the time. The percentages drop pretty dramatically after that.

3) Second half wonders – RBs who had a good second half (increased their FPPG by 40% or more) will do well in the next year if they stay healthy and are a starter. Look for high yards per carry the previous season (4.2+), as this gets noticed by the coaches.

WRs

1) Look for a WR that had lots of receptions and good yardage the year before (50+ receptions and 850 yards). This is true for any WR, regardless of his years in the league.

2) Look for WRs in their 2nd-5th year (who are 1st round NFL picks) who had 40+ receptions, 2+ TDs, 400+ yards and that are the starters (WR1 or WR2) on their team. They should have a consistent QB throwing to them and be completely free of injury. WRs have a 25% chance of breaking out in either their 2nd, 3rd or 4th year. With a 75% chance of breaking out in one of those three years, the longer the career the greater the chance of

having a breakout year. Some break out in the 5th year as well, but breakout seasons after that are rare.

3) Rookie WRs rarely (5% of the time) break out. Rookies who do well in their first year (50+ receptions and 700+ yards) tend to break out the next year.

4) Many first year QBs will concentrate on one WR they can trust and go to him often during the season. This WR is usually on the same side as the passing hand of the QB; if he is right handed, then the WR on his right side will more than likely be his go-to guy. QBs learn to spread the ball around more as they get more experience.

5) Look for breakaway speed. Every WR in the NFL should be able to catch the ball; if the couldn't, they wouldn't have been drafted. But few have the acceleration that qualifies as breakaway speed.

6) Look for a WR with confidence. Think Chad Johnson, T.O., S. Smith and M. Harrison. Notice I did not say cocky arrogance. (Marvin would not be mentioned if I had) No, it is confidence and that confidence is displayed in various forms. The WR has to run down the field and at high speed catch a projectile hurled at him while avoiding 11 other humans trying to knock his block off. To do this play after play you need confidence. That confidence can be displayed by pulling out a Sharpie after a TD, sending your opponent Pepto-Bismol or simply getting up to hand the referee the ball like you could do this another thousand times. All the great ones have the confidence.

7) Finally, look for dedication to the craft. Look for the WRs who arrive early and stay late; the ones who practice in the off-season with their QB or take extra time before every game to practice with their QB (Harrison and Wayne). These are the ones who will provide consistent performance because it is hard to catch a pigskin thrown from a human being unless you practice it.

8) Second half wonders – WRs who had a good second half (increased their FPPG by 40% or more) will do well in the next year if they stay healthy and are a starter.

Easiest way to predict a breakout WR:
1) Start with only #1 and #2 WRs (32 x 2=64 candidates)
2) Who is the QB? Is it the same one as last year and is he a Top 15 QB? If yes, both WRs advance to the next level. (2 x 13=26) Some of the Top 15 may not be on the same teams.
3) Eliminate some teams because last year was a fluke. With this eliminator, you will lose an average of three teams. (26-6 players =20 WRs)
4) Of the remaining WRs, the ones in their 2nd-5th season who were not in Top 15 last year are your candidates. The more experienced they are, (5th year being the most experienced), the higher they should be ranked.

TEs
1) 2nd-4th year TE
2) On a team with no "go-to WR" or combo WRs (Good WR1 and WR2)
3) Good offense
4) Where he is starter and has good hands
5) Characteristics: 6' 4" and 250 lbs.

Breakdown players

RB – 30 years or older

WR – 34 seems to be the average age where WRs start to lose production. (Jerry Rice is one well-known exception to this rule.)

Overall Advice for QB, RB, WR and TE

6' 2"- 6' 5" and 210-230 pounds is the typical QB or WR. TEs are a little taller (2") and heavier (30 pounds).

Quarterbacks –

Most of the top QBs are not worth the money you pay for them. P. Manning is the one exception and even he disappointed some the year after he broke Dan Marino's record. I like P. Manning because he always plays so I do not need a good backup which makes him a valuable stud QB. Having said that, you can get some real steals in the late rounds of the draft assuming you are not in a 14- or 16-team league or have some "start two QBs" rule, etc.

Things to watch: Who is he throwing it to? How is the offensive line? What is his defense like (will he get the ball back a lot)?

You can wait on drafting a QB and still get one as good (if not better) than the one you passed on. (Wait till 8th or 9th round.) Studies have shown that if you wait to draft your QB and end up with QB5+QB19 you sacrifice 12% of the possible QB1+QB8 points. In other words, you lose 12% of the FPs at your QB position, but you hopefully make that up in the higher draft picks you have to devote to other positions. Waiting till everyone else has their QB then grabbing both of yours, QB12 and QB13, costs you 14% of the top QB FP, but only a few points more than QB5+QB19. Waiting till everyone has their QB and about half have a backup (Q18/19) and then getting your one QB costs you 22% of the Top QB FPs. Three QBs do not offer more points than any of the two QB combos, so drafting three QBs is not worth it unless you are in a start two QBs league. If you are going to draft a Top 3 QB, great, but the next best strategy is to wait and get the 10th-12th best and pair them up with another QB thereafter.

Top 10 QBs tend to be 6' 4"-6' 5" and weigh 225 lbs. QBs are more likely to rush for lots of yards and TDs in the first five years of their career. After that the wear and tear and sense of survival takes over. QBs tend to bloom at 26 or 27 years old, or four or five years into their career; about the time when they stop rushing so much and stay in the pocket. Evaluate young QBs by when they throw on 3rd and long (5 yards or more). Do they complete their passes? That will tell you something about how well they are going to do in the future in the NFL. If they do not complete them they will not be in the NFL for very long. Finally, stay away from rookies and even second year QBs, who do not generally fair too well. Injury affects this position more than you think. Most QBs miss a few games during the year (P. Manning and B. Favre are exceptions to this rule).

Running Back –

This is your franchise. Watch to see if he is an every down running back or just plays on 1st and 2nd downs. Does he get the goal line carries or does he have some vulture waiting to snatch those TDs from him? Does he catch balls well out of the backfield (B. Westbrook, Steven Jackson)? Is he stable on and off the field? Does he have a good potent offense (Indianapolis, New England) or does the team always find itself behind at halftime (Detroit Lions, Houston Texans)? What is his defense like?

RBs get hurt the most so plan accordingly. Betting the ranch on one stud RB may not be the best game plan because injury could strike him at any time. Goal line vultures will be worth something in TD-only leagues but not much beyond that. Avoid the RBBC. Injuries are the most common cause of an RBBC approach, except for the Denver Broncos who always seem to use an RBBC approach. Don't be too afraid of a rookie RB because they can learn their position more quickly than any other scoring position in the NFL. Do, however, watch the inevitable rookie hype (hint: overpriced). Historically, less than 50% of the top 3 RBs have repeated in the next year. Bottom line – do not give away the store on the top 3 "consensus" RBs whether it is in an auction and you pay top dollar or in a dynasty league and you trade for them. Chances are if you pay top dollar you will not get top dollar production back.

The typical Top 10 RBs are usually around 5' 11" and 220 lbs. Avoid RBs over 30 as most RBs who make it to their 10th year do not do as well. (Tiki Barber and John Riggins are the exceptions). RBs can be power-oriented (run-you-over type backs) or cutback runners. Big RBs that do not share time can be traded early, before they get dinged up, as they will start to falter in the second half of the season. Big RBs who share time should be saved for the stretch run as they tend to do better in the second half. RBs that are involved in the passing game tend to do as well, if not better, in the second half of season. Rookie RBs tend to outperform in the second half of the season as well.

Wide Receivers –

Lots of variation here. If you play in a TD-only league, forget about it. After the first 10 or 12 you lose all hope of consistent production for your money. Look for a great QB and the consistency that only the Top 10 can provide. The next thirty are anyone's guess and can be had for about the same amount, depending on who is making up the cheat sheets. Usually it takes 2-3 years in the NFL for players to get comfortable at this position and one year to learn a new teams system. WRs tend to break out in their 2nd or 3rd year. WRs tend to drop out of the Top 10 in their 7th or 8th year. The Top 10 WRs tend to be 6' tall and 200 lbs. They are generally not as tall as TEs, but recently tall WRs have become stars.

What kind of WR? There are two types of WRs, speed and possession. Possession receivers do not have the speed to get open deep but are surer-handed. They are the ones crossing the middle of the field, getting lots of receptions and some yardage but not as many TDs. Generally the older a receiver the more he becomes a possession receiver and must learn to find the seams in a defense and "sit down" in a scheme to catch the underneath balls. The speed (or long ball or TD) WR will stretch the field and go deep more often, thus he will have more TDs and longer yardage TDs. They will generally be the younger WRs.

Tight End –

Same criteria as WR. Same time to learn systems. Only a few top TEs around after Top 5; more choices now at 6-10 TE. After that, wait. The top ranked TEs perform consistently and prove more valuable. Expect them to go in the 3rd-5th rounds.

Chapter 24 Injuries

The human body is a wonderfully designed system. I am constantly amazed at how well everything functions. However, when we ask it to do tremendous things like running very fast, jumping high or colliding with four or five men weighing 350 pounds bent on ripping our head off, then the body will sometimes fall to these pressures and become injured. Other injuries can occur because a player simply gets angry and bangs his fist or head against a wall.

Injuries are a part of fantasy football. Knowing the types of injuries and their consequences can be a big advantage. Injuries will come into play before the season starts when evaluating players and ranking them. Your draft preparation may be influenced by decisions you make regarding players with injuries. During the season, your start/bench decisions will always require medical know-how. Likewise, any trade or free agent/waiver wire transaction can be impacted by a player's injury or recovery from an injury. Finally, in the off-season, owners in leagues with keeper options will want to know about players and their injuries and possible outcomes from them.

Injuries happen. Minor injuries include sprains, bruises and pulled muscles. These should be expected. Major injuries can be career-ending (broken neck). The key is to know which are which, how much time is expected to be missed and how the injury may affect the player in the future. Can he play with it? Can he play as well as before with it? Will he be out for the rest of the season with it? These are the tough questions that can change a season's outcome.

Some players are iron men and play regardless of their injuries. Laveranues Coles is one such player. In 2006 he played every game even though he was listed as questionable on many occasions. He finished with 91 receptions, 1098 receiving yards and 6 TDs. Todd Heap is another such player. He played every game, was hurt all season, and still had 73 receptions, 765 receiving yards and 6 TDs. He fought through injuries on a weekly basis as he was listed on the team injury report for 13 of 16 games. Back, ankle, thigh, ankle again, thigh again and foot; you name it, he had it hurting. Week 3 of 2006 he was a game time decision with an injured ankle and did not know if he could play. He played; the result: 5 catches, 36 yards and a TD. At one point in 2006 he was questionable for four weeks in a row and averaged five passes per game. Of course in 2004 he missed 10 games with a high ankle sprain. Go figure. Have you heard the old joke: Todd Heap has been so banged up that I thought his last name was questionable for the past four years (Todd Heap-Questionable).

In general there is a relationship between a player's age and his injuries. As he ages he gets more injuries. Volatility is a good proxy for risk. Some leagues do not account in any special way for injuries. Others have IR rules, while other leagues give waiver wire priority to teams with players who just went on IR. The most common injury rules are the "team QB or kicker" rules and additional IR spots on a roster. Some say the biggest single factor in fantasy football success is avoiding injuries. The only way to do that is to know more about injuries and what causes them.

NFL Injury Reports

The NFL releases weekly injury reports but that information comes from the team. Injury reports are fluid lists. They change from Wednesday to Friday to Saturday to Sunday morning to game time, so be wary of some of the information. Some coaches may list an injury and say it is more serious than it is, hoping his opponents do not plan for that player. Others underestimate the injury so that opponents waste time game-planning for that player. You need to know the coaches and the players they are talking about. Keyshawn Johnson plays, Laveranues Cole plays and Todd Heap plays. Tennessee head coach Tony Fisher has a habit of listing every player who is dinged up as questionable or out every week. There is a big difference between a player having an injury and whether that player plays the game. Avoid NFL sites for this information and find a good source that can tell you reliably what will happen.

The NFL has four terms it asks coaches to use in categorizing injuries. They are PROBABLE, which means the player has a 75% chance of playing. QUESTIONABLE, which means he has a 50% chance of playing. DOUBTFUL, which means (you guessed it) he has a 25% chance of playing that week. The last term is OUT and that means he will not play that week. Caveat: there have been a few rare instances where a player is listed as OUT but played anyway. Teams and coaches can get into big trouble if this happens because they are required to provide information to the betting public and bad information may alter the odds in one way or another. So if a team says a player is "OUT," you can trust them on that. This is not to say that you should believe the other three terms without any question.

CBS, Fox and ESPN all have a ticker on their pre-game shows that tells the weather and injury status for each of the games. Xpertsports also has a good up-to-date listing of actives/inactives prior to kick off. Also see Appendix A Websites under Injuries.

Many injuries are graded on a scale of 1-3 with one the least severe and three the most serious.

Concussions

QBs, WR and TEs tend to have the most concussions. Some of the effects are nausea, dizziness and memory loss. That is why you see the team trainers asking the QB, who just took a hit to the head, some questions before allowing him back in the game. If the QB keeps asking where his dog Fluffy is, that is a bad sign. More than one concussion can have the possibility of brain damage. This is one of the reasons the NFL has gotten tough on QB hits lately. Steve Young retired early because of the concussions he suffered at QB.

Fractures

It is critical to assess where the break is and how serious it is. For example, stress fractures can be played through in many cases because they are just small cracks in the bone. Some players play with broken bones too. L. Coles plays ever week with a broken toe since corrective surgery may end his career if he elects to have it done. Surgery may include plates or pins and would count him out for the season. You also need to know the location of the broken bone. Is it the QB's throwing hand? Ouch –count him out. Is it the defensive lineman's hand? If so, he can wear a cast and still be somewhat effective. Is it the WR's hand? He is out. Is it a finger, like T.O. had? Maybe he can play. Is it the QB's non-throwing hand? I'd go ahead and play him.

Hyperextended Elbow

QBs are impacted by this frequently. This bending back of the elbow may require up to two weeks recovery time, but even then beware. The QB will have lost some of his mechanics and timing. It may be longer before he is back up to 100% even once he takes the field.

Ligament/Tendon Injuries

Ligaments are cable-like structures which hold our bones together and allow players to run and move without falling apart. Ligaments are flexible but only to a certain point. A torn or "strained" ligament is really millions of tears of these tiny pieces. Twisting a knee, spraining a ligament or even whiplash can tear or fray these connective structures. Inflammation is actually part of the healing process to repair the injured ligament. Symptoms of healing are pain, swelling, and inability to move the joint.

Tendonitis is the inflammation of a tendon. Tendons are the white tissues that connect muscle to bone. If they are overused or impacted by injury they can cause acute pain, especially in the shoulder. Players usually recover in two weeks with rest. Symptoms are sharp pains, tenderness, swelling and restricted movement of the affected area.

Knee injuries are the most common NFL injury. Of the four ligaments in the knee (ACL, PCL, MCL and LCL), the ACL tends to have the most injuries.

1) ACL or anterior cruciate ligament – This ligament is in the middle of the knee and provides stability to the joint (holds the femur and tibia in place). The ACL stabilizes the knee during deceleration. This is important. Tears of the ACL are the worst kind and can take up to two years of recovery. Players who come back in a year may not be the same. Artificial turf accounts for many ACL injuries.

2) PCL or posterior cruciate ligament – Located in the middle of the knee, this ligament works with the ACL to resist force.

3) MCL or medial collateral ligament – Located on the inside of the knee, this ligament resists forces that push the knee medially, or toward the body. A grade 3 injury can require 5-6 weeks recovery time.

4) LCL or lateral collateral ligament – Located on the outside of the knee, this ligament resists forces that push the knee laterally, or away from the body. Injuries to the LCL are rare.

In regards to knee injuries, grade 1 is a stretch or strain and will require rest, grade 2 is a partial tear and grade 3 is a complete tear, requiring surgery to repair.

Shoulder injuries

1) Rotator cuff – This occurs when the muscles or tendons surrounding the shoulder tear from the bone. If it is a partial tear then recovery consists of a few weeks of rest. If the

muscles or tendons are completely separated from the bone then surgery will be necessary. This injury affects QBs the most and can reduce long pass distance and speed.

2) Dislocated Shoulder – A dislocated shoulder is a more extensive injury in which the upper arm bone (humerus) pops out of its cup-shaped socket. Many times as long as there are no tears, a dislocated shoulder can be "popped" back into place. However, if ligaments are torn they will have to be reattached with shoulder surgery. Again, the player would be out for 3-4 months. This injury occurs more to players in the defensive secondary.

3) Separated Shoulder – A stretch or tear of the ligaments of this joint — often due to a fall directly on the shoulder — is known as a separated shoulder

Sprains/Strains

Sprains affect ligaments and strains affect muscles and tendons. The definition of a sprain is to overstrain or wrench the ligaments of an ankle, wrist, or other joint, so as to injure without fracture or dislocation. Sprains are frequently caused by rapid changes in direction or by a collision. Common locations for sprains are your ankles, wrists and knees. The definition of a strain is a wrenching, twisting, and stretching of muscles and tendons. This type of injury often occurs when muscles suddenly and powerfully contract or when a muscle stretches unusually far. This is called an acute strain. Overuse of certain muscles over time can lead to a chronic strain. People commonly call muscle strains "pulled" muscles. Hamstring and back injuries are among the most common strains.

1) Sprained Ankle – This very common injury occurs when the foot is bent beyond its normal range and some of the ligaments within the ankle are torn. Once you sprain your ankle, recovery time can vary from one week to several months depending on the severity of the sprain. If a player has suffered a sprained ankle before, it is more likely to reoccur.

2) A high ankle sprain is a tear of the ligament above the ankle. Recovery time is much longer than for a sprained ankle because the ankle has to remain immobile for the recovery process. Earlier recoveries may result in less production potential or with a higher potential for re-injury. As with most injuries, there are three levels or grades. Grade 1 usually doesn't require any time out. Grade 2 may require a cast and 2-6 weeks out. Grade 3 requires surgery and probably a screw or pin and results in the end of the season for that player. Of course, all cases are different and can vary somewhat based on a player's pain tolerance and how fast he heals.

Turf Toe

Turf toe is an injury to the base of the big toe. It usually occurs when the toe is jammed into the artificial turf (it can occur on grass too) and bent too far back. Quick movements or direction changes often cause this injury. The main symptom is the inability to run. Time is the best healer. Some players continue to play with this nagging injury, resulting in a degradation of performance. In severe cases, surgery may be required.

Pulled Muscles/Hamstrings

One of the more common injuries is the pulled hamstring. A hamstring injury occurs when there is a tear of the muscle group that helps your knee bend and straighten when running. These muscles are at the back of the thigh and run all the way down to the shinbone. Hamstring injuries can result in various conditions. Pulled hamstrings are nagging injuries, which can keep a player out of play or hinder his performance on the field for weeks. Grade 1 consists of the smallest of tears (0-3 weeks out). Grade 2 has a greater number of muscle fibers torn which results in more pain and tenderness (1-5 weeks out). Grade 3 is a complete tear of some or all of the muscles in that group. In some cases if the tendon that attaches the muscle to the bone is torn then surgery will be required (season-ending injury). Symptoms include mild swelling and a noticeable loss of strength. Other symptoms are bruising, spasms and the loss of muscle function in that area. WRs seem to have the most hamstring problems, but RBs and TEs are also affected. The guys in the trenches (OL and DL) tend to tear biceps, triceps or pectoral muscles.

Hernias

In many cases hernias are injuries in the groin area or higher in the stomach region. Hernias are essentially tears in the body where internal organs can poke through. This can cause intense pain but on an irregular basis. If a hernia is serious then surgery will be required immediately and the player will be out for a large part of the season. Less serious hernias (where the organs can be pushed back into place) will require surgery in the off-season.

Sports hernias are a muscle tear near the pubic bone. Linemen tend to suffer these hernias most often. Strains are easier to play with than tears. Medications can counteract the pain so that a player can play with a sports hernia but eventually surgery will be required to correct the problem, bringing with it a recovery time of several months.

Meniscus Injuries

We might as well say knee injuries here. There are two meniscuses in each knee that serve as shock absorbers so the bones do not rub together. The meniscus is often torn when the foot is planted and the body tries to rotate. This tear creates bone fragments which irritate the knee joint. Symptoms include swelling, pain or the knee locking up. Arthroscopic surgery will be required to remove the loose particles from the knee. Arthroscopic surgery is where a doctor uses instruments to look inside the joint and clean out loose bone or trim cartilage. It can be used to repair tendons and ligaments as well. Players will recover quickly as long as there are no complications with the "scoping" of the knee. However, if the meniscus continues to disintegrate more particles will continue to cause problems.

Neck/Spinal Injuries

These can come in many forms. Pinched or stretched nerves are usually called stingers or burners. Stingers/burners can cause numbness or sharp pain in the extremities and may leave players unable to play. These types of injuries are more likely to happen again, so this problem can be especially detrimental to playing time. A player may miss from 1-4 weeks with a stinger. Bulging or herniated disks are painful and can cost a player an entire season. Beware of neck and spinal injuries, as they are some of the more dangerous.

Conclusions

Future advances in technology include minimally invasive ACL surgery. Current knee surgeries require an incision that is about an inch long. The player will not have to wear a cast or brace and can put weight on the leg right away. Regeneration of ACLs and rotator cuffs are the future. The technology in orthopedics will only get better and better.

Injuries will occur. That is why you need more than just your starting lineup during the season. The draft provides your best method of getting bench depth. Trades and transactions provide your other avenue of acquiring depth. Statistically speaking, studies have shown that QBs will miss three games, RBs two games and WRs only one game a year on average, due to normal wear and tear. If a player was previously injured, his chances of playing a full 16-game season are less than a player who has never been hurt. To sum it up, if a player has been hurt before, chances are he will be hurt again.

Injury Tips

Do not start "doubtful" or "out" players. It is very simple, straightforward advice. This is not to say that occasionally your stud will be listed as doubtful and then go on to score a zillion points on your bench. Such is life. More often than not though he will not play or will play to such a limited or injury plagued degree that he is not worth starting. If I play a doubtful player it is because he is a stud who has been upgraded at game time and I have no other replacement.

Questionable players should be started unless you have a good enough (equal) backup or a lesser player with a great matchup. Probable players should play unless you have an equal player that can replace them. Some players listed as probable do not play (DNP). I usually bench questionable players until I hear more on game day. Start them if you do not have an equal replacement. If your player is questionable and you have no replacement, then you can do a FA pickup; but don't drop the injured player necessarily (especially if he is a stud). Drop one of your sleepers who has not panned out. Questionable players play in about 60% of their games (a little more than the 50 percent advertised by the NFL). On average, even if your player does play when his status is questionable, his performance will suffer. NOTE: there are exceptions, but on average, his stats will suffer if listed as questionable. What is the drop in stats? If he is a QB expect fewer TDs but about the same yardage. If a RB or WR, expect half as many TDs and a drop in yardage. Players listed on the injury report in previous weeks and then downgraded to "questionable" are not good starters. Nor are players who do not practice on Thursday or Friday; unless they are someone like S. McNair or T. Owens. How a player handles the days after the game is just as important as the game itself with regards to injuries.

1) Note what decisions you have made and keep them handy while watching the pre-game shows, so you know if you need to make any adjustments based on injury upgrades or downgrades.

2) Injuries become even more significant in December when you are trying to reach the playoffs or win your championship in the playoffs. Players are more tired, have nagging injuries and are more likely to get hurt in December games. Don't take chances on injured players in December. Play it extra safe toward the end of the season as far as starting questionable players.

3) Possible signs of the imminent decline of an IDP are back and lower leg injuries.

4) Two-year rule of injuries – For RBs with a significant leg (ACL, quad or knee) injury, you should wait two years before thinking they will be back to normal and thus be worthy of a high draft pick. Many RBs will struggle the first year back from a major leg injury. If they do okay in the following year it may be because they hurt it early in the season (or even preseason), thus giving them more time to fully recover. Also, if they have had the same or a similar injury before they may be better prepared to make the sacrifices for a quicker recovery. Bottom line: Let someone else take a gamble on these risky players in the hope that they return to their former glory. Instead target them next year after their poor return.

Injury Trends

A typical RB will be expected to miss two games per year on average. A RB that runs over defenders is more likely to get as much damage as he gives. RBs have the most injuries and the most "nagging" injuries. When I say nagging I mean the kind that makes their play iffy. Their stats if they do play become erratic at best and poor at worst. QBs are not too far behind RBs in terms of injuries but recent rule changes to protect the QB may see these numbers decrease in the next few years. A scrambling QB might as well put a crosshair on his back and declare "open season." Conservative picks are RBs and QBs who are injury-averse (pocket passers, RBs who dodge the hits to save themselves) and risky picks are the players who expose themselves to injury risks. After the age of 30, many RBs will lose a step and start to break down with nagging injuries. For WRs the magic number is 32; for QBs, 35.

Having over 370 touches (count catches as ½ a touch since they are more likely to be tackled by lighter DBs and not three or four heavy linemen) seems to be the magic number for RBs to increase their potential for injury. RBs coming off a 370 touch season are more likely to miss games (at least one) than other RBs. You have a 50 percent chance of losing him for 1-3 games and a 25 percent chance of losing him for four or more games so… draft his HC or get more depth on your bench if you want to take a chance on someone who had a heavy workload last year. Also watch out for a breakdown from RBs if their carries increase significantly from the season before.

Careers in NFL

Table 24. 1 Average career lengths based on position

(http://www.dartmouth.edu/~chance/chance_news/recent_news/chance_news_11.02.html# item3)

Position	Career Length in Years
QB	6.96
RB	4.35

WR	4.54
TE	4.98
K	8.33
DT	4.71
DE	5.39
LB	5.50
CB	5.13
Safety	5.88
All positions It must be noted that this research was done for 1987-1996, so these numbers may have increased based on new medical insight, or they may have decreased due to bigger and tougher players.	5.33

**** On average a player will miss two games per year due to injury. Some will miss less, some will miss more, but the average is two games per year

QBs can have careers that are twice as long as a RB or WR simply by virtue of their protection from the wear and tear of being tackled every Sunday (See Table 24.1). WRs often will have 12+year careers whereas RBs tend to wear out after 7 or 8 seasons, usually around the age of 30. Studies also show that by the time a RB turns 30 (his 8th or 9th season) he is on the downside of performance. (My apologies to Emmitt Smith, one of the exceptions to the rule.) Most RBs have a 3-4 year productive career. Some will have more, but most do well for 3- 4 years before injuries take their toll. RBs who are over the age of 30 and have a bad year rarely make it back, they are usually done. A productive back over the age of 30 is just as likely to do well the next year, but eventually age will catch up. Some studies suggest that for every year you play you lose 100 rushes in your future career. So by the time you reach 27 (4-5 years of playing in NFL) you have lost 400-500 future rushes, basically a year or more worth of rushes. RBs who start late or who have some injuries or stars ahead of them that can delay their start,will have a better chance of lasting longer.

Chapter 25 Miscellaneous

We have covered the basics: rankings, players, draft day tips, advanced draft strategies (both traditional draft and auction draft). We explored roster management (lineups, trades, FA), rule variations, commissioner information, IDP and keeper leagues. What is left? Good question. Fantasy football myths for one. Which are true and which are false? What about a common league; is there such a standard?

Percentages

Play the percentages. You hear those words of wisdom all the time from the veterans of fantasy football. All of these statistics are probabilities and are not infallible year after year. They are the percentages. FF is not an exact science, but you can use the percentages to put your team in the most favorable position possible and thus give your team the best chance of winning. Do not bet the ranch on any of the numbers mentioned in this book because sometimes the roulette wheel of life comes up double zero. Play the percentages and the majority of the time you will come out a winner.

Fantasy Football Myths

Some are true. Some are false. Some we just do not know. You must make the call. That is why you get paid the big bucks to run the fantasy team.

1) Small RBs (under 210 lbs) cannot take the pounding of the 300-pound NFL defensive players and thus cannot handle a 16-game season. Do not count on them as starting RBs for the entire season. You need a big RB like Shaun Alexander (218), Jamal Lewis (231), Larry Johnson (228), LaDainian Tomlinson (222) or Steven Jackson (233). **False.**

Tiki Barber (200), Clinton Portis (204), Brian Westbrook (200) and Warrick Dunn (180) are all under the mythical 210 pounds and have played for many seasons in the NFL. Portis had a shoulder injury in 2006 but that was because he tried to run over a defensive player returning a turnover. Tiki, Warrick and Brian all had relatively injury-free 2006 seasons.

2) Rookies are not worth drafting. **True.**

Only rookie RBs are worth drafting in redraft leagues. Studies have shown that of the rookies drafted in the first two rounds of the NFL draft, only 6% of the QBs, RBs, WRs and TEs would finish in the top 10 of their positions. Approximately 14% would finish in the top 20 (although the top 20 for a QB and TE does not amount to much). Only one QB in the last eight years has been drafted in the first two rounds and gone on to be a top 10 QB, Peyton Manning. He represents about 3% of all the QBs drafted. I think Vince Young was close in 2006 as he finished 11th in 15 starts. Let's just say that rookie QBs are not a good choice on draft day for redraft leagues. There has only been one Peyton Manning in the past eight years but there have been a lot more busts. Somewhere close to 20% of rookie RBs are Top 20 quality and another 20% are Top 35. That means that close to 40% of the rookie RBs drafted in the first two rounds will be in the top 35 their first year (or worthy of starting). Clearly you have a better chance at a starter with a RB than a QB.

Only about 12% of WRs make the Top 35. Only 6% make the Top 20 (think R. Moss and A. Boldin). In any given year roughly 10 WRs will be drafted in the first or second NFL rounds and only one will make the Top 35; if he does, he has a good chance of being in the Top 20. If you find that gem he is rewarding, but nevertheless the chances are slim that you will draft him. Only a few rookie TEs make it into the Top 10. On average only 10% of rookie TEs are good enough to make the Top 10 each year. I believe the higher up in the NFL draft a player is drafted the better he will be his rookie year (except QBs) if he gets a chance to start. I have to think that all the high paid NFL scouts know something or they would not have their jobs. Remember that many QBs are not started unless the primary gets hurt, in which case they are rushed into a bad situation and should not do as well. QBs need more time to learn defense blitz schemes and packages, etc., so avoid rookies on principle. If you are going to take a chance, then the highest drafted rookies should do better and RBs are most likely to shine. Reggie Bush in 2006 would be a perfect example of a Top 10 rookie RB.

Why is this? If you think about it, there are only 32 NFL teams, but many more college teams (over 100 Division 1A schools), so there is quite a lot of talent trying to break into the NFL. Not to mention the players in the Arena league, NFL Europe, CFL and on the teams themselves and their practice squads. There are lots of great players trying to get their shot in the NFL. Combine this with defenses that have experienced defenders familiar with playing at the NFL level and you can see why it may take some time to adjust to the speed and complexity of the NFL and to beat out all the other people vying for a job. These rookies may have been studs in college but they were playing against opponents who were not NFL-type players. They could afford to not run precise routes and make it up with their speed or athletic ability. Not so in the NFL. In addition, the NFL is a job with more weight room training, film study and a very complex offensive scheme. Players have to adjust to this new mentality of complete dedication to their new job. Some do, some do not.

3) Third-year WR theory – It takes two years in the NFL to develop a feel for a system and get a QB rhythm going; thus most WRs break out in their third year. **Depends.**

This depends on what your definition of breakout is? Different studies have used different stats and different criteria to uncover different rules of thumb. Some say 2-4 years, others say 4 years for a potentially good WR to go to consistently great. Still others say it depends on the QB throwing to him. Is he a good WR to begin with? Some studies only looked at WRs drafted in the first three rounds of the NFL draft.

4) Players who are in the final year of their contract will play better. **False.**

First, what is an unrestricted FA and a restricted FA? Unrestricted free agents have played four or more years and when their contracts expire they are free to go anywhere. Restricted free agents have played three seasons and when their contract expires they can talk to other teams, but if another offer is made the original team gets a chance to match it.

Some believe that a player in the last year of his contract will put up better stats than in his previous years. The reasoning is because he wants to show the other 31 teams, and his own, just what he can do in order to get a more lucrative contract. Every year in the NFL is a tryout. If you do not perform in this league, you will not start. So no, I am not buying it. Yes a player may try to give a little extra effort, but he needs to do that anyway just so he will not get benched.

5) Statistics are better the more years you examine. **False.**

Three years may be the best because it incorporates the latest data and trend data. One year is too short and five years is too long since rule changes or style changes may not be reflected in the older data and could possibly skew the results.

6) RBs with 350 or more touches the previous year do not do as well next season. Don't forget catches and postseason. So 400 may be a better number to look at. Studies have shown that RBs with over 400 touches normally do not perform as well the next season. **True.**

This can be explained by several things:

A) Regression to the mean. A decrease in workload thus touches and opportunity is to be expected after a season with extended carries. B) Perhaps the coach will intentionally limit his touches next season to "save" him. C) The RB probably had a healthy season the year before when he had lots of carries and the season after the workload he just had his fair share of nagging injuries.

7) RBs with more of a workload in their past are more likely to wear out because of it. **False.**

 Studies show that if a RB does have a high workload it is because he can handle it. If you are faced with two RBs of the same age and one has had lots of touches and the other has not, do not feel like you have to go with the less worked RB for the long-term. In fact, there is probably a good reason why he has not had as many touches and that reason is usually athletic ability. There is no reason to think that he will wear out and not have as long a career as the other RB of the same age with less touches. This is definitely something to remember in keeper leagues.

8) Avoid RBs over 30. **True.**

There are always exceptions, but some studies have found that RBs peak at age 30 +/-1.5 years. Of course it depends on if you use modern-day stats, whether you include all RBs or just great RBs, etc. The average age of a RB's quality production ends at 30. They miss an average of two games a year. They carry the ball an average of 275 times a year. They will play for an average of 12 years but only the first 10 will be productive in terms of quality. Considering that they start at age 21 or 22 (some skip some college years), this adds up. Most quality RBs start in either their second or third year and never look back.

9) Kickers on poor red zone offenses produce more. **False.**

More Top 10 kickers come from average to slightly above-average red zone teams. The poor red zone teams generally do not get there that often and when they do they turn it over. The average to slightly above-average teams will drive into the red zone more and thus get into FG position more (outside the 20-yard line) and score more.

10) Don't draft Big Ten RBs as they are complete busts in the NFL. **True.**

It seems that, with few exceptions (Eddie George and Robert Smith excepted, and even Robert Smith caused many an ulcer), they are doomed to failure. I have yet to explain this with logic.

"Sports Illustrated" Jinx

Whenever a player or team is featured on the cover of "Sports Illustrated" they are jinxed or will have bad luck. This demonstrable misfortune or decline is supposed to have occurred 941 times between 1954 and 2002. Hmmm... unable to dispute this one.

Madden Curse

EA Sports Madden Football is the best-selling sports title in electronic games history. Everyone with at least a little youth in their body and the slightest amount of football knowledge knows about the game. What many FF fans do not know is the Madden Curse. Whichever player (and his team) is featured on the cover of the John Madden game each year has a sub-par season the following year.

Prior to 2000, the Madden NFL game boxes all had John Madden featured on the cover. In 2000 Barry Sanders briefly shared the cover with John Madden before retiring; thus the curse was started. The game manufacturers had enough time to substitute Green Bay RB Dorsey Levens for Barry Sanders on later shipments of the game. Dorsey suffered from a lingering bad knee and GB finished 8-8 and out of the playoffs. Dorsey Levens was cut by Green Bay after that bad season. EA then started to have players exclusively on the cover. Eddie George, RB Tennessee Titans, was the first on the cover and he too had a sub-par year (939 Rushing yards, 3.0 yards per carry average and only 5 TDs). Tennessee finished 7-9 and missed the playoffs. In 2002, Minnesota Viking QB Dante Culpepper appeared on the cover and then suffered an injury-plagued year. He missed four full games and threw for 1300 less yards and 19 less TDs than the previous year. Minnesota finished 5-11, their worst record in 18 years. In 2003, St Louis Rams' RB Marshall Faulk appeared on the cover and suffered a terrible decline in performance with a injured ankle (430 less yards and 4 less TDs). The Rams finished at 7-9. Next up was Atlanta QB Michael Vick, who broke his fibula in preseason the day after Madden 2004 hit stores. Atlanta struggled to a 5-11 record as Vick missed the first 11 games. Madden 2005 debuted with Baltimore Ravens linebacker Ray Lewis who subsequently broke his wrist, missed one full game and had his first season with no interceptions. Philadelphia Eagles QB Donovan McNabb suffered multiple injuries during the 2005 season after posing for Madden 2006. Donavan had a sports hernia and missed seven games. Philadelphia finished 6-10. The most recent is Shaun Alexander, Seattle Seahawks RB, who broke his foot after a week 3 game and was out for six weeks after being on the cover of Madden 2007.

In 2006 the Madden game had a commercial in which Dallas Clark, TE for Indianapolis Colts, was featured. In the commercial he runs a crossing route across the middle and is tackled (okay, jacked UP) by two Philadelphia defenders. The play is repeated over and over as Clark grunts at the hit, and his face shows dismay to say the least. In week 12 Indianapolis played Philadelphia on Sunday night on national TV. You guessed it, Philadelphia strong Ssafety Sean Considine tackled Clark on a short pass and his knee was injured (his ACL, in fact). Clark missed four games after that, returning in week 17.

Who will be next? Should you draft them if they are on the next cover? Ignore this curse. The Madden games pick the best athletes; the ones at their peak. Naturally most will have a below expectations season after the honor. Injuries do happen in this game and the more you play the greater the chance for some injury to happen. Likewise, most of the players selected have been RBs, which suffer more injuries than most. Finally, of course the teams they play for will naturally suffer if these superstars do suffer some bad luck and have an injury. This is simply regression to the mean.

LT was rumored to be the next on the cover, but at press time it looked like Vince Young will be on the cover for Madden 2008. If he is injured it will be because he is a mobile QB with a porous OL (thus more of a injury risk). Or maybe, just maybe, he will break the curse since he will be the youngest player in terms of career on the cover. Time will tell.

What is the most common fantasy football league?

The most common is a 12-team, H2H, redraft league with a 16-man roster. Start: 1 QB, 2 RBs, 3 WRs, 1 TE, 1 K and 1 DEF/ST.

Chapter 26 Resources

When fantasy football first came into its own in the late 1980s and early 1990s, the owners had to dig and scratch through the print media to find information. At that time, the local newspapers near the NFL teams were the best sources of information. Statistics came from the box scores in the Monday and Tuesday paper. Printed newsletters were the service providers of that era. A weekly or monthly newsletter would appear in the mail. They informed you of predictions, strategy and team decisions and how they might affect your team. Today, the fantasy football information you choose to receive can arrive from any number of sources. Magazines, and to a much lesser extent, newspapers, provide an overview of the latest and greatest off-season events and predictions of the season to come. However, it is the Internet and TV that really provide continuous, up-to-the minute information for all levels of fantasy football enthusiasts. No matter what format you choose, the cost and quality will determine how happy you are with that service. Some refuse to pay for guidance; others swear by their premium pay site.

To pay or not to pay, that is the question. Do you need to pay to subscribe to a site that will provide you with FF information that in many cases can be tailored to your league's specifics? Or do you abstain from paying for information that is free on the Internet somewhere, and just do it all yourself? For those who do it themselves, their argument is that it is all free somewhere, you just have to find it. Many of the websites that support leagues also have excellent tools, databases and injury updates. Some of these features are free, still others you must pay a fee to receive or access. Those opposed point to league-specific rules (scoring or otherwise) that cannot be projected or accounted for in "custom cheat sheets." If pay sites appeal to anyone, it may be a newbie or someone who has limited time to do all the research involved.

If you are time-limited and decide to go it alone, I suggest you focus on doing your research later in the week, if transaction rules allow (i.e. not first come, first served on free agency or when a roster has to be submitted by Friday night every week). It is best to check on injuries on Saturday night or Sunday morning, when these decisions are more likely to be finalized. Also, some of the start/bench analysis that you may use to influence your decisions comes out on Fridays. Many recommend ESPN, YAHOO, CBSSPORTSLINE and AOL as their favorite free sites.

But are Yahoo and the others really free? In most cases, to get the live stats (which many owners end up getting) you have to pay $10 each or $100+ collectively. Therefore, you really are paying for a stat service. Why not just pay $60 up-front (by collecting an extra $5 per owner) and go with one of the early bird specials at the league management sites? That way you get live stats and can customize your league anyway you want. This is definitely something to think about. Everyone says there are free sites on the Internet; and there are. But most fantasy footballers will pay a little extra to get the live stats anyway. Therefore, the free sites end up getting $10 from each owner in this "free" system. The secret is out now.

The owners who advocate not paying for information will have a schedule like this: One month before the draft analyze team changes due to injuries, player and head coach changes and philosophy changes. Print out preseason depth chart. Print out last year's stats. Make notes of players on the rise and those on the way down and under or overvalued based on team information above. Make basic projections for each player at each position that needs to be ranked. Take the amount to be drafted (# of teams x {Starters + estimated bench}). Add 3 more for mom and the kids since injuries and suspensions and retirements do happen. So in a 12-team league starting one QB and one as a benchwarmer; (12 x 2) +3 = 27 top QBs to rank. Once your preliminary rankings are done, compare to other's. If any player is very high or very low, reevaluate. During the season, use a few trusted free websites to get injuries and game time decisions and a few others for up-and-coming players/waiver wire info. Those who insist on not paying would rather die than hit the pay button to subscribe to a service. Some leagues have an honor system or an inherent code of conduct that states that if you pay for a premium service you are too "in the game for the money" and thus do not belong in the league. Besides, if someone else tells you who to pick and who to start how much fun is that?

However, those who subscribe to a service save time in getting the same info but without having to dig for it and lets face it, they get the same benefits (FPs) for finding that star. Most owners who dabble in the premium services do so because they are in multiple leagues with different scoring systems and/or have entered into some pay leagues outside of their local league. They would have scowled at the thought of a premium service when playing only in their local league ("that would be dishonest"). But since they want to play in more leagues and win more money, they have surrendered their souls to the "money" side of things and rationalize that they will make more by spending more. There is definitely a fine line between hobby and obsession. Watch out for the group think at the free services (Yahoo, ESPN, etc.) as they serve the masses so you may get some group think there versus thinking outside the box.

Get your information from a variety of different sources but do not get so many that you cannot check them all. To narrow down your choices, compare information from sites. Note the players involved, what was said and what was expected. Evaluate your sources and jettison ones that are slow, repetitive, or just plain wrong. You need to find reliable sources and ones that can take the information and speculate what its impact will be. Once you have a few trusted places, use them.

Remember that the so-called "experts" are just people like you and I who are trying to predict the future based on past results and the information at hand. There are no foolproof experts and the guys at the water cooler who play fantasy football long enough will know a lot about the NFL too. When you look at any source of information, whether it is a website, book or magazine; focus on the analysis, the explanation why. Is the author just trying to rationalize his answer or does he make a strong case?

There are so many FF magazines, websites and TV programs today, how do you pick the right one? We will discuss that next. No matter what media you choose, make sure the resource you choose "shows their work." Do not accept sites or magazines that just give you lists of names with no reasons why they are ranked where they are. Expect an explanation of why they are going to do well, bad or indifferently. What are the projections used? How many games played, etc.?

Fantasy Football Magazines

Some people insist that you do not need more than one magazine since there is so much free Internet information out there. In my opinion, you should purchase two FF magazines and only two. Be careful as you can become addicted to buying every fantasy football magazine in the search for more and better information. It starts in early June when the first magazines hit the store shelves. You rush out and get the first one, even though it is not your favorite. Then, a few weeks later, you get your favorite. The week after that you are out and see a better looking magazine and you pick that one up too. Every week there seems to be a different, better and newer magazine that is a must-have. On August 1, 2006, I counted 18 fantasy football magazines in a WaldenBooks store. Before you know it you have spent $100 and have ten magazines, one for every room in the house. Stop the madness. Focus on two magazines and only purchase two. I suggest one be your main magazine (I prefer Fantasy Football Pro Forecast, as explained below) and the other be your decoy or throw-away magazine. I will explain more about this magazine later.

Look for one that does some independent thinking. It should take a chance or two (and back it up with reasoning) rather than just churn out the same copy as everyone else. The most important thing about magazines: Remember they come out in early June so they have been published at best in early May, just after the NFL draft. **They will not be current.** You need to update them for injuries and player trades, etc. So why bother? They are expensive these days, with most cover prices in the $7-$10 range. Why buy two magazines at $17 when you just told me they were outdated? Why not use that money to go with a great web service that provides information for $25 and is always current? Good question! Call me old-fashioned but I like to hold something tangible in my hand. I also like to have it on trips so I can read something when I am away from the Internet. It just feels good to have a big magazine around. In addition, it makes you look more sociable. If you stay glued to the computer all the time, your wife, children or significant other may think you are obsessive. Try to avoid this. Buy two magazines. However, which ones?

The first rule to remember is that the first on the street is not necessarily the best on the street. If it appears in June, it is printed in early May. Second, avoid the sports magazines that just come out with a fantasy football issue ("Sports Illustrated" and ESPN special fantasy football issues come to mind), since they are only part-timers in the fantasy football game. If you are lucky they will have ten pages of fantasy information, but are most likely not going to include everything you want in a fantasy football magazine. Along the same lines, watch out for non-fantasy football magazines. These are football magazines with small fantasy sections, like "Lindy's Football." If fantasy football is not their business then skip them. Third, avoid magazines you have to buy twice. Why would you want to pay $6.95 each for two issues with about the same information, just a few months removed? You know, the ones that come out in June with an August issue and then again in August with a September issue. There is not much difference in the two magazines. The second issue was published in late July/early August to get on newsstands by early/middle August, so it is not the latest source of information either. It is better to pick a magazine that comes out in July but that updates itself via its own website or e-mail updates to registered purchasers of the magazine. Make sure the updates are often and go up until you draft. You want the latest and greatest before you head into that draft room. Finally, for my primary magazine I would skip the ones that do multiple sports. I think of this as spreading yourself too thin. If I go to a restaurant and they serve Thai, Italian and French food, how good are they really at each? Stick with a magazine that does fantasy football and nothing else, and has been doing it for a long time.

Personally, I think the two best magazines are "Fantasy Football Pro Forecast" and "Fantasy Football Index." Either one represents the best investment for your FF dollar. "Pro Forecast" is my favorite and I have been using it for more than ten years. What does it have? First, it has an article on the best player in the league that year (for 2006 it was Larry Johnson), which I generally ignore since it is the "so-called" experts picking their top choice. I don't listen to the experts. The rookie review is a good way to find out what others think this year's crop will do. Remember though, few rookies do well in their first year. However, in case you missed the draft you need to know where the rookies were drafted. Somewhere in the magazine they will talk about head coaching changes and offensive coordinator changes. This gives me fresh insight into what direction the team's offense may go this season. Do not forget about defensive coordinator changes and sometimes a QB coach can affect things too. I like the fact that "Pro Forecast" does not put this information in other places like "Team Information," etc. It is easy to find.

Next is the interview with the WCOFF champion. It is always good to get some scoop from the guy that won $200,000 and beat me last year. Know your opponent. There is always an SOS article and a quick reference chart that I can use to compare with my own or others. What makes their SOS article unique is that they look behind the numbers and breakdown matchups and players to determine how they will be affected. They also look at the critical playoff weeks.

There is always an article on draft strategy. I find this is the best way to keep up with current thinking on draft strategies. I do not always leap onboard the latest and greatest strategy, but I do like to know what others are thinking. The best thing about "Pro Forecast" is that you get multiple sources of cheat sheets. Not only do you get three individuals cheat sheets, but you also get different scoring systems (basic, combination), and some keeper league information too. In addition, 12 experts list their top 25 at each position and these results are averaged for an overall top 25 at each position. Talk about getting lots of mock drafts. This is the magazine for lots of opinions, rankings and picks. There are also the usual team reviews, but it gives OL reviews as well, which most magazines do not do. Auction values are addressed too. Very few magazines will even mention auction values. Finally, it will have a mock draft or two. The mock drafts are important because it gives an early glimpse into what this season's draft may bring. Nevertheless, be sure to check the scoring rules for the mock drafts to see how well they correspond with your scoring rules. So overall this is the best magazine for your money, in my humble opinion.

No matter what magazine you use, make sure it lists or ranks enough players at each position. For example, a 14-team league starting 3 WRs and a flex may need to draft 7 WRs per team (98 WRs). Any position at which you start only 1 player (TE, K and DEF), even though you are possibly only going to draft one from these positions, there may be other owners who are going to draft two (good on them) or three so... be ready with a ranking of at least two per team from each position, just in case. Team profiles are important in that they will give you insight into the coaching changes and off-season trades, who has a hot rookie waiting on the sidelines to replace him, etc. Read all the team profiles as they will help you build a picture of the divisions, and more importantly, the competition when it comes time to analyze the SOS. If magazines or websites do not mention IDP or auctions, I avoid them. They should rank IDPs and have auction values. If they do not, it means they are not serious enough about fantasy football, in my opinion. Depth charts are critical, but remember that they will be outdated. It is best to get them updated right before the draft so that you know who will play and who will be the backups. Look for a magazine that does updates via e-mail or a website. This way you can get current information to go along with that magazine.

Of course, a magazine must have the NFL regular season schedule, week by week, so that you can do your own SOS analysis. The schedule should also include bye weeks. The magazine must have last year's NFL stats broken down by position (with last three years, if possible). One article that some do not include is a list or discussion of players who have changed teams. Watch for this information since generally you will want to avoid these players (at least for the first half of the season). Inevitably, there will be an article or two on sleeper, or bust, candidates. File this information away as good-to-know and compare it with what others are saying. If the same player is on every sleeper list, then you know his value will increase and he may not be that much of a sleeper. In that case, he becomes a high risk/low reward player because you are paying excessively for the chance that he does prove to be valuable this year.

The other magazine should be your "decoy' magazine. This one should be the one that is most popular among the other owners in your league, or the one that comes out first at the local book stores. You want to have one magazine that others use (or you let them use) so that you can know what they think or use as their guide. Your "decoy" magazine can be left at the office for others to read, (be sure to highlight some players you will not draft, but do not tell the others this). The bottom line is that you want one magazine to be your guide ("Fantasy Football Pro Forecast" or whichever you choose) and another one to be your decoy. I like to use "Fantasy Sports Magazine" as my decoy since it comes out early and I subscribe to it, so it is mailed directly to my house. This fun, bright, popular magazine also keeps me informed about the NFFC.

Newspapers

What about newspapers? Do not get them just for their information. Everything they say is going to be on the Internet for free. The only advantage a newspaper may have is if local reporters are close to the team or follow the team and report something. In this case, local newspapers are a great source for scoops. However, even this news should be reported on a blog somewhere. I avoid the newspapers for the most part, although some still swear that you can pick up small little nuggets of information from these sources. I find it too time-consuming and rely on other people to dig through these pages for me.

TV and Radio:

Do you want the good news or the bad news? The good news is that there is more fantasy football awareness in the TV media than ever before. The bad news? It is mindless and very simple and should be ignored. Anything these days with "fantasy" in the title is 75 percent likely to be worthless to you. Instead of providing a quality fantasy football product it is more likely to be a rehash of "pick P. Manning as your QB and LT as your RB." Don't get me wrong, there is usually some eye candy on the screen giving you this advice, but I have better things to do with my time than having a cute blond read cue cards that talk down to the average fantasy footballer.

So what good programs are there in TV land? ESPN's Countdown, which comes on at 11 a.m. EST on Sundays, gives you an extra hour of information than the other pre-game shows. It also has Chris Mortensen (nice Danish name, as my wife always says) with injury updates. One technique is to tape it on DVD or DVR, and at 12:20 p.m. EST fast-forward it until Chris comes on and watch until he goes off again. Once he goes off, fast-forward again. Do this until 12:45, then get last-minute updates. Use this information to change/tweak your roster in the last few minutes before the kickoff. Why fast-forward it? Two words – Michael Irvin. He gets on my nerves. I find it hard to describe why. Maybe it is his hyperactive personality or his constant "taking up" for the players who have made mistakes. Whatever. I find that I tune out when he appears.

As far as the noontime (EST) pre-game shows, I admit to being a FOX fan. I enjoy Terry Bradshaw's humor; he is a regular guy. I also like the comedian's sketches. I find Fox does just the right amount of critical information and gives me some good laughs. Of course, I was hooked when Jillian Barberie was the weather gal. Why did she leave? I really enjoy Howie Long's commentary as well. He is articulate and to the point. When Howie talks, I listen. He does not talk just to hear himself talk. That is it. That is what I do not like about Michael Irvin. Howie is the anti-Mike Irvin. One last thing I like about FOX is Jay Glazer, the Fox NFL Expert. He gets the scoop and you get it before your starters' deadline. I do not like the fact that FOX does nothing for fantasy football except ask their game commentators for a fantasy pick. How worthless is that!

CBS, on the other hand, has a ticker that runs at the bottom of the screen during the pre-game, halftime and post-game shows that has top fantasy football players and start/bench questions. But what is it based on? What scoring system is used? It is like asking who is better – Ginger or Mary Ann? (That depends on what you are looking for!) CBS has James Brown now. Why did he leave FOX? Show me the money. I like Dan Marino and Boomer and even Deion Sanders. However, the whole show just seems too old for my taste. J.B. does a fine job prodding everyone to speak, but the flow is just not as crisp. If there is a highlight, it is Shannon Sharpe. He calls them like he sees them and is not afraid to call players out for poor play. I like Phil Simms as a play-by-play commentator also.

Things are different when the games kick off. Now I like to watch the CBS games because they have a ticker with game stats that are great for fantasy football. It goes through each game and includes QB, RB, WR, K and DEF stats. What a great system. FOX has no such ticker. They even trick you into thinking they are doing a ticker, but then it just advertises their website. DOH! I prefer to watch the games on CBS now.

NBC has the Sunday night games. What can I say? I am fond of John Madden. He is getting older (aren't we all) but he is like the football uncle I never had. I welcome him into my living room every Sunday night. Al Michaels is the consummate professional. Both of them make a great team. I just wish they would bring back the cute sideline reporter from five years ago. She left because she became pregnant. She was a University of Virginia graduate and I would walk a mile on broken glass to say "hi" to her. What was her name? Missy? No, Melissa something. It will come to me. By the way, NBC – love the Pink intro! In addition, what a bonus of picking the games you want. Smart move!

ESPN does Monday Night Football and I miss the old ESPN crew. Tony Kornheiser is okay. I like him better on "Pardon The Interruption" though. In the booth, I thought he asked some great questions, but it did seem like he had a fantasy player in every MNF game, and they were not the best players either. I wish I played in Tony's league, because either he had a terrible team or ESPN was pushing some subliminal fantasy stuff through him and his comments. I hated the intro with the blatant GMC promotions when it came out and now, after an entire season of it, I still hate it. I kept trying to see what the cheerleaders looked like before they turned into cheerleaders. Hank, as always, rocks with the theme song, but I found that I missed the country version of "I Like it, I Love it" or whatever it was at halftime that showed some highlights. Oh well. Chris Berman is my favorite. I like his humor and his energy. He does not seem to mince his words either. Another reason I like Chris is because we have grown up together; he started at ESPN in 1979 and I started FF shortly thereafter. Mike Tirico and Joe Theismann round out the MNF crew and I like Joe's attitude. There it is again, the Hendricks kiss of death. A mention in this book (Parcells, M. Schottenheimer, Theismann) gets you canned apparently. Joe is replaced by Ron Jaworski on MNF. "Jaws" should get along with Tony Kornheiser well.

NFL network entered the broadcasting of NFL games with their Thursday night games. My mom always said, "if you do not have anything good to say about something, then tell me." No, that is not what she said. Suffice it to say, I will not be commenting on Bryant Gumbel. Okay, just one comment. Like watching paint dry. Chris Collinsworth, on the other hand, always impresses me with his humility and knowledge. I like his style.

There are also weekly shows that are great for giving you fantasy insights, even though they do not cater to fantasy footballers. "NFL Live" comes on weekdays at 4 p.m. EST on ESPN during the football season. It provides 30 minutes of NFL news and commentary by Trey Wingo, Sean Salisbury and Mike Golic. It is a must-see if you do not have the NFL Network. It gets you caught up on everything that is happening around the league. It even sometimes has a fantasy twist to it. They are beginning to get the idea, as Eric Karabell has given them some great direction over the years. "Inside the NFL" on HBO is a good recap of what happened the previous week. Before the NFL Network, it was the only thing on TV to review other than ESPN News. Now with the NFL Network, I find that is my sole viewing choice. Even ESPN's Sportscenter, which used to be my lifeline to the NFL with its occasional fantasy segments, has had reduced viewing by me.

The best network for information in general has to be the NFL Network. To quote its own website: "It is every football fan's dream. Seven days a week, 24 hours a day, 365 days a year; a television network solely devoted to the most popular sport in America, professional football." YES! It is like the NFL on C-Span. They have all preseason games not shown on network TV. More access to player and coaches than anyone else. At any given moment, if you tune in you will have the latest information from around the league. It is a must-have network on cable. They even have NFL Replay to see games you missed (if you do not have NFL Ticket). And they showed Thursday and Saturday games exclusively on the network live. Then there is the Total Access program (M-F, 7 p.m.), which is your sole source of everything NFL. It includes Adam Schefter, one of my favorites, as the NFL expert. He reported that Oakland coach Art Shell would not be around in 2007 and Oakland called him a rumor monger; Oakland fired Shell a few weeks later.

To show just how much NFL information you get, the NFL Network is broadcasting the NFL Combine on five consecutive days. I would hate to get some e-mails about giving too much coverage to one side of the NFL. To be fair, the NFL Network does in-depth coverage of the NFL cheerleader playoffs as well. The NFL cheerleader playoffs consists of two cheerleaders from each of the NFL's 25 cheerleading squads. They compete for the "Champions of the Sidelines" crown. They are challenged by physical events, an NFL knowledge quiz and a dance contest. There is also extensive coverage of their "Making the Squad" shows (for those moments when you need a little break from fantasy football). The only complaint I have is that the fantasy draft on the NFL Network was very weak compared to what they could have done.

The NFL Network also has former coach Steve Mariucci as a commentator. He loves to have fun. How can you not enjoy watching that guy with his big smile? NFL Playbook on NFL Network is not a fantasy show, per se, but addresses many of our needs, including upcoming matchups, league developments and injuries.

Radio

ESPN radio show Mike and Mike in the morning (6-10 a.m. EST). Co-host Mike Golic. Great show.

Sirius NFL Radio's "Around the League."

XM Satellite Radio has a daily one-hour "Fantasy Focus" show.

Internet

The Internet has made it easier to quickly learn how to play fantasy football, in a better way. It makes bad owners average and good owners great. The advantage that a skilled, prepared owner had on draft day has diminished. Remember that no matter how much information you have, it still comes down to your gut. You have to make the call.

Premium websites provide information and analyses that save you time. Sure, you could bookmark a hundred sites and get injury updates and weather updates and coaching announcements, but it would take a lot of time. These sites give you lots of information and analysis at the push of a button. Soak up their information like a sponge and use their analysis as a great second opinion. However, remember that you make the call, you have to pull the trigger and you are responsible for all the glory and shame that goes with it. I would not have it any other way.

Narrow your focus when considering websites. Seek out sites that are fantasy football only. Try to avoid sites that do multiple fantasy sports. How good can you be at football if you also do baseball, etc.? Also be wary of the ones that say "fantasy sports" in their title. Avoid sites that have distractions, like google ads or hot babes. Nothing against hot babes, but why would a site have that distraction on their web page? If I wanted a babe distraction, then I have my own porn sites bookmarked elsewhere (just kidding). Seriously, it makes me think they are not serious about fantasy football information. Or it is the old shell game of trying to distract you while you look for the dollar under the shell. Whether you go premium or free, try to limit it to three so that you can check them regularly. A separate weather site and an injury site to look at on Sundays is fine. The three I referred to are primary information sites. One may be a pay site where you can get rankings, weather status, VBD applications, etc.; the other might be a free site where your local league is located, just to get the big picture and one could be a magazine site just for a different opinion. Look for sites that have everything you need and include e-mails with updates. Perhaps use Yahoo or CBSSPORTSLINE as a quick backup and either footballdiehards.com (that goes with the *Pro Football Fantasy Football* magazine) or the *Fantasy Football Index* website.

Free sites can also provide good sources of information. For example, a great way to get player information (including local newspaper news) without going to several different websites is to "Google" it. That's right, go to www.google.com, then select "News" at the top of the page; now bookmark this site (I call it my player news search page). Type in the player's name and presto, an instant search. It is a quick and easy search method and it allows you to scan the media source too. For example, USAToday vs. sportsbetting vs. US magazine. However, this will not give you information on the other players that support him. This information is much more likely to be found on the local newspaper websites.

Another free information source comes from MBs. Join a MB and use it to network to find like-minded FFers in other parts of the country for scoops. The national papers do not have the same type of coverage of teams as the local papers do. Either bookmark local paper sites or get a network that looks at them.

Think about web or MB posting before you post a message. Your posts need to be intelligent. Answer a question like "Who should be the number one RB this year," with a clear thought-out answer and explanation of why you think so. Be prepared to backup your thought process and bring statistics into the discussion. Your response should be more than just "LT, who else?" but more along the lines of, "I think LT will be the best RB in 2007 because his new coach will run the ball even more than 'marty ball.' LT will get more carries than last year and thus more TDs. Shaun Alexander is still without Steve Hutchinson and you saw the year he had and Larry Johnson has no blocking FB." No matter what responses come from your post, do not get hurt by other opinions or dissension and do not get dragged into a thread war of counter taunts or insults. Use it to give and get information and do not waste your time with petty infighting.

Along the same lines as posting on an MB, consider signing up for an e-mail mailing list that will send an e-mail when significant events occur. Some of these can be quite intrusive, with several e-mails a day. Avoid these, as most of the subsequent ones are just follow up e-mails telling you the same thing. Find a magazine or website that has an e-mail list and sends out at least daily or weekly. Find one that sends out "breaking" news on the big players and even sends out their cheat sheet with injury status (P, Q, O) by the players' names, so you can be reminded of making lineup changes and know the latest information.

What is the best free site? That will depend on your style and the information you seek. The ESPN website has live draft info, FPs scored against, projections, added/dropped (to give you an idea of what others are doing in other leagues), injuries, etc. Some have criticized them as being too "cookie-cutter" and trying to bring everything into "their world." I think they do a good job for what they do. Yahoo and CBSSPORTLINE are also free and provide valuable information, if you know where to look. Some "Internet shows" discuss fantasy football exclusively. Yahoo and ESPN both have these webcasts. NBC Sports has "Fantasy Fix" with Gregg Rosenthal and Tiffany Simons. Find one you like and use it regularly to keep up with events.

(See Appendix A Websites for a list of some of these sites.)

Finally, what can you get out of these resources? What should you take away from all these sites, TV shows and print devices? First, seek out expert rankings, preferably a consensus of a number of "experts." Use this as your basis for what the other owners may be using. You will take it and tweak it, to make it a far better resource, but first find a consensus expert ranking in one of the magazines floating around. If you do not have the time to create your own rankings (See Chapter 7 – Ranking Players) then use the best pre-printed cheat sheet you can find. Just make sure the scoring and starters/rosters are the same. Look at the mock drafts, they let you know where the tiers of talent are and where the huge drop offs occur. They also alert you to new players who have been undiscovered by your research. Before the season starts make sure you find the offensive depth charts. These are invaluable to see who is starting or close to starting as far as HCs and up-and-coming players.

Another tool, found on the Internet, is current ADP. Make sure it is as close to your league's parameters as possible. This will help you determine when to get players that you consider sleepers, HCs and targeted players before others do, but not so early that you pay too big a price. Say you want a RB as a HC for your RB#1. ADP says he will go in 9.7; if it is the 8th round (your pick is 8.2) and you have pick 9.11, maybe it is time to grab that HC because he probably will not be around by the time your 9.11 comes around. During the season, these sources can help with "touch" numbers, you can see how often your players are getting access to the ball. News reports on players are often just as important. You need somewhere to get all the news on the players and their teams. Not just People magazine stuff like who Tony Romo is dating, but information on how well the player did versus the same opponent the last two meetings.

Chapter 27 Fantasy Football Enjoyment

How to Enjoy Fantasy Football

Notice I said enjoy fantasy football, not win. These steps make it more enjoyable but do not necessarily give you a better chance of winning. In fact, some decrease your chance of winning but the enjoyment factor will be higher.

1) Pick players from your favorite team (ex: Washington or Minnesota)

2) Do not pick players from teams you hate to root for (ex: Dallas, Green Bay)

3) Do not pick players whom you hate to root for (ex: Terrell Owens, Mike Vick)

4) If faced with a choice between two players of equal talent and one of them is from your favorite team, go with your favorite. No only will you enjoy watching him in FF but also for rooting for your favorite team. Go Vikes!

There are a few things you can do to enjoy this great hobby even more. The easiest is to create your own team name, logo, hats, shirts, etc. Team names are the first ingredient for fun. What represents your team? What inspires you to greatness? Alliteration can be a great rallying point. Slam's Slammers or Magard's Marauders. Some team names I've seen include Liverless Lushes, Crestview Crushers, Ned's Nutters, Tok's Terminators and Bronx Bombers. How many teams with names like The Choked Chickens have you seen fold in midseason when they started 0-6? On the other hand, how many teams named "Sammy" have you seen scratch and crawl their way into the playoffs from a 0-6 start? Team names do mean something.

If you have a great team name, send it to me in an e-mail and I will try to include it in subsequent editions of this tome. info@Fantasyfootballguidebook.com

Logos are a completely different level of playing experience. You have reached diehard status once you wear the polo or t-shirt with your team's logo on it. Examples of a logo are pictures of you or relatives, something your digital camera caught on film or would rather not have caught, as the case may be. An artist's rendition (your 3rd grade daughter's drawing or a more professional one) can also work, or something you found on the Internet as a picture or design. Ultimately, a team name will be with you for the rest of the history of that league (or not, if your league allows you to change names). It will show that you are truly ready to be competitive.

Do not worry too much about scoring the second most points in a given week and losing since you played the team who scored the most points that week. In a 14-team league, there is an 8% chance of this happening. Big deal, get over it. You are just as likely to score the second lowest points and get a win because you played the team with the lowest points. It will all even out over your lifetime of playing fantasy football, so do not bore everyone else with your sob stories. Take it like a man and move on. Do some trash talking. Trash talk builds rivalries and gets others motivated to do better. Rivalries add to the game, as there is nothing better than beating an old nemesis.

You need to find ways to enjoy fantasy football and you need to find ways for others to enjoy fantasy football. This may mean changing the way you attack the game or it may mean passing the love of the game on to someone you know and love. Regardless, I hope you enjoy this great hobby for many years to come.

Observations to let you live a normal life while enjoying fantasy football

First, get Dish or Direct TV and NFL Ticket. If you are going to watch the games, do it right. This also means Super Fan, where you can switch from game to game based on whom you are playing, which of your players are important or who is in the red zone. Next pony up the $25-$30 for a website that provides all your must-know information. One convenient website is worth its weight in gold and for $25 it is worth the extra family time or girlfriend time or golf time.

No matter what, never allow your hobby (fantasy football) to cost you your job. Be careful about doing research or fantasy football work on company time. Many companies have filters that prohibit going to sites with the words "game" or "fantasy" or "Pamela Anderson" in them. Trust me, I know these things. I find it is more relaxing to do my research at home anyway. At work, on a break, you can get away with going to your favorite sports website and catching up on the latest news but do not let it get you fired.

I root for my Vikings no matter what and enjoy their wins even if it costs me a fantasy win. Some think that a fantasy championship will last a lifetime, while a Vikings win will be deflated the next time they blow it in the playoffs or Super Bowl (is it three or four times we have lost there? I lose track and try to forget the pain). So one way to fight my Vikings pain is to give fantasy football more emphasis; but I pick my NFL team first because fantasy football is just that, fantasy. I want a Viking Super Bowl more than anything and a Slammer championship is next.

I enjoy visiting my mom and going to church with her on Sundays and then rushing to her house to see the pre-game shows, but this forces me to rely on her computer to do any last minute changes. And we're waiting and we're waiting… her computer is so slow that dial-up companies use her computer in their advertisements to impress people with their speed. I watch the games with her and my sister as they sleep through some of them and I wake them with my cursing as Hines Ward drops a TD pass or Carson Palmer throws a pick. I have found that once in awhile I will start to tape the Sunday game at 4 p.m. and go for a walk with my wife or we play couples golf together. I then start the DVD where I started taping and can watch the game without commercials. True, I miss the live scoring and switching between games but without NFL Sunday Ticket many times the 4 p.m. EST game is on only one network and even with Sunday Ticket many times there are only three games at 4 p.m. Life is too short to miss the really important things in life.

I do not honestly know if football on Thursday, Saturday, Sunday and Monday night is such a good thing. In 2006, it was kind of like chocolate. You loved getting that much of it but then it made you a little nauseous afterward. I can hear the collective gasps of FFers around the world. Blasphemer!

My wife knows she is a FF widow. She loves me and knows how much I love her and FF (notice which came first) so she makes some allowances. She lets me watch football from 11 a.m. on Sunday till 11 p.m. Sunday night and then turns around and lets me plop my fat behind on the couch at 8 p.m. on Monday nights. Why? Because she loves me and knows how much enjoyment I get from watching football. I use this time as "me" time, to reflect, gather my thoughts, plan out the week and month to come. In many cases, I can multi-task during MNF. Okay, I do things during the commercials like write checks to Direct TV or to pay the electricity bills. I do not drink (much). I don't go out carousing with the boys. Poker night once a month does not count. I do not play fantasy baseball (well, very competitively; one yahoo league a year is not playing to me, it is more of a fix just to get me to FF season.) By the way, I sometimes lose my concentration on it when preseason rolls around. Therefore, I avoid fantasy baseball and fantasy NASCAR and fantasy golf and fantasy basketball. Sometimes I have a nightmare and when I wake up my wife asks, "Why are stud RBs on the same bye weeks such a bad thing?" This nightmare goes away from February-July, but then I go into withdrawals and try to bank as much hiking, golfing, shopping, and traveling as I can with my wife and family because when September arrives it is FOOTBALL for five months.

Fantasy Football Nirvana (the little things that make it all great!)

1) The NFL's kickoff weekend – Sunday at 1 p.m. EST. All my fantasy teams are tied for first place and my NFL favorite the Vikings are too. I have the remote ready to switch between all the Sunday Ticket games, I have a beverage of choice at my side and a sheet listing my fantasy team players and my opponents and what time they play. I like to put a big L by the player's names if they play 4 pm games, an S if they play on Sunday night and an M if they play on Monday night. Beside me on the coffee table is my laptop, wirelessly connected to the live stats of our web page so that I can track what is going down when I see one of my players teams has scored via the fantasy ticker at the bottom of the screen.

2) Hearing Terry Bradshaw casually mention that your starting RB has scored three TDs already today.

3) Having the guys over for the games and being able to do the "I kicked your ass" dance live for them.

4) Watching the games at your opponent's house and seeing his stud RB pulled at the goal line all day for another RB.

Don't blame others

Fantasy football is not the only thing in your life. Family, friends, neighbors and co-workers all make up who we interact with daily. You need to find the right balance between your hobby (fantasy football) and your life. As an example, take Christmas Eve 2006. I am 35th out of 600+ in the WCOFF "One and Done contest." I create my final lineup for week 16 on Friday, Dec. 22 because I know my family is coming up to spend Christmas with us. This is the first time in ten years we will be able to share Christmas at our home. I do my research but not as much as I usually do and none on Sunday morning, Dec. 24, since that is when they are arriving. So rather than spend hours in front of the computer on Sunday morning, I help with last minute things around the house. My choice! Christmas comes and goes splendidly and I end up in 22nd place (5 out of the money) due to a poor performance by T. Romo on MNF. All I needed was a TD or 80 more yards to make the money. Oh well, I tried. Later I looked at my notes and I had planned to start M. Bulger in week 16 (prepared this back in week 12 based on matchups for weeks 12-16).

He of course had a great week 16. If I had started him like I planned (but I forgot he was still available to me) then I would have won $500. I did not make the right decision. Do not blame others for your mistakes. I felt like blaming Carrie Underwood since she was on the field beforehand obviously distracting Romo, but that is not productive. I started Romo and not Bulger and I cost myself $500. You have to look on the bright side of things; I had a great Christmas and I hope my family did too. I felt like I balanced fantasy football and family with just the right amount of time. Don't get me wrong, there are commitments to playing in a FF League like turning in lineups every week, managing your rosters, planning for injuries, suspensions and byes, and discussing trade talks. These things must be done too, but the extensive research that may go into them on most weeks may have to be adjusted on special occasions (weddings, funerals, holidays, etc.). It will not drive you crazy, it will help you appreciate the little things in life more.

Play in a league with some easy competition

The league you are in will only be as competitive and fun as its members. Choose your league wisely. If you want to game the system a little, pick owners who are easy. When I say easy, I mean easy to beat. Who qualifies for this position? Married men who have lots of children or big lawns are easy marks. Either of which will guarantee that although they think they have time to play fantasy football, they really do not. The married person with children will find himself unable to log on when he needs to because little Sally is playing Donkey Kong on the computer. Single people are okay as long as they are very attractive or have a drinking problem, or better yet, both. In each case, they will spend a lot of time away from the football information or be too hung over to look at it. Another attribute will be the single person who has fallen in love. This is the kiss of death to a fantasy footballer and he will spend so much time wooing the new girl that his team will be marked for the cellar from the start. You may as well circle the matchups against him and pencil in a "W" right now. Another easy mark is the serious golfer. I hit the white ball on occasion (3-4 times a week if the weather is good and I do not have some book to write), but I am the first to admit I am no good at the game. However, I have concluded that I cannot play golf and watch football on Sundays. They are mutually exclusive. Eighteen holes of golf takes at a minimum five hours by the time you show up, warm up, tee off, play and then figure out whom to give your losing money to. Tee times start at 7:30 at the earliest so that means I am not back in my recliner until 12:30 in the best of times. God forbid we have a frost delay or end up behind a foursome playing in the US Open (sinking every two footer as if it had $250,000 riding on it). No, golf on Sundays and FF do not mix. Therefore, try to get those serious golfers to play FF. They will always miss the game time decisions before they can return home. Finally, look for either young or old players who may have early bedtimes. They will not be able to watch all of the night games and you can secure a small advantage over these owners too. Remember, easy to beat means more wins and a championship.

Avoid Too Many Teams Syndrome (TMTS)

Why not play in a number of leagues; because the more leagues that you play in, the greater the chance of crossover players. Crossover players are players that hurt you in one league (because your opponent has them) and help in another league because you have started them. I hate the feeling when I see that my starting RB is also playing against me in another league. Now you face the nightmare scenario of wanting F. Gore to be shut down in one league and in another rooting for him to have 3 TDs and 150 yards. There is nothing you can do about this problem except limit the number of leagues you play in. Ultimately, when faced with this, you must decide which league is more important and root for that leagues crossover scenario. Another problem with too many leagues is being able to give them all your full attention. There is nothing worse than having ten leagues, forgetting to change the roster on one and seeing that you started a bye week or OUT player! This is not fair to the other owners in that league. Just as you hate owners who do not set lineups or give it their all, do not do that to others. By limiting the number of leagues you play in you can focus all of your attention on those few leagues. That way you can be very competitive in those leagues.

How many leagues are too many? I know most will have a local league that they play in. More will also dabble in one of the online leagues or satellite leagues for the bigger championships. So 2-3 is the most I would recommend playing in. I played in 12 last year and regretted some of them. From now on, it is just going to be my local league and WCOFF and NFFC. And you know what, I have more fun and enjoy the games more when I am in fewer leagues.

What can tempt you to join another league? Simple flawed logic such as, "The more leagues I play in, the more fun I will have because of more chances at winning." Other temptations include different owners, different scoring system, and the need for one more draft "rush;" as in "if I schedule a draft every week until the season kicks off that will be great". But as one more league turns into three more leagues and then five more leagues you will find yourself with a growing number of leagues that all require your attention until at some point you will consider barricading yourself in your office and doing nothing but FF research 24/7. If you catch yourself in time, you will find yourself in ten leagues and not have enough time to give them all adequate attention. This means you will begin to lose in many of them for lack of input. Losing in ten FF leagues is not fun. Trust me, I have been there. Okay, almost.

If in multiple leagues, here are some steps to help with the madness:

1) Prioritize. Which league have you been in the longest? That league needs to be at the top of the list. Are there leagues that have much higher payouts? If so, the financial planner in me says that one should go to the top of the list too. Allocate limited time resource to leagues with the highest priority. All leagues must get a minimal sanity check on rosters (changing bye week, injured players, etc.) but some at the bottom of the list will get much less time than those at the top for making lineup decisions, trades, etc.

2) Stay with similar formats to make research easier. If you are in three leagues and they are all the same scoring format that will help the ranking go easier since player A in all three leagues may be about the same. Economy of scale will also help with FA since your research may discover a gem that is available in multiple leagues or at least can go on all your watch lists.

3) Share duties with a co-manager. This can help you with the workload and ease the transition into a new league or system. Perhaps after co-managing one year, you can then go it on your own the following year. Be careful of co-managing though since these arrangements can cause disagreements and friendships to become damaged. Know the other owner and have definite guidelines for who does what;

what the other owner can do independently and what they both must do together. Who sets the lineup? Who can authorize a trade? Do both have website access? Who pays what costs? Drafting duties? Best if one can focus on drafting and cheat sheets while other tracks other owners' tendencies and predicts whom the other owners will take in picks leading up to yours.

4) If you decide to walk away from a league, do it after the season is over. Never quit midseason. Never give up on a team and stop managing it. Notify the commissioner soon enough to allow him to look for another owner as soon as possible.

The Perfect League

The best way to enjoy FF is to play in a league you love. Moreover, while I enjoy my local league and WCOFF, I am always searching for the Holy Grail of Fantasy Football, The Perfect League. What is the perfect league? It is many things to many people. I am looking for some equality in the skill positions, more skill in drafting than luck and a few scoring rules that are equitable to all players.

To me, this league will have 14 teams. This way everyone plays each other once with a 13-game schedule. Having 14 teams also makes the draft that much more important since the waiver wire is a little thin at some positions when you have a big roster. Roster size is 40, based on starting 15. Two of the 40 spots must always be rookies. The league would start 1 QB, 2 RBs, 3 WRs, 1 TE, 1 Flex (RB/WR/TE), 1 K, 1 DT, 1 DE, 2 LBs, 1 S, 1 CB. Note that there are 6 IDP starters and there are no IR spots, just a deep roster.

H2H is the only way to go. There is so much excitement knowing that all is on the line in those three hours (okay, maybe 9-12 hours if we are lucky) of competition. Of course, the only way to draft is with a live auction format. The $125 entry fee buys you $200 worth of salary cap money for the auction and $50 worth of FAAB budget. Any money left over from the draft is moved to your FAAB. The minimum bid is $1. Therefore, at a minimum you can have 50 free agent transactions during the year. Trades are allowed for players, draft picks and future draft picks but all such agreements must be spelled out. There can be no "future considerations" that are not quantified. Of the entry fee, $100 goes to prizes and $25 goes to purchasing league supplies such as the draft board, paying off the 30-year loan the league took out on the draft clock and the league management service. Other activities it funds are the Super Bowl party (also known as the awards banquet) and the postseason playoff tournament. The payout of the remaining money would be 50% for 1st place, 20% for second place and 3rd place gets his entry fee back. The remaining funds are split 16 ways and go to the weekly high scoring team.

It is a minimal keeper league in that only a few of the 40 players are kept from season to season. Of those few, two are the rookies that are required to be drafted each year. Each year a team gets a single 2-year, 3-year and 4-year contract along with a rookie 2-year and 3-year contract. Each year a team gets one anchor or bridge. Additional anchors are awarded based on winning the Super Bowl or scoring the most FPs in the regular season. (Only two anchors per team per year but they are transferable).

Six teams make the playoffs; the four teams with the best record and the two remaining teams with the highest TFPs scored in the regular season. In the playoffs, the teams retain their average score from the regular season. It is not single elimination but a three-week competition to see who has scored the most over those playoff weeks (plus their average for regular season). The league should have a toilet bowl so there should also be a reason to want to win in week 16 in the toilet bowl. Finally, no first come, first served waiver wire; instead a FAAB and blind bidding on Saturday night at the 8 p.m. deadline. After that any player is available until the first kickoff, then the process closes again until Saturday's deadline (it is moved up to Wednesday at 8 p.m. on weeks with Thursday games).

The perfect scoring systems should be:

1) Realistic and reward good players for good performances. A RB rushing for 220 yards should not be beaten by a kicker kicking four 25-yard chip shots.

2) Like the NFL. Points for scoring TDs, not for how long the TD catch was.

3) FF game scores should be measurable by the owners with a pencil and paper, not calculated by two IBM computers working over time.

Therefore the perfect system is:

All TDs are worth 6 points.

QBs get 1 point for every 50 yards of passing/rushing or receiving combined. Therefore, if Peyton throws for 180 yards, rushes for 18 and catches a pass for 2 yards then his total yardage is 200 and he gets 4 points.

RBs get 1 point for every 20 yards (also all combined). So if LT throws for 18 yards, rushes for 180 and catches a 2-yard pass for 200 yards, he will get 10 points.

WRs get 1 point for every 20 yards combined plus 1 point per reception. (Note: only PPR for WRs, not RBs or QBs.)

TEs get 1 point for every 10 yards of combined yardage; plus PPR. These rule changes make TEs more productive members of the fantasy league.

Kickers get 3 points for FGs and 1 point for XPs. Kickers who get more points (points for yardage) are just too dominant for a lucky position. They are still scoring points but should be kept at 3 or 1 point. Maybe 2 bonus points for a FG of 50 yards or more.

The scoring rules allow PPR (1 point) but only for WRs and TEs. Decimals are not used and the score is divided by 4 to make it look more like the NFL. RBs and WRs end up worth about the same. QBs are worth more but there is more depth, so do you take a QB and pass on a RB or WR or wait it out? TEs become almost as valuable as the RB/WR.

Slam's World

While we are on the subject of "perfect," why not discuss my perfect world. A world where WRs get some kind of credit when they are interfered with in the end zone and a penalty is called. For example, Reggie Wayne runs 40 yards down the sideline and has his defender beat, the ball is just about to be cradled in his arms when the CB dives and grabs his hand before the ball reaches it. The team gets the ball on the 1-yard line so they have been compensated; but what about the QB and WR who have been robbed of a TD each, and yards. The next play sees the FB rumble over for a TD. Where is the justice? In my world, the QB and WR get 50% of the points awarded for a TD if there is interference called in the end zone.

In my world, church services all start at 10 a.m. from September through January. Fantasy football segments on sports shows are not insulting or useless. In my world, producers have realized that FFers are a smart bunch and do not really need to know that P. Manning is a great QB to win in FF. The information we really need to know is not even FF related but football related. Who is winning the position battles, injury status, weather updates, etc.? Use the segments not to insult our intelligence with the top 5 FF players (regardless of scoring or rules formats) but instead explore other avenues such as unique rules, leagues, etc. If one more play by play announcer tells me LT is his player of the week I will puke. In Slam's world Chris Mortenson and Adam Schefler have their own show on Sundays from 11-12.

Another great feature of Slam's world is that the NFL package is available at every house I ever visit, including my relatives' homes in Denmark. Not only that, but due to the magic of science somehow in Denmark the game comes on at 10 p.m., when everyone else is too tired to care if I watch them undisturbed. And somehow football is played every Sunday when the weather where I live is bad, allowing me to stay inside on the couch guilt free.

Have a Postseason Fantasy Football Tournament

The regular season is over, and if you were smart, you had some sort of week 17 mini-tournament to get you through that week. Now the NFL is starting the playoffs and what better way to enjoy them than by having your own Fantasy Playoff Tournament. Let's face it, after News Year's Eve and all those college bowl games, you want some more fantasy football. It's in your blood. You need a fix bad. Most of these can be opened up to non-owners in your office if you wish (attempt to seduce them with some fantasy football fun).

All of these contests award prizes based on TFPs compiled over the entire postseason, including the Super Bowl. None allow trades or adding/dropping players. Tiebreakers are Super Bowl winner, loser and then closest to TPs scored in the game. Below are several formats that can be used to hold your Postseason Fantasy Football Contest. You have two options: allow everyone to pick anyone they want (results in some of the same players on teams) or have a separate playoff draft.

1) Open Playoff Contest (any number can play)

A) Have each owner pick one player from each of the 12 playoff teams. Players can be on more than one owner's team so this is not a draft; starting rosters are 2 QBs, 3 RBs, 3 WRs/TEs, 2 Ks, 2 DEF/STs. The winner is the team with the most points after the SB is over. Every team loses players as teams are eliminated from playoffs. In the SB, every team will have two players on their team (one from each SB contestant). Fun! The third place winner would get his entry fee back, the second place winner would get double his entry fee back and the first place winner would get any remaining money. Ties go to the team with the most players at the bottom of the Super Bowl starting roster. For example, if two teams tie for first place, whichever team had the most DEF teams in the SB wins. If both have the same amount then you move on to the greatest number of kickers, and so on.

If both have the same number at the same position, the money is split between them. Another idea is to break ties by closest to pick of the SB score?

B) Use your current league's starting lineup and scoring rules (so that administration is easier). One lineup for entire playoffs, once a team is eliminated from the playoffs so are their players. Encourage others to play who are not in your league (unless entry fee in August covered this tournament). Unlike the regular fantasy football season, all players are available to every owner. If everyone wants Peyton Manning or LT then they can have him. Every game a player plays you can score points. The team with most cumulative points at end of SB wins.

C) Start with week 17 and use it to generate a lineup of any NFL players to get 1 QB, 2 RB,s 3 WRs, 1 TE, 1 K and 1 DEF/ST. Have payouts for weekly high points winners and TFPs winners (1st-3rd place). In SB week rosters are reduced by 1 RB and 1 WR since there are fewer to choose from.

D) SCORING only – Players get 6 points for passing, rushing or receiving a TD. DEF/STs get 6 points for TDs and 2 for safeties; kickers get 3 for a FG and 1 for XP. Start 1 QB, 1 K, 1 TE, 1 DEF/ST, 3 RBs and 3 WRs. No bench players; once a player is out, he is out. No more than four players from any one team (DEF do not count as one of the four). So can have your QB, RB, WR and TE from Indianapolis, but not another WR.

E) "One and Done" – Pick 1 QB, RB, WR and DEF/ST per week. But you can only use a player once. On last game (SB Sunday), force leader to name his team early so everyone else can pick some others to make it interesting

2) League Rules with playoff draft

A) Have a playoffs draft where each team can draft players from playoff teams. Start 8 players (1 QB, 2 RBs, 2 WRs, 1 TE, 1 K, 1 DEF) and draft 11 (3 bench). Once that team loses, your player stops producing. Use the same scoring system as league regular season. One disadvantage to this is that it might be hard to do in a league with more than 12 teams, since only 12 teams go to the playoffs. If you are in a 14-team league, see if some teams do not want to play (if only ten want to do it, great) or combine owners into co-teams. So if all 14 want to play, use seven co-teams with two owners on each team. Look at option B below for 14-team leagues where all want to play. Another option in 14-team leagues is to only admit the Top 12 teams into the postseason tournament (another reason not to finish in last place).

B) League rules with playoff drafts but no bench spots. Same thing as option A but no bench spots. Each team drafts eight starters. This can allow more teams to play.

Postseason Strategy

Any strategy has to be based on how many games a player will play. Success hinges more on predicting who will be going to the Super Bowl than fantasy football. You must predict ten playoff games correctly to have a good chance to win these contests.

Start by making your predictions on who will win the Super Bowl. Look at the odds of each team making it. Who is favored to win the SB (or lowest odds of winning SB)? They should be one of your teams in the SB or you should have a good reason why they will not make it. Pick who you think will be there.

Another strategy is to pick a team that is an underdog so less competition will be around if they do make it. Another strategy is to pick the strongest home team from the first round to make the Super Bowl since if they do they will have played four games.

How will they get there? Next look at the point spread for the 1st round games. Round 1 will normally favor the home team, but not overwhelmingly. Take who you think will win round 1 and then determine whom they will play in round 2. Whichever teams you think will make the Super Bowl should advance in round 2. Now predict the winners of the other two games (remember if teams have byes they usually win their first games; after that it is a coin toss for who advances into the SB).

Next, advance your SB teams in round 3 to the Super Bowl. Rank each team by how many games they will play according to your scenario. Remember you do not have to predict who will win the Super Bowl, just who plays in it. Whomever you think will make the SB should represent most of the players on your lineup. All or nothing is better than splitting players from multiple teams because they are not all going to make the SB. Only two teams will make it. Are any of the teams making the Super Bowl playing in round 1 (and thus playing four games)? If yes, load up on those teams' players. Sometimes a team that does not make the SB but that plays in round 1 and advances to round 3 (thus playing three games) can produce the same or more than a player who makes the SB but only plays in three games since he starts with a bye week.

Balance single-game potential with how deep they will go into the playoffs. Players on Super Bowl teams will have played three or perhaps four (if they were involved in round 1 of the playoffs – think Pittsburgh in 2005) games. That can be a lot of scoring depending on the scoring rules.

Things to Think About:

1) Look for teams with momentum coming into the playoffs. Has anyone won three or four in a row to make playoffs? Pittsburgh in 2005 fit this mold.
2) What has been his production per game?
3) What defenses are they likely to face?
4) Does he have a history of performance in playoffs?
5) Injuries?
6) Bench spots. If limited, you may not be able to backup each position. If this is the case, backup RB and QB as they usually score the most.

How to Have a Good Draft (or What Not to Do)

1) Be prepared. When I say this I mean have materials ready, be on time and know who is dead, retired, suspended, in the hospital, in the pokey, and generally collecting an NFL paycheck. No one enjoys telling you for the third time that J. Rice retired or that R. Williams is playing in Canada. Know the rules for starter positions. I hate to see owners draft two TEs only to realize we are a TE-optional league

2) If you have a co-manager or two, work out who does what in advance, discuss strategy in advance and talk about the players you want, need, and absolutely will not draft. Arm wrestling over T.O. on draft day does not a fun afternoon make.

3) Don't lose track of when it is your turn or who else has been picked. Some leagues penalize you when you pick a player already picked. Track who is drafted ahead of you; cross their name off your lists and move on with your life. Get over it.

4) Do not drink and draft. There is a good reason they give out free booze in Vegas.

5) Show up on time and early if possible. Nothing starts the league off worse than the 1 p.m. draft starting at 1:45. If you are going to be late, give good instructions to your most trusted confidant so that they may draft for you. When you do show up do not complain about their picks; they are only as good as the guidance you provided.

6) Leave the spouse and rug rats at home. They will not enjoy watching you draft nor will the other owners enjoy babysitting for you while you decide between R. Bush and J. Addai.

7) Do not look at other people's draft lists unless they invite you to. Returning from the draft with a black eye only serves to make your wife suspicious.

8) Do not go to the bathroom right before your pick. See #4 above about no drinking. No fluid, no tinkle.

9) Do not help Forrest Gump with his picks. He has to learn sometime that this is for big boys. Okay, you can tell him one time that T. Barber is retired, but that is it.

10) Cell phones should be off unless your wife is pregnant, then they should be off for the first four rounds only.

11) Let the commish run things. If he asks you to do your loud attention-gathering whistle, fine, other than that it is his show.

Ensure Others Enjoy Fantasy Football Too

How can you contribute to the growth of the hobby? Talk about it with others. Post messages on MBs and get involved in discussions about the issues surrounding fantasy football. This should all be positive communication not just blasting the stat service or threatening to hang the commissioner for his decision. Everyone that plays is responsible for keeping this hobby going in the right direction. This involves ethical play, introducing others to the game in a friendly, keeping-it-fun kind of way (not a give-me-your-wallet/cutthroat sharks kind of way)! I can think of no better way to communicate with the youth of this world than with fantasy football. These X-BOX warriors or Madden 2008 enthusiasts can be recruited to become couch potatoes of the next generation. Seriously, sharing fantasy football can be a way of becoming closer to some of the disenfranchised youth of today's society. The first step is introducing FF to your own children.

Enjoy Fantasy Football with others

Sports are designed to entertain the masses. Watching NFL football is no different than going to the theatre or the movies. The only real difference is that you do not have to shell out $10 for a ticket and the same amount for a bucket of popcorn and cokes. Sunday afternoons can be yours, free and with whatever accoutrements you desire. Popcorn, pizza and boneless chicken wings are my favorites. However, use it to have family time if your children are involved or invite your friends and neighbors in to make it social time. There is no better way to share the fantasy football experience than with fellow owners, watching the games together, and enjoying the roller coaster of emotions as your team scores and your opponent catches you. Good friends can find much common ground in football and friendly fantasy football competition.

Fantasy Football Etiquette in 6 Easy Steps

1) Whether you win or lose, be a man about it. Win and lose with grace. Just enjoy the camaraderie and the competition and have a good time. Do not make too many excuses. Sometimes it is fair, sometimes it is unfair. Nevertheless, it is life and you enjoy it and try to win the next year.

2) Play with sportsmanship. Sportsmanship means trying to win every game and not colluding with other teams to get them the "best team." I am disgusted at the thought of such acts.

3) Compliment others on great moves. Whether it is a great draft choice, great FA acquisition or a canny trade. Let them know your admiration. It is like applauding at a concert. And who knows, maybe others will do the same to you.

4) Don't try to back out of a trade once you hit the accept button or have sent the trade to the commish for approval; it is a done deal. Big boys do not let buyer's remorse affect their decisions.

5) Pay your dues. No one likes having to wait for their winnings or never getting their winnings because some owners conveniently forgot to pay after they started 0-4.

6) Do the right thing. If you lie, cheat or steal in fantasy football it will come back to get you. What goes around comes around. It may not be this year or next year but it will come back to haunt you. So stand by your word, do not try to trade an injured player to some unsuspecting owner. If you know they are banged up and out for the season, do not try to get something for him this year with Mr. Gullible. Personally, I do not want to win because my opponent forgot to change his bye week players; I would rather call him up and remind him, and lose, than win because he did not set a competitive lineup. Your own integrity is more important than winning a championship by any means. If you do win by deceit, is it really a win?

Don'ts

Do not be the "killjoy." The "killjoy" does the following things and it makes the league deflate like a popped basketball:

1) Whines about injuries to his team. "If M. Vick had not gone down I would have won." What he really should be saying is "I did not draft well enough to have any depth at QB, so I lost."

2) Whines about "your team had a career day the one time you played me." Everything will even itself out by the end of the season.

3) Whining about how a lucky break (three Chicago DEF/ST scores in the 4th quarter of MNF) won you the game. What they should focus on is winning and losing gracefully. When an owner repeatedly harps on a tough loss through a lucky break, it only damages their reputation. It does nothing to detract from the "W" in your column or the "L" in theirs.

4) Whines about scoring second most points in league but missing playoffs.

5) Laments how he outscored the Super Bowl champion on Super Bowl Sunday but failed to make the playoffs because of a fluke scoring play.

What the "killjoy" does not realize is that everyone has a story like these. However, most of us choose not to air it because we know fantasy football is just a great game. Moreover, if you let them, the fluky bounces of the ball will drive you nuts. No one wants to lose and no one wants to hear repeatedly about how they lost on the last play of MNF. There is plenty of time for smack talking before the game but afterward win or lose with class.

Introduce Fantasy Football to your Children

I have to admit that I have no children. I do like to play games with them and get them as wired as possible then hand them back to their parents. I enjoy children for several hours at a time, but not 24/7. There I have said it. My motto is "Cats not kids." However, I do realize that FF is a great way to have fun and share things with your children.

How do you start them out? I suggest you co-manage a team with your child and let them do all the heavy lifting. There are leagues just for children at Sports Illustrated and at www.youthfantasyfootball.com for 10 year olds and above. The right age at which to introduce them to fantasy football will depend on the child. Are you going to be co-managers? How responsible are they? I would think 7 is a good age if they were supervised properly or 10 if they were on their own.

What do they get out of it? They learn the responsibility of maintaining a team and setting a roster every week. It is a commitment (like having a pet, kind of) and takes communication. It needs to be competitive and fun for kids to stay into it. It reinforces math skills and can teach new ones as far as statistics and regression analysis goes. Reading skills can be improved by reading about the games or the analysis or the team's processes. As a commissioner, you get writing skills, organizational skills, diplomatic skills and leadership skills. In addition, you have the sheer joy of sharing something you love with someone you love. If you have worries about a live draft or even an online draft; consider an auto draft feature that will help beginners get into a league without the hassle of a draft.

Who knows, maybe you can leave your dynasty fantasy football team to a beneficiary in your will. You can pass ownership on to your children. You can groom them for the management of the team by letting them be a co-manager. Will the firstborn male (why male?) get the best teams? The team and its name will become an heirloom passed on from generation to generation. Perhaps it will spurn more reproduction as our children become less obsessed with material things and more with fantasy things. We need to make sure this hobby lasts for a lifetime and is played by future generations. One of the very best things about this hobby is that it can be shared by different age groups and diversified peoples.

The Future of Fantasy Football

The next logical step to introducing fantasy football to your children is using it in school to teach children about math, communication, authority and responsibility. Eventually fantasy football will be used in the high school classrooms and then on college campuses. One day students in high school will be taking a fantasy football math class and college students will be enrolled in FF 101. Fantasy Football 101 in the fall semester will be followed by FF 102 in the spring; both statistics classes.

What about a league for children? FF is a great teacher for children. Keep it simple at first (perhaps just three players and TDs only) then expand as the children progress through their years. More players and more rules can be added as the years go by. Competition is taught but in a mental capacity versus a physical one. Logic is also taught, as well as communication and societal skills when dealing with trades and other owners. Negotiation and working with others (committees to determine rules or scoring systems) will occur naturally. Authority is taught, as there are rules and an authority figure in the commissioner. Lest we forget the number crunching; math skills will inevitably be taught as TDs are added, turnovers subtracted and yards divided by 10. Perhaps the scoring rules can even be adapted to suit the math skills desired. Using yardage divided by 10 early on and then in subsequent years by 15. Penalties for bad behavior can open up discussions of why that behavior is bad and how it is punished. There is even a lesson in budgeting if contracts are used and free agency bidding is based on a mythical budget. Finally, draft preparation can show how to prepare for any event with planning, checklists, materials and participation.

High School Fantasy Football

Then I saw an ESPN article entitled: "Fantasy Football Adds Up for Students." It details the very future I predicted. Oops, the future is now. John Hagen uses fantasy football to teach math in his California high school classes. It is algebra for seniors. Hagen's students draft a team at the beginning of the fall semester. They can even make trades with classmates. They set lineups just like every other FF owner. However, in his leagues, the twist is math and students must plug their players' statistics into mathematical formulas to determine how many points they score. His lesson plan is based on NFL statistics. His idea is simply to have students learn math in a way that is fun to them. But John Hagen is apparently not the first to develop this idea. Therefore, that means I must be a distant third at best. Dan Flockhart wrote and published "Fantasy Football and Mathematics." His textbook provides instruction on weekly fantasy scoring sheets and math problems that vary in difficulty from the middle to high school levels. In many leagues, a TD counts as 6 points; in Flockhart's leagues it could count for one-eighth or some other far more complex value. This introduces the different math concepts to students of differing levels. The only possible problem may be the fact that females may feel like this is not math geared to them. Nevertheless, teachers have not reported major problems in this area. In fact, the girls like to compete with the boys. So add to the growing number of fantasy football fans a new breed of owner, the math student. They do not play for a trophy or $200,000 in cash but instead do battle each week to make a better math grade.

Some sample math questions that would be used in such a high school fantasy football math class might include:

1) If R. Moss scored 18 TDs in a 16-game season:

    a) How many TDs does he average per game? 18/16=1.125

    b) What if he was hurt and missed three games? 18/13=1.38

2) If LT expects to score 250 FPs next season, how many points per game do you expect him to score for you if you draft him? 250/16= 15.625

3) If the 20th ranked RB is expected to score 12.3 points per game, how much more production in terms of percentage does LT give you over the 20th ranked RB? 15.625/12.3= 1.27 =27% more.

4) Which player is paid the most per year? B. Favre with a 5-year, $35 million contract or P. Manning who makes $43 million over 7 years? Favre makes 35/5=7M a year; Peyton makes 43/7=6.14M

5) If Reggie Bush is expected to rush for 125 yards per game in the fantasy playoff weeks of 14-16 and yardage points are awarded at 1 point per 10 yards, how many points from yardage alone can he be expected to score in total for weeks 14-16? 3 games x 125 yards=375/10=37.5 points.

Look out school systems, here comes fantasy football!!!

College Course on Fantasy Football

The fantasy football college (or advanced placement high school) course can have economic principles applied too, beyond the basics of adding, subtracting, multiplying and dividing. There are, of course, statistics but also supply and demand and regression to the mean. Opportunity cost (in the draft when you pick a player, now that takes away your opportunity at another player since the other players will be drafted after you) can be shown. Other concepts that could be addressed in a college course include risk vs. reward, consistency, average, weighted averages, mean, mode, medium, calculated risks, primary trading markets, secondary trading markets as they relate to players in trades and how easy or hard it is to trade them. Seasonality and its effect on markets could be studied as some players' values will fluctuate based on when the trade for them is attempted. Declining price anomalies, budgets (auction drafts especially, but also salary cap leagues) and inflation could be lessons as well (especially if salary caps or contract prices go up year to year). Diversification can be studied as too many players from the same team is the same as too many eggs in a basket of investments. Advanced statistics could cover building web-based calculators for fantasy football; spreadsheets go with databases hand-in-hand. Finally, the valuation of objects (players, draft picks, etc.) could be analyzed. I think a college course is the next step in the fantasy football education evolution.

What next?

I predict better medical technology that will reduce the number of games missed for injured players. Instead of 2-4 months for some injuries in the future, 1-2 months will be the norm. Prize money will inevitably get bigger for the high stakes leagues. However, inflation may have more of a push on this than fantasy fans. Most participants want larger league prizes (league champions money) rather than increasing the overall prize money. WCOFF will go to $250,000 soon simply because of the significance of advertising "a quarter of a million dollars." Their current prize of $200,000, adjusted for inflation at 3%, will reach $250,000 after nine years. Last year, 2006, was WCOFF's 5th Year. I predict $250,000 before 2010.

I promise you this: expect to see more real-time fantasy football revolutions. More interactive fantasy football where the TV remote will allow you to make decisions and score points against opponents across the cable/satellite/cell phone universe. Perhaps you could only start your QB on a limited number of plays per game. Therefore, it is up to you to read the defense and decide in a few seconds whether to press the red button on your remote and lock in that play for your player. Now you have to watch the game and make decisions on when to have him on your team based on defenses, down and distance scenarios (last play of first half, ball on 50 yard line – Cincinnati will pass for a Hail Mary; do you start Palmer?) It will be high risk or reward since chances are it will be an interception, incomplete or a TD. Push the blue button to play your RB this play, red is for QB, green is for WR. Another option may be to substitute players in the middle of a game. If your QB gets hurt, in the future, you may be able to plug in his backup into your lineup. Or you may just want to bench your QB and start your backup depending on a halftime evaluation.

Weekly or yearly or quarterly (as in each quarter of a football game) contests can involve you against your neighbors, statewide or nationwide, and with the NFL pushing its international acceptance, perhaps worldwide. Another form of fantasy football during individual plays may come from choosing plays and scoring points based on how successful the plays are; 1 point for a 5-yard or less gain; 2 points for a 10-yard or less play; etc. The TV will replace the computer for your live stats updates.

I predict more "total team" fantasy football where the OL and a punter are drafted as well; all the players on the field at any given time (OL, QB, RB, WR, TE, K, IDPs, P, PR, and KR) will have been drafted. Some leagues will still even have a head coach position. But these teams will have rosters of 40 or more and start one (if not more) of every position. I do not see the OL breaking down into left guard (LG) or left tackle (LT), but who knows.

Some hint that fantasy football cannot continue to grow at the current rate. I agree. That is another easy prediction. Nevertheless, will fantasy football become so big that everyone has the same information? If so, will luck really be the only thing that determines the winners from the losers? Alternatively, will the NFL shoot itself in the foot somehow and its decline will bring fantasy football down with it? In my opinion the recent stats lawsuit came close to hurting both the NFL and fantasy football. However, give the NFL credit when it is due. The NFL has already adapted in the 21st century to the old dilemma of how do you make people care about the 2-8 Lions playing the 3-7 Cardinals on Sunday night. Answer: you creatively change the schedule so those teams meet on Sunday afternoon and move the better matchup to Sunday night. The NFL Network provides NFL replay with games shown on Tuesday and Wednesday with commentary from players and coaches. This is brilliant! More of these innovations need to happen to keep the NFL riding high and fantasy football with it.

Finally, we need a commissioner of fantasy football. By the way, I am not running for the position. He will be in charge of trying to come up with a standardized league. It does not have to be used by everyone, au contraire. However, it would give everyone a starting point or a reference point for talking about fantasy football. The NFL and all of the networks should promote FF more. Some already have with special draft shows and fantasy football players of the game. Nevertheless, more needs to be done (Fox showing a decent ticker with stats would be a start). No matter what direction fantasy football takes, I will be there. I hope to play this great game for the next 65 years. That would make me 107 (I really am predicting great medical advances in the future). Somehow, I do not think the nursing home will be very bad if I can just play fantasy football and watch some NFL games. Who knows, by then, 2070, the NFL will probably be playing every night of the week.

Appendix A: Websites

First, a caveat; some of the free sites and pay sites listed are a little of both so be forewarned. Many times they will have some free content but the good stuff has a subscription fee. I have tried to only list sites I like and use and that have good information. I also tried to avoid websites that did fantasy sports other than football. Why go with someone that is too diversified? In addition, sites under the free games listing are also good free information sites. (Yahoo, ESPN, etc.)

Free Sites

www.footballguys.com

http://www.drfootball.com/

http://www.ffcheatsheets.com/

http://www.fftoolbox.com/index.cfm

http://www.sofantasyfootball.com/

http://www.draftsharks.com

http://www.fanball.com/

http://www.dynastyleaguefootball.com/

http://www.fftoday.com/

http://www.nflfreaks.com/

http://sportsillustrated.cnn.com/football/nfl/

http://msn.foxsports.com/fantasy/football/

http://www.fantasyfootballxtreme.com/calc2.html http://footballguys.com/pickvalue.htm

http://www.thehuddle.com/

http://www.fftoolbox.com/draft_order_generator.cfm (draft order random generator via e-mail)

http://www.btgsports.com/team_links.htm (Links to NFL teams and local newspapers)

http://www.bugmenot.com (provides IDs and passwords to websites – you do not have to register with all 32)

Free Games

www.yahoo.com

www.cbssportsline.com

www.espn.com

www.nfl.com

Pay Fantasy Football Sites

www.footballguys.com

http://www.fantasyindex.com/

www.4for4.com

http://www.bfdfantasy.com/

http://www.fantasyfootballadvisor.com/

http://www.mosneaky.com/

http://www.auctionffl.com/

http://www.footballinjuries.com/

www.fantasyfootball.com

http://www.fantasyfootballadvice.com/

http://www.footballdocs.com/

FF Magazines

http://www.fspnet.com/

http://www.stats.com

http://www.fantasyindex.com

Pay Games

www.sportingnews.com

http://www.sandbox.com/

http://www.cdmsports.com/

www.fantasyfootballchallenge.com

http://www.playerschallenge.com/

Fantasy Football Information

http://ffreview.com/football.htm

www.footballdiehards.com

http://schedules.footballguys.com/

http://www.ffgeeks.com/

www.rototimes.com

www.fantasyfootballlessons.com

www.ffbookmarks.com

http://www.phenomsff.com/leagues/rules/draft.html Great place to look at rules for different types of leagues

NFL Information

http://www.sportsknowhow.com/football/

http://www.nfl.com/

http://www.sportfanatics.net/Football.htm (this is a great links page)

http://gridironfans.com/

http://www.f2fa.com/

http://www.pfcritics.com/

http://www.profootballweekly.com/PFW/default.htm

http://www.usatoday.com/sports/football/front.htm

Draft Tools

http://www.draftkit.com/

http://www.ezdraft.com/

http://www.commishkit.com

http://www.mockdraftcentral.com/index.jsp

http://www.antsports.com/ADP.asp (ADP help)

http://ultimatedraft.com/

http://www.draftclock.com/

League Hosts/Software/Managers

http://www.webleaguemanager.com/

http://www.keeperfantasyleagues.com/

http://www.net-commish.com/

http://www.xpertsports.com/

http://www.tqstats.com/leagManager/football/index.html

http://myfantasyfootball.com/

http://www.fflm.com/

http://fantasyauctioneer.com

http://www.myfantasyleague.com/

High Stakes Leagues

www.wcoff.com

www.affl.com

www.fantasyfootballchampionship.com (NFFC)

www.fftoc.com

www.paydaysports.com

NFL Statistics

http://pro-football-reference.com/

http://www.insidethestats.com/

http://www.kffl.com/stat/index.php

http://www.nfl.com/stats/

http://subscribers.footballguys.com/players/

http://sports.yahoo.com/nfl/stats/

http://sports.espn.go.com/nfl/statistics

Fantasy Stuff (logos, t-shirts, trophies, rings)

http://www.fantasysportsawards.com/f-football/

http://www.fantasyaward.com/

http://fantasyfootballshirts.com/

http://www.fantasyfootballsportswear.com/cgi-bin/shop/cp-app.cgi

http://www.fantasysportstrophies.com/

http://www.fantasytrophy.com/

http://helmet-depot.com/

http://www.nfl-football-jerseys.com/

http://www.jostens.com/sports/fan_sports/index.asp

www.footballsoftware.com

Injuries

http://www.nfl.com/injuries

http://sports.espn.go.com/nfl/injuries

Appendix B Draft Tracker

Table B.1 Draft Tracker (12 Teams, 20 Player Roster)

Pos/Team	1	2	3	4	5	6	7	8	9	10	11	12
QB1												
QB2												
RB1												
RB2												
RB3												
RB4												
RB4												
RB5												
RB6												
WR1												
WR2												
WR3												
WR4												
WR5												
WR6												
TE1												
TE2												
K1												
K2												
DEF1												
DEF2												

By tracking what positions other owners have filled, you can plan your next pick based on what they will likely pick (or not pick). Simply place an X in the square for the position an owner just drafted. Do not bother with putting a name in the box. You can see whom he drafted after the draft (or have your co-manager track that). Put an X followed by the bye week, so if S. Jackson is picked by team 3 then in the RB1 square under team 3 you would write X7.

I prefer a draft tracker that has the teams going from left to right in the order of their draft but I have also seen them with the teams starting at the top left side and going down, and the positions moving from left to right. Notice this tracker does not fill in every position, with 20 players some teams may go for 3 QBs or 7 RBs or WRs. If a team drafts an RB8 it can go in one of the blank squares under RB or WR8 under WR7; by that point in the draft all the RBs and WRs may be drafted. The point to be made is flexibility to track someones picks without forcing them to fit some pre-canned mold of 7 RBs, 4WRs, and 2 Ks.

You can create this in MS Word by going to TABLE in the pull-down menus at the top and selecting insert and then table. It will ask you for the number of columns (at top of page going left to right; # teams+1) and rows (going down page; roster limit +1). Remember to include an extra column and row for the administration of positions and teams.

Think about it. Why track individual names? It is hard work. Who cares who has T.O.? Do you really want to spend your precious draft time spelling Houshmandzadeh? Nooooo!!! Make your draft tracking easier and quicker by using the draft tracker above. Most drafts are entered into a computer later so you can get a complete printout of the draft, round by round and team by team, later. You need to know who has taken what and how many of each position are gone. The tracker above is easier to read and easier to determine if someone may pass on a certain position (he has a QB already) or player (he does not need a third RB on bye week 6).

Use it when analyzing your next pick by asking yourself:

1) How many of each position are gone?
2) Which positions are likely to be drafted before your next pick?
3) What positions can you pass on this round and still get a same tier player in the next round?

Some only use it for the starters and one backup after them. After all, many owners begin to get sleepers and HCs in the late rounds. I use it for the entire draft as sometimes I can get a K or DEF a little higher using the tracker.

Your draft position is a tool in and of itself. I love the short side spots (9-11 or 2-4 in 12-team leagues).

You can use your opponents' drafting to your advantage to maximize value.

I have included an auction budget tracker also (see Table B.2)

Table B.2 Auction Budget Tracker

Position	Budget	Range	+/-	New Value	Bye Week
QB1					
QB2					
RB1					
RB2					
RB3					
RB4					
RB5					
WR1					
WR2					
WR3					
WR4					
WR5					
WR6					
TE1					
TE2					
K					
DEF					

Appendix C: Trade Analyzer:

Table C.1 Trade Analyzer

Draft Pick	Value
1	378
2	364
3	352
4	340
5	328
6	318
7	307
8	299
9	288
10	278
11	270
12	262
13	254
14	247
15	240
16	233
17	227
18	221
19	216
20	210
21	204
22	200
23	195
24	190
25	186
26	182
27	178
28	174
29	171

30	168
31	164
32	161
33	158
34	154
35	152
36	149
37	146
38	144
39	141
40	138
41	136
42	134
43	132
44	130
45	128
46	126
47	124
48	122
49	120
50	118
51	116
52	114
53	112
54	110
55	108
56	106
57	104
58	102
59	100
60	98
61	96
62	94

63	92
64	90
65	88
66	86
67	84
68	82
69	81
70	80
71	78
72	77
73	75
74	73
75	72
76	70
77	68
78	67
79	65
80	64
81	62
82	60
83	58
84	57
85	56
86	54
87	52
88	50
89	49
90	48
91	46
92	45
93	43
94	42
95	41

96	39
97	38
98	37
99	36
100	34
110	24
120	18
150	10
175	4
190	2
200	1

Appendix D Sample Draft:

Table D.1 Sample Draft through pick 3.01

Team/rd	A1	B2	C3	D4	E5	F6	G7	H8	I9	J10	K11	L12
Rd 1	R	R	R	R	R	R	R	W	R	R	R	W
2	W	W	R	R	R	R	W	R	R	Q	W	Q
3	W											
4												
5												
6												
7												
8												
9												
10												
11												
12												
13												
14												

Opening Rounds (1-5)

Round 1: All but two owners went RB in round 1.

Team 8 broke the RB run and took his #1 WR. Not only did he get his choice of WR but he also may have kicked some other owners into the WR mode a little earlier. If so all the better so that he gets a better RB with his pick 2.05.

Team 11 wanted to get his #1 WR (team 8 took his #2 WR) but did not want to risk losing his 1st tier RB so he went RB. With hindsight he could have gone WR with his 1st pick and then gotten his RB with his 2nd pick, but he did not know team 12's intentions. On the other hand, if he knew team 12 was an INDY Homer and knew he wanted both Manning and Harrison from previous years experience, then he could have taken his WR first and reasonably assumed his RB choice would be waiting in round 2.

Team 12 went WR and QB (matching up Marvin Harrison with Peyton Manning) but this essentially forces him into a RB with the next two or three picks.

By the second round, only 5 of the 12 have gone RB-RB, so everyone is not a stud RB theory devotee.

In round 2, team 2 gambled on a WR after two WRs were drafted in round 2. He hoped to beat team 1 to that position and he did.

Team 1 went WR-WR with 2.12 and 3.01 and now is forced into RBs the next few rounds.

By the end of round 3, only 7 of the 12 have their two RBs (see Table D.2)

Table D.2 Sample draft through pick 6.05

Team/rd	A1	B2	C3	D4	E5	F6	G7	H8	I9	J10	K11	L12
Rd 1	R	R	R	R	R	R	R	W	R	R	R	W
2	W	W	R	R	R	R	W	R	R	Q	W	Q
3	W	R	W	W	W	W	R	Q	W	W	Q	R
4	R	W	T	Q	W	R	W	R	W	R	T	T
5	R	Q	Q	T	R	T	R	W	R	W	R	R
6								R	W	T	W	W
7												
8												
9												
10												
11												
12												
13												
14												

Take a look at a WCOFF sample draft in Table D.3

Table D.3 WCOFF SAMPLE DRAFT

Rd	1	2	3	4	5	6	7	8	9	10	11	12
1	R	R	R	R	R	R	R	R	R	R	W	W
2	Q	R	R	W	R	W	W	W	W	R	W	R
3	W	R	W	R	W	T	W	R	R	R	R	W
4	R	Q	W	W	W	R	R	W	R	W	R	R
5	W	W	W	T	R	R	T	W	R	W	T	R
6	T	W	Q	R	R	W	R	R	W	Q	W	W
7	W	T	R	Q	Q	W	W	Q	T	W	R	Q

8	R	Q	R	W	W	R	W	R	R	R	W	W
9	R	R	T	R	W	Q	R	W	W	W	R	T
10	W	R	W	W	W	W	W	T	W	W	W	R
11	R	W	R	W	T	W	Q	W	R	T	W	W
12	R	W	D	R	Q	Q	R	R	Q	Q	Q	R
13	R	D	R	W	R	D	R	W	R	R	R	W
14	W	W	W	W	W	T	W	R	W	R	R	T
15	Q	R	W	T	D	W	Q	D	Q	K	T	Q
16	T	W	T	Q	D	R	R	Q	K	R	Q	R
17	D	Q	K	D	T	K	W	D	W	W	R	D
18	D	K	Q	K	R	W	K	W	W	K	D	W
19	K	T	W	W	K	W	D	Q	D	D	K	K
20	K	R	D	D	W	D	W	K	W	T	K	R

QBs   26 (most went 2 QBs, 2 went with 3 QBs) (earliest 2nd, latest QB1 12th round by two teams)

RB   77 (2 teams with 5 RBs, 3 teams with 6 RBs, 7 teams with 7 RBs) (earliest 1st, latest 3rd)

WR   83 (1 team with 5 WRs, 3 with 6 WRs, 4 with 7 WRs, 4 with 8 WRs) (earliest 1st, latest 5th)

TE   21 (9 teams went with 2 TEs, 3 teams with 1 TE) (earliest TE1 3rd, latest 11th by two teams)

K   15 (9 teams went with 1 kicker, 3 teams with 2 kickers) (earliest K1 15th, latest 20th)

DEF   18 (6 went with 2 DEF, 6 went with 1 DEF) (earliest 12th, latest 19th)

CAN YOU FIND A MISTAKE BY TEAMS 2 and 3?

In the fourth round, with pick 4.11, team 2 picked a QB. In round five, with 5.02, he picked a WR. He should have picked his WR in round four and his QB in round five. Why? Because team 1 was the only team ahead of him between 4.11 and 5.02 and he already had a QB (P. Manning picked in round 2). So there was absolutely no chance that he would take a QB with either his 4.12 or 5.01. Team 2 sacrificed value by taking a QB instead of the more valuable WR with his fourth pick. Team 3 does the same thing in round six with his 6.10 pick. He takes a QB and then with pick 7.03 he takes a RB. However, team 1 and team 2 are the only teams between his 6th and 7th picks and both have a QB. Neither is likely to grab their QB2 in the 6th or 7th rounds. Luckily for him they did not take his RB with either of their two picks.

ORDER FORM

Autographed or other copies:

Postal Orders: FFGB c/o S. Hendricks

P.O. Box 80

Forest, Virginia 24551

e-mail: info@fantasyfootballguidebook.com for bulk order inquiries

Please send _____ copies of Fantasy Football Guidebook in hardback.

Please send _____ copies of Fantasy Football Guidebook in paperback.

Name: _____

Address: _____

City: _____

State: _____Zip: _____

Telephone: _____

e-mail address: _____

Special Requests :_____(annotate here if autographed book requested)

Fantasy Football Guidebook: $26.95 for hardback; $19.95 for paperback.

Sales Tax: Please add 5.0% for products shipped to Virginia (total of $28.30 for hardback or $20.95 for paperback, including tax)

Make checks payable to Samuel L. Hendricks

Add $5.00 for shipping and handling for one book, $2.00 for each additional book

My check or money order for $_____

Payment must accompany orders.

ORDER FORM

Autographed or other copies:

Postal Orders: FFGB c/o S. Hendricks

P.O. Box 80

Forest, Virginia 24551

e-mail: info@fantasyfootballguidebook.com for bulk order inquiries

Please send _____ copies of Fantasy Football Guidebook in hardback.

Please send _____ copies of Fantasy Football Guidebook in paperback.

Name: _____

Address: _____

City: _____

State: _____Zip: _____

Telephone: _____

e-mail address: _____

Special Requests :_____(annotate here if autographed book requested)

Fantasy Football Guidebook: $26.95 for hardback; $19.95 for paperback.

Sales Tax: Please add 5.0% for products shipped to Virginia (total of $28.30 for hardback or $20.95 for paperback, including tax)

Make checks payable to Samuel L. Hendricks

Add $5.00 for shipping and handling for one book, $2.00 for each additional book

My check or money order for $_____

Payment must accompany orders.

Printed in the United States
130656LV00003B/3-4/A

9 781602 640207